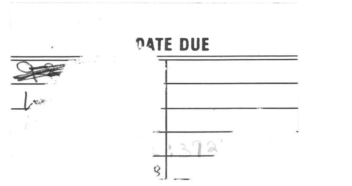

Crime and Justice

Crime and Justice
An Annual Review of Research

Edited by Michael Tonry and Norval Morris

VOLUME **4**

The University of Chicago Press, Chicago and London

The University of Chicago Press, Chicago 60637
The University of Chicago Press, Ltd., London

© 1983 by The University of Chicago
All rights reserved. Published 1983
Printed in the United States of America
90 89 88 87 86 85 84 83   5 4 3 2 1

ISSN: 0192-3234
ISBN: (cloth) 0-226-80797-5
          (paper) 0-226-80798-3

This volume was prepared under Grant Number 80-IJ-CX-0022(S1)
awarded to the University of Maryland by the National Institute
of Justice, U.S. Department of Justice, under the Omnibus
Crime Control and Safe Streets Act of 1968 as amended. Points
of view or opinions expressed in this volume are those of the editors
or authors and do not necessarily represent the official position
or policies of the U.S. Department of Justice.

Contents

Introduction

This is a trying time for the values implicit in this series, and for criminologists generally. It is a time when the public demands break-throughs in knowledge about criminals and crime and leaps in the effectiveness of crime control, but when small increments in our store of information and minor improvements in crime control are all that can be offered unless fundamental democratic values are sacrificed.

The myths of burgeoning crime overwhelming inept police, courts and correctional institutions dominate public discourse and distort political action. One can raise a cheap laugh in any company by varying George Bernard Shaw's comment about economists: "if all criminologists were laid end to end they wouldn't reach a conclusion."

This tension in criminology between belief and truth is by no means unique—it is common in the social sciences and elsewhere—but it is particularly strong here for two main reasons: first, people are born experts on the causes and control of crime; they sense the solutions in their bones. Those solutions differ dramatically from person to person, but each one knows, and knows deeply and emotionally, that his perspective is the way of truth. A peculiar blend of intuition and common sense guides everyone on these topics—clearly, firmly, and to widely divergent conclusions. Second, there is no developed discipline of criminology. Criminology is the effort to apply insights from the social and biological sciences to the causes of crime and the consequences of different crime prevention and control methods. Hence no one can possibly be an expert; the range of knowledge required is too great. Criminological insight is by consequence inherently synthetic. In such a situation—confident belief confronting uncertain glimmerings of knowledge—the strains on the synthetic discipline of criminology are substantial.

We saw one example of this confrontation in volume 3. Ted Robert Gurr's careful analysis of the historical sweep of interpersonal violence in a variety of Western societies concluded that the incidence of criminal violence has been reasonably, steadily, and substantially declining for several centuries, with occasional upturns in the declining curve—for example, in the United States in the 1850s, 1900s, and 1960s—not greatly disturbing its overall downward trend in both rural and urban areas. This truth—for truth it seems to us to be—confronts a very different belief that runs something like this: owing to the pressures of increased urbanization, profound changes in the structure of family life, and the more rapid mobility and greater anonymity of modern life, crime is increasing worldwide and in particular in the cities of the West.

Of the fine articles in volume 3, Ted Gurr's attracted by far the most attention. The press, responsible in part for the false belief, gave space to this quaint contrary view of a criminologist. There was a tone of annoyance in the commentary. It was as if Gurr was underestimating and understating the seriousness and importance of crime; as if, like most criminologists, he was seen as being on the wrong side in the battle between criminal and victim. Readers of *Crime and Justice* do not require us to demonstrate the absurdity of these reactions. Our only point is that this is a field in which we hope the hundred flowers of knowledge will be allowed to bloom amid the weeds of prejudice and passion.

Crime continues to influence seriously where and how people live. It is a scourge in blighted inner-city areas and is deeply interwoven with problems of race and class. It calls forth reactions that threaten individual freedom and equal justice and that could well do more injury to our social structure than crime could ever do. In this situation it seems to us more important than ever to adhere strictly to the aim defined at the start of this series—careful, precise statements of knowledge, not belief, information, not nostrums, about crime and its control.

Hence the menu for volume 4 presents the usual diversity of subjects. Our view on the importance of historical perspective is reaffirmed by an article on the history of juvenile corrections; essays on school violence, women as offenders and defendants, and crime and the mentally ill consider particular group problems of crime; issues of crime control are addressed in essays on the relations between gun availability and violent crime and on "target hardening"; and an examination of problems in random allocation experiments is part of our regular tribute to the long-term importance of methodology. We varied a Shaw aphorism; why not one of Churchill's? Like the pudding, this volume lacks a theme.

But please do not therefore reject it. It may be too early for overarching themes in criminology; there are no field theories here. Be content with careful state-of-the-art summaries of what is known and what are the reasonable implications of such knowledge, and be suspicious of those who claim to offer more.

Michael Tonry
Norval Morris

Jackson Toby

Violence in School

ABSTRACT

Violence in school is not new. Especially on the college level, deaths and injuries from hazing have long occurred sporadically, as have student riots. But widespread violence in public and secondary schools seems to have developed only in the past generation, especially in the United States but increasingly in other urban-industrial societies.

Two kinds of violence should be distinguished. One is violence perpetrated by predatory adolescent male trespassers who enter school buildings to steal or rob; assaults may occur to disable victims. Intruder violence is most common in the largest cities. The other type of violence is committed by enrolled students against members of the school community: teachers, fellow students, staff members. Their violent acts include robbery, especially extortion of money and valuables from fellow students, but their main motivation appears to be anger, expressed in assaults against both students and staff members.

Both these types of school violence can be understood in terms of the weakening of social control over adolescents and young adults in modern societies. Lack of family and neighborhood controls frees those youngsters not committed to the school and its values to express their predatory or aggressive impulses. This is, of course, not the whole explanation of school violence. Individual personality development explains why some persons take advantage of these opportunities for violence that are offered by a fluid society.

If modern societies are to reverse course and reduce violence in public secondary schools, they probably will have to gain greater control over adolescents. One approach to this end is to increase the voluntariness of student enrollment, thus giving students in public secondary schools a greater stake in behavioral conformity. Such an approach requires a reexamination of an established tradition of modern societies: compulsory school attendance.

Jackson Toby is Professor of Sociology and Director, Institute for Criminological Research, Rutgers University.
Revisions of an earlier draft of this article were made in response to helpful comments by Norval Morris, Albert J. Reiss, Jr., Michael H. Tonry, and Franklin E. Zimring.

I

Mass media accounts of rapes and robberies *inside* schools are especially shocking because parents send children to school to improve their minds, not to expose them to danger. Students and teachers do not expect to be assaulted or robbed in school any more than pedestrians expect motorists to aim for them as they scurry across the street. And in most public schools—as well as in the overwhelming majority of private and parochial schools—this expectation of an orderly routine is confirmed by experience. Students come to school on schedule, do more or less what their teachers ask them to do, and return home unharmed at the end of the day, possibly with assigned homework that some of them complete. Occasionally a fight breaks out in the corridor during the passing of classes, a student using a toilet is coerced into giving up lunch money, or, more rarely, an intruder robs a teacher at knife point of money and jewelry. In most schools violent crimes are unusual enough to be regarded the way pedestrians regard the possibility of being struck by an automobile: as wholly unpredictable acts of God.

But the traditional expectation that schools are safe places for children is changing, not just in the United States, but in many industrialized countries. School violence has been reported on the increase in Great Britain, Sweden, France, Israel, mainland China, and even authority-conscious Japan. In 1980 the Japanese National Police Agency announced 1,558 cases of school violence, up 20 percent from 1979 (Murray 1981). Of these, 394 were assaults on teachers. In one case, eighteen students beat a teacher with bamboo sticks. In another, several junior high school students hit a teacher after he told them to turn off a rock-music cassette tape (Associated Press 1981). School-violence data from outside the United States are mostly anecdotal press and television accounts. In the United States, on the other hand, quantitative studies exist. The National Institute of Education (NIE) conducted one national survey of victimization in 642 public secondary schools in 1975–76 (U.S. Department of Health, Education, and Welfare 1978; Gottfredson and Daiger 1979; Toby 1980a). Students and teachers from these junior and senior high schools filled out anonymous questionnaires; 31,373 student questionnaires and 23,895 teacher questionnaires were completed. Answers to questions such as the following were tabulated to provide an estimate of the amount of theft and violence in public secondary schools:

> In [the previous month] did anyone steal things of yours from your desk, locker, or other place at school?

> Did anyone take money or things directly from you by force, weapons, or threats at school in [the previous month]?

At school in [the previous month] did anyone physically attack and hurt you?

Another study was based on National Crime Survey data collected by the Bureau of the Census. The National Crime Survey conducted victimization surveys in a sample of households in twenty-six large American cities in 1974 and 1975; these data from approximately ten thousand households in each city were reanalyzed to provide information about offenses committed inside big-city schools (U.S. Department of Justice 1979). In addition, several states conducted statewide studies of school violence and vandalism; for example, in 1979 the Hawaii Crime Commission conducted a questionnaire survey of principals, counselors, teachers, and students (Hawaii Crime Commission 1980). Nearly six thousand usable questionnaires were returned, mostly from teachers and students.

This essay reviews these data on victimization at school, interprets them, and considers their policy implications. Section I presents the major findings of the two national surveys and distinguishes differential patterns of victimization in school by sex, community size, race, and whether the victims were students, teachers, or other school employees. The data suggest distinct patterns of offending by students and by "intruders," and an effort is made to identify those patterns. Section II discusses the difficult problem of disentangling the causes of school violence from its effects. Use of school security guards, for example, is associated with high rates of school violence. The explanation is probably that guards are typically hired only in schools that have experienced high rates of in-school criminality. More ambiguous is whether teachers' unwillingness to confront misbehaving students is a result of their experience with student violence or a cause of it. Section II identifies a number of these complex cause-and-effect relations and considers some of their implications for school violence. Sections III and IV explore the sociocultural and individual causes of school violence. The final section discusses alternative strategies for coping with school violence and attempts to assess the prospects for safer schools.

I. The Facts about Victimization at School and Their Interpretation

It is perhaps an overstatement to speak of the "facts" about victimization in schools. What exist are systematic data concerning victimization based primarily on two large national surveys. Since no survey is methodologically perfect, we must understand the limitations of these two surveys in order to assess the inferences drawn from them. The National Institute of Education survey had the advantage that it was specifically designed to describe the school-crime problem in the United States. It attempted to question students and teachers in a random sample of public secondary schools in different types of American communities: rural areas, suburbs, small cities, and large cities. The students in the selected schools were drawn randomly from lists of enrolled students; all the teachers in each sample school received questionnaires in their mailboxes. Nevertheless, the 31,373 students and the 23,895 teachers who filled out questionnaires were not a random sample of American students and teachers for the following reasons:

1. School systems, being under local control, had to be persuaded to cooperate with the survey; they could not be compelled. It is possible that the school systems that cooperated had less serious school crime problems than those that did not.

2. The survey design called for questionnaires from about fifty students selected at random in each of the 642 schools. It was necessary that each of these students and their parents agree in writing to participation in the survey. It was also necessary to locate the students in school on the day the questionnaires were administered or on makeup days. These requirements proved more difficult to meet in some schools than in others. Thus, in inner-city schools the proportions of the designated sample who actually filled out questionnaires were lower than in suburbs or rural areas.

3. The cooperation of teachers, like the cooperation of students, also varied from one school to another.

The Department of Justice survey of school crime, unlike the National Institute of Education survey, was not specially designed to investigate crime in school. Begun in 1972, the National Crime Survey (Sparks 1981) was designed to provide estimates of American crime rates that would supplement FBI data on crimes known to the police; the National Crime Survey tabulated victimizations reported to Census Bureau interviewers whether or not they were previously reported to the police, thereby making possible estimates of unreported crime. One component of the National Crime Survey is a countrywide survey of 72,000 households, conducted every six months, and yielding victimization data on a sample of approximately 136,000 persons 12 years of age and over. Since each survey covers only the six-month period before the household visit of the interviewer, the continuing surveys generate estimates of crime trends in the United States as a whole. In addition to ongoing semiannual national surveys, there have been city-level household surveys, a national commercial survey, and city-level commercial surveys. One question in all the surveys asks where the incident occurred, and one response category is "inside school." Thus, separating out all the victimization reports of crimes that occurred in school from all other victimizations made possible a special report on school crime. This was done for an aggregation of the data from the twenty-six city-level surveys (in Atlanta, Baltimore, Boston, Buffalo, Chicago, Cincinnati, Cleveland, Dallas, Denver, Detroit, Houston, Los Angeles, Miami, Milwaukee, Minneapolis, New Orleans, Newark, New York, Oakland, Philadelphia, Pittsburgh, Portland, San Diego, San Francisco, Saint Louis, and Washington, D.C.).

One advantage of the Department of Justice study of school crime over the National Institute of Education study is that the National Crime Survey made it possible to compare various victimizations occurring in school with those in other places. Another advantage is that the National Crime Survey dealt with the victimization in school buildings not only of teachers and students but of all other persons, such as secretaries, clerks, security guards, and custodians. (Nonteaching staff suffer an appreciable amount of victimization that is ignored in the National Institute of Education survey.) Furthermore, the Department of Justice study, dealing as it does with school crime in large cities where violent crime is most serious, is able to shed more light on school violence. But the Department of Justice study suffered from some limitations because of its origin in the National Crime Survey. Unlike the National Institute of Education study, which was conducted in public junior and senior high schools, the Department of Justice study contained victimization data from students in private secondary schools and from college students as well as from public school students. Thus it is not possible to determine from the Department of Justice study the extent to which the victims were students in private schools and colleges or to confirm the widespread belief that school violence is mainly a public school problem.[1]

Both the National Institute of Education study and the National Crime Survey study concluded that most school crime, like most crime outside school, was nonviolent. Teachers and students experienced thefts of money and valuables from unattended desks; student lockers

[1]A rough disaggregation of data for college victims and secondary school victims is possible. When student victims are looked at separately for ages 12–15, 16–19, and 20–24, it turns out that the oldest group, which contains mainly college students, had only 2 percent of all student victimizations (U.S. Department of Justice 1979, table 13).

were broken into; teachers' pocketbooks were snatched; bicycles were stolen. Other nonviolent crimes included drug sales and students smoking pot, drinking wine, beer, and hard liquor, defacing walls and desks, and starting minor fires in wastepaper baskets and toilet bowls. But both studies also revealed an appreciable amount of violent crime, mainly assaults and robberies.

A. *The Prevalence of School Violence*

Table 1 presents quantitative victimization reports from the 1976 National Institute of Education survey; it compares the rate of nonviolent theft from teachers with the rates of two violent offenses, assault and robbery. If the victimization reports can be trusted, assault and robbery of teachers were rare compared with nonviolent theft of their money or property. Even in the secondary schools of large cities, which had rates of teacher robbery and assault several times the rates in small communities, assault and robbery rates were small fractions of the rate for larceny.

A similar pattern emerges in table 2, which presents the reports of personal victimization of students from the same survey. However, the percentage of *students* claiming that they were assaulted or robbed was much greater than the rate of *teachers* reporting such violent victimizations—despite the fact that the student data covered a *one*-month period and the teacher data a *two*-month period. Probably a physical attack had quite a different meaning when the victim was a fellow student than when it was a teacher. For the same reason, "robbery" of a student did not seem like real robbery; extorting money or valuables from a fellow student by violence or the threat of violence may not have seemed to the perpetrator much different from taking the same items from the victim's locker. The line between larceny and robbery may have been clearer when the victim was a teacher. Another difference between table 1 and table 2 is that assaults and robberies of *students* occurred twice as often in junior high schools as in senior high schools, whereas assaults and robberies of *teachers* occurred at more nearly the same rate in junior and senior high schools except in schools in the very largest cities. Either junior high schools were more dangerous than senior high schools for students but not for teachers, or perhaps junior high school students were more likely than senior high school students to engage in minor attacks and petty extortions.

Still, the number of students subjected to violent victimization over the course of a school year was large. Table 2 refers only to the month previous to the survey, although multiplying the percentages by nine or

TABLE 1

Percentage of Teachers Victimized in Public Schools over a Two-Month Period in 1976

Size of Community	By Larcenies		By Assaults		By Robberies	
	In Junior High Schools	In Senior High Schools	In Junior High Schools	In Senior High Schools	In Junior High Schools	In Senior High Schools
500,000 or more	31.4% (56)	21.6% (59)	2.1% (56)	.4% (59)	1.4% (56)	1.1% (59)
100,000–499,999	24.5 (45)	22.8 (36)	1.1 (45)	1.0 (36)	0.7 (45)	0.9 (36)
50,000–99,999	21.0 (23)	19.3 (31)	0.2 (23)	0.3 (31)	0.3 (23)	0.4 (31)
10,000–49,999	20.8 (94)	16.5 (75)	0.6 (94)	0.3 (75)	0.5 (94)	0.4 (75)
2,500–9,999	16.9 (41)	19.1 (47)	0.3 (41)	0.2 (47)	0.4 (41)	0.4 (47)
Under 2,500	15.9 (42)	18.5 (53)	0.2 (42)	0.2 (53)	0.0 (42)	0.4 (53)
All communities	22.1 (301)	19.3 (301)	0.8 (301)	0.5 (301)	0.6 (301)	0.6 (301)

Note: Numbers in parentheses refer to the number of schools on the basis of which the average percentage of personal victimization was calculated for each cell.

Source: Special tabulation of data from U.S. Department of Health, Education, and Welfare 1978.

TABLE 2

Percentage of Students Victimized in Public Schools over a One-Month Period in 1976

Size of Community	By Larcenies		By Assaults		By Robberies	
	In Junior High Schools	In Senior High Schools	In Junior High Schools	In Senior High Schools	In Junior High Schools	In Senior High Schools
500,000 or more	14.8% (56)	14.9% (59)	8.5% (56)	3.7% (59)	5.7% (56)	2.8% (59)
100,000–499,999	18.0 (45)	16.8 (36)	7.8 (45)	2.7 (36)	3.6 (45)	1.9 (36)
50,000–99,999	18.0 (23)	15.3 (31)	7.7 (23)	2.9 (31)	3.8 (23)	1.3 (31)
10,000–49,999	15.5 (94)	15.8 (74)	6.8 (94)	2.7 (74)	3.3 (94)	1.4 (74)
2,500–9,999	16.1 (41)	14.6 (47)	7.4 (41)	3.1 (47)	3.5 (41)	1.4 (47)
Under 2,500	15.8 (42)	14.2 (53)	6.2 (42)	3.5 (53)	3.8 (42)	2.0 (53)
All communities	16.0 (301)	15.2 (300)	7.3 (301)	3.1 (300)	3.9 (301)	1.8 (300)

Note: Numbers in parentheses refer to the number of schools on the basis of which the average percentage of personal victimization was calculated for each cell.

Source: Special tabulation of data from U.S. Department of Health, Education, and Welfare 1978.

ten would probably exaggerate the incidence of violence; some of the same students may have been victimized every month. On the other hand, it seems likely that at least half the junior high school students in schools in the largest cities were assaulted and a third were robbed each year. Teachers were not subjected to violence to the same extent, but the assaults on and robberies of teachers probably corresponded better to the meaning of "assault" and "robbery" in the streets. Perhaps 10 percent of junior high school teachers in the largest cities were assaulted and 5 percent were robbed during the school year.

B. *Fear of School Violence*

Before turning to data on the characteristics of victims and perpetrators, let us try to place school violence in a broader perspective. We have already seen that violent school crime is quantitatively small compared with nonviolent school crime. However, there is evidence that violent school crime, though infrequent, arouses destructive fears among students and teachers. According to the National Institute of Education study, students and teachers reacted to the danger of violence by avoiding certain places in the more violent schools, such as restrooms, stairways, and corridors. Some students avoided school altogether. Four percent of all secondary school students in public schools said they stayed home out of fear at least once a month; but 7 percent of the senior high school students in the largest cities said this, as did 8 percent of the junior high school students (U.S. Department of Health, Education, and Welfare 1978, pp. 63–64). Students were more fearful in the big-city schools, where violence was more prevalent. Teachers were fearful too. Twelve percent of the public school teachers nationwide said that *within the month previous to the survey* they had hesitated to confront misbehaving students out of fear for their own safety. Twenty-eight percent of the teachers in large cities said so. Over the entire school year the percentages would doubtless have increased.

In big-city schools, instances of serious violence directed at teachers are well publicized, partly because they are unusual and therefore newsworthy, and partly because they are shocking. Thus, when a Brooklyn high school teacher intervened in a fight between two students in his homeroom, was punched by one of them, hit his head against the wall, and subsequently died of multiple skull fractures, the story received national attention (Kihss 1981). But teachers have additional sources of information about the victimization of their colleagues beyond the television and newspaper accounts known to the general public. They observe instances in their own schools (Speiser and Sanders 1979). And they learn of other cases at meetings and conferences sponsored by teachers' unions as well as through reading union reports concerning school safety.

Teachers are afraid because they sometimes are the targets of violence. Students are aware of these fears. Sometimes the threats, curses, and obscene gestures that they direct at their teachers are attempts to exploit teacher fears. In any case, such intimidating behavior is widespread in American secondary schools. Seventy-five percent of the teachers in big-city junior high schools reported that during the previous month students had sworn at them or made obscene gestures, and 36 percent reported that students had threatened to hurt them; in rural junior high schools, 43 percent of the teachers surveyed reported being sworn at or being the target of obscene gestures, and 7 percent reported being threatened (U.S. Department of Health, Education, and Welfare 1978, pp. 67–78). Curses and threats are so numerous that they must be largely discounted, but the teachers cannot be certain they are not the forerunners of violence. Particularly in schools where violent incidents have occurred, teachers may take them seriously, become reluctant to confront misbehaving students, and thereby unintentionally encourage the violence they fear.

C. *Perpetrators of School Violence: Students and Intruders*

The two main groups contributing to school violence are trespassers from the community and enrolled students. Neither of the victimization studies provided conclusive evidence on the relative proportions of trespassers and students among the perpetrators of school violence. The data came from victims; the perpetrators often escaped without being identified. In some cases, however, victims recognized perpetrators. The proportion of strangers in these victim reports was a rough indication of the proportion of trespassers—or, as school officials call them, "intruders."

The National Institute of Education study concluded that, for the entire country, intruders seemed to be a minor problem, and its aggregated data supported that conclusion. However, that conclusion was wrong, and the NIE appears to have been mistaken in its analysis. If the data had been disaggregated by size of the cities in which schools were situated, they would have shown that offenders whose identities were unknown (most of whom were intruders) were much more prominent in the largest cities. The National Crime Survey study, being concerned with school crime in twenty-six large cities, provides an opportunity to achieve this disaggregation. Table 3 shows the proportion of offenders identified by victims as strangers for various violent and nonviolent school crimes. For rape and robbery, the perpetrators were largely unknown to the victims. Aggravated and simple assaults were less likely to be committed by strangers than were robbery and rape, as might be expected for offenses that often develop outside school as a result of arguments between friends or relatives. However, in a *majority* of all offenses where the victim had an opportunity to recognize the perpetrator, the victim could not do so. This does not necessarily mean that most offenders in big-city schools were intruders. Some big-city high schools are enormous—enrolling two to four thousand students—and attendance is sporadic (Birman and Natriello 1980). The resulting anon-

TABLE 3

Estimated Percentages of Stranger Offenses in In-School Victimization, Twenty-six Cities Aggregate, 1974–75

Type of Victimization	Status of Victims	
	Students	Teachers and Others
Rape	94%[a]	100%
	(390)[b,c]	(139)[c]
Robbery	81	85
	(13,185)	(1,808)
Aggravated assault	66	71
	(6,528)	(2,900)
Simple assault	60	57
	(15,261)	(5,597)
Larceny with contact	94	92
	(4,853)	(1,095)[c]
Larceny without contact[d]	79	64
	(17,373)	(7,116)
Total[d]	74	67
	(57,590)	(18,655)

Source: U.S. Department of Justice 1979, p. 32.

[a]Percentage of stranger offenses.

[b]Numbers in parentheses are total of victimizations (stranger plus nonstranger) in the cell.

[c]Estimate, based on fewer than fifty sample cases, may be statistically unreliable.

[d]Excludes those larceny without contact victimizations in which the victim was not present at the immediate scene of the crime.

ymity makes it difficult for a victim of assault or robbery to identify even a perpetrator who is an enrolled student. Nevertheless, table 3 suggests that intruders are an important factor in the crime problem of big-city schools.

However, intruders are not a homogeneous group. The term "intruder" refers to persons who enter school buildings without legitimate business. One type of intruder is the stereotypical predator—completely alien to the school, perhaps not even a resident of the surrounding neighborhood. Such intruders are criminals who consider schools more vulnerable than stores or banks or private homes. After all, a school contains the purses and jewelry of teachers as well as valuable property belonging to the school. In underprivileged neighborhoods, these potentially stealable things are tempting prizes. The other type of intruder is no stranger to the school, although he or she may not currently be enrolled. This type of intruder may include an angry parent intent on beating up a child's teacher, friends of enrolled students who have come to visit, suspended students who prefer a warm, dry school building to the streets, or dropouts who are unemployed and bored. They may even be graduates from a few years back.

Table 4 disaggregates the data of table 3 on the assumption that most of the offenses committed by persons perceived as strangers were committed by intruders and that the remaining offenses were committed by enrolled students.[2] Table 4 omits "larceny without contact" in order to focus exclusively on violent crime. Note that the pattern of offenses was different for intruders and for enrolled students. Intruders tended to commit robberies and larceny with contact (e.g., purse snatching), whereas enrolled students were more likely to be assaultive. On the assumption that unknown perpetrators were mainly intruders, half of the crimes intruders committed against students and nearly a third of the offenses against staff members were either robbery or larceny with contact. Only a quarter of the offenses students committed against other students and only a tenth of the offenses they committed against staff members were these predatory crimes. On the other hand, nearly three-quarters of the offenses that students committed against other students and two-thirds of the offenses they committed against staff members

[2]Strictly speaking, it is not correct to infer that all the crimes committed by known persons in school were perpetrated by students. Some of the crimes may have been perpetrated by teachers, secretaries, custodians, security guards, or even intruders known to the victims. But the likelihood is that the overwhelming bulk of the known perpetrators were students.

TABLE 4

In-School Violent Offenses Inferred to Have Been
Committed by Intruders and Students, Twenty-six
Large Cities, 1974–75

	Status of Victims			
	Students		Teachers and Others	
Type of Victimization	Possibly Committed by Intruders	Committed by Enrolled Students	Possibly Committed by Intruders	Committed by Enrolled Students
Rape	1.3%	0.2%	1.8%	—
	(367)	(23)	(139)	(0)
Robbery	36.7	22.5	19.4	7.5%
	(10,680)	(2,505)	(1,537)	(271)
Aggravated assault	14.8	19.9	26.0	23.3
	(4,308)	(2,220)	(2,059)	(841)
Simple assault	31.5	54.8	40.2	66.7
	(9,157)	(6,104)	(3,190)	(2,407)
Larceny with contact	15.7	2.6	12.7	2.4
	(4,562)	(291)	(1,007)	(88)
Total	100.0	100.0	100.1	99.9
	(29,074)	(11,143)	(7,932)	(3,607)

Source: Table 3.

Note: "Intruders" are offenders perceived as strangers by the victims in table 3.
"Enrolled students" are offenders not perceived as strangers.

Numbers in parentheses are total victimizations in the cell.

were simple or aggravated assaults. Doubtless the assumption that all
offenders perceived to be strangers were intruders tends to give intruders
credit for some crimes that were actually committed by unrecognized
students. Nonetheless, the inference from table 4 of a different pattern of
offenses committed by intruders than by enrolled students seems reasonable—on the assumption that failures to identify student perpetrators
occur more or less randomly throughout the table. Another way of
looking at table 4 is to point out that the bulk of the rapes, robberies, and
larcenies with contact perpetrated against teachers and other nonstudents were committed by unknown persons, probably intruders. The
only violent crime perpetrated against staff members by an appreciable
number of students was assault.

  1. *Group violence.* In short, considerable big-city school violence can
validly be attributed to intruders. There still remains the question of

who intruders were and how they operated. For example, were intruders lone offenders, or did they enter the school in gangs and commit offenses in groups? Although table 5 does not distinguish crimes committed by known persons from crimes committed by unknown persons, it can reasonably be assumed—based on table 4—that the bulk of the perpetrators described in table 5 were intruders. Note that roughly a quarter of the robberies and assaults—of both students and staff members—involved three or more perpetrators. Close to half of the robberies of students involved two or more perpetrators.[3] Of course, violent crime *outside* schools also tends to involve groups of offenders (McDermott and Hindelang 1981, pp. 19–20). Group violence is not restricted to in-school crime.

2. *Age specificity.* Table 4 permits the inference that intruders were seven times more likely to rob students than to rob staff. However, it does not distinguish the sort of intruders who robbed students from the sort who robbed staff. Did intruders specialize? Table 6 suggests that they did. Students tended to be victimized by persons the same age or slightly older, not by persons a great deal older. Furthermore, except for a small group of student victims 20–34 years old, who were presumably college students, student victims perceived perpetrators mainly as 20 years of age or less. By contrast, about a quarter of the victimized staff members 20 years of age or more perceived the perpetrators as 21 or older. One possible interpretation of these data is that the older intruders concentrated on staff, whereas the younger intruders victimized students. Younger intruders may have been afraid to tackle older persons. Further analysis confirms this speculation; once the victimization data were disaggregated by offense, it was found that older intruders specialized in *robbing* staff persons rather than in assaultive offenses.[4] Perhaps older intruders preferred staff victims because teachers and secretaries were more likely than students to have something worth stealing. Intruders eighteen years old or older committed three-quarters of the robberies of teachers and other nonstudents, but only 21 percent of the robberies of students.

[3]Table 5 does not provide useful data concerning larcenies. In the case of larceny with contact—for example, purse snatching—about half the victims did not know how many offenders were involved. In larcenies without contact, two-fifths of the student victims and a third of the staff victims did not know how many offenders were involved. Moreover, 85 percent of the larcenies without contact occurred without any sighting of offenders by the victims. It is quite possible that gangs of intruders played an important part in larcenies as well as in robberies and assaults, but the data are not clear about this.

[4]This conclusion is based on an unpublished tabulation made for this essay by the staff of the Criminal Justice Research Center, Albany, New York.

TABLE 5

Estimated Percentages of Perceived Number of Offenders in In-School Victimization by Type of Victimization and Status of Victim, Twenty-six Cities Aggregate, 1974–75

Status of Victims and Type of Victimization	Perceived Number of Offenders					Estimated Number of Victimizations
	One	Two	Three or More	Don't Know	Not Ascertained	
Students						
Rape	76[a]	19	0	5	0	(390)[b]
Robbery	43	19	28	6	3	(13,185)
Aggravated assault	56	7	29	3	6	(6,528)
Simple assault	62	8	27	1	1	(15,261)
Larceny with contact	25	9	3	59	3	(4,853)
Larceny without contact[c]	54	3	2	40	0	(17,373)
Total[c]	52	9	18	19	2	(57,590)
Teachers and others						
Rape	87	0	0	13	0	(139)[b]
Robbery	68	8	22	0	1	(1,808)
Aggravated assault	61	5	30	2	3	(2,900)
Simple assault	78	7	14	0	0	(5,597)
Larceny with contact	40	7	7	46	0	(1,095)[b]
Larceny without contact[c]	55	7	4	33	0	(7,116)
Total[c]	64	6	13	16	1	(18,655)

Source: U.S. Department of Justice 1979, p. 35.

[a] All percentages in this table are row percentages.

[b] Estimate, based on fewer than fifty sample cases, may be statistically unreliable.

[c] Excludes those larceny without contact victimizations in which the victim was not present at the immediate scene of the crime, that is, the bulk of the larcenies without contact.

TABLE 6

Percentage Distribution of Perceived Age of Offender(s) by Age of Victim in In-School Victimization, by Status of Victim, Twenty-six Cities Aggregate, 1974–75

Status and Age of Victims	Perceived Age of Offender(s)[a]						Estimated Number of Victimizations
	Under 12	12–14	15–17	18–20	21 or Older	Don't Know	
Students							
12–15	1[b]	48	45	3	1	2	(32,809)
16–19	0	3	62	26	5	3	(12,540)
20–34	0	0	11	54	32	3	(895)[c]
Total	1	35	49	10	3	2	(46,244)
Teachers and others							
16–19	0	1	61	35	2	1	(3,312)
20–34	9	26	19	15	23	8	(7,569)
35–49	10	24	20	8	34	4	(3,191)
50 or older	19	27	38	1	14	0	(1,341)[c]
Total	8	20	30	16	20	5	(15,413)

Source: U.S. Department of Justice 1979, p. 32.
Note: Excludes those larceny without contact victimizations in which the victim was not present at the immediate scene of the crime. Also excludes those victimizations in which the victim did not know whether there was more than one offender.
[a]Includes perceived age of lone offender and perceived age of oldest group offender.
[b]All percentages in this table are row percentages.
[c]Estimate, based on fewer than fifty sample cases, may be statistically unreliable.

3. *Gender specificity.* Table 7 throws light on the relation between the sex of perpetrators and the sex of victims. The overwhelming majority of those perpetrating offenses agaist male students and male staff members were males. Two-thirds of the offenders who victimized female teachers and other female staff members were also perceived as males. But 60 percent of the large number of victimizations of female students were committed by females. It is not entirely clear what this means. Perhaps the explanation for the large proportion of females among offenders against female students but not among offenders against female staff members is that these crimes against students tended to be *assaults* committed by *fellow students* whereas the crimes against female staff members tended to be robberies and larcenies committed by *intruders*, who were mainly males. A direct check on this hypothesis was obtained by disaggregating by gender the data of table 4. It was found that half of the assaults against female students were committed by known persons

TABLE 7

Percentage Distribution of Perceived Sex of Offender(s) by Sex of Victim in In-School Victimization, by Status of Victim, Twenty-six Cities Aggregate, 1974–75

| Status and Sex of Victims | Perceived Sex of Offender(s) | | | | Estimated Number of Victimizations |
	Male	Female	Both[a]	Don't Know	
Students					
Male	96[b]	1	1	1	(28,852)
Female	33	60	4	3	(17,591)
Total	72	23	2	2	(46,443)
Teachers					
Male	80	6	3	11	(2,618)
Female	62	25	4	9	(4,024)
Total	69	17	4	10	(6,642)
Others					
Male	90	2	3	4	(4,316)
Female	63	32	3	2	(4,605)
Total	76	17	3	3	(8,921)

Source: U.S Department of Justice 1979, p. 34.
Note: Excludes those larceny without contact victimizations in which the victim was not present at the immediate scene of the crime. Also excludes those victimizations in which the victim did not know whether there was more than one offender.
[a]Group of offenders containing both male and female offenders.
[b]All percentages in this table are row percentages.

and that four-fifths of these were by females.[5] On the other hand, the predominance of male offenders in the victimization of female *teachers* could not be explained by intruders alone. Known males were also more likely than known females to assault, rob, and steal from female teachers.

4. *Racial specificity*. Table 8 addresses the race of perpetrators and victims. Overall, about 80 percent of all victimizations involved black offenders—although blacks constituted only 29 percent of the population of the twenty-six cities in which the National Crime Survey was conducted. Blacks constituted 88 percent of the offenders in cases involving black students. In view of the racial imbalance in many urban school systems, black students may well have predominated in the schools attended by black student-respondents in the National Crime Survey. Thus it is not clear whether the 88 percent black offenders who victimized black students came mainly from the student bodies of the schools involved or included intruders. The large number of black offenders who victimized white students, however, suggests either selective victimization of white students by black fellow students or a considerable number of black intruders. A pattern of black victimization of whites rather than of white victimization of blacks is not unique to schools. In the United States as a whole, the National Crime Survey reports this pattern for rape, robbery, aggravated assault, and personal larceny (Hindelang and McDermott 1981, p. 66). White teachers and white nonteaching staff tended to be victimized by black offenders to just about the same extent as white students. Table 8 shows that, generally, white offenders victimized *white* students, teachers, and other staff members. If these white offenders were students rather than intruders, the offenses they engaged in were probably assaults rather than robberies. The exception to the rule of white perpetrators victimizing fellow whites is the report from black teachers of 20 percent white perpetrators. These probably reflect the experiences of black teachers in schools with considerable white enrollment and where the teachers were victimized by enrolled students.

To sum up the inferences from these various tabulations: Intruders are an appreciable factor in big-city school crime, especially predatory crimes of violence against teachers and nonteaching staff. Intruders are likely to invade schools in groups rather than as lone individuals; they

---

[5]This unpublished tabulation was also made by the staff of the Criminal Justice Research Center.

TABLE 8

Percentage Distribution of Perceived Race of Offender(s) by Race of Victim in In-School Victimization, by Status of Victim, Twenty-six Cities Aggregate, 1974–75

Status and Race of Victims	Perceived Race of Offender(s)				Estimated Number of Victimizations
	White	Black/ Other	Mixed[a]	Don't Know	
Students					
White	30[b]	65	3	2	(30,173)
Black/other	6	88	1	5	(16,079)
Total	21	73	2	3	(46,252)
Teachers					
White	19	67	1	12	(5,609)
Black/other	20	77	0	3	(948)[c]
Total	20	69	1	10	(6,557)
Others					
White	32	65	1	3	(6,737)
Black/other	3	92	1	4	(2,163)
Total	25	71	1	3	(8,900)

Source: U.S. Department of Justice 1979, p. 33.

Note: Excludes those larceny without contact victimizations in which the victim was not present at the immediate scene of the crime. Also excludes those victimizations in which the victim did not know whether there was more than one offender.

[a]Group of offenders containing some combination of white, black, and other race offenders.

[b]All percentages in this table are row percentages.

[c]Estimate, based on fewer than fifty sample cases, may be statistically unreliable.

tend to be black males; and they are mostly in their late teens or early twenties.

In addition to intruders who get inside school buildings, there are youthful nonstudents who loiter outside the school, in playgrounds, parking lots, doorways, and on street corners. Sometimes they are waiting for friends, including girl friends who are students. Sometimes they are using the playground for recreation. Sometimes they are selling drugs. Sometimes they are looking for opportunities to steal from staff members or from students. Sometimes they are looking for a place to congregate with their friends, and loitering on school grounds is less likely to provoke the police than loitering someplace else. In the National Institute of Education survey, school principals were asked, "How much of a problem is the presence of youthful nonstudents: (*a*) in school? (*b*) around school?"

Both parts of the question offered principals the same alternatives: no problem at all; a little problem; moderate problem; fairly serious problem; and very serious problem. As might have been expected, principals in the larger cities tended to evaluate the presence of youthful nonstudents both in and around the school as more serious than did principals in the smaller cities. The statistical relation between size of city and presence of youthful nonstudents in the school was the same as that between size of city and presence of youthful nonstudents around the school.[6] Surprisingly, though, the principals considered youthful nonstudents a more serious problem *around* the school than *in* the school for every size of city, and the tendency to regard nonstudents around the school as the more serious problem was most marked in the largest cities. Thus, 58 percent of the school principals in cities of 500,000 persons or more regarded youthful nonstudents *around* the school as a moderate or serious problem; only 34 percent of them regarded youthful nonstudents *in* the school as a moderate or serious problem. Exactly what these data mean is not clear. Perhaps some principals were thinking of drug trafficking or of noise from portable stereos rather than violence. But the responses of the principals suggest that the problem of youthful nonstudents is not only an intruder problem; some of the areas near the school where youthful nonstudents congregate may not be school property. Intruders or not, loiterers may still pose a threat of violence to students and staff.

D. *Victims of School Crime: Students, Teachers, and Other Staff Members*

A comparison of the rate of violence against teachers and students shows that a much higher proportion of students than of teachers were robbed and assaulted, according to tables 1 and 2, which came from the 1976 survey of the National Institute of Education. But it is likely that the meanings of assault and of robbery were different for teachers and students. For students, robbery meant extortion of lunch money, bus passes, or articles of clothing. Students in Hawaiian public schools called this type of robbery "hijacking" (Hawaii Crime Commission 1980). For students, assault frequently meant fights in which it was difficult to disentangle victims from instigators. For teachers, robbery meant victimization by intruders, and intruders were neighborhood criminals who were more intimidating than students. For teachers, assault meant one of two seriously unpleasant experiences. Sometimes assault was a gratuitous accompaniment to a robbery, perhaps to discourage pursuit

---

[6]On a statistical measure of association, gamma, the level reached was .35.

or outcry. More often, assault was the angry response of an enrolled student after being admonished for disruptive behavior in the lunchroom, for loitering in the hallway without a pass, for fighting with other students, or for some other violation of school rules. What made a student attack on a teacher different from a student attack on another student was that this was not a quarrel between status equals. It represented a flouting of the authority system of the school as well as a prohibited act of violence. Teachers who were assaulted by students—or, even worse, their own students in their own classrooms—felt defied as well as injured.

The National Institute of Education survey provided no data on the victimization of nonteaching staff in schools. But the study of school crime based on National Crime Survey data did. In tables 3, 4, 5, and 6, data on teacher victimization and data on the victimization of "others" were aggregated, but in tables 7 and 8, data on teachers and on "others" were reported separately, as in several other tables not reproduced here. Thus it is possible to differentiate the characteristics of teacher victims from the characteristics of other staff victims of violence in big-city schools. More than 60 percent of the teacher victims were females compared with about half of the staff victims; about 85 percent of the teacher victims were white compared with three-quarters of the other staff. A somewhat larger percentage of teachers than of other staff were robbed or were victims of larceny with contact, and a somewhat larger percentage of teachers than of other staff were assaulted. These characteristics of teacher victims and staff victims may have reflected their demographic proportions in the school population rather than their differential vulnerability to victimization. Since neither the sex ratios of teachers and other staff in the big-city schools nor their racial compositions were available, it is not easy to interpret the differences found.

The meaning of the victimization data from the National Institute of Education survey is easier to interpret. *Male* students reported being assaulted or robbed twice as often as *female* students, and male teachers were somewhat more likely to be attacked than female teachers, although less likely to be robbed. If we assume that the robbery of teachers was in good part the work of intruders, the greater victimization of female teachers reflected their greater vulnerability to violent theft. Greater vulnerability may also explain other findings of the survey: younger students and the youngest, least-experienced teachers were more likely to report being robbed or attacked. But the explanation for the higher rate of violence directed at male students than at female students is obviously not vulnerability. It is, however, exactly what has been found in victimization studies in American society outside school buildings; males are more likely to be victimized than females (Hindelang 1976, pp. 116–25). It should not be forgotten that males are the main perpetrators of violent crimes, both in schools and out. That being so, the disproportionate victimization of males becomes less surprising. The assault of male students by other male students can be understood in terms of greater physical and psychological propinquity between males than between male and female students. As for the robbery of students and the assault on and robbery of teachers, it seems likely that male intruders and male students are more likely to find themselves alone with other males than with females. Thus, differential opportunity may explain the sex differences in victimization rates.

The National Institute of Education study inferred that the victims of school violence were disproportionately antisocial because, overall, victims reported more suspensions from school than nonvictims as well as less conventional attitudes toward cheating, honesty, and violence. However, this inference rested on inadequate analysis of the quantitative data; hence it was premature. It failed to consider that student victims of violence came disproportionately from the more violent schools, which tended to be in the larger cities. Such schools probably had high proportions of black and economically disadvantaged students. Student nonvictims, on the other hand, tended to come from safer schools in small cities and suburbs. Thus the comparison was not only of victims with nonvictims; it was of victims from schools in disadvantaged communities with nonvictims from schools in better neighborhoods. Furthermore, the nonvictim group was large and heterogenous; it included a small number of violent perpetrators and a much larger number of innocent bystanders. Interpreting the results was far from obvious. Although the total number of cases in the survey was large, each school contributed about fifty student questionnaires, on the average, with perhaps two or three reporting violent victimization. Aggregating the data in a meaningful way was difficult. A more valid analytical strategy would have made comparisons between black and white victims and nonvictims within cities of comparable size—and perhaps separately within junior high schools and senior high schools. Such an analysis might have shown that victims had attitudes at least as good as those of nonvictims and maybe better. In short, race and class were confounding variables. Schools in which black students predominated had rates of assault and robbery against both students and teachers twice as high as

schools where white students predominated. The large number of victims in such schools, although perhaps more likely to express attitudes
that seemed antisocial, were probably much more conventional than the
intruders or student perpetrators who victimized them. But data from
intruders were not available; and perpetrators of violence could not be
distinguished from other nonvictims because no self-report questions
about criminality were asked.

Where violent victimizations occurred was investigated in the National
Institute of Education study. But only *student* victims were asked where
the robbery or assault occurred. Student victims *were* interviewed about
their victimizations in some detail—a sample of 6,283 students were
randomly selected for intensive interviews in addition to the larger group
of respondents who filled out questionnaires. Table 9 shows where
violent victimizations occurred. Only 18 percent of the attacks and
robberies occurred in classrooms, and some of these violent acts may
have taken place in *empty* classrooms. Since schoolchildren spend a large
part of their school day in class, 18 percent seems low for classroom
violence. Maybe the presence of teachers protected students from the
violence of their classmates. Apparently, hallways and stairs (where
teacher supervision was weak) were the sites for about a third of the
violent acts, and other poorly supervised places—toilets, cafeterias, and
locker rooms—the sites for another third.

TABLE 9

Places within Junior and Senior High Schools
Where Assaults and Robberies Occur, as
Reported in Student Interviews

Place Where Offense Occurred	Percentage Of All Violent Crimes
Hallways and stairs	31
Classrooms	18
Restrooms	11
Cafeterias	11
Locker rooms/gyms	14
Athletic fields	9
Other places	8
Total	102[a]

Source: Department of Health, Education, and Welfare 1978, p. 84.
[a]Does not add to 100% because of rounding.

Poor as adult supervision is in hallways, stairs, toilets, cafeterias, and locker rooms, it is better than on the streets approaching the school or on buses carrying children to and from school. School officials do not have responsibility for children while they are on *public* buses. Even in places where children ride *school* buses, maintenance of close discipline is often difficult. The drivers, preoccupied with driving, can respond only to the most flagrant acts of violence, vandalism, or disorderly behavior. In New York City, for example, many children who ride buses feel in danger of mugging (Gaiter 1980). Some cities supply police or security guards to maintain order and safety on school buses, but in most communities adult protection is minimal for the trip to and from school in public vehicles. Neither the National Institute of Education survey nor the National Crime Survey data provided the information necessary to compare violent victimization within school buildings with victimization while traveling to and from school. Depending on how serious this problem is, especially in the largest cities, safe schools might be a practical impossibility. If getting to and from school were sufficiently dangerous in the largest cities, neither success in keeping intruders at bay nor better control over students within school buildings would be enough to change the perception of public secondary schools. Unfortunately, one study in Philadelphia showed that both black and white schoolboys regarded the streets to and from school as presenting a greater risk of being beaten or robbed than schoolyards, hallways, or classrooms (Savitz, Lalli, and Rosen 1977, p. 34).

E. *Evasive and Defiant Rule Breaking*

A useful distinction can be drawn between deviant behavior that is primarily defiant of authority and deviant behavior that is primarily evasive (see e.g. Parsons 1951, chap. 7). Assaults and robberies of teachers by students offer a clear-cut illustration of defiant deviance in the school setting. Larceny without contact with the victim illustrates evasive deviance. Much antisocial behavior in schools is less easy to classify because some deviant behavior is both evasive and defiant. The mix in a particular case is an empirical question. Vandalism in the form of graffiti surreptitiously written on walls might be considered evasive deviance. But school vandalism can go much further: firebombing classrooms or offices, ripping out plumbing, deliberately breaking walls and furniture. When destruction is massive, the perpetrators are communicating not only their lack of interest in abiding by rules but also their intention to shock the guardians of property. Substance abuse is certainly evasion of rules, but it can be more. When students drink alcohol or take drugs on school property, when the "joint" is lit in front of the vice-principal in charge of discipline, or when the neck of a bottle can be seen protruding from a paper bag, defiance is also involved. Curses, threats, and obscene gestures directed at teachers are speech, not violent acts per se, but they are disturbing to teachers, not only because they may portend future violence but because they are the functional equivalent of a slap in the face.

The motivations behind violent behavior in school are difficult to disentangle; they are the complex product of personal, social, and cultural forces. But changing attitudes toward authority in the larger society and in schools in particular appear to be involved. If defiance of teachers and principals has greater legitimacy today than it used to have, this change in cultural climate may be an important cause of greater school violence (Toby 1980b).

II. Disentangling the Causes of School Violence from Its Effects

If *intruders* contribute to school violence, especially in the largest cities, security guards are needed to keep intruders out. Security guards also help to deter *student* violence by their sheer presence. But hiring more security guards may mean having fewer teachers or less equipment and fewer supplies. How many security guards provide how much safety? This simple question requires longitudinal data of the kind that is rarely available. Ideally, a controlled experiment testing the effectiveness of security guards should begin with a high school with a high rate of violence and no guards. Each year a few security guards should be added and the effect on school violence monitored. No other changes should be made—not in the teachers, not in the students, not in the program of the school, not in the societal environment. Thus any changes in the violence rate could be attributed uniquely to changes in the security force. In practice, however, many variables affecting the rate of school violence change from year to year and even from month to month. Teachers grow older, retire, take other jobs; new, inexperienced teachers with different educational philosophies enter the system. Students move through the grade structure, drop out, transfer, graduate; new students with different interests and personality traits enter. Principals and other administrators change. The budgetary resources for education made available by the larger society change. The curriculum changes. There are changes in social rules governing lateness, absenteeism of students and teachers, class cutting, discretionary use of free periods, behavior in the lunchroom, acceptable dress, and many other things.

The difficulty of controlling a host of potentially relevant variables discourages all but a utopian from trying to assess the effect of security guards through a rigorous experiment. Instead, schools with different proportions of their resources devoted to security guards might be compared. Presumably, the contrasting violence rates would be due to the differential use of guards. The problem with this strategy is that no two schools are exactly alike. Furthermore, the chicken/egg problem confuses the issue. The schools with security guards tend to have more violence than those that do not use security guards because guards are usually hired when violence is a problem, not because someone thought it was a good idea to have a deterrent force in the school.

Thus it is difficult to tell whether security guards can reduce school violence, because violence tends to be higher in the same schools where guards are numerous, usually in the central cities, and lower in small-city schools where no one would dream of hiring them. In the same way, schools in which large proportions of teachers express reluctance to confront misbehaving students out of fear for their own safety have *higher* rates of school violence than schools in which smaller proportions of teachers express such reluctance (Department of Health, Education, and Welfare 1978, pp. 70–71). It is plausible to hypothesize that teachers' reluctance to confront misbehaving students diminishes adult control over students and thereby increases the rate of school violence over what it would otherwise be. It is also plausible to assume that teachers' reluctance to confront is an *effect* of the high level of violence in some schools. Showing that two variables are correlated does not settle the question of which is cause and which effect or of whether both are caused by an antecedent variable.

Teachers' reluctance to confront misbehaving students may be a symptom of the breakdown of informal social controls over students in big-city schools, controls that work well in smaller schools in smaller communities. To insist that the answer to school violence is stricter discipline, including the use of punishment, is to mistake the effect for the cause. True, student violence is rare in rural schools and parochial schools; and corporal punishment is common in rural schools and legendary in parochial schools. But spanking does not create an orderly atmosphere in such schools. It is the orderly atmosphere that makes corporal punishment feasible. Corporal punishment can be used by teachers and principals to discipline students only in schools that are already under informal control; attempting to use corporal punishment in a tough urban school courts violent physical retaliation from students and their parents. Another way of putting this same point is to say that the collective attitudes of students toward school—their receptivity toward learning what teachers try to teach—determine whether teachers can control students' behavior effectively. When students care what teachers think of them, teachers' approval or disapproval constitutes effective social control. When students—or intruders—feel that nothing is at stake when school rules are evaded or defied, security guards are not merely a second line of defense. They constitute formal controls that are a poor substitute for informal controls—but all that is possible in some urban schools.

Student absenteeism is another correlate of school violence. In those big-city senior high schools where a third of the enrolled students are absent on an average day, the bulk of absentees are either occasional or chronic truants.[7] What is the meaning of these high rates of truancy? Why should schools with high truancy rates also be schools with high rates of violence? As I mentioned before, the National Institute of Education survey found that appreciable numbers of students claimed to have been absent from school at least once during the previous month because they were afraid to attend.[8] One possibility, then, is that high levels of school violence generate fears that, in turn, lead to high rates of absenteeism. Another possibility is that high rates of absenteeism cause high rates of violence, perhaps through the mechanism of disrupting the educational process. Teachers as well as students become demoralized. It is difficult to teach a lesson that depends on material taught yesterday or last week when few students can be counted on to attend class regularly. Still another possibility—perhaps the most likely one—is that student absenteeism reflects the students' degree of commitment to academic effort, which depends on family and neighborhood values. These values underlie not only truancy but the school violence of stu-

[7]Truancy has become an increasingly serious problem in American high schools over the past decade (Birman and Natriello 1980). In New York City, for example, 16 out of 111 high schools had in 1975–76 average daily absence rates of 40 percent or more (Economic Development Council of New York City 1977, p. 6).

[8]Of course, those students who were truant from school when the questionnaires were administered did not have an opportunity to record themselves as being truant out of fear for their safety. Thus the statistics reported by the National Institute of Education survey for the percentage of students absent from school because of fear, high though it was, probably underestimated the problem, especially in big-city schools.

dents and intruders. In short, absenteeism may be partly a cause of school violence, partly an effect of it, and partly a reflection of values underlying coincidentally both truancy and school violence.

I mentioned the effect of high levels of student absenteeism on teacher morale. Teacher discouragement—"burnout," as it has come to be called—means that teachers stop putting forth the considerable effort required to educate even motivated students, much less uninterested students. Some quit teaching for other jobs; some take teaching positions in private or parochial schools at a big cut in pay; some take early retirement; some hold on grimly, taking as many days off as they are entitled to, including not only sick days but days in which to escape from pressure—informally called "mental health days." Thus, high rates of student absenteeism lead to high rates of teacher absenteeism. Teacher absenteeism, like student absenteeism, is partly an effect of violence and partly a cause of it. When teachers are absent, whatever the reason, substitute teachers must be found to take over their classes. In most schools, the scheduling of substitutes is part of the daily routine, and in fact quasi-permanent substitutes are attached to a school, moving from class to class on different days depending on which teacher calls in sick. In the more violent schools, however, not only must larger proportions of the teaching staff be replaced each day with substitutes, but fewer substitutes are willing to take an assignment. It is always more difficult for a substitute to maintain order than for a regular teacher. In a violent school, order may be virtually unattainable, and the substitute runs a greater risk of attack than does a regular teacher. A substitute's pay is often not worth it. With insufficient numbers of substitutes available, "study periods"—a misnomer—must be scheduled instead of regular classes. Study periods are less controlled than class periods at best; in these circumstances they are bedlam.

III. The Sociocultural Causes of School Violence

Despite the complexity of the problem and the difficulty of disentangling causes and effects, school violence is not simply the result of emotional disturbance on the part of intruders or enrolled students. Whatever the aggressive or predatory impulses of youngsters, social conditions can promote or impede their expression in behavior (Toby 1974). On one level, therefore, explaining school violence in modern societies requires explaining the sociocultural circumstances that make social control over such violence difficult. To do this, controlling school violence must be considered in the wider context of controlling deviant behavior and criminality. The same social forces that make violence more difficult to nip in the bud today than two generations ago, and more likely to be found in big-city schools than in small-town schools, also underlie the high crime rates of affluent urban-industrial societies. There are inherent difficulties in controlling deviant behavior in urbanized societies that emanate from the anonymity and mobility of urban life and the difficulty of identifying the ownership of property (Toby 1979, p. 118).

The same differential weakness of social control between more urbanized and less urbanized communities that makes robbery more than fifteen times as common in cities of one million or more as in towns of ten thousand or less (Federal Bureau of Investigation 1980, pp. 170–77) makes robbery more common in big-city schools than in small-town schools, particularly robbery of teachers. As might be expected, the disproportion in *robberies* between more urbanized and less urbanized communities is not as characteristic of *larcenies*, either in schools or in the larger society, because evasive offenses cannot be effectively controlled even in small towns. In 1979 the rate of reported larcenies was only 4 percent greater in cities of one million or more than in cities of ten thousand or less (Federal Bureau of Investigation 1980, pp. 170–71). Robberies, having a much greater defiant component than larcenies, are more effectively controlled in small towns than in big cities. Precisely the same pattern applies to schools, as tables 1 and 2 showed. The differential consequences of weak social control explains why intruders are more common in big-city schools than in small-town schools. Intruders in the schools, like robbers in the larger society, have predatory opportunities where social control is weak.

Weakness in social control also helps to explain *student* violence against teachers and against fellow students in big-city schools. While robbery of teachers might have been due largely to intruders, the higher rates of assault on teachers in schools of the largest cities cannot easily be accounted for by the incidental violence of intruder-robbers because *assaults* on teachers occurred more frequently than *robberies* of teachers. Students themselves must have attacked teachers more frequently in big-city schools than in schools in smaller communities, partly because of the effect of urban anonymity and partly because schools in the big cities were larger than schools in smaller cities. Intuitively, it seems obvious that staff control over students is weaker in the larger schools, and research seems to bear this out (Duke and Seidman 1981). Larger schools have a significantly higher incidence of student behavior problems, even when student background characteristics are controlled

(McPartland and McDill 1976, pp. 20, 30, 32). Social changes in American society have tended to reduce control generally over students in the public schools. Some of these developments have simultaneously swollen the numbers of youthful nonstudents not in the labor force and thereby contributed to the intruder problem. Others have made enrolled students less reluctant to express violent motivations. It is to these social changes that I now turn.[9]

A. *Professional-Bureaucratic Differentiation of School and Neighborhood*

Historically, the development of American public education increasingly separated the school from students' families and neighborhoods. Even the one-room schoolhouse of rural America represented separation of the educational process from the family. But the consolidated school districts in nonmetropolitan areas and the jumbo schools of the inner city carried separation much further. There were good reasons why large schools developed. The bigger the school, the lower the per capita cost of education. The bigger the school, the more feasible it was to hire teachers with academic specialties like art, music, drama, or advanced mathematics. The bigger the school, the more likely that teachers and administrators could operate according to professional standards instead of in response to local sensitivities—for example, in teaching biological evolution or in designing a sex-education curriculum. But the unintended consequence of large schools that operated efficiently by bureaucratic and professional standards was to make them relatively autonomous of the local community. The advantages of autonomy were obvious. The disadvantages took longer to reveal themselves.

The main disadvantage was that students developed distinctive subcultures only tangentially related to education. Thus, in data collected during the 1950s James S. Coleman (1961) found that American high school students seemed more preoccupied with athletics and personal popularity than with intellectual achievement. Students were doing their own thing, and their thing was not what teachers and principals were mainly concerned about. Presumably, if parents had been more closely involved in the educational process, they would have strengthened the academic influence of teachers. Even in the 1950s, student subcultures at school promoted misbehavior; in New York and other large cities, fights between members of street gangs from different neighborhoods sometimes broke out in secondary schools (Salisbury

[9]The section that follows draws extensively on Toby 1980a, pp. 26–32.

1958). However, Soviet achievements in space during the 1950s drew more attention to academic performance than to school crime and misbehavior. Insofar as community adults were brought into schools as teacher aides, they were introduced not to help control student misbehavior but to improve academic performance.

Until the 1960s and 1970s school administrators did not sufficiently appreciate the potential for disorder when many hundreds of young people come together for congregate education. Principals did not like to call in police, preferring to organize their own disciplinary procedures. They did not believe in security guards, preferring to use teachers to monitor behavior in the halls and lunchrooms. They did not tell school architects about the need for what has come to be called "defensible space," and as a result schools were built with too many ways to gain entrance from the outside and too many rooms and corridors where surveillance was difficult. Above all, they did not consider that they had lost control over potential student misbehavior when parents were kept far away, not knowing how their children were behaving. The focus of PTAs was the curriculum, and it was the better-educated, middle-class parents who tended to join such groups. In short, the isolation of the school from the local community always meant that, if a large enough proportion of students misbehaved, teachers and principals could not maintain order.

B. *Rising Expectations for Secondary and Postsecondary Education*

Another trend helping to explain how a less orderly school environment developed was the pressure to keep children in school longer—on the assumption that children needed all the education they could get to cope with a complicated urban industrial society. The positive side of this development was rising educational levels. Greater proportions of the age cohort graduated from high school and went on to postsecondary education than ever before. The negative aspect of compulsory school attendance laws and of informal pressure to stay in school longer was that youngsters who did not want further education were compelled to remain enrolled. Compulsory education laws vary from state to state. For example, Mississippi requires school attendance to age 13; four states to age 15; thirty-seven states to age 16; and nine states to age 17 or 18 (Grant and Lind 1979, p. 43). But they share an assumption that the state can compel not only school attendance but school achievement. In reality, compulsory education laws are successful only in keeping children *enrolled*, sometimes longer than the nominal age of compulsory school attendance. Parental consent was often written into the law as necessary for withdrawal from school before reaching 17 or 18 or a specified level of educational achievement, such as grade school graduation. Parents have little incentive to consent, partly because they hold unrealistic educational aspirations even for academically marginal students, partly because they recognize the difficulties faced by adolescents in the labor market and do not want their children loitering on the streets, and partly because benefits are available from programs like Aid to Families with Dependent Children for children enrolled in school.

Students also have incentives to remain enrolled, although not necessarily to attend regularly. In addition to conforming to parental pressure, they are called "students" although they are not necessarily studious, and this status has advantages. The school is more pleasant than the streets in cold or rainy weather—it is an interesting place to be. Friends are visited; enemies attacked; sexual adventures begun; drugs bought and sold; valuables stolen. There are material advantages also to being an enrolled student, such as bus passes and lunch tickets, which can be sold as well as used. Consequently, many remain enrolled although they are actually occasional or chronic truants. The existence of a large population of enrolled nonattenders blurs the line between intruders and students. School officials understand this all too well, but the compulsory school attendance laws prevent them from doing much about it.

Thus the attempt to force education on unwilling students produced a downward slide in academic and behavioral standards, which was more pronounced in schools whose predominant clientele was from ethnic groups unsupportive of academic effort. Italians were such a group in the 1930s when the heritage of rural Sicily was still strong (Toby 1957). Native Hawaiians constitute such a group today (Hawaii Crime Commission 1980). Involuntary students became bad school citizens.

C. *The Extension of Civil Rights to Children*

A third trend indirectly affecting school violence was the increasing sensitivity of public schools to the rights of children. A generation ago it was possible for principals to rule schools autocratically, to suspend or expel students without much regard for procedural niceties. Injustices occurred; children were "pushed out" of schools because they antagonized teachers and principals. But this arbitrariness enabled school administrators to control the situation when serious misbehavior occurred. Student assaults on teachers were punished so swiftly that they were almost unthinkable. Even disrespectful language was unusual. Today, as a result of greater concern for the rights of children, school officials are required to observe due process in handling student discipline (Phay 1975). Hearings are necessary. Charges must be specified. Witnesses must confirm suspicions. Appeals are provided for. Greater due process for students accused of misbehavior gives unruly students better protection against teachers and principals and well-behaved students worse protection from their classmates.

Related to the extension of civil rights in the school setting is the decreased ability of schools to get help with discipline problems from the juvenile courts. Like the schools themselves, the juvenile courts have become more attentive to children's rights. Juvenile courts are now less willing to exile children to a correctional Siberia. More than a decade ago the Supreme Court ruled that children could not be sent to juvenile prisons for "rehabilitation" unless proof existed that they had *done* something for which imprisonment was appropriate (*In Re Gault* 387 U.S. 1 [1967]). The *Gault* decision set off a revolution in juvenile court procedures. For example, more formal hearings with youngsters represented by attorneys became common practice for serious offenses that might result in incarceration. Furthermore, a number of state legislatures restricted the discretion of juvenile court judges. In New York and New Jersey, for example, juvenile court judges may not commit a youngster to correctional institutions for "status offenses"—that is, for behavior that would not be a crime if done by adults. Thus truancy or ungovernable behavior in school or at home is not grounds for incarceration in New York and New Jersey. The differentiation of juvenile delinquents from persons in need of supervision (PINS in New York nomenclature, JINS in New Jersey) may have been needed. However, one consequence of this reform is that the public schools can less easily persuade juvenile courts to act in school-discipline cases. In some cases the juvenile court judge cannot incarcerate because the behavior is a status offense rather than "delinquency." In other cases the alleged behavior is indeed delinquency, such as slapping or punching a teacher; but many judges will not commit a youngster to a correctional institution for such behavior because they have to deal with what they perceive as *worse* juvenile violence on the streets.

Increased attention to civil rights for students, including students accused of violence, was also an unintended consequence of compulsory school attendance laws. The Supreme Court held in *Goss v. Lopez* (491 U.S. 565 [1975]) (1) that the state, in enacting a compulsory school attendance law, incurred an *obligation* to educate children until the age specified in the law was reached and (2) that greater due-process protections were required for students in danger of suspension for more than ten days or for expulsion, than for students threatened with less severe disciplinary penalties. Boards of education interpreted these requirements to mean that formal hearings were necessary in cases of youngsters subject to compulsory education and in danger of severe penalties. Such hearings were to be conducted at a higher administrative level than the school itself, and the principals had to document the case and produce witnesses who could be cross-examined. In Hawaii, for example, which has a compulsory education law extending to age 18, Rule 21, which the Hawaii Department of Education adopted in 1976 to meet the requirements of *Goss v. Lopez*, aroused unanimous dissatisfaction from principals interviewed in the Crime Commission's study of school violence and vandalism (Hawaii Crime Commission 1980, pp. 322–37). They had three complaints. First, in cases where expulsion or suspension of more than ten days might be the outcome, the principal was required to gather evidence, to file notices, and to participate in long adversarial hearings at the district superintendent's office in a prosecutorial capacity, which discouraged principals from initiating this procedure in serious cases. Thus principals downgraded serious offenses in order to deal with them, expeditiously, by means of informal hearings. Second, Rule 21 forbade principals to impose a series of short suspensions of a student within one semester that cumulatively amounted to more than ten days unless there was a formal hearing. Although intended to prevent principals from getting around the requirement for formal hearings in serious cases involving long suspensions, what this provision achieved was to prevent principals from imposing any discipline at all on multiple offenders. Once suspended for a total of ten days in a semester, a student could engage in minor and not-so-minor misbehavior with impunity. Third, the principals complained that their obligation to supply "alternative education" for students expelled or suspended for more than ten days was unrealistic in terms of available facilities.

D. *The Erosion of the Authority of Teachers*

Social changes that separated secondary schools from effective family and neighborhood influences, that kept older adolescents enrolled in school whether they craved education or not, and that made it burdensome for school administrators to expel students guilty of violent behavior or to suspend them for more than ten days partially explain the erosion of the authority of the teacher. Parents and neighbors could not lend their authority to teachers without being psychologically present in the classroom.[10] Involuntary students were not nearly as likely as voluntary students to regard the teacher's edicts as sacred. And students who violated school rules and seemed to get away with it made it more difficult for teachers to respond effectively to other disciplinary infractions. *Social* changes were not the entire explanation, however. There have also been *cultural* changes undermining the authority of teachers. We have come a long way from the time when teachers were considered godlike. Doubtless, reduced respect for teachers is part of fundamental cultural changes by which many authority figures—parents, police, government officials, employers—have come to have less prestige. In the case of teachers, the general demythologizing was amplified by special ideological criticism. Best-selling books of the 1960s portrayed teachers, especially white middle-class teachers, as the villains of education, insensitive, authoritarian, and even racist (Herndon 1968; Holt 1964; Kohl 1967; Kozol 1967).

Concomitant with the erosion of teacher authority was the decline of homework in public secondary schools. When teachers could depend on all but a handful of students to turn in required written homework, they could assign homework and mean it. The slackers could be disciplined. But in schools where teachers could no longer count on a majority of students doing their homework, assigning it became a meaningless ritual, and some teachers gave up. James Coleman found that private and parochial school sophomores in high school reported doing, on the average, two hours more of homework per week than public school sophomores (Coleman, Hoffer, and Kilgore 1981). Many teachers felt they lacked authority to induce students to do *anything* they did not want to do: to attend classes regularly, to keep quiet so orderly recitation could proceed, to refrain from annoying a disliked classmate. The erosion of teacher authority was responsible for only part of the epidemic of school violence. Erosion of teacher authority had little to do with violence perpetrated by intruders. Its main effect was on students, who were less likely to commit violent acts when run-of-the-mill teachers could effectively influence behavior in their classes, in hallways, and in lunchrooms. Individual teachers still control their classes, especially those with charisma. What has changed is that the *role* of teacher no longer has

[10]Travis Hirschi (1969) uses the concept of "psychologically present" authority figures as a mechanism of social control.

the authority it once did for students and their parents; this means that less forceful, less experienced, or less effective teachers cannot rely on the authority of the role to help them maintain control. They are on their own in a sense that the previous generation was not (Rubel 1977).

E. *Sociocultural Differentiation of Schools within School Systems*

School violence occurs in all kinds of schools. However, school violence is harder to control in large urban school systems than in rural or suburban schools for two reasons. One is the intruder problem, which springs from the general weakness of social control in big cities. The other is that certain big-city public high schools are more likely to develop a critical mass of rebellious students than are high schools in smaller school systems. Large school systems tend to become differentiated into better and worse schools. In a school system with only one high school all secondary school students attend it; differentiation between schools is not possible. As a result of natural processes of social competition in big-city school systems, the least troublesome students with the best academic skills, the more stimulating teachers, and the more competent principals gravitate to one group of high schools, and badly behaved students, demoralized teachers, and administrative hacks gravitate to another.[11] This process is unplanned and often violates deliberate efforts of the central administration. But it is difficult to prevent. Schools choose and are chosen by teachers, principals, and students in a marketlike situation. For example, teachers and principals try to avoid unruly schools. The better their training and experience, the less likely they are to accept positions in disorderly schools; in turn, they are attractive to the schools that they prefer. Furthermore, union contracts often allow teachers to bid on open positions on the basis of seniority, which causes a natural gravitation to more congenial schools by higher-paid and more experienced teachers.

A slightly different marketlike process operates with students. Some urban high schools are highly selective: Bronx High School of Science, Boston Latin, Cincinnati Academy of Mathematics and Science, Chicago's Whitney Young Magnet High School, Houston High School for the Health Professions. Even vocational high schools, once the dumping ground for academic failures and behavior problems, now select students. Aviation High School in New York City, where more than two

---

[11]Junior high schools are also differentiated in big-city school systems but not as much as senior high schools because (1) they are smaller to begin with and (2) there are few selective junior high schools comparable to the selective high schools.

thousand students study aircraft maintenance, admits only seven hundred out of four thousand applicants each year, using a screening process that includes aptitude tests and personal interviews. Individual high schools within a large urban school system can be selective even though the school system as a whole is not permitted to give up on any student, no matter how unmotivated, rebellious, or handicapped he or she may be. Paradoxically, the more numerous the selective high schools within an urban school system, the more likely it is that other schools within the system will have a high concentration of troublesome students. They are attended by students not admitted to selective schools and by the failures and disciplinary problems rejected from parochial and private schools. Even in the absence of an ethnically diverse population, the differentiation process tends to be fueled by socioeconomic differences; schools containing a large proportion of middle-class children are more oriented to educational achievement and less violent than schools with many lower-class children. But ethnic diversity reinforces this socioeconomic basis for differentiation. Thus, high schools on Oahu Island of Hawaii having a high proportion of native Hawaiians tend to have lower standards of academic achievement and greater school violence than high schools with greater proportions of Japanese-American students (Hawaii Crime Commission 1980).

The history of Dunbar High School in Washington, D.C., illustrates both the possibility of creaming good students for a selective school and the deterioration of an urban high school in a high-crime neighborhood when it draws only upon its local catchment area for clientele (Sowell 1974). Dunbar recruited academically motivated black children between 1870 and 1955, worked them hard, and sent most to college. Its alumni included the first black cabinet member, a United States senator, and distinguished judges. The Dunbar record showed that an all-black high school could be both safe and academically successful, and Dunbar did it with inadequate facilities. However, Dunbar had voluntary students during this period. When Dunbar stopped being selective in 1954, when it enrolled students from its neighborhood catchment area whether they wanted to attend or not, it developed the disciplinary and academic problems that might be expected from a school serving a black population on the socioeconomic floor of American society.

When a school starts downhill as a result of these natural forces of competition that differentiate better from worse high schools, the more educationally oriented students, both black and white, accelerate the process by deciding that it is time to flee. This siphoning off of better-behaved, industrious students makes it more difficult to control those that remain. Class cutting increases, and students wander through the halls in increasing numbers. In the classrooms, teachers struggle for attention. Students talk with one another; they engage in playful and not so playful fights; they leave repeatedly to visit the toilet or get drinks of water. Some are inattentive because they have recently smoked marijuana or drunk alcohol; they become defiant or abusive when the teacher tries to maintain order. Only a quixotic teacher expects students to do homework or to take books home and study assigned lessons. A teacher is lucky when students come to class and remain reasonably quiet. Occasional interest is a victory.

IV. The Individual Causes of School Violence

Whatever the sociocultural roots of school violence, some students are more prone to violence than others. Sociocultural variables operate through family and neighborhood socialization experiences to produce some violent students in middle-class suburban schools and some high academic achievers from the black ghetto of Chicago's South Side. In short, however they are produced, the personalities of some students are more violent than others and are more likely to lead to violent behavior. In addition, some students, because of their attitudes and interests, are less responsive to the informal controls consisting of the approval and disapproval of teachers and other authority figures in the school. Having less stake in conformity (Toby 1957), they are freer to engage in deviant behavior of all kinds, including violence.

Although personality disturbances make some children more prone than others to engage in violent behavior, school systems have been too ready to infer personality disorders from violent behavior (Cressey 1954). Even psychiatric experts have a difficult time putting adolescent misbehavior into clear-cut diagnostic categories because personality disturbances in young people are more amorphous than in older people. And the rules governing "special education" in the public schools have compounded the confusion between compulsive violence and violence that may be deliberate. Part of the confusion arises because "special education" serves a heterogeneous group of students, some with physical handicaps, others with behavior problems from which emotional handicaps may be inferred.

In 1975 Congress passed Public Law 94-142, the Education for All Handicapped Children Act. This law provided "not only that every handicapped child is entitled to a free public education, but that such an education shall be provided *in the least restrictive educational setting*" (Hewett and Watson 1979, p. 305).[12] Thus the philosophy of mainstreaming handicapped children—"exceptional" children, as they are sometimes called—became national policy. Some of the handicaps are verifiable independent of classroom behavior: deafness, blindness, motor problems, speech pathologies, retardation. But learning disabilities and behavior disorders, especially the latter, are much more ambiguous. Does a child who punches other children in his classroom have a behavior disorder for which he should be pitied, or does he deserve punishment for bad behavior? The state of Hawaii ran into this dilemma in attempting to implement Public Law 94-142. The Board of Education promulgated Rule 49.13, which asserted that "handicapped children in special education programs may not be seriously disciplined by suspensions for over ten days or by dismissal from school for violating any of the school's rules" (Hawaii Crime Commission 1980, p. 339). This meant that there were two standards of behavior, one for ordinary students and one for "handicapped" students. But students who were classified as handicapped because of a clinical judgment that they were "emotionally disturbed"—usually inferred from "acting out" behavior— seemed to be getting a license to commit disciplinary infractions.

> [I]t was the consensus of fourteen principals from the Leeward and Central School Districts of Oahu . . . that the special disciplinary section under Rule 49 created a "double standard" between regular students who were subject to varying degrees of suspensions and special education students who were not. These principals believe that such an alleged double standard fosters a belief among special education students that they are immune from suspension under regular disciplinary rules and, therefore, can engage in misconduct with impunity. (Hawaii Crime Commission 1980, p. 340)

In short, "special education" students who are placed in that category because of diagnosed emotional disturbance may have violence-prone personalities. On the other hand, they may only be assumed to have such personalities because they have engaged in inexplicably violent behavior. Lack of precision in the diagnosis of personality pathologies in adolescents complicates the problem of controlling student misbehavior. The ordinary student and the "emotionally disturbed" special education student may be misbehaving in similar ways in the same classroom, yet different rules apply to them. And it is not clear why one is considered

---

[12]Italics in original.

sick and therefore less responsible for misbehavior whereas the other is subject to ordinary school discipline. Regardless of whether a scientific justification exists for classifying some youngsters as "handicapped" by virtue of emotional disturbance, the better strategy from a social control point of view is to assume that self-control is possible for an emotionally disturbed youngster. Failure to make this assumption undercuts the effectiveness of social control. In formulating Rule 49.13 the Department of Education of the state of Hawaii has been more explicit about denying responsibility to certain misbehaving youngsters, but the same tendency can be observed in other school systems. It seems unjust to hold a child responsible for violent behavior that he cannot help. Yet failure to hold children responsible means that they are more likely to engage in violence than they would otherwise be.

V. Alternative Strategies for Restoring Order
in Violent Schools

Most public schools are reasonably orderly. Even in the largest cities, where school violence is statistically most frequent, the number of schools that are truly dangerous is small. But though only a minority of big-city schools are chaotic, chaotic schools are highly visible through mass-media reports. They give all public schools a bad name and thereby promote the flight of educationally oriented students to private and parochial schools. One reason the descent into violence is difficult to reverse is that, from the point of view of nonviolent students and their parents, it seems simpler to transfer to a safer school than to wait and see whether the downward slide can be reversed. Of course this is not a solution from the point of view of the community as a whole. Most parents are not affluent enough, cunning enough, or concerned enough to transfer their children out of violent schools.

From the point of view of American society as a whole, the solution is to upgrade the disorderly schools, not only so that the children attending them feel safe, but also so that intellectually able students can use them as stepping-stones to further educational and occupational opportunities. At least three strategies are possible.

A. *Charismatic Administrative Leadership*

A charismatic principal can maintain order in a difficult urban school, but it requires enormous energy. The principal must be everywhere, talking with students in halls and classrooms, explaining to teachers why due-process requirements mandated by the courts make it difficult to back them up in disciplinary cases, watching for intruders, mollifying parents, controlling by effort what was possible by decree a generation ago. Such dedication is rare. The personal cost is great. Principals burn out too. Not only do principals burn out, but some are more competent and diligent than others to begin with.

B. *Redistribution of Behavior Problems within Large School Systems*

One aspect of the problem of disorderly schools is the concentration of educationally uninterested, violence-prone students in certain schools of large school systems. Redistributing these difficult cases uniformly through the system instead of permitting them to pile up in a few schools might at least improve the most troublesome schools. This strategy is in fact attempted. Central administrations set quotas of emotionally disturbed "special education" students for high schools whether the principals want them or not. Disciplinary transfers of students are made, partly to give problem students a fresh start in a new milieu but also to help principals cope with a high concentration of violence problems. Students are also transported into schools they have not selected and that are not near their homes in order to achieve racial balance in the school system as a whole—and incidentally to prevent some schools from being more violent than others and less committed to academic values. Nevertheless, no school system has come close to equalizing behavior problems within its constituent schools.

There are several reasons for this failure. In the first place, school boards are not insulated from political pressure in a democratic society, especially one like the United States, where education is primarily a local responsibility. Parents strenuously resist the introduction of large numbers of problem students into a tranquil school that their children attend—and resist even more strenuously the transfer of their children into a violent school. Second, big-city school systems are unwilling or unable to do away with selective high schools, probably because powerful constituencies demand such educational resources. These constituencies tend to oppose allocating a fair share of problem students to such schools as the Bronx High School of Science. In short, it is difficult to impose a political solution in a pluralistic society with a strong tradition of individual choice. Students cannot readily be forced to attend schools they or their parents consider unsafe, because alternatives exist: not only private and parochial schools but illegal evasions of official assignments. Some parents establish a fictitious residence far from their actual home, perhaps by installing a telephone at the home of a friend or relative and using the bill as "proof" that they live there; their children then commute to the "safer" public school. And, if all else fails, the family can relocate to another school district. Short of imposing controls on residential mobility as well as freedom of transfer to private schools, it seems unlikely that the stratification of schools within large school systems can be abolished.

Perhaps this is just as well. An equitable distribution of behavior problems throughout an urban school system might well spread violence into more schools and accelerate the decline of the public school system as a whole. Historically, the opposite distributive strategy has proved more feasible; allow some schools to become excellent and others terrible, and at the same time track students within schools so that even bad schools have islands of academic achievement and safety. That tradition produced special schools for disciplinary problems as well as "vocational" schools that functioned essentially as places to which problem students could be exiled. In recent years "alternative" schools have played somewhat the same role as the vocational schools of a generation ago, but on a smaller scale. However, this has been perceived as an elitist strategy and, workable or not, is not likely to be implemented in the present ideological climate. The implications of the philosophy of "mainstreaming" are that comprehensive schools are more desirable than specialized ones and that tracking should be used only as a last resort.

C. *Establishing Minimum Behavioral Standards for Continuing Enrollment*

A third strategy is to establish minimum behavioral standards for students in public schools that are enforceable by credible threats, including possible termination of enrollment. Such a strategy is an affront to the ideological tradition that children need an education whether they want one or not. Terminating enrollment for failure to meet minimum behavioral standards violates the philosophy of the compulsory attendance laws. Note that minimum behavioral standards are what make private schools successful. As Albert Shanker, president of the American Federation of Teachers, has pointed out, the superior academic achievement of private schools found in the recent Coleman study (Coleman, Hoffer, and Kilgore 1981), results from their ability to restrict enrollment to students who meet their behavioral standards.

> Parents choose to pay for private schools rather than send their children to free public schools for the same reason that thousands of teachers who once taught in public schools are now teaching at lower

salaries in private schools. The learning atmosphere may be better. There are fewer disruptions. There is much less fear of violence. There is, in a word, discipline. But that discipline does not come from superior teachers, administrators or programs. It comes from simply refusing to take in the school those students who are discipline problems—and expelling those who behave anti-socially. (Shanker 1980)

An obstacle preventing public schools from imitating private schools in insisting on nonviolent behavior from students is the lack of integration between laws defining juvenile delinquency and authorizing state action to cope with it and laws compelling school attendance. Unless a juvenile court judge decides to send a juvenile offender to a correctional institution, thereby removing him or her from the public schools, the youngster is still required to attend school. Even if the offense is a violent one committed at the school where the offender is enrolled, the juvenile court is not expected to consider the consequences for teachers and fellow students of the offender's continued presence. For example, a boy who has slapped his teacher or extorted money from his classmates may be treated by a juvenile court judge in terms of his own needs and the protection of the larger society but not in terms of the school as an important social institution. In their internal disciplinary procedures, school systems face the same problem. Even when school officials think that no appreciable educational benefits to the offender will result from his remaining enrolled in school and that considerable harm will be done to the educational process, the mechanism for making an exception to the compulsory attendance rule is so cumbersome that the youngster usually remains enrolled.

Compulsory attendance is treated, at least implicitly, as more important than promoting an orderly classroom environment. Yet everyone recognizes that the physical presence of the youngster in a building called a school is only a *prerequisite* for education, not a guarantee that it will take place. In order to require studious behavior on the part of students—regular attendance, completion of homework, reasonable attentiveness in class, nonviolent behavior toward teachers and classmates—the assumption that enrollment guarantees education would have to be changed. Youngsters would have to do certain things and refrain from doing others to remain students in good standing. Those who fail to maintain student status in this sense would be politely invited to interrupt their enrollment until they are ready to make a commitment to education.

Determining at what age youngsters are mature enough to be given the responsibility for an achieved identity as a student rather than an ascribed identity is, ultimately, an empirical question. Given the tradition of compulsory education in the United States until approximately 16 years of age, 15 might be a reasonable choice. If it turned out that there were still too many involuntary "students" to enable order to be restored in the worst big-city schools, consideration might be given to lowering the age of compulsory attendance to 14.

Lowering the age of compulsory school attendance will not necessarily tempt thousands of teenagers onto the streets to become addicts, prostitutes, or drug pushers. Most youngsters presented with a choice between going to a real school, which involves educational effort and self-control, and becoming a nonstudent, with the attendant stigma resulting from not being employed and not attending school, opt for education. Even in neighborhoods where the drop-out rate is already high, parental pressure works in favor of continued school enrollment. The choice between continued school enrollment and dropping out might shift in favor of continued enrollment if it implied genuine education. It does not imply education now for many children enrolled in urban secondary schools, particularly disorderly schools. The choice for them is fooling around in school or fooling around on the streets.

To be sure, insisting that enrolled students meet minimum behavioral standards instead of requiring all youngsters to attend school, no matter what they do and how little they learn, represents a shift in educational philosophy. It would mean that schools would no longer be multipurpose institutions, part educational, part recreational, part incarcerative. The paramount orientation of the school would be educational. Youngsters not interested in education would temporarily lose their enrollment—on the understanding that, as soon as they felt ready to use the school for its proper purpose, they should hasten to return. Withdrawal would be an episode, a temporary one, not a tragedy, because the expectation would be that eventually all youngsters would recognize that they *need* education. Since a recognition of the importance of education might be rekindled at any age, the reentry of 16-, 17-, and 18-year-olds to high school would be quite normal. Students would be freer to leave school than they are at present and more welcome when and if they return. For example, special arrangements might be made to encourage students to return to enrollment even in the middle of a semester, as soon as they felt willing to work on their own educational development.

It would be useless to redefine the mission of the school and to insist that enrolled students be committed to education if those who choose not to remain enrolled can infiltrate school buildings at will. It will be even more necessary than at present to be vigilant about intruders so that street youths are prevented from making disruptive forays into school buildings. The cost of choosing not to be educated must be that the benefits, as well as the burdens, of school citizenship are lost. Only when the lines are sharply drawn between education and the streets will it be possible to tell whether increasing the voluntariness of public education can reduce school violence appreciably.

VI. The Prospects for Reducing School Violence in the United States

The genie cannot be stuffed back into the bottle. Now that school violence has become a national concern and the public schools are in danger of losing the universal educational appeal that was their virtue, it is difficult to accept violent schools with fatalistic resignation. Experiments will be tried and laws will be changed in order to bring school violence under control, not in private or public selective schools but in inner-city schools enrolling disadvantaged minorities. Eventually, solutions to the problem of school violence will be discovered. The alternative would be the erosion of public secondary education.

REFERENCES

Associated Press. 1981. "Violent Activities on Upsurge in Japan's Schools," *Honolulu Star-Bulletin*, 11 April.
Birman, Beatrice F., and Gary Natriello. 1980. "Perspective on Absenteeism in High Schools: Multiple Explanations for an Epidemic." In *School Crime and Violence*, ed. Robert Rubel. Lexington, Mass.: D. C. Heath.
Coleman, James S. 1961. *The Adolescent Society*. New York: Free Press of Glencoe.
Coleman, James S., Thomas Hoffer, and Sally Kilgore. 1981. *Public and Private Schools*. Washington, D.C.: Educational Resources Information Center, National Institute of Education.
Cressey, Donald R. 1954. "The Differential Association Theory and Compulsive Crimes," *Journal of Criminal Law, Criminology and Police Science* 45: 35–38.
Duke, Daniel L., and William Seidman. 1981. "School Organization and Stu-

dent Behavior: A Review." Mimeographed. Palo Alto: Stanford University Department of Education.

Economic Development Council of New York City, Inc. 1977. "Truancy in New York City's Public Schools: Its Nature, Costs, and Implications for the Future." New York: Economic Development Council of New York City, Inc.

Federal Bureau of Investigation (U.S. Department of Justice). 1980. *Crime in the United States—1979*. Washington, D.C.: U.S. Government Printing Office.

Gaiter, Dorothy J. 1980. "For Some City Pupils, to Ride a Bus Is to Risk a Mugging," *New York Times*, 15 September.

Gottfredson, Gary D., and Denise C. Daiger. 1979. *Disruption in Six Hundred Schools: The Social Ecology of Personal Victimization in the Nation's Public Schools.* Baltimore: Center for Social Organization of Schools, Johns Hopkins University.

Grant, W. Vance, and C. George Lind. 1979. *Digest of Education Statistics.* Washington, D.C.: U.S. Government Printing Office.

Hawaii Crime Commission. 1980. *Violence and Vandalism in the Public Schools of Hawaii.* Honolulu: Hawaii Crime Commission.

Herndon, James. 1968. *The Way It Spozed to Be.* New York: Simon and Schuster.

Hewett, Frank M., and Philip C. Watson. 1979. "Classroom Management and the Exceptional Learner." In *Classroom Management*, ed. Daniel L. Duke. Chicago: University of Chicago Press.

Hindelang, Michael J. 1976. *Criminal Victimization in Eight American Cities: A Descriptive Analysis of Common Theft and Assault.* Cambridge, Mass.: Ballinger.

Hindelang, Michael J., and N. Joan McDermott. 1981. *Juvenile Criminal Behavior: An Analysis of Rates and Victim Characteristics.* Washington, D.C.: U.S. Government Printing Office.

Hirschi, Travis. 1969. *Causes of Delinquency.* Berkeley and Los Angeles: University of California Press.

Holt, John. 1964. *How Children Fail.* New York: Pittman.

Kihss, Peter. 1981. "Student, 16, Is Charged in Death of Teacher Trying to Halt a Fight," *New York Times*, 7 April.

Kohl, Herbert. 1967. *Thirty-six Children.* New York: New American Library.

Kozol, Jonathan. 1967. *Death at an Early Age: The Destruction of the Minds and Hearts of Negro Children in the Boston Public Schools.* Boston: Houghton Mifflin.

McDermott, N. Joan, and Michael J. Hindelang. 1981. *Juvenile Criminal Behavior in United States: Its Trends and Patterns.* Washington, D.C.: U.S. Government Printing Office.

McPartland, James M., and Edward L. McDill. 1976. *Violence in Schools: Perspectives, Programs, and Positions.* Lexington, Mass.: D. C. Heath.

Muir, Edward. 1978. *Annual Report of the School Safety Committee for the 1977–1978 School Year.* New York: United Federation of Teachers.

Murray, Geoffrey. 1981. "Japan's School Discipline Crumbles," *Christian Science Monitor*, 18 March.

Parsons, Talcott. 1951. *The Social System.* Glencoe, Ill.: Free Press.

Phay, Robert E. 1975. "The Law of Suspension and Expulsion: An Examination of the Substantive Issues in Controlling Student Conduct." National Organization on Legal Problems of Education 7. Washington, D.C.: ERIC Clearinghouse on Educational Management.

Rubel, Robert J. 1977. *The Unruly School: Disorders, Disruptions, and Crime.* Lexington, Mass.: D. C. Heath.

Salisbury, Harrison. 1958. *The Shook-up Generation.* New York: Harper.

Savitz, Leonard D., Michael Lalli, and Lawrence Rosen. 1977. *City Life and Delinquency—Victimization, Fear of Crime, and Gang Membership.* Washington, D.C.: U.S. Government Printing Office.

Shanker, Albert. 1980. "What's the Attraction of Private Schools?" *New York Times,* 8 June.

Sowell, Thomas. 1974. "Black Excellence: The Case of Dunbar High School," *Public Interest* 35:1–21.

Sparks, Richard F. 1981. "Surveys of Victimization—An Optimistic Assessment." In *Crime and Justice: An Annual Review of Research,* vol. 3, ed. Michael Tonry and Norval Morris. Chicago: University of Chicago Press.

Speiser, Lester B., and Irving Sanders. 1979. "When a Student Attacks a Teacher," *New York Times,* 29 December.

Toby, Jackson. 1957, "Hoodlum or Business Man: An American Dilemma." In *The Jews: Social Patterns of an American Group,* ed. Marshall Sklare. Glencoe, Ill.: Free Press.

———. 1974. "The Socialization and Control of Deviant Motivation." In *Handbook of Criminology,* ed. Daniel Glaser. Chicago: Rand McNally.

———. 1979. "Delinquency in Cross-Cultural Perspective." In *Juvenile Justice: The Progressive Legacy and Current Reforms,* ed. LaMar T. Empey. Charlottesville: University Press of Virginia.

———. 1980a. "Crime in American Public Schools," *Public Interest* 58:18–42.

———. 1980b. "Where Are the Streakers Now?" In *Sociological Theory and Research,* ed. Hubert M. Blalock. New York: Free Press.

U.S. Department of Health, Education, and Welfare. 1978. *Violent Schools—Safe Schools: The Safe School Study Report to the Congress.* Washington, D.C.: National Institute of Education.

U.S. Department of Justice. 1979. *Criminal Victimization in Urban Schools.* Washington, D.C.: U.S. Government Printing Office.

Philip J. Cook

The Influence of Gun Availability on Violent Crime Patterns

ABSTRACT

The spectacular increases in violent crime that began in the mid-1960s continue, and Americans are currently being murdered, robbed, and raped at historically unprecedented rates. Firearms are used in a minority of violent crimes but are of special concern because more than 60 percent of the most serious crimes—criminal homicides—are committed with firearms. This essay presents a variety of evidence to the effect that the widespread availability of firearms contributes to the criminal homicide rate and influences violent crime patterns in several other respects as well.

A gun is usually superior to other weapons readily available for use in violent crime; even in the hands of a weak and unskilled assailant, a gun poses a credible threat and can be used to kill quickly, from a distance, and in a relatively "impersonal" fashion. Guns are particularly valuable against relatively invulnerable targets. Hence, gun availability facilitates robbery of commercial places and lethal assaults on people who would ordinarily be able to defend themselves against other weapons. Some of the patterns of gun use in violent crime can be readily interpreted in terms of relative vulnerability of different types of victims.

Guns are also more dangerous than other weapons, in the sense that victims of robbery and assault are more likely to be killed if the assailant uses a gun. On the other hand, the victim is *less* likely to be injured in a gun robbery than in other robberies, since the gun robber usually does not feel the need to employ physical force.

This analysis suggests a number of predictions concerning the effects of gun availability on the number, distribution, and seriousness of violent crimes. In principle, these predictions could be tested directly by observing the effects of changes in gun availability on statistical characterizations of violent crime patterns. Not much research of this sort has been done,

Philip J. Cook is Associate Professor of Public Policy Studies and Economics at Duke University.
This essay is a substantial revision of my earlier paper entitled "The Role of Firearms in Violent Crime: An Interpretive Review of the Literature, with Some New Findings and Suggestions for Future Research." This revision owes a great deal to the editors of this volume.

in part because it is difficult to find a suitable measure for gun availability. Future research should be directed toward remedying this problem. In the meantime, it seems fair to conclude from the available evidence that the type of weapon is not an incidental aspect of violent crime, but rather has a substantial influence on the nature of the encounter and its likely consequences.

Approximately 682,000 violent crimes were committed with firearms in 1977, including 11,300 criminal homicides, 367,000 assaults (ranging from criminal threats with a gun up to attempted murder), 15,000 rapes, and 289,000 robberies (Cook 1981b). This high volume of gun-related crime is a reflection of two unarguable facts: first, the rates at which people attacked and threatened each other with any and all types of weapons reached unprecedented levels during the 1970s; second, a large fraction of the United States public has ready access to firearms.

There are at present 100–140 million firearms in private possession, of which 30–40 million are handguns (Wright et al. 1981).[1] These numbers are the result of a decade of growth in the private inventory of firearms; the total volume of handgun import and manufacture for the past decade has exceeded the total volume for the preceding six decades combined, and new sales of long guns have also been high during recent years. Surprisingly, the fraction of households owning one or more firearms has remained constant (at about 50 percent) since 1959; the rapid influx of new guns is accounted for by the growth in the number of households during the 1970s and by a tendency for gun-owning households to increase their average inventory. The most important aspect of this tendency is the increase in the number of households that own handguns; by 1978 about half of all gun-owning households (24 percent of all households) possessed at least one handgun, whereas in 1959 only about one-quarter of gun-owning households possessed handguns.[2]

---

[1]The other statistics in this paragraph are also taken from Wright et al. (1981). Their calculations are based on careful analysis of both national survey data and data on manufacturing and import. Cook (1982) presents a more detailed analysis of the commercial flows of new handguns in a recent year.

[2]Some handguns are of course being sold to households that have never previously owned a gun, but this is the exception rather than the rule—75 percent of households that own handguns also own at least one rifle or shotgun (Cook 1982). Hobbyists and sportsmen continue to dominate the statistics with respect to firearms ownership: I estimate that the top one-third of handgun-owning households (about 7.5 percent of all households) own more than 60 percent of all handguns, and the top one-third of all long-gun-owning households (about 14 percent of all households) own more than 60 percent of all long guns (Cook 1982).

I believe that the widespread availability of firearms has a profound influence on violent crime patterns. The principal purpose of this essay is to explain and justify this highly controversial assertion. The secondary purpose is to summarize the descriptive statistical information concerning the role of firearms in violent crime. Section I presents a brief overview of trends and patterns in firearm use in the four major types of violent crime—criminal homicide, aggravated assault, robbery, and rape. Sections II–IV present and interpret some of the evidence suggesting that the type of weapon used in a violent crime is not an incidental or inconsequential aspect of the event, but rather one that influences the choices made by both criminal and victim and the likely consequences of these choices. First, section II sets out a conceptual framework for thinking about weapon use in violent crime. Major elements of this framework include the *vulnerability hypothesis* (firearms are more useful and more likely to be employed against relatively invulnerable targets) and the *objective dangerousness hypothesis* (the probability of death in an assault or robbery is greater if the assailant uses a gun than if he uses another weapon). These hypotheses, together with several others, provide a concise explanation for observed weapon-related patterns in violent crime and provide a basis for predicting the effects of changes in the availability of firearms. Sections III and IV present some of the statistical evidence relevant to evaluating the vulnerability and objective dangerousness hypotheses; most of this evidence is confirmatory, though much research remains to be done. The most direct approach to testing these hypotheses is systematic analysis of the effects of changes in gun availability on violent crime patterns. Section V presents a brief discussion of the problems entailed in conducting such tests, focusing on the preliminary problem of defining "gun availability" in an operational fashion. Finally, section VI suggests a modest agenda for future research.

It should be noted at the outset that the crime of rape is virtually ignored in this essay, even though it obviously deserves equal treatment with robbery and assault. The reason is simply the absence of pertinent information on the role of weapons in rape.

I. Trends in Violent Crime Rates

The postwar "baby boom" cohorts have been responsible for an extraordinarily rapid increase in violent crime rates. Between 1965 and 1974, the police-reported rates of criminal homicide, rape, and aggravated assault each doubled, and the robbery rate tripled. After a brief

respite between 1975 and 1977, violent crime rates began increasing
again, and the most recent data suggest that they reached an all-time high
in 1980 and are continuing to increase.

A decade ago it was popular among criminologists to discount these
trend data, primarily on the grounds that they might be reflecting an
upward trend in the fraction of violent crimes reported to the police (and
thence to the FBI) rather than an increase in the "true" crime rates. One
problem with this argument is that it does not apply to the criminal
homicide rate, which is believed to reflect nearly a 100 percent reporting
rate. Since criminal homicides are *known* to have been increasing rapidly
during the violent decade beginning in 1965, it seems entirely reasonable
to take the trend data shown in table 1 on other violent crimes at near face
value.

The effects of this incredible growth in violent crime are varied and
surely profound, ranging from substantially reduced life expectancy and
enhanced disability rates for some demographic groups to the widespread adoption of costly efforts to minimize victimization risk. Indeed,
the effects are much more obvious than the ultimate causes. One possible
cause is the increased availability of guns during the past fifteen years, an
issue to which the data in table 2 are germane.

In recent years, firearms have been used in more than 60 percent of the
criminal homicides, and in about two-fifths of the reported robberies and
one-quarter of the reported aggravated assaults. (The *Uniform Crime
Reports* offer no data on weapon use in rape.) Most of these gun-related
crimes involve handguns. Since handgun ownership has become much
more widespread over the past two decades, it is reasonable to suppose
that increased gun availability has exacerbated the violent crime problem
in recent years. Although I believe this conclusion is correct, it is far

TABLE 1

Percentage Increases in Violent Crime Rates

Year	Nonnegligent Manslaughter and Murder	Aggravated Assault	Robbery	Rape	Burglary
1965–70	53	48	141	54	64
1970–75	23	40	27	44	43
1975–80	6	28	12	38	9
1965–80	100	165	242	206	156

Source: Computed from data in Federal Bureau of Investigation, *Crime in the United States*, 1970, p. 65; *Crime in the United States*, 1980, p. 41.

TABLE 2

Trends in Violent Crime Rates and Gun Use in Violent Crime

Year	Nonnegligent Manslaughter and Murder			Aggravated Assault		Robbery	
	Rate/ 100,000 (1)	Fraction with Firearms (2)	Fraction with Handgun (3)	Rate/ 100,000 (4)	Fraction with Firearms (5)	Rate/ 100,000 (6)	Fraction With Firearms (7)
1965	5.1	.57		109.5	.17	71.3	
1966	5.6	.60	.44	118.4	.19	80.3	
1967	6.1	.64	.48	123.0	.21	102.1	.36
1968	6.8	.65	.50	141.3	.23	131.0	
1969	7.2	.65	.51	151.8	.24	147.4	
1970	7.8	.65	.52	162.4	.24	171.5	
1971	8.6	.65	.51	178.8	.25	188.0	
1972	9.0	.66	.54	188.8	.25	180.7	
1973	9.4	.67	.53	200.5	.26	183.1	
1974	9.8	.68	.54	215.8	.25	209.3	.45
1975	9.6	.66	.51	227.4	.25	2.8.2	.45
1976	8.8	.64	.49	228.7	.24	195.8	.43
1977	8.8	.63	.48	241.5	.23	187.1	.42
1978	9.0	.64	.49	255.9	.22	191.3	.41
1979	9.7	.63	.50	279.1	.23	2.2.1	.40
1980	10.2	.62	.50	290.6	.24	243.5	.40

Source: Federal Bureau of Investigation, *Crime in the United States*, various issues.
Note: Firearms use in robberies is not available between 1968 and 1973. Handguns were used in about 96 percent of firearms robberies in 1967.

from a complete explanation for the increase in violent crime. The data in table 2 indicate that gun crimes did increase faster than nongun crimes from 1965 to 1973, but that since 1973 nongun crimes have been increasing at least as fast as gun crimes. Taking the period 1965–80 as a whole, we see that gun-related criminal homicide increased 118 percent while nongun homicide increased 77 percent. The force behind the crime surge since 1965 pushed both gun and nongun rates up to unprecedented levels; increased gun availability probably played some role in the late 1960s and early 1970s, but apparently did not in subsequent years.

The propensity to use guns in violent crimes differs widely across geographic areas. For example, the 1973–74 gun fraction in assaultive homicides (i.e., homicides excluding felony-related murders) ranged among large cities between 42 percent (Newark) and 83 percent (Baton Rouge); the 1974–75 gun fraction in robberies ranged from 28 percent (Boston) to 72 percent (Houston).[3] Furthermore, these gun fractions for robbery and assaultive homicide are highly correlated with each other across the 49 largest cities; the correlation coefficient is .70. This geographic pattern in gun use is also reflected in the suicide statistics; the intercity correlation between gun fractions in criminal homicide and suicide was .82 in 1973–74. Cook (1979, table 5) presents evidence that these intercity differences in the propensity to use guns in killings and in robbery are clearly related to intercity gun ownership patterns. The cities with the lowest rate of firearms ownership are in New England and the mid-Atlantic region. The cities with the highest gun ownership rates are in the South Atlantic, South Central, and Mountain regions. The fractions of criminal homicides, suicides, and robberies involving guns follow this same regional pattern.

What can we conclude from this brief description of violent crime patterns? First, Americans are currently being murdered, robbed, and raped at greater per capita rates than at any time in the fifty years of national recorded crime statistics, owing to the spectacular increases in these rates that began in the mid-1960s. Second, firearms are used in a minority of violent crimes but are of special concern because more than 60 percent of the criminal homicides involve firearms. Third, cities differ widely with respect to the fraction of violent crimes (and suicides) that involve guns, and this geographic pattern is roughly congruent with the geographic pattern of gun ownership. These results serve to set the stage

[3]These and subsequent statistics in this paragraph are calculated from unpublished FBI data. A complete description of sources and methods is available from the author.

for the detailed exploration of gun use in violent crime presented in the next three sections.

II. Conceptualization

The most important question considered in research on the criminal use of weapons is how the availability of dangerous weapons, especially firearms, influences the incidence and seriousness of violent crime. The observed patterns of weapon use in violent crime suggest a number of testable hypotheses concerning the potential effects of changes in gun availability. These hypotheses are motivated and stated in sections III and IV. The theoretical framework that guides this discussion is summarized here, without reference to sources or supporting evidence. This bare statement of the main ideas serves as a reader's guide to the more cluttered presentation of subsequent sections.

In addition to "gun availability" there are three basic elements to the theoretical framework, as depicted in figure 1: (1) the perpetrator's intent, or choice of task (e.g. which target to rob); (2) the type of weapon he uses in the crime; and (3) the outcome (Was the victim wounded, killed, or unharmed? Was the robbery successful?). There is some interrelation between the type of weapon used in a violent crime and the criminal's intent or choice of task; the causal process goes both ways. The actual outcome of the crime is of course influenced both by the perpetrator's intent and by his choice of weapon, as shown in figure 1. The fourth element of the theoretical framework, gun availability, influences weapon type and also has an effect on the quality of opportunities confronting the violent criminal.

A gun has a number of characteristics that make it superior to other readily available weapons for use in violent crime: even in the hands of a weak and unskilled assailant, a gun can be used to kill. The killing can be accomplished from a distance without much risk of effective counterat-

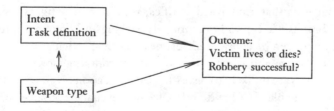

Fig. 1. The elements of a theoretical framework. The vulnerability pattern: relation between task and weapon type.

tack by the victim, and the killing can be completed quickly without sustained effort and in relatively "impersonal" fashion. Furthermore, because everyone knows that a gun has these attributes, the mere display of a gun communicates a highly effective threat. In most circumstances, a gun maximizes the probability of success for a would-be robber, rapist, or murderer.

The value of a gun as a tool in violent crime is closely related to the vulnerability of the victim. A victim who is unarmed, alone, small, frail, or impaired by alcohol or drugs is highly vulnerable. Against a vulnerable victim, the probability of perpetrating a successful robbery or murder is only slightly affected by the type of weapon employed. But a gun is essential for murdering a policeman or robbing a bank. The value of a gun in a crime will influence the probability that a gun will be the weapon actually used in that crime. Hence we have the *vulnerability pattern*: the fraction of robberies involving guns is inversely related to the vulnerability of the victim. The same pattern is characteristic of murder.

A variety of possible explanations can be given for the vulnerability pattern. Two explanations are of special interest: (1) "The tool determines the task." A robber's choice of target will be influenced by the type of weapon immediately available to him. In robbery or other confrontations, the impulse to kill is more likely to be acted on if an adequate weapon is available. (2) "The task determines the tool." In robberies and murders that involve some planning and preparation, the perpetrator will have a chance to equip himself with an adequate weapon. What he considers "adequate" will depend on the vulnerability of the victim. There is no need to choose between these two explanations—both no doubt have some validity.

A gun is usually the most effective weapon for launching a deadly attack or for generating a convincing threat of deadly attack. But in most violent confrontations, the assailant's intent is not to kill (or threaten death), but rather to hurt or gain control over the victim. Casual observation suggests that schoolyard scuffles, routine family fights, even barroom brawls are typically completely lacking in homicidal intent and would not even be considered "crimes" by the participants or (in practice) the police and courts. In violent confrontations of this sort, the protagonists are unlikely to resort to deadly weapons even when they are readily available. Husband and wife may exchange punches or throw dishes any number of times, yet refrain from reaching for the carving knife or shotgun. These commonsense observations suggest that the assailant's choice of weapon is a good indicator of his intent in assault offenses. The correlation between intent and weapon deadliness is by no means perfect, since weapon availability is an important intervening variable. Nevertheless, the assailant's intent is a major determinant of his choice of weapon. The assailant who clearly intends for his victim to survive will not fire a gun at him. The assailant who is determined to kill his victim probably will use a gun if one is available. Weapon choice in the intermediate case, in which the assailant's intent is ambiguous, may be governed by immediate availability.

A. *The Objective Dangerousness Pattern: Outcome*
    as a Function of Intent and Weapon Type

The details of this causal process differ somewhat between assault and murder, on the one hand, and robbery and rape on the other. These two crime categories are hence treated separately here.

1. Assault and murder. Whether the victim survives a serious assault with a deadly weapon depends in part on his ability to defend himself—his vulnerability relative to the nature of the attack. But in a large proportion of assaults with deadly weapons, the assailant ceases his attack by choice, rather than because of effective victim resistance. We can infer, in unsustained attacks of this sort, that the assailant's intent is to injure or incapacitate the victim—there is no deliberate, unambiguous intent to kill. Whether the victim does in fact die in such cases is largely a matter of chance—whether the first blow happens to strike a vital organ. Ambiguously motivated gun attacks are more dangerous than ambiguously motivated attacks with other weapons. This is the *objective dangerousness pattern*: gun attacks have a higher probability of killing the victim than do knife attacks in otherwise similar circumstances, and the difference is especially large when the intent of the assailant's attack is ambiguous.

2. Robbery violence. In robberies in which the robber's intent is to complete the robbery successfully, using force only as necessary to forestall or overcome victim resistance, the likelihood of physical attack or victim injury will be inversely related to the lethality of the robber's weapon—victims are less likely to attempt resistance to a gun than to other weapons. I have labeled this inverse relation the *instrumental violence pattern* in robbery.

While the instrumental violence pattern is evident in robbery statistics, it is nonetheless true that some robbers engage in unnecessary violence. They injure or kill victims who are cooperating with their demands. This *excess violence pattern* accounts for a large fraction of serious injuries and deaths for each of the weapon categories in robbery. The robber's intent in these cases is evidently to complete the robbery successfully *and*, as a separate matter, to injure or kill the victim.

The type of weapon employed has an important independent effect on the probability of victim death in robbery as well as assault. There is some evidence that most robbery murders are deliberate, and hence a reflection of the excess violence pattern. It may be that the type of weapon at hand influences the robber's decision making during the course of the robbery; the relative ease of executing a victim with a gun encourages this course of action when a gun is at hand.

B. *Inferences concerning the Effects of Gun Availability*

As indicated above, the type of weapon used in a violent crime is closely related to a number of the observable characteristics of the crime, including the vulnerability of the victim, the likelihood that the crime will be successful, and the seriousness of injury to the victim. These statistical patterns are interesting primarily as a basis for generating hypotheses (predictions) concerning the likely effects of a change in the availability of guns to violent offenders.

Suppose a jurisdiction is successful in reducing gun availability to robbers and violence-prone individuals (or in increasing the cost of using guns in crime). I postulate two effects: a pure *weapon substitution* effect, and a *selective deterrence* effect.

1. Weapon substitution: Pure weapon substitution occurs when the criminal simply substitutes a knife or club for the gun he would have preferred to use, without modifying his basic decision of what target to rob, or whether to attack someone he wants to hurt or kill. As suggested by the objective dangerousness pattern, this type of substitution will reduce the fraction of violent attacks that result in the victim's death. By the instrumental violence pattern, substitution will increase the victim injury rate in robbery.

2. Selective deterrence: In addition to weapon substitution, we expect a reduction in gun availability to forestall some types of violent crime, as suggested by the vulnerability postulate. The commercial robbery rate should be reduced, since the probability of failure of a nongun robbery against a commercial target is high (hence the high fraction of gun use in commercial robbery). Since there may be some displacement to noncommercial targets, it is not clear whether the noncommercial robbery rate will fall or increase.

A reduction in gun availability should reduce the criminal homicide rate by discouraging some homicidal attacks. The vulnerability pattern suggests that the murder victimization rate will fall the most (proportionately) for the least vulnerable victims. Controlling for the vulnerability of the victim, the murder offense rate should fall the most for the weakest potential killers (women, youths, elderly people). These predictions are predicated on the assumption that the reduction in gun availability is uniform across relevant subgroups of the population.

These predictions, which follow from an analysis of the offenders' capabilities, may have to be modified somewhat if the intervention that deprives offenders of guns also reduces gun availability to potential victims. If there is a general reduction in gun availability, then potential victims will be less likely to be armed with guns and hence will be more vulnerable to robbery or assault. In effect, a general reduction in gun availability changes the quality of opportunities available to criminals. One effect may be to increase the rate of (nongun) assault; individuals will be more likely to give vent to violent impulses if they are confident that their intended victim lacks a gun. There may also be some effect on robbery patterns, although not enough is known about self-defense in robbery to permit specific predictions. In any event, it should be clear that some legal interventions will have little effect on general availability of guns (e.g. sentencing enhancements for criminals who use guns), and others will be very broad (e.g. an increase in the federal tax on handguns). Predictions should of course be tailored to the precise nature of the intervention.

In sum, we are concerned with the effect of gun availability on three dimensions of the violent crime problem: (1) the *distribution* of robberies, aggravated assaults, rapes, and criminal homicides across different types of victims—for example, commercial versus noncommercial robbery; (2) the *seriousness* of robberies, rapes, and aggravated assaults; and (3) the overall *rates* of each type of violent crime. Patterns in the violent crime data support a number of predictions concerning these effects.

III. Evidence on the Vulnerability Hypothesis: Patterns of Gun Use in Robbery and Criminal Homicide

Firearms were used in 62 percent of the murders, 40 percent of the robberies, and 24 percent of the aggravated assaults reported to the police in 1980 (see table 2). These percentages have varied over time and differ across jurisdictions, as documented in section I. This section focuses on the patterns of gun use across the different circumstances in which these crimes occur. What characteristics of the assailant, the victim, and the immediate environment of the criminal act influence the likelihood that a gun will be employed? Since this question has been more prominent in the literature on robbery than on murder, I begin with an analysis of gun use in robbery.

A. *Robbery*

Robbery[4] is defined as theft or attempted theft by means of force or the threat of violence. The robber's essential task is to overcome through intimidation or force the victim's natural tendency to resist parting with his valuables. A variety of techniques for accomplishing this task are used in robbery, including actual attack (as in "muggings" and "yokings") and the threatening display of a weapon such as a gun, knife, or club. Whatever the means employed, the objective is to gain the victim's compliance quickly or render him helpless, thereby preventing him from escaping, summoning help, or struggling. The amount of what could be called "power" (capability of generating lethal force) the robber needs to achieve these objectives with high probability depends on the characteristics of the robbery target (victim), and in particular on the vulnerability of the target. The most vulnerable targets are people who are young, elderly, or otherwise physically weak or disabled (e.g. by alcohol), who are alone and without ready means of escape. The least vulnerable targets are commercial places, especially where there are several customers and clerks and possibly even armed guards—a bank being one extreme example.

A gun is the most effective tool for enhancing the robber's power. Unlike other common weapons, a gun gives a robber the capacity to threaten deadly harm from a distance, thus allowing him to maintain a buffer zone between himself and the victim and to control several victims simultaneously. A gun serves to preempt any rational victim's inclination to flee or resist.[5] Skogan (1978) documented the effectiveness of a gun in forestalling victim resistance in his analysis of a national sample of

---

[4]The perspective of this section was first developed in Conklin's (1972) seminal work on robbery in Boston. Cook (1976) dubbed it "strategic choice analysis" and was the first to employ large victimization survey data sets in documenting weapon use patterns of this sort. Other important contributions are cited in subsequent notes.

[5]Conklin (1972) analyzes the gun's usefulness in terms of the ability it provides the robber to (1) maintain a buffer zone; (2) intimidate the victim; (3) make good the threat, if necessary; and (4) ensure escape (pp. 110–11).

victim-reported robberies:[6] only 8 percent of gun robbery victims resisted physically in noncommercial robberies, compared with about
15 percent of victims in noncommercial robberies involving other
weapons.[7] Other types of resistance (arguing, screaming, fleeing) were
also less common in gun robbery than in robbery involving other
weapons.

It seems reasonable to assume that, from the robber's viewpoint, the
value of employing a gun tends to be inversely related to the vulnerability of the target. A gun will cause a greater increase in the likelihood of
success against well-defended targets than against more vulnerable targets. A strong-arm technique will be adequate against an elderly woman
walking alone on the street—a gun would be redundant with such a
victim—but a gun is virtually a requirement for a successful bank
robbery. Skogan (1978) provides evidence supporting this claim: he finds
little relation between robbery success rates and weapon type for personal robbery but a very strong relation for commercial robbery. He
reports that success rates in commercial robbery were 94 percent with a
gun, 65 percent with a knife, and 48 percent with other weapons.[8]

In economic terms, we can characterize robbery as a production
process (Cook 1979, pp. 752–53) with weapons, robbers, and a target as
"inputs." The "output" of the production process can be defined as the
probability of success. This probability increases with the number and
skill of the robbers, the vulnerability of the target, and the lethality of the
weapons. For given robber and target characteristics, the "marginal
product" of a gun can be defined as the increase in probability of success
if the robber(s) substitutes a gun for, say, a knife. The evidence pre-

[6]Skogan used incident reports collected from the National Crime Panel on robberies
that occurred during calendar year 1973. This and subsequent citations to Skogan's work
refer to an unpublished manuscript that was subsequently published in abbreviated form
as Skogan (1978). It should be noted that any analysis of victim survey data relies on the
victim's impression of the nature of the weapon that was employed in the robbery. In some
cases the "gun" may be a toy, or simulated; Feeney and Weir (1974, p. 33) report that of
fifty-eight "gun" robbers interviewed in Oakland, three claimed to have used toys and four
to have simulated the possession of a gun.

[7]Block (1977) found from studying robbery police reports in Chicago that victims who
resisted with physical force typically (68 percent) did so in response to the robber's use of
force. Other types of resistance typically (70 percent) preceded the robber's use of force.

[8]McDermott (1979) presents evidence that there is a similar pattern in rape. She
analyzed the National Crime Panel victimization survey data for twenty-six cities. From
the statistics she presents on pages 20 and 21 of her report, it can be calculated that success
rates in rape were 67 percent when the assailant used a gun, 51 percent when he used
another weapon, and only 15 percent when he was unarmed. These percentages exclude
rapes perpetrated by nonstrangers.

sented above suggests that the marginal product of a gun is small against vulnerable targets and relatively large against well-defended targets. We can go one step further and define the "value of a gun's marginal product" as its marginal product (increase in success probability) multiplied by the amount of loot if the robbery is successful. Since, for obvious reasons, targets with greater potential loot tend to be better defended against robbery,[9] the *value* of the gun's marginal product is even more strongly related to target vulnerability than is its marginal product. The conclusion can be put in the form of a proposition:

> The economic value of a gun in robbery tends to be greatest against commercial targets and other well-defended targets, and least against highly vulnerable targets.

It makes good economic sense, then, for gun use in robbery to be closely related to target vulnerability. Cook (1980a) demonstrates that this is indeed the case, on the basis of tabulating results of more than 12,000 robbery reports taken from victim survey data gathered in twenty-six large cities. These results are reproduced in table 3.

From table 3 (part A) we see that 55 percent of gun robberies committed by adults, but only 13 percent of other adult armed robberies, involve commercial targets. Those gun robberies that were committed against people on the street are concentrated on relatively invulnerable targets—groups of two or more victims or prime-age males—while street robbery with other weapons was more likely to involve women, children, or elderly victims. Skogan (1978) provides further detail for commercial robberies, reporting that the likelihood that a gun is present in such robberies is only 44 percent for commercial places that have only one employee, but 68 percent for commercial places with two or more employees.[10]

What is the process that produces these patterns in gun robbery? There are two plausible explanations, both compatible with the evidence presented above: (1) robbers who aspire to well-defended, lucrative targets equip themselves with guns to increase their chances of success; or (2) robbers who happen to have guns are more tempted to rob lucrative, well-defended targets than robbers who lack these tools.

---

[9]It is obvious that commercial targets tend to be more lucrative than noncommercial ones, and that a group of two or more victims will be more lucrative on the average than a single victim. Feeney and Weir (1974) report the not so obvious result that robberies of male victims resulted in a much higher median take ($50) than robberies of female victims (less than $20) (p. 24).

[10]Calculated from the statistics reported in table 3 of Skogan's article.

TABLE 3

Percentage Distributions of Robberies by
Location and Victim Characteristics

	Gun	Knife or Other Weapon	Unarmed
A. *All Robberies across Locations*			
Commercial	55.1	13.3	19.1
Residence	6.4	10.4	8.5
Street, vehicle, etc.	38.5	76.3	72.4
Total	100.0	100.0	100.0
B. *Street Robberies by Victim Characteristics*			
Male victim aged 16–54	59.8	53.8	41.1
Two or more victims	10.5	5.8	3.7
All others (young, elderly, and/or female victim)	29.7	40.4	55.2
Total	100.0	100.0	100.0

Source: Adapted from Cook 1980a, p. 43. The distributions are calculated from National Crime Panel victimization survey data on twenty-six cities.

Note: All incidents involved at least one male robber age 18 or over. Entries in the table reflect survey sampling weights.

The first explanation suggests that the observed relation between gun use and target choice is the result of differences between the kinds of people who rob lucrative targets and those who commit relatively petty street robberies—a difference reminiscent of Conklin's (1972) distinction between "professionals" and "opportunists." Victim-survey evidence does suggest that gun robbers as a group have more of the earmarks of professionalism than other armed robbers: beside the fact that they make bigger "scores," gun robbers are older, less likely to rob acquaintances, and less likely to work in groups of three or more (Cook 1976; Skogan 1978). Cook and Nagin (1979, p. 25) demonstrated that the factors that determine a robber's choice of weapon have some tendency to persist: a cohort of adult men arrested for gun robbery in the District of Colombia showed a greater propensity to use guns in subsequent robberies than a corresponding cohort arrested for nongun robberies.[11]

[11]Based on 541 adult male gun robbery arrestees and 761 nongun robbery arrestees. This cohort, which was arrested in 1973, was tracked through 1976 through PROMIS (Prosecutor's Office Management Information System). The robbery rearrest rate for the gun cohort was 0.43, of which 58 percent were gun robberies. The robbery arrest rate for the nongun cohort was 0.45, of which 40 percent were gun robberies. The two cohorts had

It seems reasonable to hypothesize, then, that robbers who engage in planning and who seek out big scores will take pains to equip themselves with the appropriate weapon—usually some type of firearm. The extent to which other less-professional robbers use guns, and hence the kinds of targets they choose, may be more sensitive to the extent to which such people have access to guns and are in the habit of carrying them, for whatever reason. Increased availability of guns may then result in some target switching by this group—substitution of more lucrative, better-defended targets for more vulnerable targets. Increased gun availability may also result in weapon substitution for a given type of target, implying an increase in the fraction of street robberies committed with a gun; that is, guns will be put to less valuable uses as they become "cheaper." These hypotheses can be stated more precisely as follows.

> An increase in gun availability in a city will have the following effects:
> —increase the fraction of noncommercial robberies committed with a gun;
> —increase the fraction of robberies committed against commercial and other well-defended targets.

B. *Criminal Homicide and Assault*

The qualities of a gun that make it the most effective robbery weapon, particularly against well-defended targets, are also of value to a killer. A decision to kill is easier and safer to implement with a gun than with other commonly available weapons—there is less danger of effective victim resistance during the attack, and the killing can be accomplished more quickly and impersonally, with less sustained effort than is usually required with a knife or blunt object. As in robbery, a gun has greatest value against relatively invulnerable victims, and the vulnerability of the victim appears to be an important factor in determining the probability that a gun will be used as the murder weapon.

The least vulnerable victims are those who are guarded or armed. All presidential assassinations in United States history were committed with handguns or rifles. Almost all law enforcement officers who have been murdered in recent years were shot: between 1970 and 1979, 94 percent of the 1,078 murdered policemen were killed by firearms (FBI, *Crime in the United States* 1979, p. 312).

---

the same rearrest rate for burglary (0.13), but the nongun cohort was much more likely to be rearrested for assaultive crimes (0.22, as opposed to 0.13 for the gun cohort). See table 9 of Cook and Nagin (1979).

Physical size and strength are also components of vulnerability. In 1977, 68.5 percent of male homicide victims were shot, compared with only 51.0 percent of female homicide victims (*Statistical Abstract* 1978). The age pattern, shown in figure 2, is strikingly regular: about 70 percent of victims aged 20–44 are shot, but this fraction drops off rapidly for younger and older—more vulnerable—victims.

Vulnerability is, of course, a relative matter. We would expect that the lethality of the murder weapon would be directly related to the *difference* in physical strength between the victim and killer, other things being equal. To investigate this hypothesis, I used the FBI data coded from the supplemental homicide reports submitted for 1976 and 1977 by police departments in fifty large cities. These data include the demographic characteristics of the victim and (where known) the offender, as well as the murder weapon, immediate circumstances, and apparent motive of the crime. Tables 4 and 5 display some results that tend to confirm the relative vulnerability hypothesis. First, from table 4 we see that women tend to use more lethal weapons than men to kill their spouses: 97 percent of the women, but only 78 percent of the men, used guns or knives. The gun fractions alone are 67 and 62 percent—admittedly not a large difference, but one that is in the predicted direction. This result is especially notable since women typically have less experience than men in handling guns and are less likely to think of any guns kept in the home as their personal property. Table 4 also shows that women who kill their "boy-

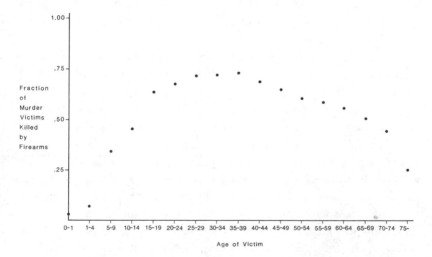

Fig. 2. The fraction of murder victims killed by firearms, 1978, by age of victim. From *Uniform Crime Reports*, 1978.

TABLE 4

Weapon Choice in Homicides Involving
Spouses and Intimates

Weapon	Identity of Victim			
	Husband	Wife	Boy Friend	Girl Friend
Gun	67.1%	61.6%	58.4%	53.5%
Knife	29.8	16.3	38.0	19.1
Blunt object	1.6	4.9	1.4	5.3
Other	1.4	17.2	2.3	22.0
N	553	547	216	209

Source: FBI Supplemental Homicide Reports, fifty cities, 1976 and 1977 combined.
Note: "Husband" and "wife" classifications include common-law relationships. Arson
cases are omitted.

friends" are more likely to use a gun than men who kill their "girl
friends."

Table 5 focuses on killings that resulted from arguments and brawls in
which both the killer and the victim were males. The gun fraction
increases with the age of the killer and is inversely related to the age of the
victim: the highest gun fraction (87 percent) involves elderly killers and
youthful victims; the lowest gun fraction (48 percent) involves youthful
killers and elderly victims. Since age is highly correlated with strength
and robustness, these results offer strong support for the relative vulnerability hypothesis.

Why are less vulnerable murder victims more likely to be shot than
relatively vulnerable victims? A natural interpretation of this result is
that intended victims who are physically strong or armed in some fashion
are better able to defend themselves against homicidal assault than are
more vulnerable victims—unless the assailant uses a gun, the "great
equalizer." The "vulnerability pattern" can then be explained as resulting from some combination of three mechanisms: (1) homicidal attacks
are more likely to fail against strong victims than against weak ones, and
the difference in the likelihood of failure is greater for nongun attacks
than for attacks with a gun. (2) The likelihood that an individual will act
on a homicidal impulse depends in part on the perceived probability of
success. The intended victim's ability to defend himself acts as a deterrent to would-be killers—but this deterrent is much weaker if the
killer has a gun. (3) In the case of a planned murder, the killer will have

TABLE 5

Gun Use in Murders and Nonnegligent Homicides
Resulting from Arguments or Brawls,
Male Victim and Male Offender

Age of Victim	Age of Offender		
	18–39	40–59	60+
18–39	68.0%	79.6%	87.2%
N	1,906	368	47
40–59	54.5%	64.1%	66.7%
N	398	245	57
60+	48.3%	49.2%	63.3%
N	58	61	30

Source: FBI Supplemental Homicide Reports, fifty cities, 1976 and 1977 combined (unpublished data).

Note: The sample size (the denominator of the fraction) is given in each cell. Cases in which the age of the killer is not known are excluded.

the opportunity to equip himself with a tool that is adequate to the task. Against well-defended victims, the tool chosen will almost certainly be a gun, if one can be obtained without too much difficulty.

Each of these mechanisms is compatible with the prediction that a reduction in gun availability will cause a reduction in murder, a reduction that will be concentrated on killings that involve a victim who is physically stronger than the killer. A number of specific hypotheses are suggested by this observation, including the following.

A reduction in gun availability will:
—reduce the male/female victimization ratio in murders of spouses and other intimates;
—reduce the fraction of murder victims who are youthful males;
—reduce the fraction of murderers who are elderly.

A number of similar hypotheses can be generated from the same perspective.

For a large percentage of violent crimes, it is in the assailant's interest to take care to *avoid* killing the victim. Robbery murder, for example, is a capital crime in many jurisdictions—even if the killing was an "accident" or a spontaneous reaction to victim resistance. Conklin (1972, p. 111) interviewed several robbery convicts who used an unloaded gun for fear they might end up shooting their victims. In other violent confrontations, such as fights between family members, this same concern may deter the combatants from reaching for a gun—even when there is one readily available. A loaded gun is not an appropriate weapon when the assailant's intent is to hurt, not kill, the victim. Phillips (1973) reasoned on the basis of such considerations that weapon choice in aggravated assault will be influenced by the probability and severity of punishment for criminal homicides; controlling for gun availability, the fraction of assaults committed with a gun should be inversely related to the perceived severity of sanctions. The results of his regression analysis of state level data is compatible with this prediction.[12]

IV. Evidence on the Objective Dangerousness Hypothesis

A. *The Role of Weapon Type in Determining the*
   Outcome of Violent Attacks

The main lessons from the previous section are common sense. Guns are more lethal than other readily available weapons. Killing with a gun requires less skill, strength, energy, and time than killing with a knife or club. A gun attack is harder to escape from or otherwise defend against than are attacks with other weapons. For these reasons, guns are the most effective weapons in robbery and murder and are especially valuable (from the assailant's viewpoint) against victims who are relatively invulnerable. It is not surprising, then, that the likelihood that a gun will be used to commit robbery and murder is systematically related to the vulnerability of the victim. The task is chosen to suit the tool, or the tool is chosen to suit the task. Either way, the "vulnerability pattern" is the result.

These observations are reasonable and fit the data, but they do not tell the whole story, especially for murder. A large proportion of serious attacks are ambiguously motivated—the "task" is not clearly defined in the mind of the assailant. The outcome of such attacks appears to be largely a matter of chance. The probability that the victim will die as a result of such attacks (in my interpretation) reflects conscious choices made by violent criminals—the "objective dangerousness" pattern, on the other hand, is a probabilistic phenomenon.

I begin the discussion of objective dangerousness with a discussion of aggravated assault and murder. The use of violence in robbery needs a separate treatment, which is presented subsequently.

---

[12]One flaw in Phillips's analysis is that he omitted from his regression specification of sanction severity for aggravated assault. Deterrence theory suggests that it is not the absolute severity of sanctions for criminal homicide that is salient to the choice of weapon, but rather the *difference* between sanction severity in assault and murder.

1. Intent and the probability of death in serious attacks. The fraction of serious gun assaults that result in the victim's death is much higher than for assaults with other weapons. Block (1977, p. 33), for example, found that of all aggravated assaults resulting in injury to the victim (and reported to the Chicago police), 14 percent of the gun cases, but only 4 percent of the knife cases, resulted in the victim's death.

One explanation for this result is that an assailant who intends to kill his victim is more likely to equip himself with a gun than an assailant who merely intends to hurt his victim. While this explanation may be valid for those murders in which there is some planning and preparation,[13] it is not a plausible explanation for the large proportion of deadly attacks that occur as the immediate result of an altercation or other provocation.

Zimring (1972) has demonstrated that a large proportion of murders are similar to serious assaults in that the attacks are unsustained—the assailant does not administer the coup de grace, the blow that would ensure the death of his victim. Indeed, the victim was shot only once in about two-thirds of the gun murders in Zimring's Chicago samples. These cases differ very little from serious assaults: for every death resulting from a single wound in the head or chest, Zimring found 1.8 victims with the same type of wound who did not die[14]—victims who were apparently saved not by any differences in the gunman's intent, but rather just by good luck with respect to the precise location of the wound.

Evidently, some proportion of gun murders are not the result of a clear intent to kill; given that the majority of murders are the immediate result of altercations, often involving alcohol and rarely much thought, it seems unlikely that many killers have *any* clearly formulated "intent" at the time of their attack. The assailant's mental state is characterized by an impulse—to punish, avenge an insult, stop a verbal or physical attack—backed by more or less cathexis. The immediate availability of a gun makes these circumstances more dangerous than would a less lethal weapon, because an unsustained attack with a gun—a single shot—is more likely to kill.

Zimring buttressed the conclusions from his first study, which compared knife and gun attacks, with a later (1972) study comparing attacks with large- and small- caliber guns. Even after controlling for the num-

[13]Wolfgang (1958) concludes from his study of homicide in Philadelphia: "The murderer who carefully plans his felonious, willful, and malicious assault is more likely to employ a weapon that performs his intended task quickly and efficiently. In such a situation a pistol or revolver probably will be used. During a drunken brawl, or in the white heat of passion, an offender uses whatever weapon is available" (pp. 80–81).

[14]Computed from Zimring (1972), table 7, p. 104.

ber and location of wounds, he found that attacks with .38 caliber guns were more than twice as likely to kill as attacks with .22 caliber guns. It appears, then, that weapon dangerousness has a substantial independent influence on the death rate from serious assaults.

Zimring's seminal work in this area supports several important propositions, including two testable hypotheses:

—A restrictive gun control policy that caused knives and clubs to be substituted for guns would reduce the death rate in serious assault.[15]
—A gun control policy focused on handguns may increase the death rate from gun assault if shotguns and rifles are substituted for handguns as a result.[16]

There is also an important normative proposition: In setting prosecution and sentencing priorities for aggravated assault cases, gun assaults should be viewed as more serious than assaults with other weapons, ceteris paribus, since there is a higher probability of the victim's dying in the gun assaults. This is Zimring's "objective dangerousness" doctrine.[17]

Block (1977) extended Zimring's work on instrumentality by comparing death rates in aggravated assault and robbery cases. He concludes that "the relative fatality of different weapons in violent crime may be a technological invariant . . . the probability of death given injury and a particular weapon remains relatively constant and unrelated to the type of crime committed" (p. 32). The notion that the number of deaths per hundred criminal attacks is a "technical" constant, largely determined by the lethality of the weapon, is not supportable, however. Zimring demonstrated that the type of weapon was *one* important determinant of the outcome of serious attacks but did not claim it was the only determinant. Presumably the weapon-specific death rates in such attacks will differ

[15]Zimring (1967) titled his original article "Is Gun Control Likely to Reduce Violent Killings?" His work was a response to a view espoused by Wolfgang (1958): "It is the contention of this observer that few homicides due to shootings could be avoided merely if a firearm were not immediately present, and that the offender would select some other weapon to achieve the same destructive goal (p. 83)"—a viewpoint expressed more succinctly by the bumper sticker: "Guns don't kill people; people kill people."

Seitz (1972) attempts to test Wolfgang's substitution hypothesis directly by calculating the correlation coefficient between total homicide rates and firearms homicide rates across states. For 1967 this correlation coefficient is .98. Seitz claims that the substitution hypothesis predicts that this correlation should be about zero. The problem with Seitz's inference, of course, is that he makes no attempt to control for the underlying etiological factors that largely determine both the gun and the nongun homicide rates in a state—indeed, these are highly positively correlated with each other.

[16]This implication has been pointed out by Kleck and Bordua (1981).

[17]"In the generality of cases, how likely is it that conduct such as that engaged in by the offender will lead to death?" (Zimring 1972, p. 114).

across jurisdictions and vary over time depending on the mix of circumstances, the quality of medical care, and so forth. Swersey (1980) presents an interesting case in point.

Swersey reports that the number of assaultive (as opposed to felony) gun homicides in Harlem increased from nineteen in 1968 to seventy in 1973, and then fell back to forty-six in 1974. Much of the change between 1968 and 1973 was due to an increase in intentional killings resulting from disputes involving narcotics activities. The importance of changes in the intent of violent perpetrators during this period is indicated by the fact that the death rate in gun attacks more than doubled between 1968 and 1973, then fell back in 1974. He shows that these changes reflect changes in murder—changes in intent to kill, rather than changes in the availability and quality of weapons and their spontaneous use. This conclusion is supported by observations on the circumstances and apparent motives of the murders.[18] Swersey concludes that more than 80 percent of the rise and fall in Harlem homicides was due to changes in the number of deliberate murders. He finds a similar pattern for the rest of New York City.

Swersey's findings do not undermine Zimring's position. Zimring did not deny that some killings were unambiguously motivated, or that the importance of intent in murder was subject to change over time, or that intent might be more important in Harlem than in Chicago. In any event, Swersey's results are useful in documenting these possibilities.

Calculations from the FBI's supplemental homicide reports file confirm that death rates in gun assault often vary over time by enough to have a substantial effect on the overall homicide rate. Table 6 reports death rates from gun assault for selected cities. Atlanta and Detroit exhibit the most extreme fluctuations during the period 1965–75. The death rate drops in all of these cities between 1972 and 1975, which is interesting given the widely noted reductions in big-city homicide rates during this period.

My conclusions can be briefly stated. The likelihood of death from a serious assault is determined, inter alia, by the assailant's intent and the lethality of the weapon used. The type of weapon is especially important when the intent is ambiguous. The fraction of homicides that can be viewed as deliberate (unambiguously intended) varies over time and

---

[18]Swersey also notes several other indications of an increasing fraction of deliberate murders in the homicide statistics for New York City as a whole. During the 1970s, the clearance rate declined for homicide, as did the fraction of homicides occurring on the weekend and the fraction involving family members.

TABLE 6

Percentage of Gun Assaults Resulting in Death,
Selected Cities

City	1965	1970	1972	1975
Atlanta	15.8	22.4	15.1	7.4
Chicago	13.2	12.5	12.2	10.6
Cleveland	14.7	14.1	15.4	10.7
Detroit	8.4	17.4	18.4	13.6
New York	9.4	9.2	9.7	7.5
Philadelphia	15.2	13.4	11.9	10.0

Source: FBI Supplemental Homicide Reports (unpublished data file) and unpublished FBI data on assaults.

Note: The numerator of each entry is the number of gun murders and nonnegligent manslaughters, excluding felony or suspected felony-type murders. The denominators are the sum of this murder count and the number of aggravated assaults with guns reported to the police.

space but is probably fairly small as a rule. The fraction of gun assaults that result in the death of the victim is one indication of the relative prevalence of deliberate gun murders.

2. *Weapon dangerousness in robbery.* The principal role of a weapon in robbery is to aid the robber in coercing the victim (either by force or by threat) to part with his valuables. If the threat is sufficiently convincing, physical force is not necessary. For this reason it is hardly surprising that the use of force is closely related to the weapon type in robbery, being very common in unarmed robbery and relatively rare in gun robbery. Table 7 documents this pattern for both commercial and noncommercial robberies committed by adult males. As shown in this table, gun robberies are less likely than other armed robberies to involve physical violence, and furthermore are less likely to injure the victim.[19] These patterns are compatible with the notion that violence plays an instrumental role in robbery—that it is employed when the robber believes it is needed to overcome or forestall victim resistance, and that this need is less likely to arise when the robber uses a gun.

There is evidence, however, that this "instrumental violence" pattern can account for only a fraction of the injuries and deaths that result from robbery (Cook 1980a). Three observations are relevant in this respect: first, more than two-thirds of the victims injured in noncommercial gun robberies do not resist in any way—even after the attack (Cook 1980a,

[19]Other sources on this pattern include Conklin (1972), Cook (1976), and Skogan (1978).

TABLE 7

Likelihood of Physical Attack and Injury in Robbery

	Gun[a]	Knife	Other Weapon	Unarmed
Noncommercial robbery[b]				
Victim attacked	22.1%	39.4%	60.4%	73.5%
Victim required medical treatment[c]	7.2	10.9	15.5	11.1
Victim hospitalized overnight	2.0	2.6	2.7	1.6
N	892	841	1,060	1,259
Commercial robbery				
Victim required medical treatment	4.8%	10.8%	17.9%	5.1%
Victim hospitalized overnight	1.5	3.5	6.0	0.4
N	2,307	288	117	570

Source: National Crime Panel victimization surveys of twenty-six cities. This table is excerpted from Cook 1980a, table 2.

Note: All incidents included in this table involved at least one male robber age 18 or over. Entries in the table do not reflect the survey sampling weights (which differed widely among the twenty-six cities).

[a]Many robberies involve more than one type of weapon. Incidents of that sort were classified according to the most lethal weapon used.

[b]Robberies occurring on the street, in a vehicle, or near the victim's home.

[c]Only about one-third of the injured gun robbery victims were actually shot. Two-thirds of the injured knife robbery victims were stabbed.

p. 36); similarly, twenty out of thirty victims killed in gun robberies in Dade County, Florida, between 1974 and 1976 did not resist the robber (p. 29); second, the likelihood that the victim will be injured in an armed robbery is much higher if the robbery is committed by a gang of three or more than otherwise; since victims are *less* likely to offer resistance to a group of three or four robbers than to a lone robber, this result is clearly incompatible with the "instrumental violence" hypothesis; and, third, judging from rearrest statistics for a large cohort of adults arrested for robbery in Washington, D.C., it appears that robbers who injure their victims tend to be more violence-prone than other robbers (Cook and Nagin 1979, p. 39).[20] These findings are different aspects of an "excess violence" pattern: much of the violence in robbery is not "necessary," in the sense of being an instrumental response to anticipated or actual

[20]The subset of the robbery arrest cohort that had injured their victims were less likely to be rearrested for robbery than the remainder of the cohort—but members of this subset were much more likely to be rearrested for assault and for murder.

resistance by the victim. Rather, it is motivated by objectives or impulses that have little to do with ensuring successful completion of the theft. In particular, street robberies committed by large groups (which typically have a low "take") are best viewed as a form of recreation, and the high incidence of gratuitous violence against victims may be just part of the fun.

Given these findings, it is useful to attempt a distinction between robbery with intent to injure or kill, and robbery without such intent (in which violence would be used only to overcome victim resistance). The latter form of robbery dominates the statistics—most victims are not in fact injured, and the likelihood of injury is less with guns than with other weapons. However, the more vicious strain of robbery, involving an intent to injure, apparently accounts for a high percentage of the serious injuries and deaths that do occur in the robbery context. Furthermore, the incidence of excess violence in robbery is subject to change over time, as Zimring (1977) demonstrated in his study of robbery murder in Detroit. He found a sharp discontinuity in 1972 in the fraction of victims killed in armed robbery: after ten years of stable weapon-specific death rates, this fraction doubled between 1971 and 1973 for gun robberies and increased even more during this period for other armed robberies.

Are gun robberies more dangerous than other armed robberies, in the sense of being more likely to result in the victim's death? Victims are killed in a higher fraction of gun robberies than others: based on victim survey and homicide data in eight cities, I calculated that there are 9.0 victim fatalities for every 1,000 gun robberies, compared with 1.7 victim fatalities per 1,000 nongun armed robberies (Cook 1980a, p. 39). Furthermore, it appears that the type of weapon plays an independent role in determining the likelihood of robbery murder; in a cross-section analysis of fifty cities, I found that the fraction of robberies resulting in the victim's death is closely related to the fraction of robberies that involve firearms (Cook 1979, p. 775).[21] Thus the objective dangerousness pattern

[21]The regression equation is as follows:
Robbery murders/1,000 robberies = 1.52 + 5.68 Gun robberies/1,000 robberies.
                                    (1.16)   (2.38)
A closely related result uses the per capita (rather than "per robbery") murder rate:
Robbery murders/100,000 = − .284 + .907 Gun robberies/1,000 + .136
                                              Nongun robberies/1,000.
                          (.232)   (.089)   (.072)
(Numbers in parentheses are the standard errors of the ordinary least-squares regression coefficients.) The data for fifty cities are 1975–76 averages.
The second question has an $R^2 = .82$, suggesting that robbery murder is very closely

applies to robbery as well as assault, for reasons that remain a bit obscure.

Why does the presence of a (loaded, authentic) gun in robbery increase the probability of the victim's death? My studies of robbery murder in Atlanta (Cook and Nagin 1979) and Dade County, Florida (Cook 1980a), indicated that in at least half of the cases the killing was deliberate: for example, the victim was tied and then executed or shot several times from close range. But insofar as intent could be ascertained from police reports, it appears that these intentional killings were not premeditated, but rather decided on during the course of the robbery. Perhaps the explanation for why these spontaneous decisions are more likely to occur when the robber is holding a gun is related to Wolfgang's (1958) suggestion: "the offender's physical repugnance to engaging in direct physical assault by cutting or stabbing his adversary, may mean that in the absence of a firearm no homicide occurs" (p. 79).

The principal testable hypothesis derived from the discussion above is this:

A reduction in gun availability will increase the robbery injury rate (Skogan 1978) but reduce the robbery murder rate.

The evidence also supports a normative proposition: given the excess violence pattern in robbery, the robbery cases in which the victim is injured should be allocated special emphasis in establishing criminal prosecution and sentencing priorities (Cook 1980a). In a high proportion of these crimes, the attack that caused the injury was not instrumental to the robbery, but rather was a distinct act. A relatively severe judicial response to such cases might act as a deterrent to excess violence in robbery.

3. Coercion and assault. Does the instrumental violence pattern in robbery have any parallel in assault? I suspect the answer is yes, but I know of no empirical evidence.

Some (unknown) fraction of assault cases are similar to robbery in that the assailant's objective is to coerce the victim's compliance—the assailant wants the victim to stop attacking him (physically or verbally), or stop dancing with his girl friend, or get off his favorite barstool, or turn down the stereo. And, as in the case of robbery, the probability of a

---

linked to robbery. Including the assaultive murder rate in this equation as an independent variable does not affect the other coefficients much—and the coefficient on the murder variable is not statistically significant. I conclude that robbery murder is more robbery than murder.

physical attack in such cases may be less if the assailant has a gun than otherwise, because the victim will be less inclined to ignore or resist a threat enforced by the display of a gun. (It may also be true that the assailant would be more hesitant to use a gun than another weapon to make good his threat.) If this reasoning is correct, it supports the following:

A general increase in gun availability will reduce the number of assault-related injuries.

B. *Conclusion*

Sections II–IV have described and labeled several patterns that have been discovered in the violent crime data. These patterns, interpreted in the context of what we know or suspect about the nature of violent encounters and the motives of criminals, suggest a number of hypotheses about the effects of a change in gun availability on the distribution, incidence, and seriousness of violent crime. While these hypotheses are plausible extrapolations from the data, our confidence in them would be increased if they were supported by direct evidence—observations on changes in gun use patterns associated with changes in gun availability. A few direct tests of this sort have been conducted, and the next section discusses some of these studies. They have all confronted the initial problem of developing a suitable operational definition of "availability." Section V begins with an analysis of the alternatives in this regard.

V. Gun Availability

Casual discussions of gun availability usually begin and end with statistics on the number of guns (or handguns) in private hands. The numbers are impressive—perhaps 40 million handguns and as many as 100 million long guns. Nevertheless, guns are nowhere near as prevalent as, say, kitchen knives. Only a quarter of all households possess a handgun, and the prevalence of handguns is even less in urban areas, where most of the violent crime occurs. Most handguns are expensive,[22] and someone seeking to obtain one may have to overcome or circumvent fairly substantial legal barriers. The point is that despite the vast arsenal of guns in private hands, guns remain a scarce commodity. This scarcity surely prevents some criminals from obtaining them or using them in violent

---

[22]For example, among the cheapest of the popular handgun models is the Ruger Standard, which retailed at a suggested price of $92 in 1980 (Cook 1982, table 3).

crime—why else would two-fifths of the criminal homicides and three-fifths of the reported robberies be committed with less effective weapons? Furthermore, it is reasonable to suppose that the terms on which guns are available to potential criminals vary over time and differ rather widely among jurisdictions at any point in time. These variations and differences in gun availability provide a potential basis for testing hypotheses concerning the effects of gun availability on violent crime patterns. The first problem in conducting such tests is to develop one or more statistical indicators of gun availability.

Defining "availability" for an individual is easier than defining this concept for a group. For any single individual, "availability" denotes the amount of money, effort, legal risk, and delay entailed in acquiring a gun. In economic terms, availability is the sum of money price and transactions cost: what Moore (1977) calls the "effective price." Transactions costs are a more important consideration for guns than for other commodities because gun transactions are extensively regulated by law, and a number of important groups (youths, convicted felons, etc.) are legally prohibited from purchasing guns. Within a single jurisdiction, then, the effective price of obtaining a gun will range from near zero (for those who already possess a suitable gun) to some large number (for those who are legally proscribed from buying a gun and lack ready access to people who would be willing to lend or sell them one). The notion of availability when applied to an entire group denotes some sort of average of the effective prices for the individuals who make up the group. This average effective price is closely related to the prevalence of gun ownership. In areas where gun ownership is relatively widespread, individuals who "need" a gun for use in a violent crime are comparatively likely to own one or be able with relative ease to buy, borrow, or steal one from a friend or family member. Furthermore, prevalent gun ownership is likely to be associated with an active black or gray market supported by hand-to-hand transfers and guns stolen in burglaries (Moore 1981).

The prevalence of gun ownership is not the sole determinant of average effective price, however. Legal restrictions designed to discourage gun transfers to certain population subgroups, or to raise the money price of a gun through, for example, taxes or minimum quality requirements, may increase the average effective price associated with a given prevalence of gun ownership.

These indicators of gun availability—prevalence of gun ownership and stringency of legal restrictions on gun commerce—are discussed in detail in the next two sections.

A. *The Prevalence of Gun Ownership*

One rather surprising finding from national surveys is that the fraction of United States households owning guns has remained roughly constant for two decades. Gallup polls in 1959, 1965, 1966, and 1972 and the National Opinion Research Center (NORC) General Social Surveys in 1973, 1974, 1976, and 1977 all found that about half of United States households own at least one gun. This statistic differs a bit from poll to poll but shows no discernible trend over this twenty-year period. Reported *handgun* ownership rates increased slightly (from 12.6 percent in 1959 to 15.4 percent in 1972) in the Gallup polls; the NORC General Social Surveys find a higher, untrended rate of about 20 percent between 1973 and 1977.[23] Two large national surveys conducted in 1978 by Decision Making Information, Inc. (DMI) and Cambridge Reports, Inc., found virtually identical handgun ownership rates of 23 percent (DMI) and 24 percent (Cambridge Reports).[24] Reasonable conclusions from these polls are: (1) About half of United States households own guns, and this fraction has not changed much since 1958. (2) About half of the gun-owning households currently own handguns, and this fraction appears to have increased considerably since 1959. (3) The increase in the total stock of guns has been absorbed without an increase in the fraction of households that own guns by (*a*) an increase in the average number of guns per gun-owning household and (*b*) an increase in the number of households (Wright et al. 1981).[25]

One implication of the survey-based estimates of the private gun inventory is that there are more than three guns for every gun-owning household. Table 8 summarizes the results of the DMI survey in 1978 on number of guns owned by the 47 percent of all households who reported they owned at least one gun. These data permit a rough estimate of the degree of ownership concentration. A conservative estimate[26] is that the top one-third of handgun-owning households (about 7.5 percent of all households) own more than 60 percent of all handguns; the top one-third of all long-gun-owning households (about 14 percent of all households) own more than 60 percent of all long-guns.

[23]These results were provided by James Wright in private correspondence.

[24]See Wright (1981) for a discussion of these two polls.

[25]Wright et al. (1981) give evidence that some substantial portion of the increase in the handgun sales was the result of increased demand by local police departments.

[26]I assume that household respondents that admit owning guns of the specified sort but refuse to say how many are distributed similarly to other households. I also assume that the average number of guns in the open-ended category is twelve. Both of these assumptions are highly conservative, in the sense that they probably lead to an underestimate of the degree of concentration in ownership.

TABLE 8

Number of Guns Owned by Gun-Owning Households, 1978

Number	Handguns	Rifles and Shotguns
None	46%	14%
One	30	29
Two	8	21
3–4	4	16
5–9	1	5
10+	1	2
Yes only	8	9
Refused	4	4

Source: "Attitudes of the American Electorate toward Gun Control 1978," by Decision Making Information, Inc., Santa Ana, California, as reported in James D. Wright, "Public Opinion and Gun Control: A Comparison of Results from Two Recent National Surveys" (University of Massachusetts, Amherst, 1979).

Another inference from the statistics in table 8 is that about three-quarters of the households that own handguns also own long guns. It seems likely, then, that much of the recent growth in handgun ownership has involved households that already owned rifles or shotguns.

In each of the years 1975 through 1979, the annual sum of handgun imports and domestic manufacture has been between 2.0 and 2.3 million units (Cook and Blose 1981). The total volume of import and manufacture for the past decade has exceeded the total volume for the preceding six decades combined (Wright et al. 1981), and there is ample reason to believe that the current volume is supporting a continuing buildup in the private inventory of handguns. However, the increase in the private inventory in any one year is substantially less than the number of units manufactured and imported. For example, approximately 2,224,000 handguns were manufactured or imported in 1975. Of these, fewer than 1,750,000 were sold to private (household and business) domestic buyers. Furthermore, these new additions to the private inventory were compensated for by the loss of more than 150,000 handguns to the police (i.e., handguns confiscated by the police and not returned) and probably larger (but unknown) numbers that were lost through normal attrition. There may also be a significant number of illegal (and hence uncounted) exports associated with the international trade in illegal drugs, in which handguns are sometimes the medium of exchange. My conclusion is that we lack the data necessary to develop good estimates of year-to-year changes in the private inventory of handguns.

The incidence of firearms ownership is not uniform across society. Wright and Marston (1975) found that the fraction of households owning guns increased with income, decreased with city size, and was higher in the South than elsewhere. The same patterns are observed when the analysis is limited to handguns only. I (Cook 1979) analyzed regional patterns of ownership for residents of large cities, using NORC polls taken in the mid-1970s and found a range for handgun ownership from 5 percent for residents of large cities in New England and the Mid-Atlantic region up to 34 percent for residents of the Mountain region cities (Denver, Tucson, Phoenix). The southern region cities were relatively high—about 24 percent—and the Pacific and North Central cities low— about 13 percent. Similar regional patterns were also obtained for long-gun ownership by urban residents in these regions: only 10 percent of urban households in Boston and the Mid-Atlantic cities owned any type of firearm, compared with about half of urban households in the Mountain cities.

This brief review suggests that gun "availability," in the sense of the extent of ownership, has not been increasing over the past twenty years. Handgun ownership has become more widespread over this period, however. The private inventory of firearms is perhaps as high as 140 million, but this inventory is highly concentrated in the relatively small fraction of households that own three or more guns. Finally, gun "availability" differs widely across regions and by city size.

These results are interesting as a global overview of gun availability patterns, but they lack the detail and precision needed for statistical analysis of the relation between gun availability and violent crime patterns. Several researchers have attempted to develop statistical proxies for gun availability, which, unlike manufacturing or survey data, can be measured for a number of jurisdictions. Of these, the only validated proxy measure is that developed in Cook (1979).

In constructing this index, I first calculated the gun fractions for suicide and assaultive homicide for each of fifty large cities, combining 1973 and 1974 data for each. The distributions of suicides and murderers differ from each other rather dramatically in terms of race, age, socio-economic status, and so forth, and of course the immediate circumstances in which these acts occur are very different. Nevertheless, the gun fractions for suicide and assaultive homicide are highly correlated across these fifty cities (.82), suggesting that environmental determinants of weapon choice for both types of violent acts are similar. I assumed that the underlying environmental determinant was gun availability (prevalence of ownership) and constructed an index of gun availability by averaging these two fractions in each city. The validity of this index was tested by the following technique: the fifty cities were divided into eight regional subsets and an "urban regional index" was constructed by combining the indexes for each city. This urban regional index was then compared with the fraction of urban households in each region that reported owning a gun in three of the recent NORC General Social Surveys (three surveys were combined to achieve sufficiently large sample sizes).[27] My index proved completely compatible with the survey results.

This index was then used as a measure of gun availability in a regression analysis of robbery rates.[28] Controlling for other variables important in explaining intercity differences in robbery, the principal results were as follows: (1) a 10 percent reduction in the number of handguns in a city is associated with about a 5 percent reduction in the robbery rate; (2) the overall robbery rate is not discernibly influenced by gun availability in a city; and (3) a 10 percent reduction in the number of handguns in a city is associated with about a 4 percent reduction in the number of robbery murders. Thus gun density influences weapon choice in robbery but not the overall robbery rate. Weapon choice is important because it influences the likelihood that a robbery victim will be killed. These results are compatible with the discussion in sections II–IV and tend to confirm two of the hypotheses stated there.[29]

B. Regulation of Handgun Commerce

Restrictions on handgun transfers have become more stringent in some states and cities since the mid-1960s. The overall effective price of a handgun may have increased in these jurisdictions as a result.

The federal Gun Control Act of 1968 imposed a national ban on mail-order purchases of firearms except by federally licensed dealers, and it restricted interstate commerce in other ways as well. The intended effect of these regulations was to insulate the states from each other, so

[27]Survey-based estimates of this sort are not strictly valid, since the sampling frame is not constructed to produce representative samples in these regional city clusters.

[28]This index has also been used by Moore (1980) and by Sherman (private communication). Sherman finds a high correlation between this measure of gun availability and the number of police killed in a city.

[29]A number of other proxies for gun availability that have appeared in the literature are summarized and analyzed in Cook (1982).

that the stringent regulations on firearms commerce adopted in some states would not be undercut by the greater availability of guns in other states.

A number of states have adopted significant restrictions on commerce in firearms, especially handguns. About half the states, including two-thirds of the United States population, currently require that handgun buyers obtain a permit or license (or at least send an application to the police) before taking possession of the gun (Cook and Blose 1981). In most of these states, the objective of the permit or application system is to prevent felons and other undesirables from obtaining handguns without infringing substantially on the majority's ability to purchase and possess them. These state systems differ with respect to the fee, the waiting period, the involvement of state (as opposed to local) agencies, the thoroughness of the criminal record check, and so forth. Perhaps more important in practice are differences among states with respect to law enforcement efforts aimed at plugging the inevitable "leaks" between the entitled and proscribed sectors: thefts, black-market sales, illegal sales by licensed dealers, and so forth. A transfer system that appears stringent on paper may be quite lax in practice if law enforcement officials view enforcement activities in this area as being of low priority.

All but a few state transfer control systems are "permissive," in the sense that most people are legally entitled to be issued a permit and obtain a handgun. In a few jurisdictions, however—New York, Boston, Washington, D.C.—it is very difficult to obtain a handgun legally. Washington, D.C., is the most restrictive jurisdiction in this respect; only law enforcement officers and security guards are legally entitled to obtain handguns there under current law (Jones 1981).

The effect of a transfer control system is to increase the effective price of a legally purchased handgun by requiring a permit fee, a waiting period, or both, and by requiring applicants to do some paperwork and submit to a criminal record check. A number of states and cities adopted or strengthened requirements of this sort during the 1970s. A transfer control system may discourage some people from purchasing handguns and motivate others to evade the transfer regulations by purchasing from nondealers. (Transfer requirements usually apply to purchases from nondealers but are very difficult to enforce for such transactions.) While it is certainly possible to evade transfer requirements and the costs thereof, purchase from a nondealer may be costly in other ways—nondealer sources are typically less reliable and less accessible than dealers.

Major changes in gun regulations, or in the effort devoted to enforcing such regulations, are "natural experiments" that may be analyzed for evidence concerning the effect of gun availability on violent crime patterns. Such changes can be evaluated even in the absence of a valid measure of gun availability: if introducing a stringent restriction on gun sales results in a reduction in the gun robbery rate, then it can be assumed that the effect was transmitted through a reduction in gun availability, even if there is no direct statistical evidence on availability. A case in point is Operation DC, a short-lived experiment by the Bureau of Alcohol, Tobacco, and Firearms (BATF) to interdict the illegal flow of firearms into the District of Columbia. BATF enforcement staff in the District was increased from seven to between thirty-five and fifty special agents for the first six months of 1970. According to Zimring (1975), the gun murder rate dropped significantly during this period and rebounded thereafter, while the nongun murder rate remained roughly constant throughout. This result is highly supportive of the claim that gun availability is sensitive to law enforcement efforts, and further, that gun availability influences the gun murder rate and the overall murder rate. However, this picture is clouded somewhat by the fact that the gun assault pattern shows no corresponding pattern during the period when Operation DC was in effect.

Other important innovations in gun regulation that have been evaluated include the Gun Control Act of 1968 (Zimring 1975) and Massachusetts' Bartley-Fox Amendment (Pierce and Bowers 1981; Deutsch and Alt 1977).

C. *Conclusion*

A major stumbling block in testing the effect of gun availability on violent crime patterns is developing an operational measure of gun availability that can be implemented from existing data. Several proxies for gun availability have been utilized by researchers, but only one meets normal standards for measurement validity—and that only for cross-sectional comparisons. It is possible to circumvent this measurement problem by taking advantage of "natural experiments"—policy innovations that are designed to change gun availability. Any observed changes in violent crime patterns resulting from the policy innovation can then be attributed to the resulting change in gun availability. Several published evaluations of major policy innovations support the hypotheses developed in preceding sections, although the evidence is not conclusive for any one of these changes in law or enforcement policy.

VI. Notes on a Research Agenda

It is my impression that social scientists tend to ignore each other's suggestions for future research unless they are funded and come in the form of a request for proposals. Rather than suggest specific research projects, my objective in this review has been to demonstrate that the technology of violent crime is an interesting and important topic—a topic that is eminently researchable and yet has been largely neglected by social scientists qua scientists. The choice of weapon by the assailant in a violent criminal encounter is not just an incidental aspect of this encounter, but may be every bit as important in shaping the encounter and determining the outcome as the underlying motivation and state of mind of the assailant, the relation between assailant and victim, the location of the attack, and so forth. More generally, the extent to which firearms are available to violent criminals may have a profound influence on the nature and seriousness of violent crime. I submit the following list of propositions as a credible summary of the likely effects of gun availability on violent crime:

—Gun availability does not have much effect on the rates of robbery and aggravated assault, but it does have a direct effect on the fractions of such crimes that involve guns.
—Since gun attacks are intrinsically more deadly than attacks with other weapons, gun availability is directly related to the homicide rate.
—Increased gun availability promotes a relative increase in robberies and homicidal attacks on relatively invulnerable targets.

There is some evidence available supporting these propositions, which I have reviewed above. More work is needed.

If funding were available for research in this general area, I would recommend that highest priority be given to three types of projects:

1. Analysis of the victim survey and homicide data to determine if the crime of rape is characterized by the same weapon-related patterns as robbery (e.g. the vulnerability, objective dangerousness, and instrumental violence patterns).

2. Fine-grained evaluations of the effect of gun regulations.

3. Interviews with violent criminals to gain greater insights into the notion of gun availability:

—Where and how do criminals obtain guns? How do state and local ordinances affect the distribution of sources of guns?

—Do violent criminals who use other weapons have ready access to guns? If so, why do they not use them? In particular, why are fewer than half of all robberies committed with guns?

—Why are handguns used in such a high percentage of gun-related crime, given that long guns are more widely available and generally more effective?

—What is the mix of motives that results in the decision of many criminals to carry a gun?

This is enough of a "shopping list," given the current austerity of funding for criminal justice research.

I have not emphasized the policy relevance of research in this area, in part because I thought it was important to stress that the role of weapons in violent crime should be of as much interest to criminologists as to policy analysts and polemicists. Ultimately, however, the policy implications cannot be ignored. It is not too far-fetched to hope that the accumulation of knowledge in this area will encourage the adoption of wiser and more effective policies.

REFERENCES

Beha, James A., III. 1977. "'And Nobody Can Get You Out': The Impact of a Mandatory Prison Sentence for the Illegal Carrying of a Firearm on the Use of Firearms and the Administration of Criminal Justice in Boston," parts I and II, *Boston University Law Review* 57: 96–146, 289–333.

Block, Carolyn, and Richard Block. 1980. *Patterns of Change in Chicago Homicide: The Twenties, the Sixties, and the Seventies.* Chicago: Law Enforcement Commission.

Block, Richard. 1977. *Violent Crime.* Lexington, Mass.: Lexington Books.

Brearly, Harrington C. 1932. *Homicide in the U.S.* Chapel Hill: University of North Carolina Press.

Brill, Steven. 1977. *Firearm Abuse: A Research and Policy Report.* Washington, D.C.: Police Foundation.

Bruce-Briggs, B. 1976. "The Great American Gun War," *Public Interest* 45 (fall): 1–26.

Bureau of Alcohol, Tobacco, and Firearms. 1976. *Project Identification: A Study of Handguns Used in Crime.* ATF P 3310.1 (5/76). Washington, D.C.: Bureau of Alcohol, Tobacco, and Firearms.

Burr, D. E. Scott. 1977. "Handgun Regulation." Final report to the Bureau of Criminal Justice Planning and Assistance, Florida.

Campbell, Donald, and Julian C. Stanley. 1966. *Experimental and Quasi-Experimental Designs for Research*. Chicago: Rand McNally.

Clotfelter, Charles T. 1982. "Crime, Disorders, and the Demand for Handguns: An Empirical Analysis," *Law and Policy Quarterly*, in press.

Conklin, John E. 1972. *Robbery and the Criminal Justice System*. Philadelphia: J. B. Lippincott.

Cook, Philip J. 1976. "A Strategic Choice Analysis of Robbery." In *Sample Surveys of the Victims of Crimes*, ed. Wesley Skogan. Cambridge, Mass.: Ballinger.

————. 1979. "The Effect of Gun Availability on Robbery and Robbery Murder: A Cross Section Study of Fifty Cities." In *Policy Studies Review Annual*, vol. 3, ed. Robert H. Haveman and B. Bruce Zellner. Beverly Hills, Calif.: Sage.

————. 1980a. "Reducing Injury and Death Rates in Robbery," *Policy Analysis* 6(1):21–45.

————. 1980b. "Research in Criminal Deterrence: Laying the Groundwork for the Second Decade." In *Crime and Justice: An Annual Review of Research*, vol. 2, ed. Norval Morris and Michael Tonry. Chicago: University of Chicago Press.

————. 1981a. "The Effect of Gun Availability on Violent Crime Patterns," *Annals of the American Academy of Political and Social Science* 455 (May):63–79.

————. 1981b. "Guns and Crime: The Perils and Power of Long Division," *American Journal of Public Policy and Management*, in press.

————. 1982. "The Role of Firearms in Violent Crime: An Interpretive Review of the Literature, with Some New Findings and Suggestions for Future Research." In *Criminal Violence*, ed. Marvin Wolfgang and Neil Weiner. Beverly Hills, Calif.: Sage.

Cook, Philip J., and James Blose. 1981. "State Programs for Screening Handgun Buyers," *Annals of the American Academy of Political and Social Science* 455 (May):80–91.

Cook, Philip J., and Daniel Nagin. 1979. *Does the Weapon Matter?* Washington, D.C.: Institute for Law and Social Research.

Curtis, Lynn A. 1974. *Criminal Violence*. Lexington, Mass.: Lexington Books.

Deutsch, Stuart Jay, and Francis B. Alt. 1977. "The Effect of Massachusetts' Gun Control Law on Gun-Related Crimes in the City of Boston," *Evaluation Quarterly* 1(4):543–68.

Etzioni, Amitai, and Richard Kemp. 1973. "A Technology Whose Removal 'Works': Gun Control." In *Technological Shortcuts to Social Change*, pp. 103–51. New York: Russell Sage Foundation.

Feeney, Floyd, and Adrianne Weir. 1974. *The Prevention and Control of Robbery: A Summary*. Davis: University of California, Center on Administration of Criminal Justice.

Fisher, Joseph. 1976. "Homicide in Detroit: The Role of Firearms," *Criminology* 14(3):387–400.

Geisel, Martin S., Richard Roll, and R. Stanton Wettick, Jr. 1969. "The Effectiveness of State and Local Regulation of Handguns: A Statistical Analysis," *Duke Law Journal* 1969:647–76.

Gendreau, Paul, and C. Thomas Surridge. 1978. "Controlling Gun Crimes: The Jamaican Experience," *International Journal of Criminology and Penology* 6(1): 43–60.

Heumann, Milton, and Colin Loftin. 1979. "Mandatory Sentencing and the Abolition of Plea Bargaining: The Michigan Felony Firearm Statute," *Law and Society Review* 13:393–430.

Hindelang, Michael J., Michael R. Gottfredson, and James Garofalo. 1978. *Victims of Personal Crime: An Empirical Foundation for a Theory of Personal Victimization.* Cambridge, Mass.: Ballinger.

Hoffman, Frederick L. 1925. *The Homicide Problem.* Newark, N.J.: Prudential Press.

Jones, Edward D., III. 1980. "Handguns, Gun Control Laws, and Firearm Violence: A Comment." Mimeographed. U.S. Department of Justice, Office for Improvements in the Administration of Justice.

———. 1981. "The District of Columbia's 'Firearms Control Regulations Act of 1975': The Toughest Handgun Control Law in the United States—Or Is It?" *Annals of the American Academy of Political and Social Science* 455 (May):138–49.

Kleck, Gary, and David Bordua. 1981. "The Assumptions of Gun Control." Unpublished manuscript. School of Criminology, Florida State University.

Krug, Alan S. 1968. *The True Facts of Firearm Legislation—Three Statistical Studies.* Washington, D.C.: National Shooting Sports Foundation.

Loftin, Colin. 1980. "'One with a Gun Gets You Two': Mandatory Sentencing and Firearms Offenses in Detroit." Unpublished manuscript. Center for Research on Social Organization, University of Michigan, Ann Arbor.

Loftin, Colin, and David McDowall. 1981. "'One with a Gun Gets You Two': Mandatory Sentencing and Firearms Violence in Detroit," *Annals of the American Academy of Political and Social Science* 455 (May):150–67.

Lundsgaarde, Henry P. 1977. *Murder in Space City.* New York: Oxford University Press.

McDermott, M. Joan. 1979. *Rape Victimization in Twenty-six American Cities.* Washington, D.C.: U.S. Government Printing Office.

Magaddino, J. P. n.d. "Towards an Economic Evaluation of State Gun Control Laws." Unpublished manuscript. California State University, Long Beach.

Moore, Mark. 1977. "Managing the Effective Price of Handguns: A Conceptual Basis for the Design of Gun Control Policies." Unpublished manuscript. Kennedy School of Government, Harvard University.

———. 1979. "The Supply of Handguns: An Analysis of the Potential and Current Importance of Alternative Sources of Handguns to Criminal Offenders." Unpublished manuscript. Kennedy School of Government, Harvard University.

———. 1980. "The Police and Weapons Offenses," *Annals of the American Academy of Political and Social Science* 452 (November):22–32.

———. 1981. "Keeping Handguns from Criminal Offenders," *Annals of the American Academy of Political and Social Science* 455 (May):92–109.

Murray, Douglas R. 1975. "Handguns, Gun Control Laws, and Firearm Violence," *Social Problems* 23(1):81–93.

Newton, George D., Jr., and Franklin E. Zimring. 1969. *Firearms and Violence in American Life*. Washington, D.C.: U.S. Government Printing Office.

Phillips, Llad. 1973. "Crime Control: The Case for Deterrence." In *The Economics of Crime and Punishment*, ed. Simon Rottenberg. Washington, D.C.: American Enterprise Institute.

Phillips, Llad, Harold L. Votey, Jr., and John Howell. 1976. "Handguns and Homicide: Minimizing Losses and the Costs of Control," *Journal of Legal Studies* 5(2):463–78.

Pierce, Glenn L., and William J. Bowers. 1979. "The Impact of the Bartley-Fox Gun Law on Crime in Massachusetts." Unpublished manuscript. Northeastern University, Center for Applied Social Research.

———. 1981. "The Bartley-Fox Gun Law's Short-Term Impact on Crime in Boston," *Annals of the American Academy of Political and Social Science* 455 (May):120–37.

Rushforth, Norman B., A. B. Ford, C. S. Hirsh, N. M. Rushforth, and L. Adelson. 1977. "Violent Death in a Metropolitan County: Changing Patterns in Homicide (1958–74)," *New England Journal of Medicine* 297(10):531–38.

Seitz, Steven Thomas. 1972. "Firearms, Homicides, and Gun Control Effectiveness," *Law and Society Review* 6 (May):595–611.

Silberman, Charles E. 1978. *Criminal Violence, Criminal Justice*. New York: Random House.

Skogan, Wesley G. 1978. "Weapon Use in Robbery: Patterns and Policy Implications." Unpublished manuscript. Northwestern University, Center for Urban Affairs.

Swersey, Arthur J. 1980. "A Greater Intent to Kill: The Changing Pattern of Homicide in Harlem and New York City." Unpublished manuscript. Yale School of Organization and Management.

U.S. Conference of Mayors. 1980. "The Analysis of the Firearms Control Act of 1975: Handgun Control in the District of Columbia." Mimeographed.

Verkko, Veli. 1967. "Static and Dynamic 'Laws' of Sex and Homicide." In *Studies in Homicide*, ed. Marvin Wolfgang. New York: Harper and Row.

Weber-Burdin, Eleanor, P. H. Rossi, J. D. Wright, and K. Daly. 1981. *Weapons Policies: A Survey of Police Department Practices and Related Issues*. Amherst: University of Massachusetts, Social and Demographic Research Institute.

Wolfgang, Marvin E. 1958. *Patterns in Criminal Homicide*. Philadelphia: University of Pennsylvania Press.

Wright, James D. 1979. "Public Opinion and Gun Control: A Comparison of Results from Two Recent National Surveys." Unpublished manuscript. University of Massachusetts, Amherst.

———. 1981. "Public Opinion and Gun Control: A Comparison of Results from Two Recent National Surveys," *Annals of the American Academy of Political and Social Science* 455 (May):24–39.

Wright, James D., and Linda L. Marston. 1975. "The Ownership of the Means of Destruction: Weapons in the United States," *Social Problems* 23(1):81–107.

Wright, James D., P. H. Rossi, K. Daly, and E. Weber-Burdin. 1981. *Weapons, Crime, and Violence in America: A Literature Review and Research Agenda*.

Amherst: University of Massachusetts, Social and Demographic Research Institute.

Zimring, Franklin. 1967. "Is Gun Control Likely to Reduce Violent Killings?" *University of Chicago Law Review* 35:721–37.

———. 1968. "Games with Guns and Statistics," *Wisconsin Law Review* 1968:1113–26.

———. 1972. "The Medium Is the Message: Firearm Calibre as a Determinant of Death from Assault," *Journal of Legal Studies* 1(1):97–124.

———. 1975. "Firearms and Federal Law: The Gun Control Act of 1968," *Journal of Legal Studies* 4(1):133–98.

———. 1976. "Street Crime and New Guns: Some Implications for Firearms Control," *Journal of Criminal Justice* 4:95–107.

———. 1977. "Determinants of the Death Rate from Robbery: A Detroit Time Study," *Journal of Legal Studies* 6(2):317–32.

Ilene H. Nagel and John Hagan

Gender and Crime: Offense Patterns and Criminal Court Sanctions

ABSTRACT

The relation between gender and criminality is strong, and is likely to remain so. Women have traditionally been much less likely than men to commit violent crimes, and that pattern persists today. Rates of female involvement in some forms of property crime—notably petty theft and fraud—appear to be increasing. However, while the relative increase in women's property crime involvement is significant, female participation even in these crimes remains far less than that of men.

The relation of gender to case processing decisions in the criminal justice system varies from stage to stage. Although the pertinent literature is plagued by methodological and interpretive problems, several tentative conclusions can be offered. Women are more likely than men, other things equal, to be released on recognizance; however, when bail is set, the amount of bail does not appear to be affected by the defendant's gender. There is no clear evidence that the defendant's gender systematically affects prosecution, plea negotiation, or conviction decisions. In sentencing, however, women appear to receive systematic leniency except when they are convicted of high-severity offenses.

In the formative years of criminology, a major emphasis in theory and research was on understanding the causes of crime. Despite a plethora of theories on the typology of crime, no consensus was ever reached; each new causal theory was subjected to a fresh round of criticism of both method and substance. In part, the frustration of being unable to set forth one overarching theory to account for all criminal behavior stimulated a shift in emphasis. Whereas the early crime-causation tradition was characterized by attention to commonalities among criminals in

Ilene H. Nagel is Associate Professor of Law and Sociology in the School of Law, Indiana University. John Hagan is Professor of Sociology and Law at the University of Toronto.

The authors wish to express their gratitude to Richard Berk, Sheldon Plager, and Doug Smith, who read and commented on earlier versions of this essay.

psychological attributes, physiological characteristics, socialization patterns, and social backgrounds, the new tradition gave its attention to the commonalities of those formally labeled "criminals" in courts of law.

One reason for this shift was the hypothesis that overrepresentation of the socially disadvantaged might be explained by bias in the labeling process. Thus it might not be true that the socially disadvantaged commit more crimes. An alternative thesis could be that commission of crimes was equally distributed in the population but that, for a variety of political reasons, those empowered to categorize some as criminal and others as not would attach the stigmatizing label of criminal only to the powerless and the weak.

It was the intersection of these two traditions that provided the link between, on the one hand, the study of offenses and alleged offenders and, on the other hand, patterns of decisions resulting in criminal court sanctions. From then on, when race, sex, social class, or ethnicity were found to correlate highly with crime statistics, the question had to be asked: Were these groups really committing more or fewer crimes, or were they being discriminated against in the criminal courts, or both?

In the decade of the sixties, the increased sensitivity to issues of race, sex, and class bias reached new heights. One consequence was a renewed interest in the search for evidence of racism, sexism, and class bias in the law. In particular, the application of criminal laws and sanctions received considerable attention. The American system of justice is symbolized by a blindfold woman, carefully balancing a set of scales. The symbolic meaning is clear. All men (and women?) are equal before the eyes of justice; and the relevant facts, and only those, will be judiciously weighed on the juridical scales. To the extent that justice is not blind and, worse, favors or disfavors defendants because of status attributes over which they have no control, the abuse must be exposed and the system righted.

The concern for sexism in the law and its application has been especially slow in coming. Whereas race was identified early as an inappropriate consideration, the classification of sex as similarly inappropriate has not yet been resolved. Furthermore, unlike claims of racism in the application of laws and sanctions, there is no general presumption that women have historically been subjected to a consistent pattern of discrimination.

Only in the past two decades has the connection between sexism and the law begun to receive widespread attention. With respect to criminal law in particular, attention to the relation between gender and patterns of offense, and gender and patterns of criminal court sanctions, has been especially lacking. One purpose of this review is to assess the depth and breadth of that lack.

As we conceptualize the issues, two questions must simultaneously be addressed. First, What is the relation between gender and patterns of crime? We consider the way the relation varies as a function of the particular way crime and patterns of criminal offenses are measured. Second, What is the relation between gender and patterns of criminal court outcome decisions? Here we consider the way the relation varies as a function of a particular criminal court decision stage being examined (e.g. pretrial release, conviction, plea, sentence). Although we present our review in two separate sections, the two are interrelated. Patterns of crime statistics are affected by the decisions of criminal justice personnel. Without consideration of the policeman's decision to arrest, the prosecutor's decision to prosecute, or the judge's decision to sentence, criminal justice statistics on the sex of defendants alleged to have committed certain offenses lose much of their meaning. Similarly, in the absence of an appreciation of who commits what alleged offenses, decisions of police, prosecutors, and judges can easily be misunderstood. Unfortunately, despite the conceptual interrelation of these two issues, we know of no practical way to integrate our examination of the extant research, because it has developed largely without drawing this connection. Thus we present our review as if the research traditions were distinct, as they indeed appear in the literature. But in the end we will come back to our starting point and wrestle with the juxtaposition of these research literatures.

Section I examines the relation between gender and patterns of crime, as indicated by official crime statistics. We examine this same relation as revealed in self-report data, victimization data, and research based on field observations and archival record data.

Section II reviews the attention given to gender as a relevant determinant of criminal court outcome decisions and follows with a discussion of why such attention is theoretically important. Subsequently, we review the research on the relation between gender and decision outcomes for pretrial release, the decision to prosecute fully toward conviction, the decision on the acceptability of a plea bargain, the adjudication of guilt or innocence, and sentencing. Throughout, our concern is to ascertain whether the sex of a defendant systematically affects decision outcomes, and whether male defendants and offenders are treated differently than are female defendants and offenders.

In section III we speculate about the interrelation of the patterns noted in the two previous sections and juxtapose these findings in an effort to set forth a research agenda for the future.

I. The Criminal Behavior of Women

Research on crime by women focuses primarily on three issues: the extent of gender differences in criminal behavior, whether these differences show signs of declining, and the comparability of the criminal behavior patterns of men and women.

Data on differential patterns of offending by sex are available from several sources: public and private crime control agencies, victim surveys, self-report studies, field observations, and archival research. Each of these sources is imperfect, but their individual failings need not be collectively fatal. Credible estimates can be obtained through triangulation from the various sources. If several data sources produce comparable results, this may warrant confidence. Of course, to the extent that the sources disagree, our skepticism should increase.

The data on crime by women indicate several clear patterns. Women are much less likely than men to commit violent crimes or serious property crimes. With the exception of peculiarly female crimes such as prostitution and infanticide, and various "victimless crimes" on which credible statistical data are seldom available, "traditional female crimes" tend to be minor property offenses like shoplifting and fraud. There appear to have been increases in the rates of female criminality compared with rates for men, but the notable increases are for those minor offenses that are traditionally female crimes. Female crime rates remain, in absolute terms, far below those for men. These points can be illustrated with the following kinds of data.

A. *Public Agency Data*

Public agency data can tell us only part of the story of crime and gender, but it is an important part and is remarkably consistent: men are nearly always shown to be much more involved in criminal activity than are women. The annual *Uniform Crime Reports* (UCR) published by the FBI are the major source of national data on criminality. Data reported annually on arrests provide the nearest thing available to a national criminality register. These data are far from perfect. They provide at best only a distorted image of crime patterns: not all people arrested are guilty; the likelihood of arrests given involvement in crime varies enormously between offenses and over time; the data are vulnerable to conscious and inadvertent manipulation by the police departments that report them; and so on. Such problems of official arrest data are well known (for example, see Nettler 1978, chap. 4). Still, arrest data are the closest we can get on a large scale to actual offending. As Hindelang has observed: "researchers who refuse to examine even a blurred reflection of the phenomenon may be discarding an opportunity to reduce ignorance about the phenomenon in question" (1974, p. 2).

We begin our examination of female offending, then, by looking at UCR arrest data; we later consider whether the lessons we draw from these data are confirmed by the findings of victimization surveys, self-report studies, and other data. Table 1 shows arrest rates and ratios per 100,000 population by sex for selected property offenses for the period 1960–75. From the pioneering explorations of official crime statistics by Quetelet (1842) to the more modern tabulations by Radzinowitz (1937), Pollak (1950), Adler (1975), Simon (1975), and Smart (1977b), such statistics have consistently shown that men are more criminal than women. However, although this pattern is apparent in table 1 as well, it is also the case that the *ratio* of male to female arrest rates has declined in recent years. For example, we see in table 1 that between 1960 and 1975 the ratio of male to female rates of index property crimes (combining the offenses of burglary, larceny, and auto theft) decreased from 9.43 to only 3.93. Similar declines in the ratio of male to female rates are also apparent in table 1 for the individual crimes of burglary, larceny theft, auto theft, fraud/embezzlement, and stolen property. The question commonly asked of these kinds of data is whether the gap between males and females in rates of property crime has therefore declined.

Different answers have been given to this question, and there is reason to think that the differences derive from the kinds of measures applied. Steffensmeier (1978, 1980) notes that disparities between the sexes can be measured in absolute and relative terms. He advocates the former. Some ratio and percentage measures of relative differences, he argues, can be misleading because, if the starting point is low, small absolute changes will look *relatively* large. This may often be the case with female crime rates. Furthermore, he notes that percentage or ratio measures of relative change may be unstable when the measure is premised on part-to-part rather than part-to-whole comparisons. In place of the part-to-part ratio measure, Steffensmeier calculates the percentage that the female rate contributes (% FC) to the male rate *plus* female rate for each offense. He also calculates absolute differences between male and female rates. These various kinds of measures are presented in table 2 to

TABLE 1
Property Crime Rates and Ratios per 100,000 for Females and Males, 1960–75

Year	Three Property Crime Index			Burglary			Larceny Theft		
	Female	Male	Male/Female	Female	Male	Male/Female	Female	Male	Male/Female
1975	421.2	1657.1	3.93	31.0	588.4	18.98	379.6	913.8	2.41
1974	428.1	1708.0	3.99	31.7	592.9	18.70	384.5	930.5	2.42
1973	339.6	1364.7	4.02	25.4	479.6	18.88	303.6	706.8	2.32
1972	327.0	1387.4	4.24	23.6	464.8	19.70	293.3	743.6	2.54
1971	321.8	1470.1	4.57	23.4	468.1	20.00	286.7	786.3	2.74
1970	298.7	1400.5	4.69	20.8	455.3	21.88	267.8	742.9	2.77
1969	252.1	1313.3	5.21	18.4	434.8	23.63	222.8	667.0	2.99
1968	213.7	1265.0	5.92	17.6	434.1	24.66	186.0	620.3	3.33
1967	200.9	1210.0	6.02	16.0	406.8	25.42	176.6	602.7	3.41
1966	183.2	1128.5	6.16	13.6	361.1	26.55	162.0	576.6	3.56
1965	176.6	1138.1	6.45	13.4	369.2	27.55	155.4	579.6	3.73
1964	156.0	1102.0	7.06	12.7	355.1	27.96	135.6	563.2	4.15
1963	134.9	1044.3	7.74	10.9	342.5	31.42	117.6	529.8	4.51
1962	134.0	1040.5	7.76	11.9	342.7	28.80	115.5	530.8	4.60
1961	112.3	1002.9	8.93	10.9	349.3	32.04	96.0	502.3	5.23
1960	101.9	961.3	9.43	9.8	324.7	33.13	87.3	487.4	5.58

Year	Auto Theft			Fraud/Embezzlement			Stolen Property		
	Female	Male	Male/Female	Female	Male	Male/Female	Female	Male	Male/Female
1975	10.6	155.0	14.62	67.1	142.2	2.12	13.7	124.9	9.12
1974	11.9	184.5	15.50	53.7	121.0	2.25	13.4	127.3	9.50
1973	10.5	178.4	16.99	41.9	101.0	2.41	10.5	101.2	9.64
1972	10.1	179.1	17.73	44.2	113.9	2.58	10.1	101.0	10.00
1971	11.8	199.6	16.92	44.0	119.3	2.71	10.6	111.0	10.47
1970	10.1	202.3	20.03	35.5	104.1	2.93	8.9	93.3	10.48
1969	10.9	211.5	19.40	29.6	92.0	3.11	6.5	75.0	11.54
1968	10.2	210.6	20.65	24.3	84.6	3.48	4.8	61.6	12.83
1967	8.3	200.5	24.16	24.2	87.8	3.62	3.6	46.9	13.03
1966	7.7	190.7	24.77	22.0	86.4	3.92	2.9	36.6	12.62
1965	7.7	189.2	24.50	21.7	92.5	4.27	2.9	33.9	11.69
1964	7.7	183.8	23.66	19.1	87.4	4.58	3.3	32.3	9.79
1963	6.3	171.9	27.29	18.7	90.9	4.86	2.4	28.7	11.96
1962	6.6	167.0	25.30	16.7	87.4	5.23	2.5	28.8	11.52
1961	5.5	151.3	27.50	16.1	89.7	5.57	2.4	27.3	11.38
1960	5.4	149.2	27.62	14.7	87.9	5.98	2.3	26.3	11.43

Source: Steffensmeier 1978, table 1, reformulated.

illustrate the point that a *relative* gap in crime rates between the sexes can narrow while the *absolute* gap actually widens.

Indeed, for all crimes except forgery and embezzlement in table 2, the relative gap does decline, while the absolute difference increases. Using larceny as an illustration, the arrest rate for females was 87.3 in 1960 and 376.2 in 1978. For males it was 487.4 in 1960 and 870.4 in 1978. The two relative measures of change presented in this table both indicate a narrowing of the male/female gap: the ratio of rates declined from 5.58 to 2.31, and the % FC increased from 15.2 to 30.2. However, Steffensmeier's point is that only limited significance can be attached to these changes because, during the same period, the absolute difference between male and female rates widened to 493.6 (870.4–376.8) from 400.1 (487.4–87.3). Based on the kinds of calculations presented in table 2, Steffensmeier concludes that the relative gains made by women in their rates of crime are often more apparent than real. However, there are important differences of opinion on this point.

Rita Simon, whose work (e.g. 1976a, b) may have had the greatest influence in this area, offers a convergence theory in which patterns of criminality for women increasingly resemble those for men. For example, she has analyzed arrest statistics for a forty-year period (1932 to 1972) and concluded that: (1) the proportion of all persons arrested in 1972 who were women was greater than was the case one, two, or three decades earlier; (2) the increase was greater for serious offenses than for other kinds of offenses; and (3) the increase in female arrest rates among the serious offenses was caused almost entirely by women's greater participation in property offenses, especially larceny. Simon (1976b) extrapolates from the latter findings and states that "if present rates in these crimes persist, approximately equal numbers of men and women will be arrested for fraud and embezzlement by the 1990's, and for forgery and counterfeiting the proportions should be equal by the 2010's. The prediction made for embezzlement and fraud can be extended to larceny as well."

Steffensmeier is most at odds with Simon on these last points. He finds that arrest rate projections for larceny show a *widening of the absolute gap* with each passing decade to the year 2000, with similar results for fraud and forgery. He concludes (1980, p. 1098) that "female gains have been leveling off in recent years and it is likely that crime will be as much a male-dominated phenomenon in the year 2000 as it is in 1977." Still, this does not deny Simon's more fundamental point that, in *relative* terms, women are now significantly more involved in crime than they were in the past.

In terms of crime patterns, Simon emphasizes that the relative increases in adult women's crime rates are concentrated in the area of property crime. This point is important to Simon's theoretical argument that as women increase their participation in the labor force, their opportunity to commit certain types of crime also increases. Steffensmeier does not reject this argument; rather, he seeks to diminish its significance. His point is that, while the female contribution to property crime generally, and again in a relative sense, has increased, the amount of this increase that is occupationally related (e.g. embezzlement) is small. A problem here involves the vagueness of general offense categories like larceny. When such categories are broken down, Steffensmeier argues that the greater contributions of women are in the areas of petty theft and fraud.

Some support for Steffensmeier's suggestions is provided in table 2. This table includes a division between "masculine" and "petty property" crimes. As both Steffensmeier and Simon suggest, "masculine" crimes like robbery, burglary, and auto theft remain predominately male phenomena, in spite of some recent relative increases in female participation. In contrast, the petty property crime rates of women have increased notably, and the absolute differences between the male and female rates for petty crimes like forgery and embezzlement have actually declined: between 1960 and 1978 the sex difference in forgery rates declined from 42.8 to 36.8, and for embezzlement from 11.3 to 4.7. Still, the absolute differences between male and female rates of other petty property crimes like larceny and fraud have increased over this period, and it may be important to note that embezzlement represents only a very small part of female arrests: one-tenth of one percent in 1978, down from a similarly small three-tenths of one percent in 1964. Steffensmeier's point is that women are being arrested for traditionally female kinds of larceny like fraud rather than for nontraditional kinds of female crime such as embezzlement. However, this does not make the nontraditional gains any less important; indeed, in terms of dollars and the threat posed to the economic order, these nontraditional female crimes may be very important. Simon and Steffensmeier here offer different interpretations of similar empirical findings.

Last, there is the issue of female involvement in violent crime. Simon's findings seem to contradict Adler's predictions of growing female vio-

TABLE 2

Arrest Rates and Ratios per 100,000 Males and Females for Petty Property Crimes and for Masculine Property Crimes, 1960 (64) and 1977[a]

Type of Crime	Female Rate	Male Rate	Male/ Female	% FC	AD[b]	% of All Female Arrests	% of All Male Arrests
Petty							
Larceny							
1960	87.3	487.4	5.58	15.2	400.1	8.5	5.4
1978	376.2	870.4	2.31	30.2	494.2	9.0	22.2
Fraud							
1964	16.3	73.4	4.50	18.2	57.1	1.6	0.9
1978	100.3	185.3	1.85	35.1	85.0	5.9	1.9
Forgery							
1960	9.2	52.0	5.65	15.0	42.8	0.9	0.6
1978	23.8	60.6	2.55	28.2	36.8	1.4	0.6
Embezzlement							
1964	2.8	14.1	5.03	16.5	11.3	0.3	0.2
1978	2.1	6.8	3.23	23.6	4.7	0.1	0.1

Masculine							
Robbery							
1960	3.5	76.5	21.86	4.4	73.0	0.3	0.9
1978	10.9	154.7	14.19	6.6	143.8	0.6	1.6
Burglary							
1960	9.3	324.7	34.91	2.8	315.4	0.9	3.6
1978	32.7	536.1	16.39	5.7	503.4	1.9	5.5
Auto theft							
1960	5.4	149.2	27.6	3.5	143.8	0.5	1.7
1978	14.0	165.2	11.8	7.8	151.2	0.8	1.7
Arson							
1964	0.9	9.4	10.44	8.7	8.5	0.1	0.1
1978	2.4	18.7	7.79	11.4	16.3	0.1	0.2
Vandalism							
1964	8.6	142.3	16.55	5.7	133.7	0.8	1.7
1978	20.5	240.6	11.74	7.9	220.1	1.2	2.5
Stolen property							
1960	2.3	26.3	11.43	8.2	24.0	0.2	0.3
1978	13.5	177.5	13.15	10.3	104.0	0.8	1.2

Source: Steffensmeier 1981, table 1, reformulated.
Note: In some cases 1964 data were used because this was the earliest year for which data were reported separately for these categories.
[a]Percentage of female contribution.
[b]Absolute difference.

lence. Other sources of data seem to be consistent with Simon's position as well, at least for adult women (see Noblet and Burcart 1976; Harris and Hill 1981; Steffensmeier 1980). Thus the violence of adult women is clearly patterned differently from the violence of men (Ward, Jackson, and Ward 1969; Wolfgang 1958), and this patterning has not shown much sign of change. However, this point is less clear for adolescent women. Noblet and Burcart (1976, p. 655) find that arrests for violent crimes and property crimes increased equally among adolescent women between 1960 and 1970, and Harris and Hill (1981) report sex ratio drops between 1963 and 1974 in the population under 18 for a variety of violent crimes. We will return below to the issue of changing patterns of violence among adolescent women.

B. *Victimization Surveys*

Since many criminal acts involve victims as well as perpetrators, victims too can be a source of information about crime. Surveys of victims began in the United States in the mid-1960s (Biderman et al. 1967; Ennis 1967), and the American government has since inaugurated a regular surveying program on a national scale, the results of which we consider here.

Victimization surveys are limited, of course, in their subject matter: they are concerned explicitly with *crimes*, committed by *individuals*, against *persons* and their *property*. They are not concerned with "victimless crimes" such as gambling, prostitution, public disorder offenses, and alcohol and drug abuse. Added to this limitation, there are several deficiencies of method (see Sparks 1979), at least one of which—the reluctance of victims to report sexual assaults and crimes deriving from family quarrels—may particularly involve women. The existence of these deficiencies must be weighed against the unique findings that victimization surveys provide (Bowker 1981) and the short history of the techniques involved.

Hindelang (1979) has analyzed data on the sex of offenders reported by victims derived from the 1973 through 1976 surveys of American crime victims, called the National Crime Surveys (NCS). The findings of these surveys are summarized in table 3 along with 1976 *Uniform Crime Reports* data. A comparison of the NCS and UCR data (see table 3) reveals a very similar picture, leading Hindelang (1979, p. 152) to surmise that "in general, it appears that even at the earliest stage in the offending process for which data are available, the conclusions we can draw about sex and involvement in crime from victimization survey data are essentially the

TABLE 3

Estimated Percentages of Offenders Reported by Victims to Have Been Females, by Type of Crime in National Crime Survey, 1972–76, and Female Arrests in *Uniform Crime Reports*, 1976 Only

Type of Crime	NCS 1972[a]	NCS 1973[a]	NCS 1974	NCS 1975	NCS 1976	UCR 1976
Rape	0%	1%	0%	3%	1%	1%
	(232,845)[c]	(203,733)	(223,721)	(222,050)	(161,000)	
Robbery	6%[a]	4%[a]	7%	4%	4%	7%
	(2,365,176)	(2,070,110)	(2,122,945)	(2,248,777)	(2,126,622)	
Aggravated assault	8%	8%	7%	6%	8%	13%
	(1,895,089)	(2,191,050)	(2,086,011)	(1,982,910)	(1,986,360)	
Simple assault	15%	15%	15%	15%	14%	14%
	(3,047,491)	(3,364,001)	(3,228,297)	(3,283,535)	(3,374,864)	
Burglary	5%	5%	4%	7%	5%	5%
	(563,470)	(493,526)	(604,949)	(458,304)	(502,293)	
Motor vehicle theft	3%	3%	4%	2%	5%	7%
	(127,933)	(161,621)	(87,213)	(69,030)	(110,205)	
Larceny[b]	14%	14%	14%	15%	17%	
	(2,039,625)	(1,636,759)	(1,709,704)	(1,818,003)	(1,670,439)	
Personal larceny	11%	11%	11%	11%	14%	—
	(409,217)	(351,611)	(380,437)	(507,332)	(383,957)	
Larceny from household	15%	16%	16%	14%	17%	—
	(695,064)	(568,833)	(535,966)	(515,022)	(507,345)	
Larceny of unattended property	14%	15%	16%	19%	19%	—
	(935,344)	(716,315)	(793,301)	(795,649)	(779,137)	

[a]Commercial robberies for 1972 and 1973 (or about one-fifth of all robberies) have been excluded because the raw data were not available for analysis. Female offenders generally constitute fewer than 2 percent of the commercial robbery offenders; hence, if they were included in the 1972 and 1973 robbery data, the robbery percentages for females might decline by half a point.

[b]The UCR and NCS larceny categories are not comparable (see Hindelang 1979, p. 148).

[c]Number of cases in parentheses.

same as those derived from arrest data for the same types of crimes."
Thus these data indicate (1) women offenders are a small portion of all
offenders reported by victims (e.g. in 1976 they accounted for 4 percent
of all robberies, 8 percent of all aggravated assaults, 14 percent of all
simple assaults, 5 percent of all burglaries, and 5 percent of all motor
vehicle thefts reported by victims), and that (2) what increase in female
involvement in crime has occurred during the short period of these
surveys is most conspicuously in the area of larceny offenses (women
accounted for 14 percent of all larcenies reported by victims in 1972, and
17 percent of these larcenies in 1976). Again, these data indicate that
petty property crimes are the "traditional female crimes," and that they
are the crimes in which increases in female involvement are most clearly
occurring. Finally, Hindelang reports that, when the sex of the victim
was held constant in his analyses, there was no evidence that male
chivalry (males' reluctance to report crimes against them by women) had
the effect of reducing the number of female-offender victimizations
reported to the police. In sum, victimization data seem to confirm the
picture of women and crime portrayed in public agency data.

C. *Self-Report Studies*

Self-report studies use paper-and-pencil instruments and interviews
to ask (usually male) respondents to confess, in Kinseylike fashion, the
quality and quantity of their criminal and delinquent indiscretions. The
problems of self-report research are reviewed comprehensively elsewhere (Hindelang, Hirschi, and Weis 1978). Here it may be important
to note that self-report research often involves students, and disproportionately middle-class ones at that. Even urban secondary-school
student samples are skewed toward the middle class because of high
drop-out and truancy rates. The weaknesses of the self-report approach
also include memory lapses, deceit among subjects, vaguely stated survey items, and indefinite periods of coverage. Nonetheless, self-report
data are suggestive of the volume and social location of various kinds of
crime and juvenile delinquency, and, if appropriate questions and sampling procedures are used, it may be possible to generalize from these
findings and to make comparisons with official data sources.

The gender-crime patterns we have seen in public-agency and
victimization data reappear in the self-report studies, but with significant
variations in degree. For example, official arrest ratios by sex are substantially higher than the sex ratios by offense found in self-report
surveys. Nye and Short (1958) find a sex ratio among adolescents of 2.42

in a midwestern setting and 2.82 in a western setting. Wise's (1967) New England study yields an adolescent differential of 2.30; Hindelang's (1971) California data yield a sex ratio of 2.56; Kratcoski and Kratcoski (1975) report a 2.00 sex ratio; and Cernkovich and Giordano (1979) find a ratio of 2.18 (see also Hagan, Simpson, Gillis (1979); Jensen and Eve 1976). In each of these instances, males exceed females in self-reported delinquencies by more than two to one. However, this figure is still considerably less than that indicated by public agency data. The 1975 FBI *Uniform Crime Reports* indicate that the male/female arrest ratio for those under 18 years of age is 3.72. One explanation for this disparity is that police are more sensitive and responsive to male delinquencies.

In an attempt to estimate how police selection practices might influence delinquency sex ratios, Feyerherm (1981) has calculated a series of "transition probabilities" that reflect the likelihood that male and female adolescents will be processed through a series of steps beginning with police contact and leading to arrest. The results of these calculations reveal that, while the ratio of male to female delinquency at the stage of self-report was on the order of 1.70 to 1, at the point of arrest this ratio had increased to 3.88 to 1, more than doubling the apparent difference between males and females and approximating the figures found in public agency data.

Two explanations are offered: (1) that police are biased in their arrest practices, and (2) that male adolescents are involved in more serious kinds of delinquency. This brings us to the *kinds* of self-reported activities in which male and female adolescents are involved.

The important point to be made here is that, while female adolescents may be more "versatile" in their delinquencies than female adults are in their criminal behavior, nonetheless, as the seriousness of the events increases, so also do the differences between levels of male and female participation, among both adolescents and adults. A first indication that female adolescents may be unexpectedly versatile in their delinquencies is found in the work of Hindelang (1971). Hindelang reports that, while males may be much more delinquent than females, female delinquencies, much like those of males, still are spread across a broad range of activities. However, more recently Feyerherm (1981) has pointed out that the seriousness of these activities may differ substantially by sex. Thus, in Feyerherm's data, three levels of theft are examined, with the following results: in the lowest level, under $10, the ratio of male to female participation is 1.80; between $10 and $50 the ratio increases to 4.56; over $50, it increases to 22.00. The conclusion (p. 88) is that "since the sets of arrest statistics most often examined are designed to deal primarily with serious offenses, this tendency may explain why arrest information is more likely to show strong male-female differences."

A key difference between the self-report studies and those based on public agency data is that the former are generally time bound in their coverage. This makes it more difficult to answer questions about change over time when using self-report data. Fortunately, however, Smith and Visher (1980) have brought together many of these studies, along with those focusing on public agency data, and have offered a "meta-analysis" of the data they review. Their analysis indicates that the relative involvement of males and females in crime is trending toward similarity for *both* self-report and official measures, but that the rate of the trend is significantly greater for the self-reported measures. Beyond this, Smith and Visher report that, although women are closing the gap in terms of *minor* forms of crime and delinquency, there is no indication that equal gender representation in the area of serious criminal behavior has yet occurred. Finally, and perhaps most significantly, they note that, while the gender-deviance relation is diminishing for both youths and adults, their data indicate that this trend is stronger for youths.

The last point is significant because, as Smith and Visher (1980) note, "It is at least plausible that shifting sex-role ideologies may be more salient for younger females and, thus, may have a greater impact upon the behavior of this group." This hypothesis and an analysis of public agency data in support of it are found in the work of Harris and Hill (1981).

D. *Private Agency Data, Observational Studies, and Archival Research*

There remain three other sources of data on women and crime. First, the records of the internal security departments of corporate entities have been used to study shoplifting and the crimes of employees against these bureaucracies. The studies of shoplifting indicate that this is a traditionally female crime in that it has involved large numbers of women for some time (Cameron 1964). Of greater interest is the question whether women shoplifters are reported by private security personnel to police at the same rate as are men shoplifters. Because so many women are apprehended for shoplifting, this is a good offense to test for police bias. Cameron reports from the Chicago department store data she analyzed that only 10 percent of the women shoplifters, compared with 35 percent of the men shoplifters, were reported to the police. However, Hindelang (1974) finds no disparity by sex when the retail value of goods stolen was taken into account in a sample of shoplifting cases processed in California between 1963 and 1965. Of the two studies, Hindelang's is the more recent and the more methodologically sound.

Employee theft is another area in which private agency data have been put to interesting use. Franklin (1979) reports, in a study based on the reports of a large retail organization, that although a majority of the employees were women, the majority of employee thieves were men. Similarly, it is also found that the greater the value of the theft, the greater the likelihood that it was committed by a male employee. Indeed, the female thefts were relatively petty, with 81 percent of the thefts committed by females valued between $1 and $150. These private agency data, then, seem to further confirm the impression that women continue to be involved in the "traditional" types of female crime.

The latter point is made in a somewhat different way by observational case studies of different types of criminal behavior. Miller (1973) reports on the basis of his work with street corner gangs that females continue to play largely ancillary roles. As Steffensmeier (1980, p. 1102) notes, this does not mean there have been no serious and significant female criminals: there are now and always have been cases of female professional thieves, robbers, and so on (Block 1977; Byrnes 1886; Ianni 1974; Jackson 1969; Lucas 1926; Reitman 1937). However, the female role, then and now, has typically been as an accomplice to a male who both organized the crime and was the central figure in its execution (although see Giordano 1978).

There is, finally, one additional study based on archival records that puts much that precedes into a broader historical perspective. This study, by Cernkovich and Giordano (1979), is based on police blotters from the city of Toledo, Ohio, for the years 1890–1975. The length of the time period covered is unique to this study, and these conclusions were drawn: (1) women are now being arrested for offenses that are increasingly similar to those for which males are arrested; (2) female rates of arrest are increasing more rapidly than are male rates; and (3) male-to-female ratios are declining for many offenses. This changing character of female crime is noted in qualitative as well as quantitative terms. Thus, notes made by police officers in the margins of these blotters indicate that, whereas in the earliest periods a high percentage of the total number of women arrested were somehow tied to "houses of ill fame" (see also Heyl 1979), by the 1930s there began to be a more active, independent-from-hearth-and-home (as well as from house-of-prostitution) quality to the offenses. Indeed, the 1930s show significant increases in such property offenses as robbery, burglary, theft, and embezzlement. The significance of the timing of this shift is that it also marks the onset of the Great Depression, a time that was particularly precarious for women. Thus Giordano, Kerbel, and Dudley (1981) conclude that "this analysis of offense types as well as the characteristics of women arrested suggests that the increases may reflect the fact that certain categories of women (e.g., young, single, minority) [were] now in an even more unfavorable position in the labor market at the same time they [were] . . . increasingly expected to function independently."

We are now in a position to draw some conclusions about the relation between gender and crime. We have noted that this relation is strong and that it is likely to remain so into the near future, at least in an absolute sense. On the other hand, in a relative sense, there is evidence that women are becoming more like men in their levels of involvement in crime, with this being particularly true of younger women and in the area of property crime. The areas of female criminality that are changing fastest are those that have been traditionally female, including petty forms of theft and fraud. These changes are important not only to our understanding of crime as a behavioral phenomenon, but also to our understanding of changes that may be occurring in the sanctioning of women offenders. As we will see in the following section, research on sanctioning has not done a good job of drawing this connection. We emphasize this point in the conclusion. First, however, we review the research that has been conducted on women and the sanctioning process.

II. The Role of Gender in Court Outcome Decisions

Our purpose here is to examine the research on *the role of gender in criminal court outcome decisions*. To organize our presentation, we divide this section into six subsections: (*a*) changes in the level of attention given to gender in court outcome research; (*b*) the theoretical relevance of including gender as a potential decision outcome determinant; (*c*) the role of gender in pretrial release decisions; (*d*) the role of gender in decisions to prosecute fully toward conviction rather than to terminate through some form of dismissal, discharge, or diversion; (*e*) the role of gender in plea negotiation/bargains; and (*f*) the role of gender in conviction and sentencing decisions. Because our focus is on the role of gender in *criminal court* decisions, we exclude research on juveniles and juvenile court dispositions (see e.g. Chesney-Lind 1973; Datesman and Scarpitti 1980; Kratcoski 1974; Scarpitti and Stephenson 1971; Terry 1970; Thornberry 1973), research on decisions that precede (e.g. arrest) or follow (e.g. parole) processing in the court, research based on data drawn from jurisdictions not within the United States (e.g. Smart 1977b), and research focusing on discrimination in criminal statutes (e.g. Armstrong 1977; Babcock 1973; DeCrow 1974; Frankel 1973; Singer 1973; Temin 1973). While some of this literature is relevant to the discussion here, it does not fall directly within our review mandate. Finally, we exclude research on the imposition of the death penalty, not because it falls outside the boundaries of our review, but because there have been too few empirical studies where the gender of the offender was examined (for exceptions, see Bedau 1964; Judson et al. 1969).

A. *Changes in the Attention Given to Gender in Court Research*

Rasche, in an essay on the female offender as an object of criminological research, contends that "the vast bulk of criminological research, unquestionably, has concerned itself with male offenders" (1975, p. 9). To explain this, she notes that women constitute only a minute proportion of those imprisoned, that they appear to be less violent, and that as research subjects they seem inherently less interesting. As we noted in section I, the actual number of women arrested, prosecuted, convicted, and imprisoned is indeed considerably smaller than the number of males, especially for violent crimes and major property offenses. This has two important consequences. First, because there are so few women offenders, researchers have generally presumed that they can safely be ignored in the search for important patterns of decision making. Moreover, the smallness of their numbers makes inclusion of women a problem in data analysis.

> Small populations of female offenders mean that researchers interested in them will have fewer subjects for study, complicating statistical findings and, of course, lowering the generalizability of the data. (Rasche 1975, p. 11)

Second, women typically have not been prosecuted and convicted for the more serious or violent crimes such as robbery, burglary, assault, and auto theft. They have more often been prosecuted and convicted for property-related misdemeanors such as shoplifting. Researchers have not included women in their more focused efforts to model decision making for the outcomes of serious, violent offenders. Finally, the importance of gender as a salient independent variable for sociological inquiry has only recently been recognized. While the social science journals of the 1970s are filled with publications on sex differences in labor force participation, occupational mobility, scientific accomplishments, and the like, no comparable research tradition can be found in the journals of the 1950s or 1960s. Thus the inattention to sex in court outcome research probably reflects the more general pattern of inattention to gender in social science research before the onset of the women's liberation movement.

The inattention to gender in court outcome research raises several important interpretative issues. First, it is unclear whether the patterns discerned for samples of male defendants hold for samples of female defendants. Harris (1977, p. 3) argues that "general theories of criminal deviance are . . . no more than special theories of male deviance." From this perspective it follows that including females in the research samples used to model court outcome decisions might dramatically change current conceptions. Second, to the extent that including gender in models of decision outcomes changes the relation among other independent variables (e.g. the defendant's race, age, occupation, social class) and the court outcome under study, extant theory and research may need to be reexamined.

Our review of the research on the role of gender in court outcomes reveals a major change after 1970. Before 1970 the inattention to gender was almost universal. In Hagan's 1974 review of studies relating extralegal offender characteristics to judicial sentencing, nineteen of the twenty studies reviewed were published before 1970. Only five of the nineteen included a defendant's sex in the research; in two of those five there were too few women to draw any inferences (Bedau 1964; Judson et al. 1969). Both were studies of the imposition of the death penalty. Since 1970, we can identify more than twenty studies that consider a defendant's sex. What is noteworthy is that only a handful of researchers and their students seem to have done most of this work. Thus, despite the relative gains in the apparent attention to gender, relative to other status characteristics of defendants such as race or social class, gender is still largely ignored. Moreover, with few exceptions, there are virtually no studies that go beyond noting that males, or females, receive preferential treatment at one decision point or another. The research by Nagel, Cardascia, and Ross (1980) on sex differences in the processing of state court defendants is the only study we can identify where the question raised by Harris—Are there different models of decision making by sex?—is directly addressed. It appears that the repeated calls for an end to the inattention to gender (see e.g. Adler 1975; Babcock 1973; Brodsky

1975; Harris 1977; Simon 1975; Ward, Jackson, and Ward 1969) have not yet been answered.

B. *The Theoretical Relevance of Gender as a Decision Outcome Determinant*

Current perspectives in the sociology of law and deviance provide strong theoretical justification for expecting a defendant's gender to affect criminal court outcome decisions. These perspectives draw attention to social power, social rank, the defendant's ability to negotiate the imposition of a criminal label, and stereotypic expectations and responses to criminal defendants.

With respect to power, conflict theorists (e.g. Chambliss and Seidman 1971; Quinney 1970, 1973, 1977; Turk 1969) and labeling theorists (e.g. Lofland 1969) argue that the relative power of an individual is an important factor in the determination of criminal court decision outcomes. Less powerful members of society, they contend, will be more likely to receive unfavorable treatment. In Black's (1976) terms, the quantity of law will vary with the social rank and power of the individual. In other words, sanctions will more likely be imposed on the less advantaged members of society. Women can be assumed to be less powerful by virtue of their weaker ties to the economic means of production, their lesser status roles in the work force, their underrepresentation in politics, and their general underrepresentation in positions of economic, social, and political leadership. If one simply applied the thesis that the less powerful are more likely to receive the least favorable outcomes, one would predict that women will fare less well than men in court outcome decisions.

We believe, however, that power is situational, and in the context of the criminal court the relative powerlessness of women in society would be more an advantage than a disadvantage. We contend that this is so because the powerlessness of women is not accompanied by a diminution in value and rank. Rather, one societal view is that the proper role of women is one of powerlessness and dependency, but that this role deserves respect, protection, and value. Thus a simplistic application of the conflict perspective would erroneously predict that women would be treated more harshly than men. We predict instead to the extent that there is a consistent pattern—that women will be less likely to be detained pretrial, prosecuted fully to conviction, unfavorably treated in plea negotiations, or sentenced to imprisonment.

With respect to a defendant's ability to negotiate away the imposition of a criminal label, Blumberg (1967), Bernstein et al. (1977), and Schur (1971) argue that certain status attributes, life experiences, or court experiences enable some defendants to evade criminal labels more easily. Warner, Wellman, and Weitzman (1971) suggest that women may be better negotiators since they can use their "femininity" to manipulate actors to respond favorably to them. Some social psychological research testing hypotheses deduced from attribution theory (see e.g. Landy and Aronson 1969; Stephan 1975; Weiten and Diamond 1980) supports this supposition, since it is generally reported that jurors and judges (simulated or real) are less likely to attribute criminal liability to attractive defendants. Further, on the assumption that most criminal court decisions are made by males, one would again predict that female defendants are likely to receive more favorable decision outcomes.

With respect to values and expectations, Becker (1963), Erikson (1964), Kitsuse and Cicourel (1963), Rubington and Weinberg (1978), Schur (1971), and Swigert and Farrell (1977) argue that criminal court personnel hold certain values and expectations that are shaped by the ascribed and achieved status of defendants. Since sex is a major ascribed status for shaping behavior and expectations, typifications based on gender can be expected to affect criminal justice decision making.

A consideration of gender is clearly consistent with, and indeed central to, some of the assumptions of the variety of theoretical perspectives that frame court outcome research. Yet the specific role of gender in these perspectives has not been well developed. While hypotheses of differential treatment by sex can be derived, it is not at all clear what the direction of the hypotheses should logically be, or how the hypotheses would change when the same questions are addressed for women defendants as for men. There are, however, two theoretical perspectives, the chivalry thesis and the evil woman thesis, that focus specifically on differential treatment, by gender, within the legal system. Both emphasize the importance of specific expectations of, and tolerances for, female criminality. What is curious is that, while the two positions make different assumptions about the motive of decision makers (i.e., punitive versus protective), the outcomes they predict are not clearly dissimilar. And, in the most recent literature, *both* the punitive and the protective (chivalry) patterns are attacked as evidence of sex discrimination (see e.g. Datesman and Scarpitti 1980; Moulds 1980).

1. The chivalry/paternalism thesis. The first perspective is ordinarily termed the *chivalrous* or *paternalistic* thesis. It is meant to explain the preferential treatment of women on the basis of chivalrous or paternalistic responses of judges, prosecutors, magistrates, and the like. The thesis that women are given chivalrous treatment in the criminal justice system was first noted by Thomas (1907). In his book *Sex and Society* he states:

> man is merciless to woman from the standpoint of personal behavior, yet he exempts her from anything in the way of contractual morality, or views her defections in this regard with allowance and even with amusement. (Thomas 1907, p. 234)

Despite the relatively early date of its origin, the chivalry thesis was largely ignored until Pollak revived it in his classic (1950) work on female criminality. Pollak (1950, p. 151) states the thesis quite clearly:

> One of the outstanding concomitants of the existing inequality between the sexes is chivalry and the general protective attitude of man toward woman. This attitude exists . . . on the part of the officers of the law, who are still largely male in our society. Men hate to accuse women and thus indirectly to send them to their punishment, police officers dislike to arrest them, district attorneys to prosecute them, judges and juries to find them guilty.

After Pollak, many years passed before the chivalry thesis reappeared in the literature. With the exception of Nagel (1969), Nagel and Weitzman (1971), and Reckless and Kay (1967), each of whom claim to find some empirical support for the thesis that women are chivalrously or paternalistically treated, the chivalry/paternalism thesis was not really elaborated upon until 1975 when Simon revived it in her monograph on women in crime. A review of the post-1975 literature suggests that the chivalry thesis is now wholly accepted. Anderson (1976), Crites (1978), and, most recently and perhaps most comprehensively, Moulds (1980) elaborate on the propositions and implications of the thesis. Moulds makes the most important contribution because she tries to draw conceptual distinctions between chivalry and paternalism. Tracing the historical and etymological derivations of each term, she finds the roots of the chivalry concept in the Middle Ages. Then it was an institution of service rendered by the crusading orders to the feudal lords, to the divine sovereign, and to women (Moulds 1980, p. 279). Knights were sworn to protect women against dragons and devils. While the formal practice was ultimately discontinued, the legacy lived on in an informal set of conventions and a code of manners. What Moulds does not point out, but we believe to be equally important, is that chivalry dictated that women were to be put on a pedestal and treated with the most gallant of manners, while being presumed to be weak and in need of protection. There is little, however, that one can consider "negative" in chivalrous treatment or a chivalrous attitude *if* one interprets the behavior in its temporal context.

Paternalism is, as Moulds aptly points out, very different from chivalry. By definition, paternalism is meant to imply a power relationship; the term has always had a pejorative connotation. Webster defines paternalism as "a relation between the governed and the government, the employed and the employer, etc., involving care and control." For Moulds the key element in paternalism is the likening of the female to a child. Paternalism presumes that one is dealing with a defenseless, propertyless individual who cannot be held responsible for his or her own actions, who is incapable of assessing information, and who is incapable of making a proper decision. Such a person is in need of guidance and protection. It follows that, if such a person "strays"—commits a crime—it is wholly appropriate to assume that, like a child, he or she is not responsible. Moulds (1980, p. 282) summarizes the difficulties with such a paternalistic attitude:

> It is important to be wary of a society which permits paternalism to color the perceptions of those who make and enforce the law. Those perceptions profoundly affect behavior of those in power and the behavior of those paternalized in a manner that is inconsistent with the operation of a democratic state. A basic denial of self-determination is what is taking place.

In sum, the chivalrous treatment of women in the arms of the law does not have the same negative implications as does paternalistic treatment. Unfortunately, Moulds does not provide a basis for identifying whether preferential treatment, as she observes it in California, results from a paternalistic or a chivalrous response.

Our own reading of the literature suggests that there is one additional implication of consciously or implicitly drawing the theoretical distinction between chivalry and paternalism. To the extent that researchers who found preferential treatment for female defendants in decisions at pretrial (e.g. Nagel 1981), plea (Crites 1978), and sentencing (e.g. Nagel 1969; Nagel and Weitzman 1971; Simon and Sharma 1978) assumed such preferential treatment was reflective of a chivalrous or even a mixed chivalrous/paternalistic response, there were no strident calls for redress or reform. Nor did the authors view these results as egregious examples of sex discrimination. However, to the extent that the same preferential patterns are interpreted as reflective of a purely paternalistic response—

see, for example, Datesman and Scarpitti (1980) and Moulds (1980)—
then the findings are seen as consistent with other evidence of sex
discrimination, and different reform measures are proposed.

We believe that future research should seek empirical evidence of the
bases for the preferential treatment of females, and the conditions under
which it is most and least pronounced. Hagan, Hewitt, and Alwin
(1979), Kruttschnitt (1981), and Nagel, Cardascia, and Ross (1980) have
begun to investigate the conditions under which females are more or less
likely to be preferentially treated. But to our knowledge there is no
research that provides empirical data to link the preferential treatment of
women specifically with any of the following assumptions: Women (*a*)
are less culpable; (*b*) are more emotional and less responsible for their
actions; (*c*) commit crimes that are ephemeral and not part of a general
criminal pattern; (*d*) are not dangerous; (*e*) are easily deterred without
harsh sanctions; (*f*) are amenable to rehabilitation outside the prison;
(*g*) are too sensitive to withstand severe sanctions that are harsh and
traumatic. Until preferential responses are linked to particular assumptions, we will not be able to resolve whether preferential treatment stems
from notions of chivalry or paternalism or from some combination. More
important, the theoretical implications of preferential treatment, and the
consequent appropriate policy suggestions, remain unclear.

2. *The evil woman thesis.* Despite widespread acceptance of the view
that female defendants receive preferential treatment, whether reflecting
chivalry or paternalism, there is a counterthesis—*the evil woman thesis*—
that hypothesizes that women are more harshly treated in the arms of the
law. One problem with this thesis is that it has been conceptually
muddied by the evidence used to support it. It is argued that, under the
guise of paternalism, female juveniles, and some adult women, are
incarcerated for longer periods than are equivalent males (see e.g. Chesney-Lind 1977; Kratcoski 1974; Singer 1973; Smart 1977*b*; Velimesis
1975 for elaborations on this theme). The result is said to stem from the
courts' belief that women who commit crimes are evil and must be
"helped" to see the error of their ways. But if the evil woman thesis is the
antithesis of the chivalry/paternalism thesis, then paternalistic responses
that generate harsher outcomes cannot logically be used to substantiate
the evil woman thesis.

The above notwithstanding, the evil woman thesis hypothesizes that
women will be more harshly sanctioned because their criminal behavior
violates sex stereotypic assumptions about the proper role of women. It
follows that if women accrue benefits from a presumption that they

cannot commit wrongdoings, then, if that presumption is shown to be false, the benefits accrued will now be lost. Furthermore, such a loss might well be accompanied by an overreaction to their "falling from the pedestal." Rasche (1975) observes:

> The few references made about women in this regard show clearly that women were generally considered morally corrupt (as opposed to evil) when they transgressed the law, but were not taken seriously as a danger to society. Hence the terms "fallen" or "errant" which were so often applied to females who pursued criminal careers; women were seen as essentially virtuous unless they "fell" from their pedestals or were "led astray" by others. Very few women were labeled "evil," but when such labeling occurred, it was with a vengeance. Often, "evil" women were portrayed as supernatural, or as witches, and therefore, no longer deserving of the protection or politeness normally extended toward women. (1975, p. 15)

In assessing the empirical support for the evil woman thesis, there are two hypotheses that might be tested. The first is the generalized statement that female defendants will fare less well than male defendants in terms of the severity of court outcomes. Since all crimes committed by women can be seen as violating sex stereotypic assumptions about the proper role of women, female defendants will be sanctioned not only for their offenses, but also for their inappropriate sex role behavior. This prediction comes from a rather simplistic interpretation of the evil woman thesis. At a minimum, we would refine the hypothesis to state that female defendants will retain the advantage of being female until after such time as evidence of their law-violating behavior has been presented. Accordingly, we would predict that females will be preferentially treated in pretrial, full prosecution, and plea negotiation decisions. Only after an extensive evidentiary hearing, that is, posttrial, would the benefit of their female status be lost. Thus, at the time of conviction and sentencing, one might predict a reversal in the pattern. The second prediction consistent with the evil woman thesis assumes, as did the chivalry thesis, that females, relative to males, will fare better in general in terms of court outcome decisions. However, when one compares females with other females, those whose offense pattern most dramatically departs from sex role stereotype assumptions (e.g. those prosecuted for armed bank robbery, auto theft) will fare less well than their more traditional female counterparts (e.g. those prosecuted for shoplifting or embezzlement).

To assess the empirical support for the evil woman thesis and for the chivalry/paternalism thesis earlier discussed, we turn now to a review of the extant research on each of the major decision stages. Before presenting our review, we need to note three special problems that may affect the results reported in the research reviewed. First there is the potential problem of sample selection bias. Specifically, it may be that preferential treatment of women in the early decision stages results in the women who continue to conviction and sentencing decisions being the most serious and violent offenders. Thus a comparison of the effects of gender across decision outcome stages would, in the absence of a statistical control for this potential bias, not be fair. Second, if women do cluster at the less severe end of offense categories, then even when the nature of the crime is considered it might be appropriate for them to be more advantageously treated to reflect their less severe offenses. Unfortunately, most of the research reviewed will not provide data in sufficient detail to explore this issue. Third, most of the research reviewed contains no data on motive. This may be especially important since it is increasingly presumed that a substantial number of assaults and murders by females are motivated by self-defense. If the presumption of self-defense is justifiable, this might explain a finding of preferential treatment for women. With these limitations in mind, we proceed to our review.

We organize our review around decision stages because we believe that the determinants of decision outcomes change as a function of the particular decision being examined, the statutory and case law surrounding the making of that decision, and the general social context in which the decision is made (for an elaboration of this perspective, see Nagel 1981 and Nagel and Hagan 1983).

C. *The Role of Gender in Pretrial Decisions*

For most criminal defendants, the first decision of major consequence is the determination of the terms under which defendants may be free during the interim between arrest and the disposition of the case against them. "Bail" is the term commonly used to denote this stage of court processing, a term that refers to the amount of money necessary to obtain pretrial liberty. In fact, the pretrial release decision is at least two-tiered, and the amount of bail is the second tier. In most jurisdictions, the first decision concerns the type of release conditions offered the defendant. If the defendant meets the conditions of release, he or she may remain at liberty during the preadjudication period. Options range from release on personal recognizance, that is, an unsecured promise of the defendant to return for all scheduled court appearances, to the outright denial of bail, a decision that denies the defendant any opportunity to be released. The second decision, the amount of money requested, is relevant only for those defendants for whom a monetary deposit is the release condition. The two most common monetary conditions are the request for a surety bond and the request for a cash deposit. The latter is often an alternative to the former. The former requires the sponsorship of a bail bondsman; the latter does not. In either case the critical issue is the amount of money requested. For our purposes, the important question is whether a defendant's sex affects the type of release condition offered or the amount of money requested.

In trying to assess the empirical evidence for these questions, one is immediately struck with three problems. First, many of the more robust studies that seek to model the bases upon which pretrial decisions are determined (e.g. Landes 1974) fail to include women in their sample. Second, the methods by which pretrial release decisions are measured vary dramatically from study to study. This makes it difficult to draw summary conclusions. Third, the samples of defendants vary, from those that focus on serious felony cases to those that focus on misdemeanor cases only. Also, the number and type of control variables other than sex—for example, prior record, nature of offense—vary as well. These problems notwithstanding, we note two general patterns. It is not unusual for researchers to report that gender has no effect on pretrial decisions, especially decisions on the dollar amount of cash or surety bond requested. To the extent that there are sex differences, female defendants are more likely to receive the less restrictive release options, such as release on recognizance.

Nagel (1969; also see Nagel and Weitzman 1971) examined pretrial outcomes for a sample of 11,258 defendants prosecuted in 1962, drawn from 194 counties across 50 states. Focusing on felonious assault and grand larceny, Nagel concludes: "male defendants in assault and larceny cases are much less likely than female defendants to be released on bail they can afford" (1969, p. 92). An analysis of his data suggests that this conclusion may not be fully supportable. First, females represent approximately 7 percent of his felonious assault ($N = 846$) and grand larceny ($N = 1,103$) cases. Thus inferences are drawn from patterns based on very small samples. Second, no factors other than a defendant's sex are taken into account. The analyses include no control for prior record, age, family composition, race, employment, and so forth, many of which have been shown to mediate the relationship between gender and court outcomes. Third, the way the pretrial outcome variable is measured—Did the defendant make bail or not?—merges the judicial decision on type of release condition offered with the amount requested (if a monetary amount was requested) and the defendant's ability to raise the money (if money bail was the condition). Thus, while one can conclude that females were more likely to be released on bail they can afford, it is unclear whether this is because they were offered less restrictive options, or lower bails, or because they were more successful in raising bail money. Most important for our purposes, the research contributes little toward an understanding of whether, and how, gender affects pretrial decisions.

Swigert and Farrell (1977), in a study of persons arrested for murder between 1955 and 1973 in a large eastern state, improve somewhat upon Stuart Nagel's early research. Swigert and Farrell use a multivariate mode of analysis to examine pretrial release decisions for 444 defendants. However, they too confound the analysis by merging judicial decisions with defendant resources when they code the pretrial variable as released/detained. Thus their conclusion that males are more likely than females to be detained before trial is not particularly useful as evidence of the role of gender in pretrial judicial decisions. Again, if the question is whether judges accord preferential treatment to women on the basis of sex, one has to examine the decision unconfounded by other resources the defendant brings to subsequent outcomes. The pretrial decisions are the type of release and the amount of money requested. Whether a defendant meets the release conditions—for example, makes bail—may be a function of the amount requested, the amount the defendant can raise, the degree to which a bondsman may want to sponsor a defendant, or some combination thereof.

Three studies that do contribute more to our understanding of whether gender affects pretrial decisions are Goldkamp's (1979) study of 8,326 defendants prosecuted in Philadelphia in 1975, Nagel's (1981) study of 5,594 defendants prosecuted in New York between 1974 and 1975, and Nagel and Hagan's (1983) research on 9,068 defendants prosecuted in ten federal jurisdictions between 1974 and 1977.

Goldkamp looks first at whether the defendant was released on recognizance or if some other release condition was required. Examining the relation between sex and release on recognizance, he observes that in Philadelphia 62 percent of the female defendants were released on recognizance compared with 45 percent of the male defendants. This pattern is similar to that reported by Nagel (1969). But when Goldkamp introduced into the analysis the host of other variables ordinarily expected to affect pretrial decisions (e.g. age, race, income, employment, type of charge), the effect of gender became negligible. In fact, Goldkamp finds that ascribed status characteristics of defendants, as a set, have very little influence on pretrial release decisions. Turning his attention next to the mean dollar amount requested from those asked to post money bail, when a variety of factors in addition to sex are simultaneously considered, Goldkamp finds gender to have no significant effect.

Ilene Nagel's (1982) study focuses on three pretrial decisions: (1) whether a defendant is released on recognizance or bail is set; (2) if money bail is requested, the amount requested; and (3) whether a cash alternative, lower in dollar value than the surety bond, is offered. Controlling for such factors as race, ethnicity, age, education, primary speaking language, severity of the charged offense, prior record, and the particular judge before whom the defendant appears, she notes the following results. For the decision whether to release the defendant on personal recognizance or to set bail, female defendants are more likely to be released than to have bail set. The effects of gender are statistically significant for those prosecuted for both more and less serious offenses. However, gender has no effect on the dollar amount of bail requested. Similarly, the decision whether to offer a cash alternative is not affected by a defendant's sex.

Finally, in some preliminary analysis of pretrial decisions for federal defendants, Nagel and Hagan (1983) analyze three pretrial decisions: (1) the type of release condition, ordered according to restrictiveness from release on recognizance through surety bond; (2) the amount of surety bond requested from those for whom surety bond is the release condition; and (3) the amount of cash deposit requested from those for whom a cash deposit is the release condition. The authors report a pattern similar to Nagel's (1982) findings for defendants prosecuted in New York State. For federal defendants, gender affects the first decision on type of release, with females being more likely to receive the less restrictive release options. Gender has no effect on the subsequent decisions concerning the amount of dollars requested.

In summary, with respect to our initial question, Does gender affect pretrial decisions? our review suggests the answer is a limited yes. There is support for the thesis that female defendants fare better in pretrial decisions. With respect to the circumstances in which this preferential treatment is more or less pronounced, we note that preliminary reports by Nagel, Hagan, and Smith (1982) find greater advantages for women in small federal jurisdictions in southern states. We note too that there is some pattern of difference according to the particular pretrial decision being examined. While gender apparently has some effect on the decision between release on recognizance and bail, no study reported a significant effect of gender on the amount of money requested if money, either surety bond or cash, was requested (see Goldkamp 1979; Nagel 1982).[1]

We might speculate that these early findings suggest that, for decisions that can be ordered from low to high severity (e.g. type of release condition, type of sentence), the decision to give female defendants more of the least severe options can be empirically supported. However, as defendants become more similar in offense/offender patterns and are pushed along the conveyor belt of criminal justice processing, the effect of gender is reduced to insignificance. Finally, we note that, with the exception of the ongoing work of Nagel, Hagan, and Smith (1982), there is no known research that seeks to ascertain whether the determinants of pretrial decisions differ for males and females, nor is there research that explains, with empirical support, the rationale that gives rise to the patterns of preferential treatment noted.

D. *The Role of Gender in the Decision to Prosecute Fully toward Conviction*

Between the initial prosecutorial decision to charge a suspect with a crime and the adjudicative decision of guilt or innocence, be it by trial or by plea, the prosecutor continuously has the option to prosecute toward conviction or to terminate the case through a dismissal, deferral, nolle prosequi, discharge, or some other dispositionary tactic. In many state jurisdictions, upward of 40 percent of defendants' cases terminate in some form of a dismissal (see e.g. Hagan 1975; Zeisel, de Grazia, and Friedman 1975; Bernstein et al. 1977). In federal jurisdictions the number is similarly high. Accordingly, any effort to assess the effect of the defendant's sex on court outcomes must encompass the interim processing decision of whether to continue to prosecute toward conviction.

The primary problem in assessing the role of gender at this stage is that reliable information on the strength of the prosecutor's case is seldom included in the research literature. We, like Miller (1969), believe that

[1] One possible explanation for women's being less likely to be asked to post bail is that requesting bail often translates to detention, especially among the indigent. Detaining women, however, presents a special problem in that space is often not available.

the strength of the evidence in the case, along with other unmeasured variables, probably accounts for most of the variance between why some are prosecuted toward conviction and others are deferred, discharged, or otherwise diverted. Our review of the literature disclosed virtually no studies that included measures of evidence, or measures of the other factors highlighted by Miller as most important to the outcome—for example, attitude of the victim, cost to the system, harm to the suspect, alternative modes of disposition, and the general fit between the decision to prosecute fully any single case and prosecutorial priorities and case-load. Accordingly, we hesitate to draw conclusions about the role of gender at this stage, since it is always measured in a model of analysis that is likely to be misspecified. Nonetheless, for the sake of continuity, we review the extant research.

Pope (1976), in a study of 1,196 defendants prosecuted for burglary in California between 1972 and 1973, examined the decision to terminate prosecution before trial. While the decision to dismiss is theoretically predicated on the assumption of a low probability of conviction, he finds that cases against female defendants are more likely to be terminated. This finding is robust even when the defendant's prior record is introduced as a control variable, although it varies somewhat depending upon the nature of the record. That is, when both males and females had no prior record, the cases against female defendants were proportionately more likely to be terminated. However, when they both had records, the sex differences in the termination rate disappeared.

Simon and Sharma (1978), in an analysis of defendants prosecuted in 1974 and 1975 in Washington, D.C., similarly report an interaction effect when examining the relation between sex and dismissal, controlling for the nature of the offense. They report that prosecutors are more willing to drop charges against females than males when the defendants are prosecuted for violent crimes. Conversely, when the prosecution is for a victimless crime, prosecutors are more willing to drop charges against males than females. For all other offense categories, no difference between sex and the dismissal rate was noted.

Myers (1977) studied the prosecution of 1,050 cases in Indiana between 1974 and 1976. In an analysis that included (1) the sex of the defendant, (2) the occupation, employment, age, and sex of the victim, (3) the victim's prior record, (4) a measure of the victim's helplessness, negligence, and degree of provocation, (5) the relationship between the defendant and the victim, (6) a host of other characteristics of the

defendant, such as occupation, employment, and age, and (7) characteristics associated with the charged offense, she finds a defendant's sex to
have no notable effect on the decision to dismiss felony charges.

> The prosecutor's commitment to prosecute fully did not depend on
> the seriousness of the charge, the harm sustained by the victim, the
> defendant's relative status [the category in which sex was examined],
> predisposition outcomes and defendant threat. Full prosecution was
> more likely only if the victim was willing to prosecute, non-negligent
> and employed in a low status occupation. (1977, p. 181)

Parenthetically, in support of our earlier contention that many of the
models of the decision to prosecute fully are misspecified, we note that
Myers, using the same set of independent variables for the analysis of
each stage of decision making, finds she can explain only 12 percent of
the variance in the decision to prosecute fully compared with 30 percent
of the variance in the conviction outcome and 59 percent in the type of
sentence. Of interest too is that Myers finds the influence of gender to be
significant in the conviction decision and sentence severity, although, as
noted, she does not find it significant in the decision to prosecute fully
toward conviction.

Moulds (1980), in an examination of 1974 rates of disposition for
267,904 felony arrests in California, notes:

> A very large number of felony arrests each year are subsequently
> charged as misdemeanors or dropped altogether from the courts.
> These cases never reach Superior Court. . . . the percent of male
> felony arrests reaching Superior Court in California in 1974 (16.6%)
> and the percent of female felony arrests reaching Superior Court
> (13.5%). (1980, p. 289)

While no multivariate analysis is done, and therefore no conclusions can
appropriately be drawn, Moulds's data do conform to the pattern of
slight preferential treatment for women. Whether these differences
would be significant when other variables are controlled is doubtful.

Nagel, Cardascia, and Ross (1980), in a study of 2,972 male and
female defendants prosecuted in New York in 1974 and 1975, directly
address the question of sex differences in the decision to prosecute fully
versus the decision to dismiss. Looking first at the relation between
gender and the decision to prosecute toward conviction, they note that
57 percent of the male defendants have their cases dismissed compared

with 66 percent of the female defendants. However, when a multivariate analysis is employed that includes, in addition to gender, the severity of the arrest charge, the type of arrest charge, the defendant's prior record, release status pending adjudication, the particular court (criminal versus supreme) in which the case was prosecuted, and a host of other variables, the effect of gender is not significant. Moreover, like Myers (1977), they find they can explain very little of the variance in the decision to prosecute fully toward conviction. Again, since their model does not include measures of the strength of evidence and the other variables highlighted by Miller (1969), it is probably similarly misspecified. While the authors separately modeled decisions for male and female defendants for the sentencing decision, they did not do so for the decision to prosecute toward conviction because sex had no additive effect on the full prosecution outcome and because their set of independent variables taken together failed to predict well on this outcome.

To summarize, our conclusion is that, in the absence of research that includes measures of strength of evidentiary materials, and lacking other indicators such as the value to the prosecutor of obtaining a conviction in the case, we cannot at this time assess whether gender plays a role in the decision to prosecute fully toward conviction. The above notwithstanding, we can hypothesize that gender has no substantial influence on the decision to prosecute fully. Our hypothesis is based on our finding that the more comprehensive research efforts that include the greatest range of independent variables in addition to sex (e.g. Myers 1977; Nagel, Cardascia, and Ross 1980) report that gender has no significant effect. We would, however, add the following caveat: while in the aggregate, and perhaps in the great majority of cases, the sex of the defendant makes little difference in the decision to prosecute toward conviction, were research to be done where cases were sorted according to the strength of the evidence, we might hypothesize that, among those cases where the evidence is weakest, females may have a slight advantage in being offered more alternatives to prosecution, (e.g. nolle prosequi, deferred prosecution), especially at the early stages of prosecutorial discretion. This hypothesis is based on observational data we collected as part of our research on the processing of criminal defendants in federal district courts (Nagel and Hagan 1983). We would further point out that a finding that gender has little influence on the decision to prosecute fully toward conviction might reflect a pattern of early decisions by prosecutors not to charge women with crimes unless the crime is serious enough to warrant full prosecution.

E. *The Role of Gender in the Favorability of Plea Bargains*

Despite a rich tradition of research on court outcome decisions, a review of the particular decisions examined to test questions of equality and justice, discrimination, and hypotheses deduced from the variety of theoretical perspectives earlier discussed (e.g. labeling, conflict, attribution) reveals a dearth of quantitative research on the favorability of plea bargains. This dearth is particularly important since upward of 90 percent of all cases are disposed of by a plea of guilty, and the outcome of the plea negotiation has a substantial effect on sentence severity (see Hagan, Nagel, and Albonetti 1980). The absence of a substantial body of research on the favorability of the plea bargain stems, in part, from two major sources. First, and probably most important, it is difficult to obtain the necessary data. Most research on decision outcomes is limited to data made available from court records. Most of these data sets contain *either* the charge at arrest, the charge at arraignment, the charge at the preliminary hearing, *or* the charge for which the defendant was convicted. Few include the charge(s) at each point. Since measures of the favorability of the plea require data on changes in charges, the requisite data are not often available.

Second, for reasons not always obvious, research traditions have a way of developing in nonparallel ways. Sentencing decisions have been the most thoroughly researched, and most of the research is quantitative. Research on plea bargains and plea negotiations has only recently become abundant, and most of this research is qualitative. For example, there is an enormous wealth of descriptive data provided in the work of Alschuler (1968); Bequai (1974); Blumberg (1967); Buckle and Buckle (1977); Cressey (1968); Eisenstein and Jacob (1977); Hagan and Bernstein (1979); Heumann (1978); Katz (1979); Mather (1979); Rosett and Cressey (1976); and Utz (1978). Yet, with few exceptions (e.g. Eisenstein and Jacob 1977) most of this research is more qualitative than quantitative. For our purposes in this review, this means that in much of this research literature there is no easy way to assess the influence of gender, relative to other considerations, on the favorability of the negotiated plea.

There are, however, three studies that we can identify. The first is a study by Bernstein et al. (1977) examining the favorability of pleas for 1,435 male and female defendants prosecuted for burglary, larceny, assault, or robbery in New York State between 1974 and 1975. The data are separately analyzed for defendants whose cases were settled at their first court appearance and for those whose cases included several court appearances. The favorability of the plea is measured two ways: (1) by a measure of the magnitude of the reduction in charges, constructed by subtracting the statutorily prescribed maximum severity of the final charge for which the defendant is convicted from the maximum severity of the charge at first court presentation and dividing that by the maximum severity of the lowest charge for which the defendant might have been convicted, subtracted from the maximum severity of the charge at first court presentation; (2) by the maximum severity of the most serious charge for which the defendant was convicted.

Looking first at the correlation between sex and the two outcomes measuring the favorability of the final measures of plea, the authors conclude that being male is correlated with less reduction, relative to what is possible, and that being male is correlated with being convicted for a *less* serious offense. However, when other variables are controlled (e.g. type of crime, number of charges, whether a weapon was involved, whether the defendant was charged with resisting arrest, prior record) gender turns out to have no significant effect on the magnitude of the reduction in charge severity, relative to the reduction possible. Gender does have an effect on the severity of the final charge for which the defendant is convicted, but only for cases not disposed of at first presentation. Somewhat surprisingly, male defendants were more likely to be convicted of the less severe charges. If we presume that only the more serious cases are not disposed of at first presentation, it is possible that this surprising finding may have occurred because females charged with more serious offenses were compared with males charged with less serious offenses. This would mitigate the authors' conclusion that their findings are consistent with the evil woman thesis. Alternatively, this may be an instance in which the propositions of the evil woman thesis are in effect.

The second study, Sterling and Haskins (1980), includes an analysis of data for 2,600 felony cases filed between 1974 and 1977 in Denver, Colorado. All 2,600 defendants were charged with robbery, burglary, theft, murder, assault, narcotics, forgery, or fraud. (Cases filed as misdemeanors, cases dismissed, or cases reduced to misdemeanors before or during the preliminary hearing were not included.) Charge reduction was categorized as no reduction, reduction to a lesser felony, or reduction to a misdemeanor. Controlling for type of counsel, age, race, education, prior record, employment status, pretrial status, and the like, Sterling and Haskins conclude that sex has trivial effects on charge reduction compared with the other factors considered. As before, the fact that the potential for sample selection bias has not been controlled limits the robustness of the conclusions.

Finally, Crites (1978), in a review of research on women in the criminal court, refers to a study conducted in Alabama in 1974, analyzing data on male and female defendants prosecuted in seven judicial circuits. Although no primary data are presented, Crites (1978, p. 164) reports the following:

> An interesting finding of the study was the comparative percentages of women and men who had charges against them reduced. In cases of grand larceny and violations of the Alabama Uniform Controlled Substance Act, almost three times as many women as men had their charges reduced.

Without access to the original research publication, we can only report that Crites's review suggests that prior record and type of offense may have been entered as control variables.

This concludes our review of research on the favorability of plea bargains. Since there are so few studies that report quantitative data on the influence of gender on the favorability of the negotiated plea, it is difficult to draw conclusions. The two studies that used multivariate analyses, Sterling and Haskins (1980), and Bernstein et al. (1977), were limited to studies of decisions in single jurisdictions. Both focused on defendants prosecuted for serious violent offenses. Accordingly, we do not know whether the same results would hold if defendants prosecuted for a greater variety of offense categories were included, especially if there were greater representation of those prosecuted for property offenses and misdemeanors. Moreover, as was the case for research on the decision to prosecute fully toward conviction, the role of evidence was not considered. Clearly, more research is needed on the favorability of plea bargains and on the factors that affect how favorable any bargain is. With respect to the role of gender, we suggest that future researchers include in their studies samples of cases from a variety of types of offense (e.g. embezzlement, narcotics, theft, fraud, robbery) and examine sex differences within offense categories. The same strategy might be adopted for levels of offense severity. If our early speculation has any merit, we can expect sex differences to be more pronounced in the bargaining of misdemeanor cases and in the bargaining of nonviolent property offenses.

F. The Role of Gender in Conviction and Sentencing Decisions

We group these final two decisions not because we believe that conviction and sentencing decisions should be aggregated, but because much of the research aggregates these two disparate decisions into single variables. We strongly disapprove of any such aggregation, for we believe each decision occurs in a social and legal context that differentiates it from all others. Thus, while the study of decisions to arrest and to prosecute fully and the favorability of a negotiated plea may be complementary to studies of sentencing, the contextual setting is so different that it is essential to analyze each decision separately.

1. Adjudication. There are four relevant studies related to the question of the adjudication of guilt. Chiricos, Jackson, and Waldo (1972) report research on a pattern perhaps unique to Florida, that is, a decision to withhold an adjudication of guilt despite the establishment of guilt by plea, by judge, or by jury. In examining dispositions for 2,419 felony cases filed between 1969 and 1970, the authors find that the Florida statute, section 948.01—adjudication withheld—is not affected by the gender of defendants. The authors report surprise at their finding, since it is commonly believed that women are preferentially treated. To explain their finding, they suggest that sex differences may occur in the earlier sifting of cases. However, when only the serious cases are left, such as at the point of adjudication, sex differences may be muted by concerns for prior record and other offense-related variables.

The next two publications, by Farrell and Swigert (1978) and Swigert and Farrell (1977), derive from analyses of one body of data. Data for a sample of 444 defendants prosecuted for murder in New York State between 1955 and 1973 are examined. The analysis considers the role of the defendant's sex. While Swigert and Farrell report that females are preferentially treated, the way they code their dependent variable is open to question. Specifically, they create one single ordered dependent variable that includes dismissal, acquittal, conviction for first-degree misdemeanor, conviction for second-degree felony (voluntary manslaughter), conviction for first-degree felony (second-degree murder), and conviction for first-degree murder. This coding decision creates interpretative problems because there are at least three conceptually distinct decisions included in this one ordered variable. Dismissals are related to the decision to prosecute fully toward conviction. As noted, that decision may be substantially affected by the strength of evidence and by prosecutorial values and priorities. Moreover, previous research has shown that it is not affected in the same way or by the same variables as are sentencing decisions (see e.g. Myers 1977; Bernstein, Kelly, and Doyle 1977). Acquittals are an option only for cases that go to trial; yet the vast majority of dispositions are by pleas of guilt. Furthermore, acquittal decisions, because they result from trials, are far more affected by evidence and other factors related to the trial (e.g. jury composition) than are sentencing decisions. Finally, the seriousness of the final charge for which a defendant is convicted is also likely to be affected by evidence, especially if all defendants were initially charged with the same offense, as in the Swigert and Farrell (1977) sample. Swigert and Farrell include no measure of the strength of the evidence. In sum, the coding of their dependent variable limits our confidence in their conclusions. They conclude that sex is related to the severity of disposition, with females receiving preferred outcomes.

The fourth study is a comprehensive work by Myers (1979c). Her research focuses on the adjudication decision for 201 felony cases tried by jury in Marion County, Indiana, between 1974 and 1976. Controlling for seven measures of evidence (as inferred from data in the court records rather than directly observed), indicators of witness credibility (e.g. defendant's and victim's prior record of convictions), defendant and victim status characteristics (e.g. age, employment) and a host of other variables, Myers concludes that the sex of defendants has no significant effect on the adjudicative decision.

2. *Sentencing: Tabular studies.* This brings us to the final outcome decision—sentencing. Of the variety of court outcome decisions, sentencing decisions are most studied, and studied by the most sophisticated techniques. Our review led us to sixteen studies of sentencing that considered gender as one of the independent variables. Since the number of studies is so much greater than those identified for the earlier decisions reviewed, we organize our review by the methodological approaches used to analyze the data. We do so because many of the studies that base their results on tabular analyses, where few variables in addition to sex have been considered, report findings that fail to hold up under more rigorous statistical tests.

Looking first at the group of studies that relies on bivariate analyses of sex by sentence severity, or tabular analyses of sex by sentence severity, controlling perhaps for prior record or nature of the offense, we find two fairly consistent patterns. First, to the extent that there is preferential treatment by gender, it is the female defendants who receive the more favorable outcomes. Second, when preferential treatment is observed, it is more pronounced in the least severe sentencing options. More women are given suspended sentences or probation, whereas fewer sex differences are noted when examining variation in the harsher outcomes, such as imprisonment or length of incarceration.

Martin (1934), in an early study of sentencing, concluded that females were no more likely than males to be sentenced to prison terms. However, females were more likely to receive suspended sentences. Green

(1961) reported that females more often receive probation, fines, and suspended sentences; and they were sentenced more often to indeterminate terms of imprisonment, whereas males were given determinate terms. However, males were more likely than females to be sentenced to imprisonment. When Green controlled for prior felony convictions and the severity of the convicted offense, he found that the preferential treatment for females held only for misdemeanor cases.

Nagel (1969) and Nagel and Weitzman (1971) report that male offenders are more likely to be sentenced to incarceration, whereas female offenders are more likely to be given probation. Those sentenced to imprisonment for less than one year are more likely to be females than males (45 percent to 33 percent).

Baab and Furgeson (1967), in analyzing the sentences of 1,720 felony offenders convicted between 1965 and 1966 in one of twenty-seven Texas courts, create a twelve-category ordered variable of sentence severity. They conclude that gender does affect sentence severity. Their results show a definite pattern of preferential treatment for female offenders.

Pope (1975), in an analysis of felony offenders convicted in California, does tabular analyses, controlling for race, age, prior record, criminal status, charge at arrest, and gender, to examine simultaneously the relation between two and three variables in the decision to sentence an offender to probation, to jail, or to some other sanction. He also examines the determinants of the length of probation and the length of jail term. He reports the following:

1. Among offenders sentenced in misdemeanor court, females are preferentially treated, especially when convicted in urban areas.

2. Among offenders sentenced in misdemeanor court, females are more likely to receive probation; females are less likely to be sent to jail, especially when convicted in an urban area.

3. Among offenders sentenced in felony court, there are no differences in the sentence by sex.

4. In the length of jail term, males are more likely to receive a longer term when sentenced in felony court; there are, however, no differences by sex in the misdemeanor court sentences.

5. In the length of probation, there are no differences by sex.
To summarize Pope's findings, the pattern of preferential treatment for females is somewhat more pronounced in the courts that deal with less severe offenses—lower courts—and in the giving of less restrictive sen-

tences (e.g. probation). But, the pattern is not wholly consistent; males sentenced in felony court—superior court—are more likely to receive longer jail terms.

More recent studies reporting bivariate relationships and results based on tabular analyses include Crites (1978), Simon and Sharma (1978), Moulds (1980), and some preliminary work reported by INSLAW (1981). Crites (1978) finds no difference by sex when she examines offenders given suspended sentences. Yet she finds that the mean sentence length for females is lower than that for males, except for those convicted of violations of drug laws. Simon and Sharma (1978) find that women are more likely than men to be sentenced to probation and less likely to receive long terms of imprisonment for some offense categories, such as robbery. Generally, this is the predominant pattern. However, for other offense categories, for example, victimless crimes, they find females less likely to receive probation than males. And for still other offense categories, for example, violent crimes, males and females are reported to be approximately equal in their likelihood of receiving long terms of imprisonment. Simon and Sharma's research suggests that sex interacts with the type of offense in its effect on the type of sentence. It also suggests that sex differences vary, depending on whether one is examining the type of sentence or the length of imprisonment.

Moulds (1980), looking at adult felons arrested in California between 1970 and 1974, finds that females receive comparatively gentler sentences. Forty-two percent of the female offenders received probation compared with 20 percent of the males. Moreover, even when the defendant's race, offense type, and prior record were controlled, the pattern of preferential treatment for women held. Finally, INSLAW (1981), in a preliminary draft summarizing the results of their study of sentences for offenders prosecuted for one of eleven offenses between 1974 and 1978 in federal jurisdictions ($N = 5,781$), reports that male offenders are more likely than female offenders to be sentenced to incarceration or to longer terms of imprisonment.

3. Sentencing: Multivariate studies. This brings us to the final set of studies, those that control for a variety of variables in addition to sex in multivariate analyses of the determinants of sentence severity. These studies vary in the way they measure sentence severity, in the particular set of independent variables included, and in the nature of the samples studied. Nonetheless, we see three patterns, each with limited support: (1) to the extent that gender is found to affect the sentencing decision significantly, female offenders receive preferential treatment (for an exception, see Myers 1979*b*);[2] (2) the pattern of preferential treatment noted for female offenders is more pronounced in the receipt of the less severe sentence outcomes; that is, female offenders are more likely to receive probation, suspended sentences, or fines; (3) in examining the determinants of the most severe outcomes, such as imprisonment, when all other variables have been controlled, (e.g. prior record, type of offense) gender has little if any effect.

In a reanalysis of data from twenty studies of sentencing, Hagan (1974) concluded that the demonstrated effect of gender was negligible. Rhodes (1976), in a study of felony cases closed during 1970 in two county courts in Minnesota, controlling for race, age, sex, type of crime, number of charges, plea, judge, and the like, found that among offenders convicted of burglary, narcotics possession, larceny, or forgery, men were more likely than women to receive sentences of imprisonment. Rhodes coded sentences as imprisonment or some other sentence. He did not, however, include controls for prior record, a variable often found to mediate the relation between gender and sentence.

Hagan, Hewitt, and Alwin (1979) analyze data for 504 felons convicted in the state of Washington in 1973. In an attempt to be sensitive to the way the coding of the sentencing variable may affect results, they code sentence severity in two ways. First, they examine the antecedents of the decision to give an offender a *deferred sentence versus the decision to sentence* him or her *to any other sentencing term*. Second, they examine the antecedents of the decision to sentence the offender to *incarceration versus all other sentencing terms*. By coding the variable in these two ways, they can explore differences between results obtained when one examines the least severe option versus all others and the most severe option versus all others. For the first outcome, deferred sentence versus all other sentences, the authors report that the zero-order correlation between gender and deferral (.258) is substantially reduced when other variables are added to the multivariate model as controls (.082). However, although the effect of gender decreases, females remain significantly more likely than males to be deferred. But when they examine the second outcome, incarceration versus nonincarceration, the zero-order correlation between gender and incarceration of .09 is reduced to .025 in the regression model when other variables are added. The effect of gender (.025) is *not*

[2] In analyzing her data, Myers finds female offenders slightly more likely than male offenders to be sentenced to prison. She carefully notes, however, that her sample of eleven female offenders is so small as to preclude any sweeping conclusions.

statistically significant. Thus, for the incarceration decision, gender ultimately has no significant influence.

Nagel, Cardascia, and Ross (1980) similarly explore the effect of different codings on their results. In looking at the sentencing decision, where probation and incarceration are coded as the harsh sentence and fines, suspended sentence, and deferred prosecution (a judgment of guilt that can be expunged if the offender commits no new crimes in a specified period following the conviction) are coded as the less harsh sentence, they report that males are more likely than females to be sentenced to the harsher outcomes.[3] The authors subsequently examined the effect of gender on the question whether the defendant spent any time imprisoned, either before or after conviction. Here the effect of gender was far more substantial. Controlling for other factors, the effect of gender in the harsh/gentle sentence analysis was .04; for the variable "any time imprisoned," the effect was .10.

In addition to the above, the authors explored the question of sex differences in the bases upon which these two outcome decisions were made. They concluded:

1. In the variable harsh versus lenient sentence, there were few differences between males and females in the determinants of the decision. That is, the decision structures were basically the same. Moreover, they were consistent with prior research based only on male samples.

2. In the variable "any time imprisoned," there were several significant differences between the way the decision was determined for females and the way it was determined for males. These differences included:

a) the advantage of being married was much stronger for female defendants than for male defendants;

b) the adverse effect of a prior record was stronger for male defendants than for female defendants;

c) the adverse effect of having a case pending in another court was stronger for male defendants than for female defendants;

d) whereas the statutorily defined severity of the charged offense had a strong effect for male defendants, it was not significant for female defendants;

---

[3]The authors categorize probation *or* imprisonment as harsh in accordance with interview data. Their interviewees argued that for this sample of misdemeanor defendants, probation was considered harsh. Both probation and imprisonment were deemed harsher sentences than fines, suspended sentences, deferred prosecution, or the other sentencing alternatives.

e) whereas female defendants charged with personal crimes fared less well than females charged with property crimes, this was not so for male defendants.

Nagel, Cardascia, and Ross's (1980) interpretation is that while women are preferentially treated compared with men, when women are compared with one another, those whose offense/offender patterns most depart from sex role stereotypes fare least well. Thus, while their research provides some support for the chivalry thesis, some support is also provided for the evil woman thesis, within the context of comparing women with one another. The theoretical implications of this may be that the chivalry thesis should not be pitted against the evil woman thesis. Rather, future research might best explore the conditions under which evidence of both patterns is simultaneously manifest.

Finally, Hagan, Nagel, and Albonetti (1980), in a study of sentences given 6,562 offenders convicted in ten federal district courts, find additional support for the preferential treatment of women. In an analysis focusing on differences in the sentencing of white-collar offenders versus others, they find that gender affects sentence severity, controlling for such variables as prior record, severity of the charged offense, number of charges, ethnicity, physical health, age, education, and type of offense. While gender is not the most salient influence, it is nonetheless consistently significant.

Clearly, the research on sentencing produces the strongest evidence for the thesis that gender does affect court outcome decisions and that women receive preferential treatment. The effect of gender is small relative to other factors (e.g. statutory seriousness of the charged offense, prior record), yet it is demonstrably present.

III. Summary

However measured—with official agency data or alternative sources—the relation between criminal behavior and gender is strong and is likely to remain so. This does not mean that the involvement of women in crime is unchanging. For property crime, especially petty forms of theft and fraud, and particularly for younger women, changes *are* occurring. However, these changes are more significant in terms of relative than of absolute numbers—from very small absolute frequencies to slightly higher frequencies. The relative change in these areas may be large, but the absolute involvement is still small. An unanswered question is how these changes have affected and will affect sanctioning decisions.

The defendant's sex appears to affect decisions differently at different stages in the criminal process. At the pretrial stage, the research suggests that gender affects the decision to release on recognizance rather than to set bail. However, once the decision to set bail is made, gender does not appear to affect the amount of surety bond or cash requested. With reference to decisions to prosecute fully toward conviction, to plea bargain, or to convict, there is no clear evidence that gender makes a systematic difference. It is at the sentencing stage that the best evidence of significant gender differences is found. As was true at the pretrial stage, it is differential leniency that is most often observed. Although this effect is small, it nonetheless frequently withstands control for a variety of other variables. These findings tentatively support the proposition that where decisions can be clearly ordered from low to high severity (e.g. type of pretrial release condition, type of sentence), and particularly where careful attention can be given to less severe options, female defendants can be found to receive more of the less severe sanctions.

The theoretical implications of our review for the evil woman versus chivalry/paternalism debate are not easily determined. First, there is the problem discussed earlier about the lack of conceptual clarity among the terms evil woman, chivalry, and paternalism. Second, there is a lack of agreement on the proper measurement of these terms and what they suggest for proposed reform. Despite these difficulties and in an effort to advance the debate, we offer the following conclusions, pending further research.

When court outcomes for male defendants are compared with those meted out to female defendants, females are more likely to receive the more favorable outcomes. This supports the chivalry/paternalism thesis. This pattern is more pronounced when the courts are responding to defendants charged with less severe offenses and when the option is whether or not to give the least harsh outcome (e.g. release on recognizance, probation).

This may suggest that the evil woman thesis is not contrary (opposite) to the chivalry/paternalism thesis, but rather its corollary. Thus it may be that women are preferentially treated, compared with men, until such time as the basis for that preferential treatment—chivalry or paternalism—is rendered inappropriate. Then, by virtue of the seriousness of the offense charged, the lessening of the presumption of innocence, and the evidence of deviation from traditional female patterns of behavior, the woman is moved into the evil woman category, and preferential treatment ceases. This would be consistent with our finding that women charged with more serious offenses or women placed in the harsher categories for further decision (e.g. those asked to post bail, those required to serve long sentences) are treated no differently than are comparable men.

High on the agenda for future research should be a planned inquiry into the relation between outcomes, the sex of the defendant, and assumptions based on sex made by criminal court personnel.

We have been careful to emphasize that the patterns we have observed may vary by type of offense, and that the factors that lead to decisions may be different for women and men. Thus we have found some evidence that gender-based leniency is more likely for less severe crimes, and that women thought evil in terms of other attributes are more likely to receive severe treatment. However, research to date has not extensively examined these possibilities. They remain important avenues for future research.

What is most striking about the two bodies of research literature we have reviewed is that they remain disconnected. Research on the criminal court processing of women has given little or no attention to changing patterns in the involvement of women in crime. Yet, if there are indeed gender differences in criminal sanctioning, they presumably have their base in sex role attitudes. Among the best reflections of changes in these attitudes are changes in the involvement of women in crime. We would therefore expect gender-based patterns of criminal sanctioning to be sensitive to these changes. One way to focus future research better is to pay increased attention to those particular crimes that are showing the greatest signs of change (for example, petty theft and fraud), ideally by considering those time periods in which significant changes have occurred. We have noted already that these crimes are among those where differential leniency has been most frequently observed. One hypothesis that we offer for further research is the suggestion that gender-based disparities may be decreasing alongside these changes. That is, as women are seen to be increasingly like men in these areas of criminality, the sanctions imposed may be converging as well.

Also valuable would be direct measurement of the sex role attitudes of decision makers. As noted, patterns of chivalry and paternalism are difficult, if not impossible, to separate in sanctioning decisions. Moreover, aggregations of decision makers who vary individually in their sex role attitudes may conceal disparate patterns in the treatment of men and women. Direct measurement of these attitudes and correlation with decisions made would allow exposure of these patterns, as well as changes in them, if considered over time.

Finally, there is need for research that is sensitive to variations in jurisdictional context. There is good reason to believe that sex role attitudes vary by region; jurisdictions in the South, for example, may be different from those in the North or West. Similar arguments might be made about urban and rural jurisdictions. Federal court jurisdictions, involving an identical body of law that is differently applied in a wide variety of settings, provide an ideal opportunity to examine these kinds of possibilities.

In the preceding pages we have explored a variety of ways to build variation in sex role attitudes into the data sets used to study gender and criminal sanctioning. This body of research may have reached the point where accumulating additional single-setting studies may no longer appreciably increase our understanding of this issue. Studies that systematically vary the social context in which sanctioning occurs are much more likely to yield results that are informative and generalizable. This is true not only of studies that focus on gender and criminal sanctioning, but of those that focus on other status attributes as well. We will come to understand the criminal law better as we observe its operation in the variety of social contexts that give it form and character.

REFERENCES

Adler, Freda. 1975. *Sisters in Crime*. New York: McGraw-Hill.
Alschuler, Albert W. 1968. "The Prosecutor's Role in Plea Bargaining," *University of Chicago Law Review* 36:50–112.
Anderson, Etta A. 1976. "The Chivalrous Treatment of the Female Offender in the Arms of the Criminal Justice System: A Review of the Literature," *Social Problems* 23:350–57.
Armstrong, Gail. 1977. "Females under the Law—'Protected' but Unequal," *Crime and Delinquency* 23 (April):109–20.
Baab, George William, and William Royal Furgeson. 1967. "Texas Sentencing Practices: A Statistical Study," *Texas Law Review* 45:471–503.
Babcock, Barbara. 1973. "Introduction: Women and the Criminal Law," *American Criminal Law Review* 11:291–308.
Becker, Howard S. 1963. *Outsiders: Studies in the Sociology of Deviance*. New York: Free Press.

Bedau, Hugo A. 1964. "Death Sentences in New Jersey," *Rutgers Law Review* 19:1–55.

Bequai, August. 1974. "Prosecutorial Decision Making: A Comparative Study of the Prosecutor in Two Counties in Maryland," *Police Law Quarterly* 4:34–42.

Bernstein, Ilene Nagel, William Kelly, and Patricia Doyle. 1977. "Societal Reaction to Deviants: The Case of Criminal Defendants," *American Sociological Review* 42:743–55.

Bernstein, Ilene Nagel, Edward Kick, Jan Leung, and Barbara Schulz. 1977. "Charge Reduction: An Intermediary Stage in the Process of Labelling Criminal Defendants," *Social Forces* 56:362–84.

Biderman, A. D., et al. 1967. *Report of a Pilot Study in the District of Columbia on Victimization and Attitudes toward Law Enforcement.* Washington, D.C.: U.S. Government Printing Office.

Black, Donald. 1976. *The Behavior of Law.* New York: Academic Press.

Block, Alan. 1977. "Aw—Your Mother's in the Mafia: Women Criminals in Progressive New York," *Contemporary Crisis* 1:5–22.

Blumberg, Abraham. 1967. "The Practice of Law as Confidence Game: Organizational Co-optation of a Profession," *Law and Society Review* 1:15–39.

Bowker, Lee H. 1981. "Women as Victims: An Examination of the Results of L.E.A.A.'s National Crime Survey Program." In *Women and Crime in America*, ed. Lee Bowker. New York: Macmillan.

Brodsky, Annette M., ed. 1975. *The Female Offender.* Beverly Hills, Calif.: Sage Publications.

Buckle, Suzann R., and Leonard G. Buckle. 1977. *Bargaining for Justice: Case Disposition and Reform in the Criminal Courts.* New York: Praeger.

Byrnes, Thomas. 1886. *Professional Criminals of America.* New York: Cassell.

Cameron, Mary Owen. 1964. *The Booster and the Snitch.* Glencoe, Ill.: Free Press.

Cernkovich, Stephen A., and Peggy C. Giordano. 1979. "A Comparative Analysis of Male and Female Delinquency," *Sociological Quarterly* 20:131–45.

Chambliss, William J., and Robert B. Seidman. 1971. *Law, Order and Power.* Reading, Mass.: Addison-Wesley.

Chesney-Lind, Meda. 1973. "Judicial Enforcement of the Female Sex Role: The Family Court and the Female Delinquent," *Issues in Criminology* 8 (fall):51–59.

———. 1977. "Judicial Paternalism and the Female Status Offender: Training Women to Know Their Place," *Crime and Delinquency* 23(2):121–30.

Chiricos, Theodore G., Phillip D. Jackson, and Gordon P. Waldo. 1972. "Inequality in the Imposition of a Criminal Label," *Social Problems* 19:553–72.

Cressey, Donald R. 1968. "Negotiated Justice," *Criminologia* 5:5–16.

Crites, Laura. 1978. "Women in the Criminal Court." In *Women in the Courts*, ed. Winifred Hepperle and Laura Crites. Williamsburg, Va.: National Center for State Courts.

Datesman, Susan K., and Frank R. Scarpitti, eds. 1980. *Women, Crime and Justice.* New York: Oxford University Press.

DeCrow, Karen. 1974. *Sexist Justice.* New York: Random House.

Eisenstein, James, and Herbert Jacob. 1977. *Felony Justice: An Organizational Analysis of Criminal Courts.* Boston: Little, Brown.

Ennis, Philip H. 1967. *Criminal Victimization in the United States: A Report of a National Survey*. Washington, D.C.: U.S. Government Printing Office.

Erikson, Kai T. 1964. "Notes on the Sociology of Deviance." In *The Other Side: Perspectives on Deviance*, ed. Howard S. Becker. New York: Free Press.

Farrell, Ronald A., and Victoria Lynn Swigert. 1978. "Prior Offense as a Self-Fulfilling Prophecy," *Law and Society Review* 12(3) 437–53 (special issue on criminal justice).

Feyerherm, William. 1981. "Gender Differences in Delinquency: Quantity and Quality." In *Women and Crime in America*, ed. Lee H. Bowker. New York: Macmillan.

Frankel, Marvin S. 1973. *Criminal Sentences*. New York: Hill and Wang.

Franklin, Alice. 1979. "Criminality in the Work Place: A Comparison of Male and Female Offenders." In *The Criminology of Deviant Women*, ed. Freda Adler and Rita Simon. Boston: Houghton Mifflin.

Fuller, Lon L. 1934. "American Legal Realism," *University of Pennsylvania Law Review* 82:429–62.

Giordano, Peggy C. 1978. "Guys, Girls and Gangs: The Changing Social Context of Female Delinquency," *Journal of Criminal Law and Criminology* 69(1):126–32.

Giordano, Peggy C., and Stephen A. Cernkovich. 1979. "On Complicating the Relationship between Liberation and Delinquency," *Social Problems* 26(4):467–81.

Giordano, Peggy C., Sandra Kerbel, and Sandra Dudley. 1981. "The Economics of Female Criminality: An Analysis of Police Blotters, 1890–1976." In *Women and Crime in America*, ed. Lee H. Bowker. New York: Macmillan.

Goldkamp, John S. 1979. *Two Classes of Accused: A Study of Bail and Detention in American Justice*. Cambridge, Mass.: Ballinger.

Gottfredson, Michael R., and Donald Gottfredson. 1980. *Decision Making in Criminal Justice: Toward the Rational Exercise of Discretion*. Cambridge, Mass.: Ballinger.

Green, Edward. 1961. *Judicial Attitudes in Sentencing*. London: Macmillan.

Hagan, John. 1974. "Extra-Legal Attributes and Criminal Sentencing: An Assessment of a Sociological Viewpoint," *Law and Society Review* 8:857–84.

———. 1975. "Parameters of Criminal Prosecution: An Application of Path Analysis to a Problem of Criminal Justice," *Journal of Criminal Law and Criminology* 65:536–44.

Hagan, John, and Ilene Nagel Bernstein. 1979. "The Sentence Bargaining of Upperworld and Underworld Crime in Ten Federal District Courts," *Law and Society Review* 13:467–78.

Hagan, John, and Kristin Bumiller. 1981. "Making Sense of Sentencing: A Review and Critique of Sentencing Research." Draft presented at July 1981 Meeting, National Academy of Sciences Panel on Sentencing Research, Woods Hole, Mass.

Hagan, John, John Hewitt, and Duane Alwin. 1979. "Ceremonial Justice: Crime and Punishment in a Loosely Coupled System," *Social Forces* 58(2): 506–27.

Hagan, John, Ilene Nagel, and Celesta Albonetti. 1980. "The Differential

Sentencing of White-Collar Offenders in Ten Federal District Courts," *American Sociological Review* 45:802–20.

Hagan, John, John Simpson, and A. R. Gillis. 1979. "The Sexual Stratification of Social Control: A Gender-Based Perspective on Crime and Delinquency," *British Journal of Social Science* 30(1):25–38.

Harris, Anthony. 1977. "Sex and Theories of Deviance: Toward a Functional Theory of Deviant Type-Scripts," *American Sociological Review* 42:3–16.

Harris, Anthony, and Gary Hill. 1981. "Changes in the Gender Patterning of Crime, 1953–77. Opportunity v. Socialization," *Social Science Quarterly*, in press.

Heumann, Milton. 1978. *Plea Bargaining: The Experiences of Prosecutors, Judges, and Defense Attorneys*. Chicago: University of Chicago Press.

Heyl, Barbara. 1979. "Prostitution: An Extreme Case of Sex Stratification." In *The Criminology of Deviant Women*, ed. Freda Adler and Rita Simon. Boston: Houghton Mifflin.

Hindelang, Michael J. 1971. "Age, Sex and Versatility of Delinquent Involvement," *Social Problems* 18:522–35.

———. 1974. "The Uniform Crime Reports Revisited," *Journal of Criminal Justice* 2(1):1–17.

———. 1979. "Sex Differences in Criminal Activity," *Social Problems* 27(2):143–56.

Hindelang, Michael J., Travis Hirschi, and Joseph Weis. 1978. *Measurement of Delinquency by the Self-Report Method: Interim Report*. Bethesda, Md.: Center for Studies of Crime and Delinquency, National Institute of Mental Health.

Ianni, Francis. 1974. *Black Mafia*. New York: Simon and Schuster.

Institute for Law and Social Research (INSLAW). 1981. "Federal Sentencing: Toward a More Explicit Policy of Criminal Sanctions." Draft prepared for the Federal Justice Research Program of the Department of Justice by INSLAW and Yankelovich, Skelly and White, 20 March 1981, Washington, D.C.

Jackson, B. 1969. *A Thief's Primer*. New York: Free Press.

Jenson, Gary, and Raymond Eve. 1976. "Sex Differences in Delinquency: An Examination of Popular Sociological Explanations," *Criminology* 13:427–48.

Judson, Charles J., James J. Pandell, Jack B. Owens, James L. McIntosh, and Dale L. Matschullat. 1969. "A Study of the California Penalty Jury in First-Degree-Murder Cases," *Stanford Law Review* 21:1297–1497.

Katz, Jack. 1979. "Legality and Equality: Plea Bargaining in the Prosecution of White-Collar and Common Crimes," *Law and Society Review* 13:431–59.

Kitsuse, John I., and Aaron V. Cicourel. 1963. "A Note on the Uses of Official Statistics," *Social Problems* 11:131–39.

Kratcoski, Peter C. 1974. "Differential Treatment of Delinquent Boys and Girls in Juvenile Court," *Child Welfare* 53 (January):16–22.

Kratcoski, Peter C., and J. Kratcoski. 1975. "Changing Patterns in the Delinquent Activities of Boys and Girls: A Self-Reported Delinquency Analysis," *Adolescence* 10:38–91.

Kruttschnitt, Candace. 1981. "The Social Status and Sentences of Female Offenders," *Law and Society Review* 15:247–63.

Landes, William H. 1974. "Legality and Reality: Some Evidence of Criminal Procedure," *Journal of Legal Studies* 4:287–337.

Landy, D., and E. Aronson. 1969. "The Influence of the Character of the Criminal and His Victim on the Decisions of Simulated Jurors," *Journal of Experimental Social Psychology* 5:141–52.

Llewellyn, Karl. 1930. *The Bramble Bush.* New York: Columbia University Law School (privately published for use by Columbia University law students).

Lofland, John. 1969. *Deviance and Identity.* Englewood Cliffs, N.J.: Prentice-Hall.

Lucas, Netley. 1926. *Crook Janes: A Study of the Woman Criminal in the World Over.* London: Stanley Paul.

Martin, Roscoe. 1934. *The Defendant and Criminal Justice.* University of Texas Bulletin, no. 3437. Austin: Bureau of Research in the Social Sciences.

Mather, Lynn M. 1979. *Plea Bargaining or Trial? The Process of Criminal Case Disposition.* Lexington, Mass: Lexington.

Miller, Frank W. 1969. *Prosecution: The Decision to Charge a Suspect with a Crime.* Boston: Little, Brown.

Miller, Walter B. 1973. "The Molls," *Society* 11:32–35.

Moulds, Elizabeth F. 1980. "Chivalry and Paternalism: Disparities of Treatment in the Criminal Justice System." In *Women, Crime and Justice,* ed. Susan Datesman and Frank Scarpitti, pp. 277–99. New York: Oxford Press.

Myers, Martha A. 1977. "The Effects of Victim Characteristics in the Prosecution, Conviction and Sentencing of Criminal Defendants." Ph.D. diss., Indiana University.

———. 1979a. "Rule Departures and Making Law: Juries and Their Verdicts," *Law and Society Review* 13:401–17.

———. 1979b. "Offended Parties and Official Reactions: Victims and the Sentencing of Criminal Defendants," *Sociological Quarterly* 20 (autumn): 529–40.

———. 1979c. "Common Law in Action: Differences in the Prosecution of Felonies and Misdemeanors." Presented at the 1979 Annual Meetings of the Law and Society Association, San Francisco.

Nagel, Ilene H. 1982. "The Legal/Extra-Legal Controversy Revisited: A New Look at Judicial Decisions," *Law and Society Review,* forthcoming.

Nagel, Ilene, John Cardascia, and Catherine E. Ross. 1980. "Institutional Sexism: The Case in Criminal Court." In *Discrimination in Organizations,* ed. Rudy Alvarez. San Francisco: Jossey-Bass.

———. 1981. "Sex Differences in the Processing of Criminal Defendants." In *Women and the Law: The Social Historical Perspective,* ed. Kelly Weisberg. New York: Schenkman.

Nagel, Ilene H., and John Hagan. 1983. *Federal Defendants in District Court: Criminal Process and Outcome Decisions.* New York: Academic Press, forthcoming.

Nagel, Ilene H., John Hagan, and Doug Smith. 1982. "Pre-Trial, Plea and Sentencing: The Impact of Sex on Court Decisions." Unpublished manuscript, Indiana University School of Law, Bloomington.

Nagel, Stuart. 1969. *The Legal Process from a Behavioral Perspective.* Homewood, Ill.: Dorsey Press.

Nagel, Stuart, and Lenore Weitzman. 1971. "Women as Litigants," *Hastings Law Journal* 23:171–98.

Nettler, Gwynn. 1978. *Explaining Crime.* New York: McGraw-Hill.

Noblet, George W., and Janie M. Burcart. 1976. "Women and Crime: 1960–70," *Social Science Quarterly* 56 (March):651–57.

Nye, F. Ivan, and James F. Short. 1958. "Scaling Delinquent Behavior," *American Sociological Review* 22 (June):326–32.

Pollak, Otto. 1950. *The Criminality of Women.* Westport, Conn.: Greenwood Press.

Pope, Carl E. 1975. *Sentencing of California Felony Offenders.* Washington, D.C.: U.S. Department of Justice.

————. 1976. "Post Arrest Release Decisions: An Empirical Examination of Social and Legal Criteria." Presented at the 1976 Annual Meeting of the American Society of Criminology, Tucson, Ariz.

Pound, Rosco. 1908. "Mechanical Jurisprudence," *Columbia Law Review* 605:609–10.

Quetelet, Adolphe. 1842. *A Treatise on Man.* Edinburgh: William and Robert Chambers.

Quinney, Richard. 1970. *The Social Reality of Crime.* Boston: Little, Brown.

————. 1973. *Critique of Legal Order.* Boston: Little, Brown.

Radzinowicz, Leon. 1937. "Variability of the Sex Ratio of Criminality," *Sociological Review* 29:76–102.

Rasche, Christine. 1975. "The Female Offender as an Object of Criminological Research." In *The Female Offender*, ed. Annette Brodsky. Beverly Hills, Calif.: Sage Publications.

Reckless, Walter C., and Barbara A. Kay. 1967. *The Female Offender.* Consultant's Report Presented to the President's Commission on Law Enforcement and Administration of Justice.

Reitman, B. 1937. *Sister of the Road: The Autobiography of Box-Car Bertha.* New York: Macaulay.

Rhodes, William M. 1977. "A Study of Sentencing in the Hennepin County and Ramsey County District Courts," *Journal of Legal Studies* 6:333–53.

Rosett, Arthur, and Donald Cressey. 1976 *Justice by Consent.* Philadelphia: Lippincott.

Rubington, Earl, and Martin S. Weinberg. 1978. *Deviance: The Interactionist Perspective.* 3d ed. New York: Macmillan.

Scarpitti, Frank R., and Richard M. Stephenson. 1971. "Juvenile Court Dispositions: Factors in the Decision Making Process," *Crime and Delinquency* 17:142–51.

Schur, Edwin M. 1971. *Labeling Deviant Behavior.* New York: Harper and Row.

Simon, Rita J. 1975. *Women and Crime.* Lexington, Mass.: D.C. Heath.

————. 1976a. *The Contemporary Woman and Crime.* Washington, D.C.: U.S. Government Printing Office.

————. 1976b. "American Women and Crime," *Annals AAPSS* 423 (January): 31–46.

————. 1977. *Women and Crime*. Lexington, Mass.: D.C. Heath.

Simon, Rita James, and Narvin Sharma. 1978. *The Female Defendant in Washington, D.C.: 1974 and 1975*. Washington, D.C.: Institute for Law and Social Research.

Singer, Linda R. 1973. "Women and the Correctional Process," *American Criminal Law Review* 11:295–308.

Smart, Carol. 1977a. "Criminological Theory; Its Ideology and Implications Concerning Women," *British Journal of Sociology* 28:89–100.

————. 1977b. *Women, Crime and Criminology*. London: Routledge and Kegan Paul.

Smith, Douglas, and Christy Visher. 1980. "Sex and Involvement in Deviance/ Crime: A Quantitative Review of the Empirical Literature," *American Sociological Review* 45:697–701.

Sparks, Richard F. 1979. "'Crime as Business' and the Female Offender." In *The Criminology of Deviant Women*, ed. Freda Adler and Rita Simon. Boston: Houghton Mifflin.

Steffensmeier, D. 1978. "Crime and the Contemporary Woman: An Analysis of Changing Levels of Female Property Crime, 1960–75," *Social Forces* 57: 566–84.

————. 1980. "Sex Differences in Patterns of Adult Crimes, 1965–77: A Review and Assessment," *Social Forces* 58:1080–1108.

————. 1981. "Patterns of Female Property Crime, 1960–78: A Postscript." In *Women and Crime in America*, ed. Lee H. Bowker. New York: Macmillan.

Stephan, C. 1975. "Selective Characteristics of Jurors and Litigants: Their Influences on Juries' Verdicts." In *The Jury System in America*. Beverly Hills, Calif.: Sage Publications.

Sterling, Joyce S., and Mary Haskins. 1980. "Plea Bargaining: Responsive Law or Repressive Law." Paper presented at the American Sociological Association Convention.

Swigert, Victoria, and Ronald Farrell. 1977. "Normal Homicides and the Law," *American Sociological Review* 42:16–32.

Temin, Caroline. 1973. "Discriminatory Sentencing of Women Offenders: The Argument for ERA in a Nutshell," *American Criminal Law Review* 11:355–72.

Terry, Robert M. 1970. "Discrimination in the Handling of Juvenile Offenders by Social Control Agencies." In *Becoming Delinquent: Young Offenders and the Correctional System*, ed. Peter G. Garabedian and Don Gibbons. Chicago: Aldine.

Thomas, W. I. 1907. *Sex and Society*. Boston: Little, Brown.

Thornberry, Terence. 1973. "Race, Socio-Economic Status, and Sentencing in the Juvenile Justice System," *Journal of Criminal Law and Criminology* 64:90–98.

Tittle, Charles R., Wayne J. Villemez, and Douglas A. Smith. 1978. "The Myth of Social Class and Criminality," *American Sociological Review* 43:643–56.

Turk, Austin T. 1969. *Criminality and the Legal Order*. Chicago: Rand McNally.

————. 1979. "Analyzing Official Deviance: For Nonpartisan Conflict Analyses in Criminology," *Criminology* 16:459–76.

Utz, Pamela J. 1978. *Settling the Facts: Discretion and Negotiation in Criminal Court.* Lexington, Mass.: Lexington.

Velimesis, Margery. 1975. "The Female Offender," *Crime and Delinquency Literature* 7:94–112.

Ward, David, Maurice Jackson, and Renee E. Ward. 1969. *Crimes of Violence by Women.* Crimes of Violence 13, Appendix 17. Washington, D.C.: President's Commission on Law Enforcement and Administration of Justice.

Warner, Steve, David Wellman, and Lenore Weitzman. 1971. "The Hero, the Sambo, and the Operator: Reflections on Characterizations of the Oppressed." Paper presented at the American Sociological Association Convention.

Weiten, W., and S. S. Diamond. 1980. "A Critical Review of the Jury Simulation Paradigm: The Case of Defendant Characteristics," *Law and Human Behavior* 3(1/2):71–93.

Wise, Nancy. 1967. "Juvenile Delinquency among Middle-Class Girls." In *Middle Class Juvenile Delinquency.* New York: Harper and Row.

Wolfgang, Marion. 1958. *Patterns of Criminal Homicide.* New York: Wiley.

Zeisel, Hans, Jessica de Grazia, and Lucy Freidman. 1975. *A Criminal Justice System under Stress.* New York: Vera Institute of Justice.

John Monahan and Henry J. Steadman

Crime and Mental Disorder:
An Epidemiological Approach

ABSTRACT

The analytic framework of epidemiology can be used to study the relation between crime and mental disorder, distinguishing between the *true* rates of crime and mental disorder, that is, the rates at which crime and mental disorder actually occur, and their *treated* rates, that is, the rates at which the criminal justice and mental health systems respond to them.

The conclusion that emerges is that rates of true and treated criminal behavior vary independently of rates of true and treated mental disorder when appropriate controls are made for such demographic factors as age, gender, and social class and for such life history factors as prior experience in the mental health and criminal justice systems. When these controls are not applied, rates of true and treated mental disorder are higher among criminals than among the general population, and rates of true and treated crime are higher among the mentally disordered than among the general population. When these controls are applied, the observed relations tend to dissipate.

"The main problem in discussing any relationship between criminal behaviour and mental disorder," John Gunn (1977, p. 317) has written, "is that the two concepts are largely unrelated." That they are not *completely* unrelated, however, may be the source of even more difficulty. A person who commits a criminal act while disordered to the point of legal "insanity" is held not to be responsible for that act. Indeed, the very adjudication of criminal guilt is not possible where a defendant's mental disorder is of such a nature as to render him or her "incompetent" to

John Monahan is Professor of Law, University of Virginia. Henry J. Steadman is Director of the Special Projects Unit, New York State Office of Mental Health.

Preparation of this chapter was supported in part by a grant to the authors from the National Institute of Justice, "The Movement of Offender Populations from Correctional to Mental Health Facilities" (79-N1-AX-0126). We wish to express our appreciation to Michael Tonry, Norval Morris, Seymour Halleck, Shari Diamond, Stephen Morse and an anonymous reviewer for detailed and insightful critiques of an earlier draft.

stand trial. Other forms of mental disorder, believed to predispose toward certain crimes, can result in the complete bypassing of the criminal process and the invocation of special civil procedures, such as those for "mentally disordered sex offenders." Just as the criminal law is shaped by the perception that criminal behavior and mental disorder interact in some cases, so the civil law governing the commitment of the mentally disordered to hospitals is now and historically has been based on the belief that some of the mentally disordered, if left to their own devices, would commit dangerous or criminal acts.

Contemporary public policy, no less than historic legal doctrine, is premised on the assumption that a population exists in which mental disorder and criminal behavior converge. This orienting assumption, with its roots in the enduring public perception that the mentally ill are prone to violence (Nunnally 1961; Fracchia et al. 1976; Olmstead and Durham 1976), provides support for the construction of prisonlike secure treatment facilities for civil mental patients and the offering of mental health services to convicted offenders in prisons and jails. Selective media reporting of instances in which mental illness and criminal behavior appear to be linked (Steadman and Cocozza 1978) feeds this perception.

In this essay we review and organize existing empirical estimates of the relation between criminal behavior and mental disorder in adult populations in the United States. We believe that refinement of law and reformulation of public policy profitably could be informed by the assembled body of descriptive and analytic research. We thus hope to supplant the "myth-information" (Fracchia et al. 1976) that detracts from rational discourse in this area.

We have chosen an epidemiological framework to analyze estimates of the relation between crime and mental disorder. Originally developed for the study of such diseases as cholera, plague, and yellow fever, epidemiology has expanded in this century to address conjoint social and biological problems such as injuries (Baker and Dietz 1979) and disasters (Logue, Melick, and Hansen 1981). Epidemiologists have developed a distinction between the *true* and *treated prevalence rates* of a "pathological" condition that is useful in exploring the relation between crime and mental disorder. A *prevalence rate* is simply the number of known cases of a condition at a given time divided by the size of the population from which the cases are drawn.

It became clear early in the development of epidemiology that ascertaining the prevalence rate of a disease by counting the number of cases presented for treatment at a health facility provided little information on the actual or "true" prevalence rate in the population at large. Many personal factors, such as denial of symptoms, and system factors, such as inaccessibility of health facilities or prohibitive cost of treatment, affected which of those with the "true" disease would be treated for it.

It is now commonplace to apply this true/treated distinction to the epidemiology of mental disorder. The Midtown study (Langner and Michael 1963), for example, reported that 23 percent of a random sample of adults interviewed at home in Manhattan displayed "severe" symptoms of mental disorder. Yet fewer than 2 percent of the total sample were receiving treatment for those symptoms.

The true/treated distinction has been less explicitly invoked in the study of criminal behavior. That true crime prevalence cannot be inferred from the prevalence rates of crime treated by the criminal justice system, however, has in some form long been acknowledged. Indeed, it has been the principal impetus to the development of self-report measures of criminality, premised on the belief that an individual's own admission of having committed crime is a more accurate indicator of whether he or she "truly" committed it than is knowledge of whether the individual was arrested, prosecuted, or convicted (Hirschi, Hindelang, and Weis 1980). The true/treated distinction is also implicit in the rationale for criminal victimization surveys (Hindelang, Gottfredson, and Garofalo 1978). Self-report measures of criminality attempt to estimate the "true" crime rate from statements made by offenders; victimization surveys estimate "true" crime rates from statements made by victims. Both are then typically contrasted with the much lower official crime rates.

The true/treated distinction is particularly apposite to analyzing the relationship between crime and mental disorder because it helps disentangle the legal and policy issues involved. Debates over the insanity defense and the doctrine of incompetence to stand trial, for example, concern the *true* prevalence rates of mental illness among persons being *treated* for criminal behavior. The choice of civil commitment policy, particularly deinstitutionalization, is often argued in terms of the *true* prevalence rates of criminal behavior among populations *treated* for mental disorder. Procedures for transferring prisoners to mental hospitals, as in the recent United States Supreme Court decision *Vitek v. Jones* (445 U.S. 480 [1980]), implicate estimates of the *treated* prevalence rates of mental disorder among those also being *treated* for criminal behavior. The fourth and final permutation—the interrelation of *true* crime and *true* mental disorder—is most relevant in the contexts of etiology and prevention.

Before reviewing the empirical literature on crime and mental disorder according to this epidemiological approach, we must set out a number of definitions and indicate what we mean by the terms *crime* and *mental disorder*, *true* and *treated* prevalence, and *pure* and *mixed* cases. In addition, some comment on the implications for our analyses of the ambiguity and elasticity of some diagnostic categories that pertain to mental disorder is essential.

I. Preliminary Issues

A. *Crime and Mental Disorder*

Merely to discuss the definition of mental disorder for the purpose of relating it to criminality is to risk unfavorable mention in the writings of Thomas Szasz. Szasz (e.g. 1978), of course, holds that no criminals are mentally ill, as a corollary of his general position that mental illness does not exist. Karl Menninger's early writings anchor the other end of the spectrum: "The time will come," he stated in 1928, "when stealing or murder will be thought of as a symptom, indicating the presence of a disease" (p. 373).

The definition of crime, no less than the definition of mental disorder, has been the subject of intense debate. "Labeling theory" (e.g Lemert 1951; Schur 1980) tends to shift the study of crime to the reactions of functionaries in the criminal justice system rather than the behavior of the individual to whom they are reacting.

We will not attempt to review the social reaction perspective on crime and mental disorder here. We raise it because it is seemingly inconsistent with an epidemiological approach. That is, the societal reaction theorist would state that "treated" prevalence rates are all that exist, since "primary deviance" is not "crime" or "mental disorder" *until it is so labeled (in our usage, treated) by the criminal justice or mental health systems*. To the extent that one emphasizes the true rates of crime or mental disorder in the population, one is at least implicitly discounting societal reaction as the sole focus of intellectual interest in the field.

Our own view is that *both* the behavior of individuals and the reactions of others to that behavior are worthy of scholarly attention (Gove 1980). We believe it is both possible and desirable to estimate rates of "primary deviance" (i.e., "true" crime and mental disorder) as well as "secondary deviance" (i.e., "treated" rates of crime and mental disorder).

There is one technical problem with an epidemiological approach to crime and mental disorder. For reasons of legal theory, some of the mentally disordered cannot commit a "criminal" act. A mentally disordered person who murders someone, for example, may be found not guilty of a criminal act by virtue of his or her mental disorder. This is because the definition of "crime" has both a "mental" and a "behavioral" component. Those mentally disordered persons lacking the mental component are, by legal definition, not "criminals." While this definition of a crime may be important for legal theory, it is confounding for epidemiological purposes, since it leads to the conclusion that the true and treated prevalence rates of criminal behavior among certain "insane" groups of the mentally disordered are zero. Therefore we consider as "crime" for the mentally disordered not only acts that are treated as such by the criminal justice system (or, in the case of true prevalence rates, acts that would be treated as such if discovered), but also acts that *but for* the mental disorder of the perpetrator would be crimes. If a mentally disordered person intentionally kills someone but is found not guilty of murder by reason of insanity, for example, we consider that person both mentally disordered and criminal.

B. *True and Treated Prevalence*

The distinction between true and treated forms of crime and mental disorder is straightforward at the extremes. Self-reports are an index of true crime; imprisonment is an index of treated crime. A reliable diagnosis of mental disorder made during an epidemiological community survey is an index of true mental disorder; indefinite confinement in a mental hospital is an index of treated mental disorder. It is the middle range—behavior more affected by official processing than self-reported acts or random diagnostic assessments and less affected by "system variables" than adjudicated confinement in a correctional or mental health facility—that presents classificatory issues.

One might reasonably take rates of formal *adjudication* of crime or mental disorder as an index of treated status. In the mental health system, legal adjudication of mental illness at a civil commitment hearing is done only to institute or continue confinement, so every case of adjudicated mental illness would also be a case of institutionalization for mental illness.

In the criminal justice system, however, formal adjudication—that is, *conviction*—for crime is not always followed by imprisonment. Probation and suspended sentences account for a substantial portion of criminal dispositions, especially for relatively minor crimes and for first offenders. Nevertheless, conviction appears to be an appropriate index of "treated" criminal behavior. Even when it is not followed by imprisonment, conviction represents the official adjudication that an individual "is" a criminal. The resulting social stigma and legal disabilities (e.g. disbarment of attorneys convicted of certain crimes) support its classification as treated criminality.

The principal dilemma is whether *arrests* should be considered an index of true or of treated criminality. Clearly an arrest is one way to "treat" an offender. It is an official notice that at least one component of the criminal justice system—a police officer—believes that a person qualifies for further treatment. Numerous biases affect who among those who commit crimes are arrested, including availability of witnesses, ingenuity of the offender, cooperation by the victim, and police workloads. Even in the case of violent crimes, for example, it appears that two of every three that occur in the United States are reported to the police, and one of these results in an arrest (Monahan 1981, p. 35). So it is not difficult to claim that arrest is a highly selective treatment applied only to a minority of true criminal incidents.

Nonetheless, while arrest may reflect selective treatment *for any given criminal act*, it may also be a reasonably accurate indicator of *those who are true criminal actors*. The central question in this regard is: Who commits the true criminal acts that do not result in arrest? One answer is that those arrested for crimes are most often the same persons who have committed other unreported or unsolved crimes. As Shinnar and Shinnar (1975, p. 597), for instance, concluded, "The important question is who commits the 70 percent of crimes which are never solved . . . [T]he most likely possibility is that they are committed by the same group of recidivists who commit the 30 percent of crimes which are solved."

We have chosen here to consider the arrests of the mentally disordered as one index of their *true* criminal behavior. We do not believe that all true criminal acts are committed by persons who eventually are arrested, or that all arrested persons "truly" did the act for which they were arrested. However, arrested persons *are*, as a group, responsible for much more true crime than that for which they were arrested (Wolfgang 1978), and the overwhelming proportion of persons arrested for crime *did commit* a true criminal act (e.g. Heumann 1978). Both observations support our classificatory decision. Readers who believe otherwise should transpose studies using arrest data from the "true" to the "treated" category of crime.

The central issue in the epidemiological study of "true" mental disorder is the reliability of diagnostic classification. One cannot hope to understand the relation between true mental disorder and crime without a modicum of agreement on who is truly mentally disordered.

Research conducted in the 1950s and 1960s on the reliability of psychiatric diagnoses tended to conclude that it was "a hopeless undertaking" (Grove et al. 1981). But more recent studies, employing highly trained interviewers using standardized interview schedules, have found interrater concordance (i.e., agreement) to be in the 70–80 percent range (Helzer et al. 1977a, 1977b). Given this "quantum jump in the magnitude of psychiatric reliability in the last decade," Grove et al. (1981, p. 412) have concluded that "[i]t no longer seems necessary to apologize for poor diagnostic reliability in psychiatry." They qualify this lack of apology, however, in the case of "milder mental illnesses like personality disorders, minor depression, and hypomania," which "all show poorer reliability than do major diagnoses" (p. 413).

We shall therefore focus in this review upon the relation between "major" or "serious" mental disorders and crime. Findings regarding diagnoses of less severe—and therefore less reliable—conditions, where given for the sake of comprehensiveness, should be interpreted with appropriate caution.

Each of the four types of relation between true and treated crime and mental disorder that we review is bidirectional. The relation between treated crime and treated mental disorder, for example, involves both questions of the rate of mental hospitalization among persons imprisoned for crime and questions of the rate of imprisonment for crime among persons in mental hospitals. Therefore each of the four types of relations has two subcategories. A temporal component is also often at issue. The temporal sequence of the epidemiological relation—Did imprisonment precede or follow hospitalization?—is specified within each relevant subcategory.

C. "Pure" and "Mixed" Cases

We have found clarity of interpretation to be enhanced by separating the studies into those addressing "pure" cases of criminal behavior or mental disorder and those dealing with the "mixed" cases of "mentally disordered offenders" who are being treated *simultaneously* both for crime and for mental disorder. This latter group consists of persons found incompetent to stand trial or not guilty by reason of insanity, mentally disordered sex offenders, and prison-to-mental hospital transfer cases.

D. *Overview*

The conclusion to which our review is drawn is that the relation between either type of crime—true or treated—and either type of mental disorder can be accounted for largely by demographic and historical characteristics that the two groups share. When appropriate statistical controls are applied for factors such as age, gender, race, social class, and previous institutionalization, whatever relations between crime and mental disorder are reported tend to disappear. The correlates of crime among the mentally ill appear to be the same demographic and life-history factors that are the correlates of crime among any other group. Likewise, the correlates of mental disorder among criminals appear to be the same things that correlate with mental disorder in the general population. When research fails to control for demographic and life-history factors, a relation between crime and mental disorder is reported. When research does control for demographic and life-history factors, no relation or, at best, a much weaker relation is found.

In both section II, which considers "pure" cases of crime *or* mental disorder, and section III, which considers "mixed" cases of crime *and* mental disorder, we divide the research among the four possible permutations of the two dichotomies—crime versus mental disorder and true versus treated status—that we have constructed. Thus we inquire into the relations between (*a*) true criminal behavior and true mental disorder, (*b*) true criminal behavior and treated mental disorder, (*c*) treated criminal behavior and true mental disorder, and (*d*) treated criminal behavior and treated mental disorder. This organizing format is displayed in table 1.

II. "Pure" Cases of Criminal Behavior
or Mental Disorder

We have called "pure" those cases in which rates of mental disorder are ascertained from groups of true or treated criminals, and those cases in which rates of crime are computed for groups of the truly or treated mentally disordered. That is, we begin by taking people who are "purely" in one category—criminal or mentally disordered—and inquiring as to the proportion who fall into the other category as well. The studies reviewed in this section are summarized in table 2.

A. *The Relation between True Criminal Behavior*
   and True Mental Disorder

1. *Rates of diagnosed mental disorder among persons who self-report crime or who are arrested.* There are no studies assessing mental disorder among

TABLE 1

Mental Disorder and Criminal Behavior as a Function of Epidemiological Status

Mental Disorder

	Epidemiological Status	True	Treated
Criminal Behavior — True	True	A	B
	Treated	C	D

persons who self-report criminal behavior, and there is only one study providing estimates of it among samples of newly arrested persons (in distinction to jail populations).

Monahan, Caldeira, and Friedlander (1979) surveyed police officers concerning their perceptions of the degree of mental disorder, if any, present in a random group of persons arrested for criminal behavior (excluding public drunkenness). The police "diagnosed" 2 percent of the persons they arrest as "severely" mentally ill, 10 percent as "moderately" mentally ill, and 18 percent as "somewhat" mentally ill. If one assumes that police assessments, at least of severe mental disorder, comport with psychiatric assessments (a major, but not an unreasonable, assumption), these data are not inconsistent with those from community surveys of mental disorder. As discussed below, the median rate of psychoses reported in community surveys is 1.7 percent (Neugebauer, Dohrenwend, and Dohrenwend 1980), compared with 2.0 percent of severely mentally ill persons reported by police officers among the people they arrest.

We conclude, therefore, that *there is very little evidence on the rates of severe mental disorder among people arrested, but that that little evidence suggests that the rates are no higher than for the general population.*

2. *Rates of self-report or arrest for crime among persons who are diagnosed as mentally disordered.* An exhaustive search of the epidemiological literature, including correspondence with the leading researchers in the field, has revealed no study of the prevalence of true mental disorder in the general population that has inquired whether the individuals identified as mentally ill were ever arrested for, or admit to ever having committed, criminal acts. Nor have these "truly mentally disordered" persons ever been monitored to assess their subsequent criminal behavior. One study directed by Lee Robins of Washington University assessing true crime in

TABLE 2

Summary of Studies on "Pure" Cases of Criminal Behavior or Mental Disorder

Relation at Issue	Amount of Evidence	Findings Compared with Matched Groups in the General Population
A. True criminal behavior and true mental disorder		
1. True disorder among true criminals	Little	No higher
2. True crime among truly disordered	None	—
B. True criminal behavior and treated mental disorder		
1. True crime among treated disordered	Much	No higher
2. Treated disorder among true criminals	None	—
C. Treated criminal behavior and true mental disorder		
1. True disorder among treated criminals	Much	No higher
2. Treated crime among truly disordered	None	—
D. Treated criminal behavior and treated mental disorder		
1. Treated disorder among treated criminals	Little	No comparison data
2. Treated crime among treated disordered	Little	Unclear

a community survey of true mental disorder is in progress and should provide the first empirical estimates in this area of basic research.

B. *The Relation between True Criminal Behavior and Treated Mental Disorder*

1. *Rates of self-reported crime or arrest among mentally hospitalized persons.* In the research on treated mental disorder and true criminal behavior, "treated" means almost exclusively "treated in a state mental hospital." With one exception, all the follow-up studies on criminal behavior after some sort of mental health treatment focused only on patients released from state, municipal, or Veterans Administration mental hospitals. Thus, at the outset it is crucial to note that in this section we examine only certain segments of all persons treated for mental disorder. No persons treated either privately or in public outpatient facilities have been studied. As a result, the rates of criminal behavior that will be examined might be expected to be higher than would be the case for the entire group of persons who have been treated for mental disorder, because persons treated in state mental hospitals tend to be of lower social class than those treated in outpatient or private facilities (Hollingshed and Redlich 1958), and many studies find a correlation between criminal behavior and lower social class (e.g. Wolfgang, Sellin, and Figlio 1972; Braithwaite 1981).

There is a temporal dimension to the issue of true criminal behavior among the treated mentally disordered. Current research interest has focused on the subsequent criminal behavior of patients released to the community. For the most part, prior criminal behavior of patients has been of interest only insofar as it relates to subsequent arrests.

Since 1965 there has been a series of studies in the United States on the arrest rates of former mental patients. These studies have been provoked by the controversies surrounding the deinstitutionalization of the mentally disordered from state facilities to a "community care" that for the most part has been illusory.[1] This series of studies, as well as prior

---

[1] It has been claimed, for example, that restrictions on who can be civilly committed and for how long have increased the number of mentally disordered people who are arrested (Bonovitz and Guy 1979). That mentally disordered people are arrested rather than receiving the "community care" (e.g. outpatient treatment, halfway houses) that was to be the hallmark of the "community mental health movement" may be because, in practice, "community care" has often come to mean "no care." According to Scull (1977, p. 153), deinstitutionalized mental patients are dumped into "newly emerging 'deviant' ghettoes,' sewers of human misery and what is conventionally defined as social pathology within which the (largely hidden from outside inspection or even notice) society's refuse may be repressively tolerated." Even those who do not share Scull's structural framework agree

research on the criminal behavior of persons treated in state mental hospitals, has been incisively and exhaustively reviewed by Rabkin (1979) and will not be reviewed again here. We will highlight her conclusions and supplement her data with the two subsequently published studies.

In the four reports published before 1965 (Ashley 1922; Pollock 1938; Brill and Malzberg 1954; Cohen and Freeman 1945), released mental patients were found to have rates of arrest lower than those of the general population. In contrast, in the six studies published since 1965 (Rappeport and Lassen 1965, 1966; Giovannini and Gurel 1967; Zitrin et al. 1976; Durbin, Pasewark, and Albers 1977; Sosowsky 1978), mental patients were found to be arrested more often than the general population. There was no consensus among the latter researchers on the causes of the change in rates. Most explanations emphasized one facet or another of the deinstitutionalization movement, which was seen as putting more persons at risk in the community who formerly would have been housed in state mental hospitals.

An alternative explanation was put forth in a series of articles published after Rabkin's review (Steadman, Cocozza, and Melick 1978; Melick, Steadman, and Cocozza 1979; Cocozza, Melick, and Steadman 1978), although the core data from these articles were included in her review on the basis of an earlier in-house report. The data in these studies were derived from a random sample of all patients released from New York State mental hospitals in 1968 and 1975. There were 1,920 patients in the 1968 group and 1,938 in the 1975 group. As is evident in table 3, in every offense category for both years, except sex crimes in 1968, the former patients as a group were arrested more often than the general population. This is consistent with the other studies reviewed by Rabkin.

What was not consistent with the previous work was the interpretation of the possible causes of these changes. Rather than relying on factors related to system *output* changes such as deinstitutionalization putting more persons at risk, the data suggested system *input* changes. The argument developed from the finding of significant differences in the rates of arrest of the former mental patients based on their prior arrest records. Not surprisingly, the two factors that were most associated with

that the "community care" provided deinstitutionalized patients "is often illusory; they may have less community and less care where they live than they had in their state hospitals where at least food, clothing, shelter and the presence of other people were routinely available" (Rabkin and Zitrin 1982; see also Monahan 1982; Scull 1981; Warren 1981).

TABLE 3

Annual Arrest Rates per 1,000 for Felonies for the General Population, Total Patient Samples, and Patients with Zero, One, and Two or More Prior Arrests, 1968 and 1975 Samples

Crime	General Population	Total Patient Sample	Patients with No Prior Arrest	Patients with One Prior Arrest	Patients with Two or More Prior Arrests
			1968 Sample		
	(N = 13,822,300)	(N = 1920)	(N = 1552)	(N = 129)	(N = 239)
Total arrests	27.53	67.59	9.34	170.93	437.57
Arrests for violent crimes	2.29	5.58	2.03	9.77	26.36
Arrests for potentially violent crimes	1.85	3.94	0.81	19.53	15.82
Arrests for sex crimes	0.42	0.33	0.00	0.00	2.64
			1975 Sample		
	(N = 12,320,540)	(N = 1938)	(N = 1428)	(N = 187)	(N = 323)
Total arrests	32.51	98.50	22.05	138.00	413.50
Arrests for violent crimes	3.62	12.03	2.21	3.37	60.46
Arrests for potentially violent crimes	2.83	6.18	0.88	3.37	31.21
Arrests for sex crimes	0.45	2.60	0.44	6.74	9.75

Source: Steadman, Cocozza, and Melick 1978.

subsequent arrest were younger age and more prior arrests. The importance of prior arrest is clearly evident when the 1975 overall group annual arrest rate per 1,000 of 98.50 is broken into those with no prior arrests (22.06), those with one prior arrest (138.00), and those with multiple prior arrests (413.50). Note that the arrest rate for the 75 percent of the patients released in 1975 who had no police records before admission (22.06 per 1,000) is actually lower than that of the general New York State population (32.51 per 1,000).[2]

Having ascertained the strong effect of a prior arrest record, we compared our 1968 and 1975 data with 1947 data in the Brill and Malzerg (1954) study. Their report dealt only with males and found that, of all males released, 15 percent had a prior record of arrest. Among the males released in 1968, however, 32 percent had prior arrests, and fully 40 percent of the 1975 males had prior arrests. Another ongoing study by the authors found that, of patients admitted to New York State mental hospitals in 1978, 51 percent had at least one prior arrest. The pattern of these New York State data suggests that the composition of the clientele of state mental hospitals has been changing, bringing more persons with criminal histories into the mental health system. Thus there are changes in system inputs, rather than a simple change in system outputs that may have exposed more persons to the risk of arrest. Further, these results suggest that the issue of criminal behavior among the treated mentally ill might better be framed in traditional criminological terms rather than in the context of mental health. In other words, crime among those treated for mental illness may result primarily from the same factors as crime among any other subgroup.

Another interpretation of these data is that Community Mental Health Centers, nursing homes, private proprietary homes, and the like have "creamed" persons without arrest records from the pool of those susceptible to mental hospitalization, leaving in the pool primarily persons with arrest records. One of us (Steadman 1981) has rejected this argument on the basis of both New York State data suggesting similari-

---

[2]The arrest rate for the 80 percent of the patients released in 1968 who had no police records before admission (9.34 per 1,000) is *much* lower than that for the general New York State population of that year (27.53 per 1,000). Thus from 1968 to 1975, the arrest rate for the general New York State population increased 18 percent (from 27.53 to 32.51 per 1,000), and the arrest rate for released mental patients with no prior arrests increased 136 percent (from 9.34 to 22.06 per 1,000) (Lawrence Greenfeld, personal communication). While it is unclear what accounted for this great increase in the arrest rate of released mental patients with no prior arrests, the arrest rate for this group was *still* lower than that for the general New York State population in 1975.

ties in admission characteristics (other than arrest history) over time and the literature strongly suggesting that Community Mental Health Centers have developed a new constituency of their own rather than diverting the traditional clientele of state mental hospitals.

Sosowsky (1980) has urged caution on generalizing from these findings to other jurisdictions. He compiled data from 301 patients released from Napa State Hospital in California from 1972 to 1975. He found that their overall arrest rate for violent crimes was 34.2 per 1,000, which was about ten times that of the general population for San Mateo County, California (3.5 per 1,000). As in our New York State data, those patients with prior arrest records were much more often arrested than patients with no prior arrests (18.5 per 1,000). However, unlike the New York data, the arrest rate for released patients with no prior arrests was more than five times that of the general population.

We find one aspect of Sosowsky's data and inferences troublesome. He compared the arrest rate of San Mateo County residents with the arrest rate of all patients released from Napa State Hospital. This may not be the appropriate comparison. San Mateo, a largely middle-class county, has a lower arrest rate than the general catchment area of Napa State Hospital, which includes inner-city San Francisco and Oakland. According to the most recent data available from the California Bureau of Criminal Statistics and Special Services (1980) the total arrest rate in San Mateo County in 1979 was 31.17 per 1,000. This was less than half the arrest rate in San Francisco County (70.41) and in Alameda County (Oakland; 66.63). San Francisco and Alameda counties—with double the arrest rate of San Mateo County—sent more than ten times as many patients to Napa State Hospital in fiscal year 1979 as did San Mateo County (a total of 1,106 compared with 109) (personal communication, Napa State Hospital, Napa, California).

To say, therefore, that residents of Napa State Hospital, upon their release and return to their "home" communities, have a higher arrest rate than the general population of San Mateo may reveal much about arrest rates in San Francisco and Oakland but little about how patients released from Napa State Hospital compare with their peers in the geographically matched catchment area.

In spite of this potential confounding, and possibly other problems (Diamond 1981; Adams 1981; cf. Sosowsky 1981), Sosowsky found no association between any psychiatric diagnosis and arrest. The factors that were associated with arrest were past crime, age, and legal status (with involuntary patients having a higher arrest rate than voluntary ones). These findings, together with Steadman, Cocozza, and Melick's (1978) similar findings of the lack of association between diagnosis and arrest (controlling for age) and a strong associaton between prior arrest, age, and subsequent arrest, all suggest support for an explanatory framework for criminal behavior among the treated mentally disordered that relies more on the traditional perspective of criminology than on psychiatric considerations.

The second issue of true criminality among the treated mentally disordered has to do with reported rates of arrest or self-reports of crime *before* hospitalization. In discussing the strong association between prior and subsequent arrests in the New York State data, it was noted that the proportion of all males released from New York State hospitals with prior arrests had dramatically increased from 15 percent in 1947–48, to 32 percent in 1968, to 40 percent in 1975, and to 51 percent in 1978. No comparable figures are available for women. Only one other of the subsequent arrest studies of former mental patients reports the proportion who had been arrested before hospitalization (Sosowsky 1980). Of the 301 patients admitted to Napa State Hospital in 1972–75, 160 (53 percent) had previous arrests. Without data from additional sites, it is impossible to assess how generalizable these figures may be. Given the pace of deinstitutionalization in New York and California and the level of urbanization in New York State and northern California, it might be expected that many other areas in the United States would have substantially lower proportions of mental patients with previous arrests.

It should be reiterated that state mental hospital populations are not representative of all persons treated for mental illness. State mental patients are unrepresentative for precisely those factors that statistically would increase their probability of both prior and subsequent arrest (e.g. lower socioeconomic status). All that can now be asserted is that the proportion of state mental hospital patients with prior arrests may be increasing and that there appears to be a strong relationship between prior and subsequent true criminality among this group of the treated mentally ill.

Throughout this section, while discussing "true" criminality, both before and after hospitalization, we have relied upon arrest rates as our index of true criminality. This is because we assume that arrest is a valid index of true crime and also because there is little else with which the questions of true crime among those treated for mental illness can be addressed. The "little else" involves four diverse studies, plus some unpublished data we have collected. The published studies deal with the issue of behavioral incidents associated with civil hospitalization that could have been considered criminal acts *but for* the initiation of mental hospitalization.

The first of these studies was Levine's (1970). This work examined records of 100 patients selected from an unnamed large state mental hospital. The hospital folders of these patients were reviewed by a local attorney who classified the behaviors leading to admission according to whether criminal behavior could have been alleged. Of the 100 patients, the attorney found 71 with behaviors that could have been deemed criminal. These 71 produced a total of 117 criminal charges, of which 61 (51 percent) were classified as against persons or as violence to property. None of these acts resulted in arrest. Extrapolating this figure to the whole sample would mean that 36 of the 100 patients studied exhibited behavior sufficiently violent to justify an arrest.

The second study of unreported violent and criminal behavior for the treated mentally disordered was reported by Lagos, Perlmutter, and Saexinger (1977). They relied on admission notes for 100 patients admitted to each of four state mental hospitals in New Jersey during 1974. They found that 18 percent of these patients were admitted because of actions of physical violence toward persons or objects, and another 10 percent were vaguely described as being violent. Of 115 patients reported to display some type of violent behavior, 3 (2.6 percent) had been arrested.

Skodol and Karasu (1978) examined the same set of questions with data from a sample of 416 patients representing all patients presented to the psychiatric emergency room in Bronx Municipal Hospital Center over a two-week period. Of the 367 patients who were not making return visits or did not walk out before being seen, 62 (17 percent) "were deemed violent because of outwardly directed aggressive ideation of behavior in their clinical presentations" (1978, p. 203). No indication is given of how much of the behavior could have been considered criminal.

In the final study, Tardiff and Sweillam (1980) examined all patients admitted to Nassau County and Suffolk County, New York, state mental hospitals between 1 April 1974 and 31 March 1975. For these 9,365 patients, admission notes were searched for indications of assaultive acts as presenting symptoms. In all, 21 percent of these admission notes indicated some type of assaultive behavior. No information was provided on whether any of these acts resulted in arrests.

Thus, in the three studies in which admission notes were examined, there was a relatively narrow range in the proportion of patients—17 percent, 18 percent, and 21 percent—who had exhibited assaultive behavior, although the locales and types of facilities were quite varied. In the Lagos work, when a looser criterion was used, the figure increased from 18 percent to 29 percent. In the one project where an attorney categorized the behavior (Levine 1970), the figure for violent acts was 36 percent and for all types of criminal acts was 71 percent. Only the Lagos study reported any patients ultimately being arrested, and this was only 1 percent of the total study group and 2.6 percent of those with reported violent behavior.

Before attempting to interpret these data on the preadmission criminal behaviors of civil patients, it may be useful to examine some recent self-report data we collected from former mental patients. The data are from 148 persons who had been released into Albany County, New York, from state mental hospitals. Interviews were conducted between October 1979 and June 1980. The research did not deal specifically with criminal behavior and therefore poses problems for our use here in two regards. First, there is no information on self-reports of potentially illegal property behavior. Second, the study's focus on aggressive and violent behavior categorized behaviors into (1) arguments without physical attack of any sort, (2) incidents with slapping or pushing only, (3) hitting without a weapon, and (4) attack with a weapon. It is unclear how congruent these categories are with criminality. Certainly an attack with a weapon would be criminal, but would hitting a child under the aegis of parental discipline be included?

For our purposes, the hitting and weapon categories may be the most relevant. Of the 148 former patients, 18 percent reported at least one incident of hitting, 8 percent reported a dispute involving a weapon, and 8 percent reported both. Thus a total of 26 percent had committed some type of self-reported violence that could be considered criminal. As with three of the four admission cohort studies just reviewed, we have no directly comparable arrest data. There is, however, some indirect evidence. In the New York State study on former mental patients reported above (Cocozza, Melick, and Steadman 1978), 2.7 percent were arrested for any crime against a person during their first nineteen months back in the community. These numbers, 26 percent self-reporting criminal-type behavior and 2.7 percent arrested for it, are strikingly similar to those of Lagos, who found 18 percent to 29 percent (depending on the tightness of the definition used) of their patient cohort to have committed assault-ive behavior and 1 percent to have been arrested for it.

The research on self-reported violence among the 148 mental patients also included two comparison groups: samples of released offenders and the general population. Information on the samples and more detailed analysis can be found elsewhere (Steadman and Felson 1981). For our purposes, the important finding is that the rate of self-reported crime for the mental patients is significantly lower than that for the offenders (22.3 percent compared with 48.9 percent reporting a hitting incident, and 8.1 percent compared with 15.6 percent reporting an incident involving a weapon) but significantly higher than those of the general populaton (22.3 percent compared with 15.1 percent reporting a hitting incident and 8.1 percent compared with 1.6 percent reporting an incident involving a weapon). These self-report comparisons are very similar to the arrest comparisons reported in two other studies (Steadman, Cocozza, and Melick 1978; Steadman, Vanderwyst, and Ribner 1978). In each case the offender group had the highest arrest rates, followed by the mental patients, with the general population rates being lowest. Our analyses of the self-report data suggest that the two major factors associated with the frequency of criminal incidents among the mental patients are age and education. When these factors are controlled, the offenders' rates remain high, *but the mental patient/general population differences disappear*, suggesting that the rates of self-reported criminal behavior among mental patients have more to do with demographic factors than with mental health status.

The issue of the extent to which the use of arrest statistics underrepresents true crime among the treated mentally disordered is broader than a comparison between arrest and self-report or arrest and hospital records will allow. Former mental patients or persons about to be mental patients may be *more* likely to be arrested for the same behavior than those in the general population. This would be the case where police, responding to the public perception of a link between violence and mental illness, subject former or potential mental patients to more scrutiny than they do other citizens (e.g. arresting them in "dragnet" type raids) and also where the impaired mental functioning of a former or potential mental patient renders his or her attempts at criminality less proficient than those of a similarly inclined person who is not a mental patient. The latter is sometimes referred to as the "turkey theory" of arrest. To the extent that either of these two hypotheses is correct and former or potential mental patients are more susceptible to arrest, for the same behavior, than members of the general population, then the use of arrest rates *overestimates* their true criminality relative to the general population. It is, of course, possible that arrest data underestimate everyone's true criminality but do so less for mental patients than for others.

What is clear from this review is that, as a group, those treated for mental disorders in public inpatient facilities since 1965 have substantially higher rates of arrest after release from the hospital than does the general population. These rates have increased absolutely as well as relative to the general population over time. It is also clear that released patients who have arrest records before their admission to a mental hospital have rates of subsequent arrest that are substantially higher than those of patients with no prior arrests. Given the consistent lack of relation between crime and any psychiatric diagnostic factors, the criminal behavior of mental patients may be much more closely allied to factors traditionally associated with criminal behavior in the general population than with factors linked to psychopathology. *There is no consistent evidence that the true prevalence rate of criminal behavior among former mental patients exceeds the true prevalence rate of criminal behavior among the general population matched for demographic factors and prior criminal history.*

2. *Rates of mental hospitalization among persons who self-report or are arrested for crime.* This section is an empty cell. The closest any data come to addressing these questions are those reported for prior mental hospitalizations among jail inmates that will be reviewed in the next section, which will deal with *treated* criminal behavior rather than the *true* criminal behavior that is the focus here. Here the question focuses on groups who have been surveyed at the time of arrest. Owing to the rapid turnaround in local jails as a result of bail and other diversions, many jail inmates are being treated for crime (i.e., sentenced) rather than merely suspected of having truly committed it (i.e., awaiting trial). Furthermore, no study of self-reported criminal behavior has inquired about prior mental hospitalization or other forms of treatment for mental illness among true criminals.

C. *The Relation between Treated Criminal Behavior and True Mental Disorder*

1. *Rates of diagnosed mental disorder among persons who are convicted or imprisoned.* Persons in jails and prisons have been subjected to the standard mental health diagnostic techniques of psychiatric interviews and psychological tests. Their rates of diagnosed psychosis appear to be no

higher than those of the general population. There is no consistent pattern to the data on their rates of nonpsychotic mental conditions.

The most comprehensive study of rates of psychiatric disorder among offender populations has been performed by Guze (1976). Guze's review of the literature is representative of the conclusions of others (e.g. Brodsky 1973).

> Psychosis, schizophrenia, primary affective disorders, and the various neurotic disorders are seen in only a minority of identified criminals. There is no complete agreement as to whether any of these conditions is more common among criminals than the general population, but it is clear that these disorders carry only a *slightly* increased risk of criminality if any at all. (Guze 1976, pp. 35–36; italics in original)

Guze studied 233 male and 66 female felons. He reported that only 1 percent of his prison sample was schizophrenic. Fifty-four percent of the males and 47 percent of the females were alcoholic. Five percent of the males and 26 percent of the females were drug dependent. Fully 78 percent of the males and 65 percent of the females were diagnosed as sociopathic. Overall he concluded: "Sociopathy, alcoholism, and drug dependence are the psychiatric disorders characteristically associated with serious crime. Schizophrenia, primary affective disorders, anxiety neurosis, obsessional neurosis, phobic neurosis, and brain syndromes are not. Sexual deviations, defined as illegal *per se*, are not, in the absence of accompanying sociopathy, alcoholism, and drug dependence, associated with other serious crime" (p. 124).

Diamond (1974), commenting on Guze's earlier work, notes that sociopathy, alcoholism, and drug dependence "are precisely those psychiatric states which are less easily definable and less generally agreed to be illnesses at all" (p. 448). Indeed, Guze defined "sociopathy" for the purposes of his research as follows:

> This diagnosis was made if at least two of the following five manifestations were present in addition to a history of excessive fighting . . . school delinquency . . . a poor job record . . . [and] a period of wanderlust or being a runaway. . . . For women, a history of prostitution could be substituted for one of the five manifestations. (1976, p. 35)

If all prostitutes who have ever been truant from school, or all unemployed males with a period of "wanderlust" in their history are counted as "sociopaths," it is not difficult to understand why 78 percent of all male and 65 percent of all female felons were so diagnosed. Given the lack of reliability, discussed above, attending to the diagnosis of less severe mental abnormalities—that is, the fact that other researchers might define sociopathy very differently than Guze does—we find the very high rates of sociopathy revealed in his study difficult to interpret. Indeed, "sociopathy" has been renamed "antisocial personality disorder" in the American Psychiatric Association's (1980) *Diagnostic and Statistical Manual of Mental Disorders, third edition* (DSM III). Rather than requiring two criteria in addition to "a history of excessive fighting," as in Guze's definition, a positive diagnosis of antisocial personality disorder now requires the presence of at least ten separate indicators (pp. 320–21). This tightened definition would no doubt exclude as cases of antisocial personality disorder many of the individuals diagnosed as sociopaths by Guze's criteria.

Like Diamond, we do not classify alcoholism or dependence upon other drugs, in themselves, as "mental disorders," at least for the purposes of this review. As stated in DSM III (p. 163), "there are wide subcultural variations" in the use of alcohol and other drugs, and in some groups—including those from which offenders are disproportionately drawn—"the use of various illegal substances for recreational purposes is widely accepted."

The most recent review of studies in this area (Roth 1980) concluded that "approximately 15 to 20 percent of prison inmates manifest sufficient psychiatric pathology to warrant medical attention or intervention," but that the rate of psychoses was "on the order of 5 percent or less of the total prison population" (p. 688).

Six studies have investigated rates of true mental disorder among jail, rather than prison, inmates and found low rates of psychosis and widely varying rates of less severe mental disorders. Bolton (1976) surveyed more than 1,000 adult offenders in five California county jails and reported that 6.7 percent of the inmates were psychotic, 9.3 percent had a nonpsychotic mental disorder, and 21.0 percent had a form of "personality disorder." Swank and Winer (1976) assessed 100 consecutive admissions to the Denver, Colorado, County Jail and reported that 5 percent were psychotic, 13 percent were "antisocial personalities," and 16 percent had "other personality disorders." Schuckit, Herrman, and Schuckit (1977) interviewed a random sample of 199 white males (whose major charge was not drug related) shortly after admission to the San Diego, California, County Jail. Three percent of the inmates were found to have a psychotic affective disorder, and 3 percent to have an organic brain syndrome. "Antisocial personality" was diagnosed for 16 percent of the inmates, alcoholism for 15 percent, and drug abuse for 12 percent. Borgira (1981) reported that 4 percent of the inmates in the Cook County (Chicago) Jail were classified as "psychotic, suicidal, or in a serious manic depressive or toxic state or . . . [as having] serious adjustment problems." O'Keefe (1980) studied 995 inmates in three county jails in Massachusetts. He found that 4.6 percent of those admitted were sufficiently mentally ill to be civilly committed to a psychiatrist, and an additional 6.2 percent "were noted as exhibiting signs of mental illness by jail personnel" but were not committable. Finally, the United States Department of Justice's 1978 National Jail Survey questioned a sample of 5,172 inmates in jails throughout the country (94 percent male). Inmates were asked whether they were experiencing a "nervous disorder," a "mental problem," an "emotional problem," or "depression." No definition of terms was given. Our analysis of the data tapes showed that 4.1 percent of the males and 6.4 percent of the females reported a nervous disorder; 1.6 percent of the males and 2.2 percent of the females reported an emotional problem; and 1.1 percent of the males and 2.4 percent of the females reported depression.

One is left from these studies with true prevalence rates for serious mental illness (i.e., psychoses) among offenders incarcerated in prisons or jails varying from 1 percent (Guze 1976) to 7 percent (Bolton 1976). True prevalence rates for less severe forms of mental illness (nonpsychotic mental disorders and personality disorders) vary greatly, ranging up to 15–20 percent (Roth 1980).

Some of the discrepancy in prevalence rates for both serious and less serious mental illness may reflect differences in true rates of mental illness across the various populations studied; one correctional system may actually have fewer psychotic prisoners than another correctional system. There can be little doubt, however, that much of the variation in prevalence rates reflects diversity in defining what counts as a "case" of mental disorder. Indeed, psychosis was virtually the only diagnostic category common across the various prison and jail studies, and for this category variation was relatively modest (1–7 percent). It is impossible to gain reliable estimates of the prevalence of less severe disorders when each study counts those conditions in such different ways.

The review of studies of the true prevalence rate of mental disorder in the United States by Neugebauer, Dohrenwend, and Dohrenwend (1980) for the President's Commission on Mental Health provides estimates of the rates of mental illness in "community" populations, with which the rates among prison and jail populations can be compared.

They reported rates for psychoses varying from 0.0 to 8.3 percent, with a median of 1.7 percent. For neuroses rates varied from 0.3 to 40.0 percent, with a median of 15.1 percent, and for personality disorders the rates varied from 0.1 to 36.0 percent with a median of 7.0 percent. Overall, they conclude that the range of "functional psychiatric disorder" in community populations is between 16 and 25 percent.

Most relevant for the purpose of comparing these community prevalence rates with prison and jail prevalence rates is the finding that social class strongly affects the data. Neugebauer, Dohrenwend, and Dohrenwend (1980) report the prevalence rate of psychosis to be 2.58 times higher, that of neuroses 1.3 times higher, and that of personality disorders 3.3 times higher in the lowest than in the highest social class.[3]

What, if anything, can one conclude from the existing evidence regarding the true prevalence rate of mental disorder among persons being treated for criminal behavior? If one eliminates "sociopathy" as a meaningful diagnostic category and chooses to consider alcoholism and other drug dependence as not, per se, forms of mental disorder, one is left with the two broad categories of "psychotic" and "nonpsychotic" disorders.

The prison prevalence rates of 1 to 7 percent psychotic do not differ appreciably from the community prevalence rates of 0.0 to 8.3 percent reported by Neugebauer, Dohrenwend, and Dohrenwend (1980). When one considers that, by all accounts, prisoners are drawn disproportionately from the lower social classes and that the community studies indicate that these classes have disproportionately high rates of psychosis, the weight of evidence appears to support the assertion that *the true prevalence rate of psychosis among inmate populations does not exceed the true prevalence rate of psychosis among class-matched community populations.*

The existing data speak less strongly to the prevalence rates of nonpsychotic disorders among either community or prison populations. The 9.3 percent rate of adult nonpsychotic mental disorders reported by Bolton (1976) for the California prison and jail population is less than the 15.1 percent community rate of neurosis reported by Neugebauer and his colleagues, but Bolton's 21.0 rate of personality disorders is higher

[3]It is, of course, possible that lower class is in part a *consequence* of mental disorder rather than a *cause* of it. The functional sequelae of some disorders, particularly severe disorders, may affect educational and occupational performance to the extent that persons with these disorders "drift" downward in social class. The major empirical attempts to establish the direction of causality in the frequently found inverse relationship between social class and rates of psychological disorder, however, have been unsuccessful (Dohrenwend and Dohrenwend 1969).

than Neugebauer's 7.0 percent rate. The overall rate of "sufficient psychiatric pathology to warrant medical attention" among prisoners of 15 to 20 percent reported by Roth (1980) is surprisingly close to the rate of "functional psychiatric disorder" among community populations of 16 to 25 percent reported by Neugebauer, Dohrenwend, and Dohrenwend (1980). We offer here only the cautious conclusion that *there is no consistent evidence that the true prevalence rate of nonpsychotic mental disorder is higher among inmate populations than among class-matched community populations.*

2. Rates of conviction or imprisonment among persons with diagnosed mental disorder. Whereas the previous section considered the rates of true mental disorder among persons convicted or imprisoned for criminal behavior, this section addresses the converse relationship: the conviction or imprisonment of the truly mentally disordered. Relevant here would be estimates of the rates of prior conviction or imprisonment among people identified in an epidemiological survey as mentally disordered, as well as follow-up studies of the rates of conviction or imprisonment among such persons after their identification.

Unfortunately, there appear to be no existing data that bear on either the prior or the subsequent treatment for criminal behavior of true cases of mental disorder. We have failed to locate any epidemiological survey of mental disorder that inquired, even by means of self-report, whether its subjects had ever been convicted of or imprisoned for crime. Nor have we found any estimates of the proportion of true cases of mental disorder in the community in which individuals later experience conviction or imprisonment.

D. *The Relationship between Treated Criminal Behavior and
Treated Mental Disorder*

1. Rates of mental hospitalization among persons convicted of or imprisoned for criminal behavior. There are three studies that report on the prior mental hospitalization of incarcerated offenders and no studies examining subsequent mental hospitalization rates of former inmates.

Steadman and Ribner (1980) obtained prior hospitalization records for two groups of offenders released in 1968 and two groups released in 1975 to Albany County, New York. One group in each year was from the state prison system and one from the local jail. Nineteen percent of the 91 state prison inmates released in 1968 had a history of prior state mental hospitalizations, compared with 13 percent of the 76 prison inmates released in 1975. While the proportion of state prison inmates with a history of mental hospitalization decreased over time, there was a slight increase in the proportion of jail inmates with such a history. Of the 76 jail inmates released in 1968, 9 percent had prior state mental hospitalizations compared with 12 percent of the 176 inmates released in 1975.

An unpublished study by the Massachusetts Department of Mental Health (1980) of all inmates in or admitted to three county jails during April 1980 reported that 6.4 percent of the 995 inmates examined had prior state mental hospitalization in the Massachusetts system. Adams (1980), studying a random sample of 3,426 inmates released from the federal prison system during 1970–72, found that 287 (8.7 percent) had a record of prior mental hospitalization.

Finally, some preliminary data are available from a study we are currently conducting. We are gathering data in several states on the "confinement careers" of a random sample of all inmates admitted to state prison systems. One component of these data is the history of mental hospitalization. Rates of prior mental hospitalization for inmates entering state prisons in 1978 varied from a low of 2.2 percent in Arizona to a high of 16.7 percent in Iowa. Texas (8.4 percent), New York (9.3 percent), Massachusetts (9.0 percent), and California (15.2 percent) had intermediate rates that were close to those of the other United States studies. We currently are analyzing rates of prior mental hospitalization for inmates incarcerated in 1968 to establish whether change has taken place and, if so, in what directions.

What these findings suggest are fairly low percentages of inmates with prior treated mental illness; 12 and 13 percent among the Albany County 1975 released inmates, 8.7 percent among the 1970–72 federal prison sample, 6.4 percent among the 1980 Massachusetts jail inmates, and 2.2–16.7 percent among those admitted to six state prison systems in 1978. These data represent the full range of information currently available on the amount of mental disorder previously treated by hospitalization among groups of convicted or incarcerated criminals in the United States. Unfortunately, *no comparative conclusions can be drawn on the rates of mental hospitalization among inmate populations, since there are no baseline data on the rates of mental hospitalization among groups in the general population.*

2. Rates of conviction or imprisonment for criminal behavior among persons who have been mentally hospitalized. In large part owing to the unreliability of official records of conviction and incarceration, few researchers have reported this information when studying the crime rates of mental patients. Most who have considered the issue of criminal behavior among mental patients have chosen to rely upon arrest statistics as the most accurate indicators of true criminal behavior and have been little concerned with treated criminal behavior, which must rely upon much less reliable records.

In terms of the *prior* conviction or incarceration rates, not a single study of United States mental patients from regular civil state hospitals reports these figures. There are three studies of the "criminally insane" that are presented in the next section, on "mixed" cases.

One of the few sources of information on the prior—treated criminal behavior of mental patients is our ongoing study, discussed above. In our preliminary data we find rates of prior imprisonment for random samples of persons admitted to state mental hospitals in 1978 to vary from a low of 5.8 percent in New York to a high of 13.5 percent in California. Arizona (4.0 percent), Massachusetts (3.2 percent), Texas (8.2 percent), and Iowa (13.3 percent) had intermediate rates. We know of no data on the proportion of the general population with a history of prior imprisonment with which to compare these figures.

Turning to studies that address the issue of mental hospitalization and *subsequent* conviction or imprisonment, we again find little information. Two studies by Sosowsky provide data on the subsequent conviction of state mental hospital patients and are reviewed by Rabkin (1979). His first study examined only violent crime convictions in a statewide sample of former state hospital inpatients and state hospital outpatients. Among the former inpatients the annual conviction rates per 1,000 were 1.96 for assault and 0.98 for homicide. Among the outpatient study group, the conviction rate per 1,000 was 2.57 for assault and 0.20 for homicide. The rates for both groups were substantially higher than those of the general population, which were 0.33 per 1,000 for assault convictions and 0.10 per 1,000 for homicide convictions. His second study looked at 301 admissions to Napa State Hospital. The total annual conviction rate per 1,000 for this group was 11.70. Unfortunately, these latter data are of little use, since they include both prior *and* subsequent convictions and since Sosowsky suggested that most arrests, and therefore most convictions, preceded hospitalization.

Regarding the subsequent conviction or imprisonment of released mental patients, therefore, we can say practically nothing. Much of the reason for the dearth of information has to do with gaps in state criminal justice information systems. A second contributing factor is the grave concern of researchers that differential court processing of former mental patients may preclude any valid comparison with former offenders or with the general population. We know little about what the label "former mental patient" means in terms of criminal justice system processing. This lack of understanding may affect the arrest rate data reported in the previous section in unknown ways, but it is likely to have even more effect on the conviction and incarceration data reported here. For example, Thornberry and Jacoby (1979) found that among 140 "criminally insane" cases, 29 percent had their subsequent criminal behavior disposed of through rehospitalization. Clearly this proportion of cases handled through rehospitalization rather than conviction far exceeds what would be expected among the general population or groups of former offenders.

Because it is unclear what effect being a former mental patient may have on court processes and because of irregularly reported disposition information, little attention has been given to the conviction and incarceration rates of mental patients. All we can conclude is that *there is some evidence that mentally hospitalized persons have rates of conviction and imprisonment for crime higher than the general population and that these rates— like arrest rates—may be associated with demographic rather than clinical factors.*

III. "Mixed" Cases of Criminal Behavior and Mental Disorder

We have included in our consideration above those "pure" cases of persons treated for criminal behavior *or* for mental disorder. We consider now those "mixed" cases of persons treated simultaneously for criminal behavior *and* for mental disorder. This group consists of persons in four legal categories: incompetent to stand trial (IST), not guilty by reason of insanity (NGRI), mentally disordered sex offenders (MDSO), and prison-to-mental hospital transfer (Transfers). We shall accept the common summary term "mentally disordered offenders" to refer to all four categories, despite its technical inaccuracy (e.g. the ISTs and NGRIs have not been convicted and therefore are not adjudicated "offenders"). We recently have completed a review of empirical research on each of these categories (Monahan and Steadman 1982) and here focus only on the epidemiological questions of their rates of true and treated criminal behavior and mental disorder, both before and after their designation as "mentally disordered offenders." The studies we review in this section are summarized in table 4.

It should be noted at the outset that, despite widespread public and professional beliefs to the contrary (Burton and Steadman 1978), mentally disordered offenders constitute only a minuscule proportion of either the treated mentally ill or treated criminals. A survey of all

TABLE 4

Summary of Studies on "Mixed" Cases of Criminal
Behavior and Mental Disorder

Nature of the Relation to Mentally Disordered Offenders	Amount of Evidence	Findings Compared with Matched Groups in the General Population
A. True criminal behavior	Much	No higher
B. True mental disorder	None	—
C. Treated criminal behavior	Little	No higher
D. Treated mental disorder	Much	No higher

persons admitted to or residing in United States state and federal facilities as mentally disordered offenders in 1978 found a total of 20,143 admissions and a resident population of 14,140 (Steadman et al. 1982). These data are presented by legal status and gender in table 5. Given that 278,141 persons resided in United States prisons and 158,394 in United States jails on any given day in 1978 (Weis and Kenney 1980), "mentally disordered offenders" constituted only 3.2 percent of the institutionalized offender population. The President's Commission on Mental Health (1980) reported the resident population of state and county mental hospitals to be 191,391 in 1975 (the most recent year for which data were available). Mentally disordered offenders, therefore, composed 7.3 percent of the institutionalized mentally disordered population.

A. *The Relation between Treatment as a Mentally Disordered Offender and True Criminal Behavior*

Studies of arrest or self-reported crime among populations of mentally disordered offenders generally have been performed to validate the predictions of psychiatrists and psychologists that portions of these groups will exhibit criminality upon their releases. Prior arrest has been examined primarily as a correlate of subsequent arrest.

The first of these validation studies was that of Steadman and Cocozza (1974) on what have come to be known as the "Baxstrom patients." As a result of the United States Supreme Court decision in *Baxstrom v. Herold*, 383 U.S. 107 (1966), a group of 967 patients was transferred against psychiatric advice from maximum security hospitals run by the New York Department of Corrections to regular security state mental hospitals run by the Department of Mental Hygiene. The group comprised 67

TABLE 5

Admission and Census of Mentally Disordered Offenders in United States Facilities by Legal Status and Gender (1978)

Legal Status	Admissions				Census			
	Male	Female	Gender Un-determined	Total	Male	Female	Gender Un-determined	Total
Incompetent to stand trial	3,295	266	2,859	6,420	1,945	165	1,290	3,400
Not guilty by reason of insanity	847	127	651	1,625	1,863	285	992	3,140
Mentally disordered sex offenders	753	0	450	1,203	2,437	5	0	2,442
Mentally ill inmates External mental health units	5,323	261	64	5,648	2,510	122	52	2,684
Internal prison mental health units	5,061	186	0	5,247	2,334	140	0	2,474
Total	15,279	840	4,024	20,143	11,089	717	2,334	14,140

Source: Steadman et al. 1982.

percent Transfers from regular prison units, 20 percent ISTs, and 13 percent other legal statuses. A four-year follow-up of the patients found that, of those who were returned to the community, 20 percent were rearrested. McGarry and Parker (1974) also examined a group of patients in Massachusetts who were transferred to civil mental hospitals as a result of the *Baxstrom v. Herold* decision. Of their 108 patients ultimately released to the community, 15 (14 percent) were rearrested during an average of 14 months after release. A study closely allied to the two Baxstrom follow-ups was carried out by Thornberry and Jacoby (1979) on a group of 586 patients released as a result of *Dixon v. Attorney General*, 325 F. Supp. 966 (M.D.Pa. 1971), in Pennsylvania. The *Dixon* patients also were predominantly Transfers from regular prison units (52 percent), followed by ISTs (26 percent) plus civil commitments (13 percent), NGRIs (2 percent), and others (7 percent). Of those eventually released to the community, 24 percent were rearrested, with youthful age being the primary correlate of rearrest.

These rates of subsequent arrest for mentally disordered offenders (14–24 percent) are substantially higher than those reported for the general civil mental patient population. As noted above, for example, Steadman, Cocozza and Melick (1978) found the annual felony arrest rate for persons released from New York State mental hospitals in 1975 to be 9.8 percent. However, *all* the mentally disordered offenders, by definition, had been arrested at least once before their hospitalization. The comparable arrest rate for civil patients in the Steadman, Cocozza, and Melick (1978) study with one prior arrest was 13.8 percent. There is little doubt that many of the mentally disordered offenders had been previously arrested more than once. The arrest rate for civil patients with two or more prior arrests was 41.3 percent. The subsequent arrest rates for mentally disordered offenders (14–24 percent) therefore fall precisely within the range of the arrest rates for civil patients who had either one or multiple prior arrests (13.8–41.3 percent). This underscores the similarity between civil mental patients and mentally disordered offenders in terms of the demographic or criminological correlates of true criminal behavior (e.g. age, prior crime). None of these Baxstrom-type studies found a relationship between clinical factors (e.g. diagnosis) and arrest.

In addition to the *Baxstrom* and *Dixon* studies, Kozol, Boucher, and Garofalo (1972) provide often-cited data on the rearrest rates for violent crimes of persons evaluated as "sexually dangerous persons" in Bridgewater State Hospital in Massachusetts. Thirty-five percent of those released against professional advice and 8 percent of those released in accordance with it were rearrested for violent crimes. Numerous methodological problems preclude accepting these figures as evidence of psychiatric acumen (Monahan 1973). The point here is that these rates, even if accepted at face value, are not outside the range for civil patients matched for prior criminality.

Likewise, Steadman's (1977) study of patients/inmates at Maryland's Patuxent Institution—similar in many ways to Bridgewater—found that arrest rates after release varied between 60.4 and 74.3 percent, depending upon treatment status. Considering that between 69 and 90 percent of the various Patuxent groups had a history of prior arrest, averaging between 2.5 and 4.4 arrests per person, these figures are not surprising.

The Patuxent data are very similar to those reported by Steadman (1979) for a population of 411 males found incompetent to stand trial in New York State and eventually released into the community. Forty-four percent were rearrested. While this figure, like that for Patuxent, is much higher than the arrest rate for civil mental patients, 73 percent of these persons had been arrested before the offense for which they were found incompetent to stand trial. Twenty-two percent of those with no prior arrests, 39 percent of those with one prior arrest, 47 percent of those with two prior arrests, 48 percent of those with three to nine prior arrests, and 77 percent of those with nine or more prior arrests were subsequently arrested. Age, but not diagnosis, was also related to subsequent arrest.

Two studies provide subsequent arrest rates for persons found not guilty by reason of insanity. Morrow and Peterson (1966) found that 37 percent of NGRIs were rearrested within three years of their release. Pasewark, Pantle, and Steadman (1979a) found that 19.6 percent of NGRIs released from New York State hospitals between 1965 and 1967 were rearrested. These rates, while higher than those of civil mental patients, are lower than those just cited for persons incompetent to stand trial. Since other studies (Pasewark, Pantle, and Steadman 1979b) have found NGRIs to have more prior arrests than civil patients and fewer prior arrests than ISTs, these data fit the pattern we have observed elsewhere.

We conclude that *there is great variation in the subsequent arrest rates of different types of mentally disordered offenders, and that this variation closely corresponds to the prior criminal history and demographic characteristics of each group.*

B. *The Relation between Treatment as a Mentally Disordered Offender and True Mental Disorder*

There are no studies of the rates of diagnosable mental disorder among persons before or after their institutionalization as mentally disordered offenders. Nor have any community epidemiologic surveys followed persons identified as true cases of mental disorder to ascertain the proportion later treated as mentally disordered offenders.

In one sense, the question of true mental disorder at *the time* an individual is treated as a mentally disordered offender is rhetorical: had not someone diagnosed the individual as a true case of mental disorder, the adjudication of mentally disordered offender status could not have been made. The true prevalence rate of mental disorder among mentally disordered offenders, therefore, should be 100 percent.

The reliability and validity of these diagnoses of true mental disorder, however, are open to question. Thus, among a group of 260 persons admitted to Atascadero State Hospital in California after having been diagnosed and adjudicated to be "mentally disordered sex offenders," the most frequent diagnosis upon admission was "sexual deviation." As the authors of the report on these patients (Sturgeon and Taylor 1980, p. 42) note: "Significant pathology such as psychosis, retardation, or major affective disorders, usually found among mental hospital patients, is uniformly lacking within the [mentally disordered] sex offender population. Within the category of 'sexual deviation,' the specific diagnosis given usually coincided with the commitment offense. Thus, rapists were most frequently diagnosed as 'aggressive sexuality.' . . . Child molesters whose victims were female were most frequently diagnosed as 'female pedophilia.' "

Other findings questioning the "mental disorder" in some "mentally disordered offenders" can be found in Pasewark, Pantle, and Steadman (1979b) for NGRIs, Steadman (1979) for ISTs, and Monahan and Steadman (1982) for prison-to-mental hospital transfers. The extent to which the diagnosis of mental disorder is manipulated in these cases, or is based upon feigned symptomatology ("malingering"), is unknown.

C. *The Relation between Treatment as a Mentally Disordered Offender and Treated Criminal Behavior*

The same deficiencies in criminal justice reporting practices regarding information on conviction and incarceration that have dissuaded researchers from obtaining these data when studying "pure" crime or mental disorder are also salient in the investigation of "mixed" cases of crime and mental disorder. We have been able to locate only four studies with information on prior conviction or incarceration and only two addressing subsequent treated criminality.

Steadman and Cocozza (1974) found that 51 percent of the "*Baxstrom* patients*" had a prior conviction for murder, manslaughter, or assault. Seventy percent of these patients had been previously incarcerated, with a median of 2.2 incarcerations per offender.

Steadman (1977) reported that 77 percent of the inmates of the Patuxent Institution had prior convictions, and the mean number of prior incarcerations was 2.2 per offender. Steadman (1979), in the study on incompetent defendants described earlier, also found a high rate of prior convictions and incarcerations. The mean number of prior convictions for these incompetent defendants was 1.7 each (with almost twice as many of the indicted as the unindicted defendants having such a history). Previously unpublished data from this study show that 54 percent of the incompetent defendants had prior convictions and 46 percent had prior incarcerations.

Finally, the Sturgeon and Taylor (1980) study of mentally disordered sex offenders found that 57 percent had at least one prior conviction for a property crime, 39 percent for a sexual crime, and 10 percent for a nonsexual personal crime.

What are we to make of these four studies reporting rates of prior conviction for mentally disordered offenders from 51 to 77 percent and of prior incarceration from 46 to 70 percent? Unfortunately, not very much. Indeed, studies of the process of becoming designated as a mentally disordered offender suggest that it is precisely *because* one has a history of prior conviction or incarceration that one is found to be a mentally disordered offender in the first place. Konecni, Mulcahy, and Ebbesen (1980), for example, studying the process by which one is adjudicated a mentally disordered sex offender (MDSO) in California, found that the one factor that largely determined who was and who was not an MDSO was the existence of a prior history of sex-related criminal behavior. The longer the individual's record of prior sex crimes, the more likely he was to be diagnosed a "sexual deviant" by the examining psychiatrist and found to be an MDSO by the judge. To the extent that designation as a mentally disordered offender is a *function* of prior treatment for criminal behavior, one would, of course, find high rates of

prior treated criminality among mentally disordered offender populations. Perhaps the implicit reasoning here is that the failure of the
previous convictions and incarcerations to deter the individual from
crime is itself a sign of irrationality and hence a symptom of mental
illness.

In terms of the conviction and incarceration rates of persons after their
release from confinement as mentally disordered offenders, only two
of the studies discussed above provide information. Thornberry and
Jacoby's (1979) work on the *Dixon* patients found that 19 percent were
convicted and 6.7 percent incarcerated for crimes after their release into
the community. Since these patients averaged forty-seven years of age
and had been hospitalized an average of fourteen years at the time of
release, one would not expect their subsequent treated criminality to be
high. Sturgeon and Taylor (1980) found that 29 percent of the mentally
disordered sex offenders they studied were reconvicted of new crimes
(most frequently, sex crimes) within five years after their release from the
hospital. Comparison with a group of persons imprisoned in California
for sex crimes but not found to be MDSOs revealed that the "normal"
prisoners had higher rates of subsequent conviction for sexual crimes,
nonsexual personal crimes, and property crimes than the MDSOs.
Given the prison group's generally higher rates of prior convictions,
however, these differences in subsequent conviction rates are not surprising.

We would conclude only that *there is little data on the subsequent conviction or incarceration rates of mentally disordered offenders, but the data that do
exist are not inconsistent with what would be predicted from a knowledge of their
criminal history and demographic characteristics.*

D. *The Relation between Treatment as a Mentally Disordered Offender and Treated Mental Disorder*

Numerous studies provide estimates of the rates of mental hospitalization of persons both before and after they have been found to be mentally
disordered offenders.

Four studies have produced fairly consistent estimates of the prior
hospitalization rates of persons adjudicated not guilty by reason of
insanity. Morrow and Peterson (1966) found that 34 percent of their
NGRIs from Missouri had a history of prior hospitalization. Both Cooke
and Sikorski (1974) in Michigan and Pasewark, Pantle, and Steadman
(1979a) in New York found that 43 percent had been hospitalized before

NGRI adjudication. Finally, Pasework and Lanthorn (1977) reported that 48 percent of the male and 33 percent of the female NGRIs in Wyoming had a history of mental hospitalization.

Steadman's (1979) study of 539 male defendants in New York State adjudicated incompetent to stand trial found fully 82 percent with a history of prior hospitalization.

The *Baxstrom* (Steadman and Cocozza 1974) and *Dixon* (Thornberry and Jacoby 1979) studies, described earlier, included a variety of different types of mentally disordered offenders and found that 24 percent and 43 percent, respectively, had been previously hospitalized. Why these figures differ to the extent they do is unknown.

Halleck (1966) reported that 50 percent of the prisoners transferred from the Wisconsin State Prison to the Wisconsin State Hospital for the Criminally Insane had a history of mental hospitalization predating their imprisonment.

What we have, then, is considerable variability among types of mentally disordered offenders in terms of the rates of prior hospitalization, from a low of 24 percent for the *Baxstrom* patients (Steadman and Cocozza 1974) to a high of 82 percent for incompetent defendants (Steadman 1979). Most of the studies, however, report that between one-third and one-half of mentally disordered offender populations have a history of prior mental hospitalization. Persons found incompetent to stand trial tend to rank highest in terms of prior hospitalization, and persons found not guilty by reason of insanity tend to rank lowest.

A similar pattern—incompetents highest, NGRIs lowest—appears with regard to the subsequent hospitalization of mentally disordered offenders. Morrow and Peterson (1966) reported that 37 percent of their NGRIs in Missouri were rehospitalized, and Pasework, Pantle, and Steadman (1979a) reported that 22 percent of their New York NGRIs were rehospitalized. Mowbray (1979) in Michigan and Steadman (1979) in New York found that 55 percent and 44 percent, respectively, of the released NGRIs were rehospitalized.

As with previous hospitalization, the *Baxstrom* (Steadman and Cocozza 1974) and *Dixon* (Thornberry and Jacoby 1979) studies produced discrepant results, with 45 percent of the former group and only 16 percent of the latter being rehospitalized.

The subsequent hospitalization rate for mentally disordered offenders, therefore, has been found to vary between 16 and 55 percent, with an unweighted mean of 36.5 percent. Persons found incompetent to stand trial appear to be on the higher end of this range and persons not guilty by reason of insanity on the lower end.

These data are made difficult to interpret by a lack of knowledge about what effect the designation "mentally disordered offender" has on subsequent criminal justice system processing. If persons known by the police to have been institutionalized as incompetent, insane, and so forth, are discovered to have committed a new criminal act, do they tend, independent of their mental status at the time of the crime, to be *assumed* to be mentally disordered and hence wind up being rehospitalized rather than reimprisoned? If so, these data overestimate mental disorder at the same time that they underestimate criminality.

Given that approximately one-third to one-half of all mentally disordered offenders have been mentally hospitalized before their adjudication as mentally disordered offenders and that approximately one-third to one-half of all mentally disordered offenders are rehospitalized after release into the community, and given that prior hospitalization in "pure" civil mental patients is strongly related to their subsequent hospitalization (Fairweather et. al. 1969), we offer the hypothesis—the data are not strong enough to support a "conclusion"—that the *same factors that relate to the rehospitalization of civil mental patients also relate to the rehospitalization of mentally disordered offenders.*

IV. Conclusions

The overarching impression that remains after reviewing the vast array of existing epidemiological data on crime and mental disorder is that, when one makes the appropriate controls for demographic and anamnestic factors (e.g. prior patterns of institutionalization), rates of true and treated criminal behavior vary independently of rates of true and treated mental disorder. While the unadjusted crime rate of the mentally ill is indeed higher than that of the general population, and the unadjusted rate of mental disorder among criminals is indeed higher than among the general population, both relations tend to disappear when the appropriate statistical adjustments are made for age, social class, and prior exposure to the mental health and criminal justice systems.

Put another way, the correlates of crime among the mentally ill appear to be the same as the correlates of crime among any other group: age, gender, race, social class, and prior criminality. Likewise, the correlates of mental disorder among criminal offenders appear to be the same as the correlates of mental illness among other populations: age, social class, and previous mental illness. Populations that are characterized by the common correlates of crime and mental disorder (e.g. low social class) could be expected to show high rates of both, and they do.

While the available data on treated mental disorder are limited by the omission of information from private hospitals and from public or private outpatient clinics, we doubt that access to these sources would substantially affect this conclusion. Street criminals are unlikely to frequent private hospitals and clinics, and patients at private hospitals and clinics are likely to be from the social classes that are underrepresented among street criminals.

There is one interpretation of this review that we wish to fervently guard against. We have cross-tabulated rates of criminal behavior and rates of mental disorder among various *groups* in the population. We have not sought to examine the relation between crime and mental disorder within any given *individual* in those groups. *One must not commit the "ecological fallacy" in reverse.* From a finding that there is no relation between crime and mental disorder, in the aggregate, one cannot infer that no persons are both criminal and mentally disordered. Indeed, even if there were no relationship whatever between group rates of criminal behavior and group rates of mental disorder, one would expect the distributions to overlap at chance levels. That is, if X percent of a given population were mentally disordered, and there were *no* relation between mental disorder and criminal behavior, one would still expect X percent of the criminal population to be mentally disordered. The same is true for rates of mental disorder among criminals.

It is conceptually difficult, and often legally impossible, to address the existence of criminal behavior and mental disorder within the same individuals without invoking the concept of *causality*. The legal question, as in the insanity defense, is usually put as whether the criminal behavior was a "result" of the mental disorder. There appear to be three possible causal paths that may link crime and mental disorder in given individuals: (1) mental disorder may simply *coexist* with criminality, without having any causal significance, much as an offender may have a toothache without arousing suspicions of dental determinism; (2) mental disorder may *predispose* toward criminality, as in the case of M'Naghten's delusion that he was the victim of persecution by the prime minister of England; and (3) mental disorder may *inhibit* criminality, as catatonia would inhibit a person who otherwise would commit rape.

There can be little doubt that persons exist who "fit" each of these causal paths. The relative proportion of persons who fit each path is unknown. From the general pattern of the data reviewed here, however, one might infer that paths 2 and 3 are of approximately equal frequency and therefore cancel each other out when aggregated into group rates. In more statistical terms, the mean rates of mental disorder among offender populations may be quite similar to those among appropriately matched groups in the general population, while the variances may be much greater.

One would expect that providing effective psychiatric and psychological treatment to offenders who are mentally disordered would (1) have no effect on the criminal recidivism rate of those offenders for whom mental disorder and criminal propensities merely co-exist; (2) reduce the criminal recidivism rate of those offenders whom mental disorder predisposes toward crime; and (3) increase the criminal recidivism rate of those offenders for whom mental disorder inhibits crime. Only in the latter two groups would it be relevant to take criminal recidivism as a measure of treatment efficacy.

This is not, of course, to say that psychological technology can be effective in reducing the recidivism risk only of those offenders for whom mental disorder predisposes toward crime. It is to say that, if the effectiveness of therapeutic techniques is to be measured against the criterion of reduced criminal recidivism, those techniques should be targeted directly against recidivism, not against mental disorder as an intervening variable. There may, for example, be a small group of "psychotic rapists" for whom the cure of their psychosis will result in the cessation of their raping. But there may also be a much larger group of nonpsychotic rapists—or rapists for whom psychosis and criminal tendencies coexist without being causally related—for whom psychological techniques aimed directly at reducing recidivism (e.g. training in self-control and socially appropriate forms of making sexual requests) would prove effective. The use of such techniques, of course, would leave any existing mental disorder intact.

The finding that rates of crime and of mental disorder vary independently when adjusted for demographic and historic base rates may have more scientific than policy importance. From the policy perspective, the most important fact may be that, in the "naturally" occurring ecology of crime and mental disorder, demographic and historic factors are *not* controlled. Prison wardens attempting to deal with what they correctly perceive as an abundance of psychological pathology may take little comfort in the knowledge that it is the social class, rather than the criminal behavior, of their wards that puts them at greater risk of disorder. Nor will it do for the administrators of state mental hospitals, attacked by irate legislators for the high crime rate of people they release, to paraphrase Lester Maddox and say that what mental hospitals need is a better class of patients. It appears from the data we have assembled that if one could excise approximately half the population of state mental hospitals—those with prior arrest records—the remaining half of the patients would be no more criminal upon their release than the rest of us. How this can be done, however, without shipping many of these people to jails and prisons and thereby aggravating the problems of those institutions, the data do not say.

REFERENCES

Adams, James J. 1981. "Letter to the Editor," *American Journal of Psychiatry* 138:857.

Adams, Kenneth. 1980. "Former Mental Patients in a Prison and Parole System: A Study of Socially Disruptive Behavior." Mimeographed. Criminal Justice Research Center, Albany, New York.

American Psychiatric Association. 1980. *Diagnostic and Statistical Manual of Mental Disorders*. 3d ed. Washington, D.C.: American Psychiatric Association.

Ashley, M. C. 1922. "Outcome of 1000 Cases Paroled from the Middletown State Hospital," *State Hospital Quarterly* 8:64–70.

Baker, Susan P., and Park E. Dietz. 1979. "The Epidemiology and Prevention of Injury." In *The Management of Trauma*, 3rd ed., ed. G. D. Zuidema, R. B. Rutherford and W. F. Gallingee. Philadelphia: W. B. Saunders.

Bolton, Arthur. 1976. "A Study of the Need for and Availability of Mental Health Services for Mentally Disabled Jail Inmates and Juveniles in Detention Facilities." Mimeographed. Arthur Bolton Associates, Boston.

Bonovitz, J., and E. Guy. 1979. "Impact of Restrictive Commitment Procedures on a Prison Psychiatric Service," *American Journal of Psychiatry* 136:1045–48.

Borgira, Steven. 1981. "Psych-Team," *Reader—Chicago's Free Weekly*, 10 April, pp. 1–52.

Braithwaite, John. 1981. "The Myth of Social Class and Criminality Reconsidered," *American Sociological Review* 46:36–57.

Brill, H., and B. Malzberg. 1954. "Statistical Report on the Arrest Records of Male Ex-Patients, Age 16 or Over, Released from New York State Mental Hospitals during the Period 1946–48." Mimeographed. New York State Department of Mental Hygiene, Albany, New York.

Brodsky, Stanley L. 1973. *Psychologists in the Criminal Justice System*. Urbana: University of Illinois Press.

Burton, Nancy, and Henry J. Steadman. 1978. "Legal Professionals' Perceptions of the Insanity Defense," *Journal of Psychiatry and Law* 6:173–87.

California Bureau of Criminal Statistics and Special Services. 1980. *Criminal Justice Profile—1979*. Sacramento: California Department of Justice.

Cocozza, Joseph J., Mary Evans Melick, and Henry J. Steadman. 1978. "Trends in Violent Crime among Ex-Mental Patients," *Criminology* 16:317–34.

Cohen, L., and H. Freeman. 1945. "How Dangerous to the Community Are State Hospital Patients?" *Connecticut State Medical Journal* 9:697–700.

Cooke, Gerald, and Cynthia R. Sikorski. 1974. "Factors Affecting Length of Hospitalization in Persons Adjudicated Not Guilty by Reason of Insanity," *Bulletin of the American Academy of Psychiatry and the Law* 11:251–61.

Diamond, Bernard L. 1974. "The Psychiatric Prediction of Dangerousness," *University of Pennsylvania Law Review* 123:439–52.

———. 1981. "Letter to the Editor," *American Journal of Psychiatry* 138:857.

Dohrenwend, Bruce P., and Barbara S. Dohrenwend. 1969. *Social Status and Psychological Disorder: A Causal Inquiry*. New York: John Wiley.

Durbin, J. R., Richard A. Pasewark, and D. Albers. 1977. "Criminality and Mental Illness: A Study of Arrest Rates in a Rural State," *American Journal of Psychiatry* 134:80–83.

Fairweather, George W., D. H. Sanders, H. Maynard, and D. L. Cressler. 1969. *Community Life for the Mentally Ill: An Alternative to Institutional Care*. Chicago: Aldine.

Fracchia J., D. Canale, E. Cambria, E. Ruest, and C. Sheppard. 1976. "Public Views of Ex-Mental Patients: A Note on Perceived Dangerousness and Unpredictability," *Psychological Reports* 38:495–98.

Giovannini, J., and L. Gurel. 1967. "Socially Disruptive Behavior of Ex-Mental Patients," *Archives of General Psychiatry* 17:146–53.

Gove, Walter R. 1980. *The Labelling of Deviance*. (2d ed.) Beverly Hills, Calif.: Sage Publications.

Grove, William M., Nancy C. Andreasen, Patricia McDonald-Scott, Martin B. Keller, and Robert W. Shapiro. 1981. "Reliability Studies of Psychiatric Diagnosis: Theory and Practice," *Archives of General Psychiatry* 38:408–13.

Gunn, John. 1977. "Criminal Behavior and Mental Disorder," *British Journal of Psychiatry* 130:317–29.

Guze, Samuel. 1976. *Criminality and Psychiatric Disorder*. New York: Oxford University Press.

Halleck, Seymour. 1966. "A Critique of Current Psychiatric Roles in the Legal Process," *Wisconsin Law Review* 1966:379.

Helzer, John E., Lee N. Robbins, Mitchell Taibleson, Robert A. Woodruff, Theodore Reich, and Eric D. Wish. 1977a. "Reliability and Psychiatric Diagnoses. I. A Methodological Review," *Archives of General Psychiatry* 34:129–33.

Helzer, John E., Paula J. Clayton, Robert Pambakian, Theodore Reich, Robert A. Woodruff, and Michael A. Reveley. 1977b. "Reliability of Psychiatric Diagnoses. II. The Test/Retest Reliability of Diagnostic Classification," *Archives of General Psychiatry* 34: 136–41.

Heumann, Milton. 1978. *Plea Bargaining: The Experience of Prosecutors, Judges and Defense Attorneys*. Chicago: University of Chicago Press.

Hindelang, Michael J., Michael R. Gottfredson, and James Garofalo. 1978. *Victims of Personal Crime: An Empirical Foundation for a Theory of Personal Victimization*. Cambridge: Ballinger.

Hirschi, Travis, Michael Hindelang, and Joseph G. Weis. 1980. "The Status of Self-Report Measures." In *Handbook of Criminal Justice Evaluation*, ed. M. W. Klein and K. S. Teilmann. Beverly Hills, Calif.: Sage Publications.

Hollingshed, August B., and Frederick C. Redlich. 1958. *Social Class and Mental Illness*. New York: John Wiley.

Konecni, Vladimir, Jr., Erin M. Mulcahy, and Ebbe B. Ebbesen. 1980. "Prison or Mental Hospital: Factors Affecting the Processing of Persons Suspected of Being 'Mentally Disordered Sex Offenders.'" In *New Directions in Psychological Research*, ed. P. Lipsitt and B. Sales. New York: Van Nostrand Reinhold.

Kozol, H. L., R. J. Boucher, and R. F. Garofalo. 1972. "The Diagnosis and Treatment of Dangerousness," *Crime and Delinquency* 18:371–92.

Lagos, J., K. Perlmutter, and H. Saexinger. 1977. "Fear of the Mentally Ill: Empirical Support for the Common Man," *American Journal of Psychiatry* 134:1134–37.

Langner, Thomas S., and Stanley T. Michael. 1963. *Stress and Mental Health*. New York: Free Press.

Lemert, Edwin M. 1951. *Social Pathology*. New York: McGraw-Hill.

Levine, David. 1970. "Criminal Behavior and Mental Institutionalization," *Journal of Clinical Psychology* 26:279–84.

Logue, James N., Mary Evans Melick, and Holger Hansen. 1981. "Research Issues and Directions in the Epidemiology of Health Effects of Disasters," *Epidemiological Reviews* 3:140–62.

McGarry, A. Louis, and Lawrence L. Parker. 1974. "Massachusetts Operation Baxstrom: A Follow-up," *Massachusetts Journal of Mental Health* 4:27–41.

Massachusetts Department of Mental Health. 1980. "Department of Mental Health Correctional Study Summary." Unpublished report.

Melick, Mary Evans, Henry J. Steadman, and Joseph J. Cocozza. 1979. "The Medicalization of Criminal Behavior among Mental Patients," *Journal of Health and Social Behavior* 20:228–37.

Menninger, Karl. 1928. "Medicolegal Proposals of the American Psychiatric Association," *Journal of Criminal Law, Criminology and Police Science* 19:367–73.

Monahan, John. 1973. "The Psychiatrization of Criminal Behavior: A Reply," *Hospital and Community Psychiatry* 24:105–7.

———. 1981. *The Clinical Prediction of Violent Behavior*. Washington, D.C.: U.S. Government Printing Office.

———. 1982. "Three Lingering Issues in Patient Rights." In *Patient Rights and Patient Advocacy: Issues and Evidence*, ed. B. L. Bloom and S. Asher. New York: Human Sciences Press. Forthcoming.

Monahan, John, Cynthia Caldeira, and Herbert D. Friedlander. 1979. "The Police and the Mentally Ill: A Comparison of Arrested and Committed Persons," *International Journal of Law and Psychiatry* 2:509–18.

Monahan, John, and Henry J. Steadman. 1982. *Mentally Disordered Offenders: Perspectives from Law and Social Science*. New York: Plenum. Forthcoming.

Morrow, W. R., and D. B. Peterson. 1966. "Follow-up on Discharged Offenders 'Not Guilty by Reason of Insanity' and 'Criminal Sexual Psychopaths,'" *Journal of Criminal Law, Criminology and Political Science* 57:31–34.

Mowbray, C. T. 1979. "A Study of Patients Treated as Incompetent to Stand Trial," *Social Psychiatry* 14:31–39.

Neugebauer, Richard, Bruce P. Dohrenwend, and Barbara S. Dohrenwend. 1980. "Formulation of Hypotheses about the True Prevalence of Functional Psychiatric Disorders among Adults in the United States." In *Mental Illness in the United States: Epidemiological Estimates*, ed. Bruce P. Dohrenwend, Barbara S. Dohrenwend, Madelyn S. Gould, Bruce Link, Richard Neugebauer and Robin Wunsch-Hitzig. New York: Praeger.

Nunnally, J. C. 1961. *Popular Conceptions of Mental Health: Their Development and Change*. New York: Holt, Rinehart and Winston.

O'Keefe, John. 1980. "Massachusetts Department of Mental Health Correctional Study Summary." Mimeographed. Massachusetts Department of Mental Health, Boston.

Olmstead, Donald W., and Katherine Durham. 1976. "Stability of Mental Health Attitudes: A Semantic Differential Study," *Journal of Health and Social Behavior* 17:35–44.

Pasewark, Richard A., and B. W. Lanthorn. 1977. "Disposition of Persons Utilizing the Insanity Plea in a Rural State," *Journal of Humanics* 5:87–98.

Pasewark, Richard A., Mark L. Pantle, and Henry J. Steadman. 1979a. "The Insanity Plea in New York State 1965–1976," *New York State Bar Journal* 51:186–225.

————. 1979b. "Characteristics and Disposition of Persons Found Not Guilty by Reason of Insanity in New York State, 1971–1976," *American Journal of Psychiatry* 136:655–60.

Pollock, H. H. 1938. "Is the Paroled Patient a Threat to the Community?" *Psychiatric Quarterly* 12:236–44.

President's Commission on Mental Health. 1980. *Report for the President*. Washington, D.C.: U.S. Government Printing Office.

Rabkin, Judith G. 1979. "Criminal Behavior of Discharged Mental Patients: A Critical Appraisal of the Research," *Psychological Bulletin* 86:1–27.

Rabkin, Judith G., and Arthur Zitrin. 1982. "Antisocial Behavior of Discharged Mental Patients: Research Findings and Policy Implications." In *Patient Rights and Patient Advocacy: Issues and Evidence*, ed. B. L. Bloom and S. J. Asher. New York: Human Sciences Press. Forthcoming.

Rappeport, Jonas R., and G. Lassen. 1965. "Dangerousness–Arrest Rate Comparison of Discharged Patients and the General Population," *American Journal of Psychiatry* 121:776–83.

————. 1966. "The Dangerousness of Female Patients: A Comparison of the Arrest Rate of Discharged Psychiatric Patients and the General Population," *American Journal of Psychiatry* 123:413–19.

Roth, Loren. 1980. "Correctional Psychiatry." In *Modern Legal Medicine, Psychiatry and Forensic Science*, ed. W. Curran, A. McGarry, and C. Petty. Philadelphia: Davis.

Schuckit, Marc A., Gerard Herrman, and Judith A. Schuckit. 1977. "The Importance of Psychiatric Illness in Newly Arrested Prisoners," *Journal of Nervous and Mental Disease* 165:118–25.

Schur, Edwin M. 1980. "Comments." In *The Labelling of Deviance*, 2d ed., ed. Walter R. Gove. Beverly Hills, Calif.: Sage Publications.

Scull, Andrew T. 1977. *Decarceration, Community Treatment and the Deviant: A Radical View*. Englewood Cliffs, N.J.: Prentice-Hall.

———. 1981. "A New Trade in Lunacy: The Recommodification of the Mental Patient," *American Behavioral Scientist* 24:741–54.

Shinnar, S., and R. Shinnar. 1975. "The Effects of the Criminal Justice System on the Control of Crime: A Quantitative Approach," *Law and Society Review* 9:581–611.

Skodol, Andrew E., and Toksoz B. Karasu. 1978. "Emergency Psychiatry and the Assaultive Patient," *American Journal of Psychiatry* 135:202–5.

Sosowsky, Larry. 1978. "Crime and Violence among Mental Patients Reconsidered in View of the New Legal Relationship between the State and the Mentally Ill," *American Journal of Psychiatry* 135:33–42.

———. 1980. "Explaining the Increased Arrest Rate among Mental Patients: A Cautionary Note," *American Journal of Psychiatry* 137:1602–5.

———. 1981. "Letter to the Editor," *American Journal of Psychiatry* 138:858.

Steadman, Henry J. 1977. "A New Look at Recidivism among Patient Inmates," *Bulletin of the American Academy of Psychiatry and the Law* 5:200–209.

———. 1979. *Beating a Rap? Defendants Found Incompetent to Stand Trial*. Chicago: University of Chicago Press.

———. 1981. "Critically Reassessing the Accuracy of Public Perceptions of the Dangerousness of the Mentally Ill," *Journal of Health and Social Behavior* 22:310–16.

Steadman, Henry J., and Joseph J. Cocozza. 1974. *Careers of the Criminally Insane*. Lexington, Mass.: Lexington Books, D. C. Heath.

———. 1978. "Selective Reporting and the Public's Misconceptions of the Criminally Insane," *Public Opinion Quarterly* 41:523–33.

Steadman, Henry J., Joseph J. Cocozza, and Mary Evans Melick. 1978. "Explaining the Increased Arrest Rate among Mental Patients: The Changing Clientele of State Hospitals," *American Journal of Psychiatry* 135:816–20.

Steadman, Henry J., and Richard Felson. 1981. "Differences in Self-Reported Aggression and Physical Violence among Ex-Mental Patients, Ex-Offenders and the General Population." Mimeographed. New York State Office of Mental Health, Albany.

Steadman, Henry J., John Monahan, Eliot Hartstone, Sharon K. Davis, and Pamela Clark Robbins. 1982. "Mentally Disordered Offenders: A National Survey of Patients and Facilities," *Law and Human Behavior*. In press.

Steadman, Henry J., and Steve Ribner. 1980. "Changing Perceptions of the Mental Health Needs of Inmates in Local Jails," *American Journal of Psychiatry* 137:1115–6.

Steadman, Henry J., Donna Vanderwyst, and Steven Ribner. 1978. "Comparing Arrest Rates of Mental Patients and Criminal Offenders," *American Journal of Psychiatry* 135:1218–20.

Sturgeon, Vikki, and John Taylor. 1980. "Report of a Five Year Follow-up Study of Mentally Disordered Sex Offenders Released from Atascadero State

Hospital in 1973," *Criminal Justice Journal of Western State University, San Diego* 4:31–64.

Swank, G. E., and D. Winer. 1976. "Occurrence of Psychiatric Disorder in a County Jail Population," *American Journal of Psychiatry* 33:1331–33.

Szasz, Thomas S. 1978. "Nobody Should Decide Who Goes to the Mental Hospital," *Co-evaluation Quarterly*, summer, pp. 56–59.

Tardiff, Kenneth, and Attia Sweillam. 1980. "Assault, Suicide, and Mental Illness," *Archives of General Psychiatry* 37:164–69.

Thornberry, Terence P., and Joseph E. Jacoby. 1979. *The Criminally Insane: A Community Follow-up of Mentally Ill Offenders.* Chicago: University of Chicago Press.

United States Department of Justice. 1978. *National Jail Survey.* Washington D.C.: U.S. Government Printing Office.

Warren, Carol A. B. 1981. "New Forms of Social Control: The Myth of Deinstitutionalization," *American Behavioral Scientist* 24:724–40.

Weis, J., and J. Kenney. 1980. "Crime and Criminals in the United States." In *Criminology Review Yearbook*, vol. 2., ed. E. Bittner and S. Messinger. Beverly Hills, Calif.: Sage Publications.

Wolfgang, Marvin. 1978. "An Overview of Research into Violent Behavior." Testimony before the Committee on Science and Technology, U.S. House of Representatives.

Wolfgang, Marvin, Thorsten Sellin, and Robert Figlio. 1972. *Delinquency in a Birth Cohort.* Chicago: University of Chicago Press.

Zitrin, Arthur, Anne S. Hardesty, Eugene I. Burdock, and Ann K. Drossman. 1976. "Crime and Violence among Mental Patients," *American Journal of Psychiatry* 133:142–49.

Robert M. Mennel

Attitudes and Policies toward Juvenile Delinquency in the United States: A Historiographical Review

ABSTRACT

During the past decade, the history of juvenile delinquency has attracted considerable scholarly attention. This reflects both the recent popularity of social history and the desire of some historians to become involved in the policymaking process. Generally, interpretations have emphasized the social-control motives of the founders of institutions and the juvenile court while portraying the delinquents themselves as victims of social and economic discrimination. Recent research has neglected case studies and the comparative approach. Several recent works have uncovered some popular support for institutions and shown American policies, at least in the nineteenth century, to be less disadvantageous than European formulations. These studies have also stressed the significant differences between programs and institutions in the United States. Future research can profitably examine the post–World War II era, focusing particularly on the influence of legal changes, professional study, and government policy on programs and institutions. Scholars undertaking this work can make their contributions more useful by declining to view themselves as policymakers.

The American juvenile justice system remains a topic of national concern. Peter Prescott's *The Child Savers* (1981), a bleak portrait of the New York City Family Court, is the latest in a long series of indictments. A representative sampling might include Howard James, *Children in Trouble* (1970), Albert Deutsch, *Our Rejected Children* (1952), Clifford Shaw, *The Jack-Roller* (1930), and John Peter Altgeld, *Our Penal Machinery and Its Victims* (1886) and perhaps might begin with Elijah Devoe's 1848 exposé of the New York House of Refuge. Prescott popularizes the principal policy implication of sociological labeling theory, that is, that the more fortunate youths were those who slipped off the official blotter and

Robert M. Mennel is Professor of History at the University of New Hampshire. The preparation of this essay was aided by a grant from the Central University Research Fund of the University of New Hampshire.

escaped future treatment. Traditionally, scholars and reformers who have condemned one approach have always had a new institution or mode of treatment on hand. Thus, critics of congregate reform schools promoted cottage and farm schools. Scientists distrustful of the determinism of Lombrosian criminology advocated psychological study. Even today, most of us resist the notion that little can be done or, even worse, that institutions and programs have been created in the knowledge that they will fail. We would rather think of juvenile delinquency as a symptom of larger disjunctions and inequalities in American life, of problems thus far unsolved but not insoluble.

This critical but hopeful spirit has animated the "new" social history that has been the vogue of the profession in the 1960s and 1970s. The fundamental premise, epitomized by Tamara K. Hareven, ed., *Anonymous Americans: Explorations in Nineteenth-Century Social History* (1971), was that historians had ignored "ordinary" people and vulnerable or disadvantaged groups such as women, children, and minorities. Traditional history was also indicted for minimizing ideological conflict in order to persuade readers of the benevolence and indispensability of existing institutions and power relationships. The novelty of this perspective has been questioned. More than fifty years ago, Charles and Mary Beard's *The Rise of American Civilization* exalted common people and castigated "robber barons," while Mary Beard's collection of documents, *America through Women's Eyes* (1933), helped inaugurate women's history. The Beards, however, were mavericks in a small, genteel profession, whereas contemporary social historians occupy dominant positions in a vastly larger and more complex enterprise. The difference is important and has implications for writing on the history of delinquency and correctional institutions.

The American Historical Association's recent survey of historical writing (Kammen 1980) reveals a specialized and increasingly compartmentalized discipline. One is amazed by the variety of research but sobered by the fact that a growing number of chronological and topical experts communicate more within subgroups than among them. In this context the history of crime and delinquency is but a chapter of social history. I prefer to think of it as a wave—a separate entity yet one that is inextricably connected to other topics such as the history of law, social welfare, education, and the family. Understanding of the origins of the concept of juvenile delinquency, for example, owes much to Bernard Bailyn's *Education in the Forming of American Society* (1960), which linked institutional development of all sorts to the effect of socioeconomic forces upon family government in the late eighteenth century. Thus, historians have been attracted to the topic of delinquency because of its interstitial qualities. As scholars, it challenges them to utilize a wide range of related historical work. As potential reformers, it offers a means of cooperation with presentist and policy-oriented social scientists who share their view that history is a tool to promote change. An illustrative way to date the beginning of the current era may be to note the simultaneous appearance in 1960 of Cloward and Ohlin's *Delinquency and Opportunity* (1960), a cornerstone of the War on Poverty, and Griffen's *Their Brothers' Keepers: Moral Stewardship in the United States, 1800–1865* (1960), which stressed the social control motives of urban elites responsible for the first wave of asylums, prisons, and reform schools.

This essay examines historical works on juvenile delinquency and juvenile correctional institutions. Since the literature, with several notable exceptions, is not widely known, section I briefly notes the principal scholars and includes a paragraph about my own background. Section II identifies some general characteristics and conceptual problems of contemporary scholarship. For the rest of the essay, I have adopted an approach that is both chronological and analytical. Section III begins with a discussion of interpretations of the origins and treatment of juvenile delinquency in the nineteenth century. The advent of the juvenile court is a natural midpoint (section IV), and challenges to the benevolent purposes of the court in the 1960s and the concomitant deinstitutionalization movement form section V. In crossing this terrain, I hope to offer the reader a summary view of developments, indicate interpretive controversies, and also suggest opportunities and strategies for future research.

I. Scholarship

The most prominent American historian focusing upon juvenile delinquency is David Rothman, whose two volumes, *The Discovery of the Asylum* (1971) and *Conscience and Convenience* (1980), relate definitions and institutional expressions of criminal justice, juvenile justice, and mental health to the major changes in American society from the colonial era to the eve of World War II. My own work, *Thorns and Thistles: Juvenile Delinquents in the United States, 1825–1940* (Mennel 1973b), is narrower in scope but attempts a similar transit. Joseph Hawes, *Children in Urban Society: Juvenile Delinquency in Nineteenth Century America* (1971), is yet more confined and episodic, though it does include a chapter on juvenile delinquency in children's literature.

Several studies develop their effect by utilizing the case study approach: Robert Pickett, *House of Refuge: Origins of Juvenile Reform in New York State, 1815–1854* (1969), is self-explanatory. Anthony Platt's *The Child Savers: The Invention of Delinquency* (1977a) studies child-saving philanthropy in late-nineteenth-century Chicago as a preface to an explanation of the beginning of the Illinois juvenile court, the first of its kind; Steven Schlossman, *Love and the American Delinquent: The Theory and Practice of "Progressive" Juvenile Justice, 1825–1920* (1977), follows a general analysis of doctrine with a detailed examination of the Wisconsin system and the early juvenile court in Milwaukee; Jack Holl, *Juvenile Reform in the Progressive Era: William R. George and the Junior Republic Movement* (1971), investigates an important private institution that attempted to reform children by requiring them to participate in a model "free enterprise" system. Miriam Langsam, *Children West: A History of the Placing out System of the New York Children's Aid Society, 1853–1890* (1964), examines the leading example of anti-institutional reformism. Michael Gordon, *Juvenile Delinquency in the American Novel, 1905–1965* (1971), surveys a variety of scenarios.

Assessment of the juvenile court is an important aspect of the studies cited above and has attracted separate attention as well. Ellen Ryerson, *The Best Laid Plans: America's Juvenile Court Experiment* (1978), is a general study of reformer's attitudes, while Charles Larsen, *The Good Fight* (1972), recounts the life of Ben Lindsey, America's most famous juvenile court judge.

These represent only the major studies. Examples of related works include documentary collections (Abbott 1938; Bremner 1970–74; Sanders 1970), articles (Fox 1970; Mennel 1980a, 1980b; Parker 1976a, 1976b; Teeters 1960; Wohl 1969; Zuckerman 1976), dissertations (Brenzel 1978; Pisciotta 1979; Schupf 1971; Stack 1974; Stewart 1980; Wirkkala 1973); studies with major chapters on delinquency (Katz 1968; Leiby 1967; Levine and Levine 1970); and the principal works of earlier generations (Beaumont and Tocqueville 1835; Brace 1872; Burleigh and Harris 1923; Folks 1902; Healy 1915; Hurley 1907; Reeves 1929; Shaw 1929; Snedden 1907; Thomas 1923; Thrasher 1927; Thurston 1942; Van Waters 1925; Wines and Dwight 1867, 1880).

My research interest developed from participation in the Child and State Project directed by Robert H. Bremner of Ohio State University. This work, funded by the federal government and administered by the American Public Health Association, took its name and inspiration from Grace Abbott's two-volume documentary history (1938) covering most aspects of child-state relations. The new volumes, *Children and Youth in America: A Documentary History* (Bremner 1970–74), represented a thorough restudy and expansion of the original. I edited the juvenile delinquency documents and in the process gathered material for my dissertation (Mennel 1969), which was expanded to *Thorns and Thistles* (Mennel 1973b).

II. Historiographical Issues

Michael Ignatieff's thoughtful article (1981) on the historiography of punishment raises basic issues that can help shape consideration of this topic as well. His dialectic begins with Whiggish accounts that portray the creation of systematic law codes and penitentiaries as the enlightened activity of altruistic citizens who eventually triumphed over the foul conditions and "barbaric" punishment characteristic of the medieval period and early modern age. The reformers' accomplishments were described as monuments to their benevolent intent and also harbingers of future and presumably equally reformative programs. In the 1960s, historians joined others in questioning the wisdom of some of these initiatives (psychosurgery and behavior modification, for example) and in reflecting doubts about "the size and intrusiveness of the modern state." Ignatieff notes, "The prison was thus studied not for itself, but for what its rituals of humiliation could reveal about a society's ruling conceptions of power, social obligation and human malleability" (Ignatieff 1981). Of late, however, "antirevisionists" or "counterrevisionists" have appeared on the scene to attack these accounts "for over-schematizing a complex story, and for reducing the intentions behind the new institution to conspiratorial class strategies of divide and rule." Counterrevisionism, charges Ignatieff, "abdicates from the task of historical explanation altogether," since it "merely maintains that historical reality is more complex than the revisionists assumed, that reformers were more humanitarian than revisionists made them out to be, and that there are no such things as classes." The task of future research thus becomes the development of a historiography "which accounts for institutional change without imputing conspiratorial rationality to a ruling class, without reducing institutional development to a formless *ad hoc* adjustment to contingent crisis, and without assuming a hyper-idealist, all triumphant humanitarian crusade."

Ignatieff's essay challenges revisionists including himself ("a former though unrepentant member of the revisionist school") to undertake their future research on the basis of a renewed appreciation for the volitional bases of human activity. Revisionists should question their faith that "the state enjoys a monopoly of the primitive sanction, that its moral authority and practical power are *the* binding sources of social order and that all social relations can be described in the language of power and domination." Ignatieff dismisses "counterrevisionists," generally identified as authors of case studies of French and English institutions, because they minimize the significance of the penitentiary by stressing local resistance to the rationalist ideas that produced it. Future history will be accomplished by revisionists who have seen the light.

The historiography of delinquency runs parallel to Ignatieff's account in some respects. There was a period when historians linked nineteenth-century institution founding and certainly the juvenile court to the march of American progress (Faulkner 1931; Tyler 1944). And certainly the predominant emphasis of 1960s scholarship reflected the egalitarian values and social anger of that era. The coerciveness of the elites who founded the institutions is stressed, and sympathy for the children designated delinquents is widespread. The titles of the monographs convey the message. Who "loves" a delinquent? No one. What happens to the "best laid plans"? They go astray, of course. What did the "child savers" do? They "invented" a pathology. Also like Ignatieff's scholars, historians of juvenile delinquency seldom venture beyond 1940. Whether this stems from the general tendency of the discipline to relegate the recent past to journalism or from the proliferation and complexity of government programs and professional study is impossible to say. The paucity of work is clear, however, and makes a trenchant analysis such as John Moore's article (1969) on early federal policy all the more valuable.

There have also been substantial disagreements between scholars of delinquency. Rothman's review (1974) of my book and Platt's review (1977b) of Schlossman's illustrate the sharp tone of the debate. Scholarly dialogue has been limited. My study commends certain approaches, particularly the environmentalism of the early children's aid societies and the Chicago sociologists of the 1920s. "Tony" Platt, editor of *Crime and Social Justice*, regards variations between programs expressing the nature or the nurture philosophy as less significant than the controlling inequalities of capitalist society. These are differences between a moderate and a radical, but Platt probably views the gap as unbridgeable.

Platt, Rothman, and others have acted upon their convictions and become involved in preventive work. David and Sheila Rothman, for

example, are codirectors of the Project on Community Alternatives for
the mentally disabled. These are commendable efforts. But in the dominant ahistoricism of contemporary life, the historian/policymaker faces a
dilemma beyond the bureaucratic frustrations and resource problems
common to most social programs. To illustrate: Prescott's study (1981)
bears the same title as Platt's, originally published in 1969 and revised
in 1977. This shows bad manners but is not surprising. The modern
world has little time for historians. The point here is that historians can
make their most useful contribution by writing better history. How then
should this be done?

In contrast to Ignatieff, I suggest that the demanding task is to "merely
maintain" the complexity of historical reality. To do so, the historian
must be primarily concerned with shaping the data of the past into a
plausible representation of reality. The important skills are preciseness
in describing events, sensitivity to distinctions, fairness in appraising
individuals and groups, and enthusiasm in collecting and relating material. These count more than assertiveness or conviction in propounding a
particular view. Such an approach does not require, in the case at hand,
the conclusion that reformers were humanitarian or that social classes
were illusory. Nor does it pretend to objectivity in the manner of
Leopold von Ranke and the German school of the late nineteenth century. We are the products of our own age and will surely reflect it in our
writing. But we must protest this fact. For, just as Horace Mann
proclaimed himself the lawyer of the next generation, so historians are or
should be the lawyers for generations gone by. Theory can be helpful in
addressing this work, but it must always be ready to yield to the
experiences of people who are now dead.

From this perspective there are two major shortcomings that
characterize the historical literature on juvenile delinquency: (1) the
failure to utilize the comparative approach, (2) the shortage of comprehensive case studies linking institutions and programs to the society
that produced and sustained them. The reasons for these deficiencies are
not hard to find. The language skills of American historians, never great,
have followed the general downward trend of recent years. Even studies
of European subjects written in English are ignored. Although there
have been several case studies, they are vulnerable to the objection that
they are unrepresentative. For the incipient policymaker, generalizations on the national level are important. Consequently, the preferred
method is to gather a few facts and opinions on many programs rather
than to accept the inherent contingency of the case study in exchange for

the possible reward of an understanding that is both concrete and illustrative.

III. The Nineteenth Century

Let us start by summarizing the inception of efforts to define and treat juvenile delinquency. The term itself was almost never used before 1800 because public authorities relied upon family government to correct or at least contain children who misbehaved or committed crimes. Early law codes and commentaries, such as Blackstone's, recognized mitigating circumstances for accused children, but the purpose of these statutes was not to exonerate or to categorize youthful wrongdoing but to sustain the family-based system of discipline. Colonial laws commanded parents to punish their children so that court officials would not have to intervene. By the late eighteenth century, however, the ability of family government to serve as the keystone of social control came to be doubted as villages developed into commercial towns and cities and as work left the home for the shop and factory. Families could no longer absorb vagrant youths as servants and apprentices. The children of poorer families left home, or were cast loose, to seek their way as deprived individuals. They became the source material for new definitions of crime, poverty, and juvenile delinquency.

The initial definers were established male citizens of the major East Coast cities, New York, Philadelphia, and Boston. Their sense of duty as well as their fear of impoverished, unfamiliar faces and anonymously committed crime led them to create a variety of institutions—almshouses, insane asylums, penitentiaries. They hoped these would not only isolate troublesome and indigent individuals but also provide them with the habits necessary to function as law-abiding individuals in a volatile capitalistic society.

Neglected and delinquent children were the objects of special attention because their behavior was more likely to be viewed as the product of environmental stimuli than as a sign of innate depravity. The basic fear was that children who were convicted of crimes suffered corruption by mixing with adult criminals, as did children who were released by sympathetic judges and juries. Thus, special institutions for children proliferated. These were first called houses of refuge, then reform schools, to indicate emphasis upon the growing enthusiasm for common schooling in the mid-nineteenth century. As this occurred, the concept of juvenile delinquency was born and began to come of age. Beyond describing the criminal and vagrant status of certain children, it announced the institutions that would correct, educate, and socialize apart from the ministrations of family government.

A word about the institutions themselves. The houses of refuge and many of the early reform schools were organized on a congregate basis; that is, the children lived in cells or large dormitories and followed rigid schedules based upon contract labor in central workshops. Surrounded by high walls and characterized by harsh discipline, the refuges resembled the adult penitentiaries of the day. After lengthy incarcerations, the children were considered trained "for usefulness" and were released or apprenticed, the boys to local artisans and farmers, the girls to domestic service. The proliferation of these institutions in the mid-nineteenth century was marked. In 1867, Wines and Dwight noted seven state reform schools outside of New York and local refuges and reform schools in nine eastern and midwestern cities. By 1900 all states and major cities outside the Deep South had boys' reform schools and, in most cases, separate institutions for girls as well.

By this time an alternative strategy for preventing delinquency had developed. Epitomized by the work of Charles Loring Brace and his New York Children's Aid Society (1853), this approach emphasized noninstitutional solutions such as placing out. Brace agreed with reform-school founders that the temptations of the volatile urban environment were the basis for delinquency, but, unlike them, he believed that children were born with a disposition to do good and hence did not require lengthy incarceration. "The best of all asylums for the outcast child is the *farmer's home*," said Brace, and until the agrarian depression of the late 1880s he sent railroad cars full of "street arabs" to the western states.

Brace's ideas found institutional expression with the opening of the Massachusetts Industrial School for Girls (1856) and the Ohio Reform Farm (1857). The cottage or family plan reformatory, with its agrarian location and routine and its "elder brothers," "elder sisters," or surrogate parents supervising youths divided into "families," became the dominant type of reform school in the late nineteenth century. The family organization maintained its popularity even when vocational programs shifted from farm chores to industrial training in the twentieth century.

The end result was hardly a smooth-running system. Institutionalists and advocates of placing out bickered constantly. Nativist Protestants expressed their preferences, thus hastening the development of Roman Catholic institutions. Delinquent girls did institutional housework and often were sexually abused when placed out. Negro children were initially more fortunate, since few institutions accepted them. Once admitted, they were usually segregated. By the Civil War, several institutions had experienced rioting and incendiarism, which usually began in the workshops where contract labor encouraged exploitation.

But it was a legitimized system. Institution founders and public authorities successfully defended themselves against the claims of parents who regarded reform schools and children's aid societies as usurpers of family government. In the precedent-setting decision *Ex Parte Crouse* (4 Wharton 9, Pennsylvania [1838]), the Pennsylvania Supreme Court denied the attempt of a father to free his daughter on a writ of habeas corpus from the Philadelphia House of Refuge saying, "The right of parental control is a natural, but not an inalienable one. . . . The infant has been snatched from a course which must have ended in confirmed depravity; and, not only is the restraint of her person lawful, but it would be an act of extreme cruelty to release her from it."

Historians' accounts of these developments are deficient in several respects. They gloss over the colonial era, describing the rudimentary state of institutions but relating this mainly to the still-powerful Calvinist ideology that resisted the concept of malleable human nature. They utilize the comparative method, but only to indicate the presence of seemingly similar reform activity in Europe; American institutions are usually presented as indigenous responses to the physical and social mobility of the Jacksonian era.[1] Also, scholars tend to rely upon the social control desires of elites as a sufficient causal explanation, and this blurs the variety of the institutional impulse. Of course these generalizations cannot be uniformly applied. Rothman (1971) and Mennel (1973b), for example, treat the colonial period, but in summary form. Neither gives concrete illustrations of shifting patterns of crime and family life that might have set the stage for institution building. Schlossman (1974, 1977) relates reform schools to emerging instrumentalist definitions of education, law, and even polite advice literature. The general criticisms hold, however, and can be best demonstrated by referring to a variety of studies and sources in addition to the principal monographs.

---

[1] "Jacksonian reform" is one of those phrases that historians casually accept and shouldn't. Few of the individuals who built reformatory instititutions supported Jackson; many more viewed his vigorous individualism as a prime cause of social disorder (Mennel 1973b). Furthermore, scholars do not use presidents' names to characterize reform in later periods. "Lincolnian" sounds awkward, as does "Rooseveltian," which is confusing as well. "Jacksonian" is euphonious, elastic (from the Battle of New Orleans to the Mexican War), but not very helpful to the matter at hand.

The colonial period is thinly treated because family history has become, in good measure, the property of colonial scholars, hence "warning out" modernists. Lawrence Stone's recent survey (1981) shows the increasing complexity of the subject and the intensity of its application in the pre-1800 era. He summarizes that, while the family was a key mediator in the change from traditional to modern society, it displayed a variety of types, by class, region, and religious affiliation, substantially limiting efforts to reach general conclusions. The difficulty peculiar to the study of delinquency is that the literary evidence is heavily weighted toward memoirs of genteel family life, thus favoring the definers of social problems and founders of institutions and relegating the inarticulate— that is, the clients and inmates—to demographic accounts.

This barrier may be more apparent than real. A number of studies (Ariès 1965; Bremner 1970–74; Jones 1938; Laslett 1965; Pinchbeck and Hewitt 1969–73) have confirmed important trends such as the decline of household-based apprenticeship and the proportionately increasing number of unattached young wage laborers living in cities, all of which precipitated planning for schools, missions, and houses of refuge. Moreover, the accounts of the elite bear closer reading, since they link the anxieties of affluent parents about their own children to their fears about the children of the poor. Allan Horlick (1975) has used such materials to show how New York businessmen of the 1840s, reflecting both the uncertainties of their own climb to power and the difficulty of limiting the aristocracy of the next generation to young men who endorsed charitable activity, created remedies and screening groups in the form of moralistic literature and the YMCA. The memoirs of the men who founded the first houses of refuge demonstrate that they conceived of the institutions as serving not only the court system but also a broad range of families who requested or were offered their assistance as patriarchs and neighbors (Pickett 1969; Mennel 1980a). The refuge founders placed substantial authority in the hands of the superintendents, whose conduct they expected would further exemplify their ideal of a society cemented by patriarchal families. The neighborhood orientation and local scope of the institutions (only New York and Philadelphia had refuges), as well as their quasi-public organization (state chartered but privately managed and funded by combinations of donations and public revenues), suggest a limited comparison with English institutions such as the Philanthropic Society's reformatory (1788) in London (Carlebach 1970; Heale 1976; Owen 1964; Pinchbeck and Hewitt 1969–73).

The Anglo-American connection, as illuminated by family history, provides an additional way to demarcate the first years of definition and treatment.

In the later nineteenth century, the increasing number and variety of institutions made more apparent, though it did not originate, philosophical differences on the nature and requirements of childhood. Even the management of the refuges alternated between proponents of Benthamite rationalism, who drew their inspiration from the disciplinary routines of the penitentiaries, and advocates of the Swiss pedagogue Johann Pestalozzi, who believed that children were unique individuals who became socialized by appeals to their inherently good sentiments and thoughts (Lewis 1965; Mennel 1973b; Pickett 1969; Schlossman 1977; Slater 1970). The rationalists prevailed in the refuges, but the romantic ideal, fueled by religious evangelicalism, reappeared in the family reform schools and childrens' aid societies and also animated other reform activity such as the urban missions (Banner 1973; Langsam 1964; Rosenberg 1971; Smith 1957; Sutherland 1976; Wohl 1969).

The differences between silent obedience and emotional allegiance to adult values may appear moot to some contemporary observers, but they mattered greatly to nineteenth-century people and thus appeared in related facets of American life. The trend toward instrumentalism in law, for example, reflected the rationalist faith that human conduct could be improved by public policy (Horwitz 1971; Schlossman 1974). The growing genre of children's literature increasingly portrayed the young as disposed toward the path of virtue and receptive to confirmation through adult kindness and personal attention (Kiefer 1948; Wishy 1968). Education, like juvenile reform, stood at the crossroads. Many urban schools, with their hierarchical monitorial systems and emphasis upon rote learning and compulsory attendance, displayed the social control philosophy (Kaestle 1973; Kaestle and Vinovskis 1980; Katz 1968; Lazerson 1971). But in other schools the influence of Horace Mann's ideas liberated students and teachers alike from the narrow curriculum and harsh discipline of the colonial past, and they responded eagerly to the possibilities of learning (Cremin 1961; Messerli 1973). Reform school founders conceived of their institutions as midpoints between the common school and the penitentiary. They rejected serious offenders and utilized both rationalist and romantic approaches in their attempt to change young people (Fox 1970; Mennel 1973b).

The significance of early reform schools is best revealed in a comparative setting. Pedagogues such as Horace Mann and Henry Barnard publicized the development of European institutions, giving special prominence to two family schools: Johann H. Wichern's Rauhe Haus, founded in Hamburg in 1833, and Frederic A. DeMetz's "La Colonie Agricole" in Mettray, France (1839). American institution founders visited to study their agricultural routines and the cottage organization where "elder brothers" utilized various combinations of merit badges, military drill, singing, and close personal supervision to seek the allegiance of the *colóns* to the values of their keepers. The transfer of techniques is interesting, but the comparative approach is most informative in noting differences and omissions. In the 1850s, for example, western states often ignored European innovations and copied the congregate institutions of the East, while even those who undertook pilgrimages to Mettray or Hamburg did so with only hazy knowledge of Mann's or Barnard's work (Foucault 1978; May 1973; Mennel 1980a, 1980b; Thavenet 1976).[2]

I used the comparative perspective in a case study of the Ohio Reform School for Boys (1857), one of the first cottage and farm institutions. The "Farm" was organized with reference to Mettray and other European schools, but differed from them in operation and reformatory goals. In Ohio, literacy and individual attainment were encouraged; nearly all of the entering boys could read, and half could write and cipher. Most could do all three upon release. They also had the opportunity to participate in dramatics and both solo and group singing. Education at Mettray was limited to thirty minutes a day and spent mostly on reading the catechism. Dramatics were not peformed, and the boys were allowed to sing only as a group. Released *colóns* were often illiterate or could only read. Former Mettray inmates were carefully placed, usually in the army or in menial farm labor with families other than their own. They were then kept in these positions by the supervision of local notables or the military. Ohio boys were usually released to the care of parents or friends or left to their own devices; farm labor apprenticeships were regarded as confining. The parents of American delinquents were treated permissively in another respect. Local committing jurisdictions did not pursue them to pay individual maintenance costs despite administrative and legislative injunctions to do so. European, especially En-

[2]The low rate of emigration from France to the United States contributed to the fact that Mettray was never well understood. The Rauhe Haus fared better because it was known in the Lutheran settlements where Wichern's umbrella organization, die Innere Mission, was active. However, these communities were themselves fairly well insulated from the non-German-speaking community.

glish, institutions forced parents to contribute to institutional income (Carlebach 1970; Mennel 1980a, 1980b; Pinchbeck and Hewitt 1969–73).

Institutional hierarchies and sociopolitical allegiances also present striking constrasts. At Mettray, all officers were trained, with a classical education, at the institution's Ecole Préparatoire. *Colóns* could serve as monitors (*frères âinés*) but could not aspire to higher positions. Ohio "elder brothers" were not required to have special training. Inmates could and did achieve these positions, and a few even became superintendents of other institutions. The chief obstacle to such advances was the disposition of superintendents and trustees to hire their own friends and relatives. European institutions underwrote hereditary power and privilege. Wichern consistently supported the German monarchy, while DeMetz demonstrated his loyalty by sending a contingent of *colóns* to help the national guard crush the republican forces in the revolution of 1848. On the other hand, boys and officers from the Ohio Reform Farm joined the Union army in large numbers, in part because they opposed slave-owning (Mennel 1980a, 1980b; Muller 1976; Shanahan 1954).

The comparative method helps to show some of the salient characteristics of American institutions. Americans took selective readings of European schools, purposefully or unintentionally ignoring their hierarchical characteristics and lauding their agricultural routine and small-group organization. But this is what one should expect from a country where social relations were dynamic, where urbanism was a growing but disagreeable trend, and where racism and nativism coexisted with dedication to the ideal of equal opportunity.

The further significance of American reform schools is that they were broadly publicized and, at least at first, popularly supported. Ohio Farm annual reports were printed in German and English and summarized in local newspapers. Didactic children's literature and journals of education spoke well of the institutions but also used them to caution their juvenile audience. There was only minor political opposition to the founding of the schools; in the sea of turmoil that was Ohio politics in the 1850s, the reform school was an island of consensus. During the first two decades of operation there was a waiting list, and large numbers of parents and guardians committed their own children. Boys who were released, and even some who escaped, wrote letters on their own volition praising the institutions. Discharge papers were valued because they "proved character." In the early 1870s there was even an alumni association that returned for an annual picnic (Mennel 1980a, 1980b).

What this suggests is not that reform schools were idyllic retreats, but that they may have met the needs of a variety of people, not all of whom were founders of institutions. Other scholars have contended the same thing about the juvenile court, and John Hagan has noted that truly unpopular social control movements, such as Prohibition, are repealed (Hagan 1980; Schlossman 1977; Schultz 1973). Paul Boyer's recent study (1978) has urged us to be sensitive to nineteenth-century reformers who sought to defuse broad-based fears of disorder that gained their lethal force from combining with equally popular suspicion of institutional solutions. The reform school's opponents were not academicians but country people ("Jacksonians") who regarded them as "soft" boarding schools. Labor groups complained about the contract system, while agricultural organizations such as the Patrons of Husbandry refused to cooperate with the farm reform schools because they were afraid that the status of farming would be degraded (Mennel 1980a, 1980b; Pickett 1969).

Eventually, of course, the institutions lost whatever value they had as redemptive agencies. The reasons are various. Gradual though grudging popular acceptance of industrialization secured the workshop as an organizational form and limited the development of farm schools. Workshops had been sore points from the beginning, especially when outside contractors were used. But even though the institution staff ran the shops by the 1880s, the rate of work-related death and injury continued to increase, and most fires were set there (Mennel 1973b; Pickett 1969; Rothman 1971). Thomas Bender has related the changing character of charity societies to the passing of the generation of founders who had daily contact with the presumed objects of their beneficence. Their successors, perhaps because they tended to accept more easily the prevalent social divisions, relied upon paid subordinates to organize the daily work (Bender 1975). The same trend was evident in reform schools, where the demands for routinized operation were even greater. Superintendents and staff increasingly functioned as buffers, which meant keeping the children in, since the outside world no longer viewed the institutions as novelties (National Conference of Charities and Correction 1893). Serious politicians and distinguished foreign visitors like Alexis de Tocqueville and Charles Dickens no longer came to call. However, the schools did serve occasionally as party spots for sporting trustees and state legislators. Reform school officials, emulating their superiors, began to insulate themselves from their inmates. Attendance at summer schools and charity conferences came to count more for

advancement than time spent with the children. The Ohio superintendent visited the Rauhe Haus and proclaimed his allegiance to its warm
personal style and humble cottages. To implement this ideal, he requested an appropriation to build large Gothic residence halls and an
administration building, thus permitting the demolition of the original
farm cottages.[3]

Conflict continued, but the institutions endured. And why not? Their
rise had occurred in a society where economic and social change had
rendered ambiguous the scope and authority of existing institutions,
particularly the patriarchal family. In their early careers, the schools had
accomplishments to be proud of, and even in decline they served as
conveniences that society was unwilling to abandon. But they were
blatant advertisements for social control, inappropriate for a society that
increasingly valued elaborate though unspecific warnings, particularly
to the young. Thus the opposition that began to form came less from the
inmates and their parents than from the young middle-class men and
women who promoted a more decentralized system, one that promised
broader though less intense surveillance as well as the opportunity to
apply social and psychological therapies. This interpretation has
stressed popular acceptance of the institutions and of gradual efforts to
change them and suggests that recent studies have overemphasized the
power and coerciveness of those who founded and managed the schools.

Before discussing the juvenile court and its influence, special mention
should be made of two research areas: local studies on crime, order, and
police and works on female delinquency. Recent crime and police studies
have excelled in analyzing the ecology and etiology of lawbreaking and
disorder (Johnson 1973, 1979; Lane 1967; Laurie 1973; Monkkonen
1975; Richardson 1970; Schneider 1980). Boys and young men appear
here as gang members and fire laddies, some of whom were surely sent to
institutions. But examination of reform school records reveals that only a
minority of inmates arrived via local criminal courts. County common
pleas and probate courts were more likely venues, and disputes within
families were often precipitating factors (Mennel 1980b). Local court
studies could clarify the extent to which courts and institutions served
families seeking to commit their children or citizens fearing crime and
disorder. The implication is that gangs, particularly when they were

---

[3]European institutions such as Red Hill (the Philanthropic Society's home), Mettray,
and the Rauhe Haus have retained or replicated their original buildings. At Mettray the
church occupies the central place reserved for the administration building in American
reform schools.

affiliated with local political organizations, may have been able to protect their members from classification as delinquents, while young people who conflicted with their parents and had no peer groups to support them were prime candidates for reform school.

The relative scarcity of recent studies on the history of female delinquency (Manton 1976; Brenzel 1975, 1978; Schlossman and Wallach 1978) may be explained in part by the challenges they pose on perplexing and controversial issues in the writing of women's history. On the one hand, to the degree that institutions confined women and girls on morals charges, they require censure, since these were unpunished male offenses. But criticism must be tempered for several reasons. First, as Barbara Brenzel has shown (1978, 1980), the schools did provide a degree of care and protection for homeless and abused girls. Second, and more important, women administrators took charge of female institutions in the late nineteenth century, which may be interpreted as a sign of progress in the narrative of women's history.

A complicating factor, raised though certainly not encompassed by female reform schools, is the meaning of sexual behavior. Homosexuality and lesbianism were regular features of life in juvenile institutions. After 1900, a few adult female reformatories had permissive attitudes toward lesbian relationships (Freedman 1981). In general, however, extraordinary efforts were made to suppress sexual activity, of which there was plenty. The matron at the Western House of Refuge (New York) complained that she could not prevent black and white girls from "[getting] together in bed." An 1891 investigation of the Ohio Reform School discovered many boys with venereal sores on the mouth and noted the superintendent's practice of personally applying a blistering fluid to the sexual organs of boys who were caught masturbating (Mennel 1973b, 1980b). Historians might profitably relate adult attitudes to the imperatives of the economy, which condoned gluttony and overdressing while frowning upon sex and desire. The trick is to convey the ways contemporary mores encouraged as well as dampened libidinal drives and to do so without succumbing to the vogue of intimate self-revelation and imposing one's own preferences upon the reader.

IV. The Juvenile Court
The first juvenile court opened in Illinois in 1899, and the idea spread rapidly to other states; by 1912 twenty-two states had passed juvenile court legislation, and all but two had done so by 1932. In one sense the court represented the culmination of efforts to reform children without

committing them to reform school or sending them to jail. The Illinois law combined the concept of probation, first developed in Massachusetts (1869), where children's aid societies supervised children who were awaiting trial or who had been sentenced, with several New York laws providing for separate trial sessions and detention facilities. As courts developed their own probation staffs, detention homes, and investigative services, the reform schools were relegated to places of "dernier resort," in the words of one superintendent (Mennel 1972).

The juvenile court was more than a systematic alternative to incarceration, however; Jane Addams claimed that it signified "almost a change in mores." She referred not only to the legal innovations but also to the fact that the court's leverage—that is, its administrative power to gather case histories and its generally urban location—made it a key weapon in the Progressive campaign to get government to assume a greater responsibility for social welfare (Flexner and Baldwin 1912; Lou 1927). The social and psychological facts about the children appearing before the court offered the most compelling evidence for the adoption of child labor laws, mothers' pensions, municipal playgrounds, compulsory school attendance, public health care for children, and rigorous regulation of tenement-building. Thus the popularity of the juvenile court derived in some measure from the fact that it served as a laboratory for the professional study of delinquency. Theoretical works based on empirical research flourished, with the ecological approach of the University of Chicago sociologists and the psychological studies of William Healy becoming ancestors of the type. In the daily operation of the court, this trend was manifested in the eclipse of voluntary probation officers by civil service professionals trained in the "art" of gathering desired information and supervising a client population (Levine and Levine 1970; Lubove 1965; Mennel 1973b).

An important result of this activity was to rescue the *parens patriae* doctrine from the reform schools, where its credibility was being seriously undermined. By expressing a preference for diagnosis and probation, the court implicitly downgraded incarceration, yet retained it as a judicial option. Court decisions soon ratified the new arrangement. *Commonwealth v. Fisher* (213 Pennsylvania 48 [1905]), a decision upholding the parental character of the Pennsylvania juvenile court, became the most often cited precedent, concluding, "the legislature surely may provide for the salvation of . . . a child, if its parents or guardians be unable or unwilling to do so, by bringing it into one of the courts of the state without any process at all, for the purpose of subjecting it to the state's guardianship and protection."

The court did not lack criticism even in its early days (Eliot 1914). This stemmed mostly from its imprecise, encompassing jurisdiction, a situation that was addressed by the development of family and domestic relations courts. Occasional studies such as Sheldon and Eleanor Glueck's *One Thousand Delinquents* (1934) faulted the effectiveness of the court and its agencies but did not question the institution's benevolent intent. After World War II, however, a number of investigations accused local and state governments of not providing entitled services to wards of the court. In time, legal decisions ratified this disillusion by according children who appeared in court most of the rights of adults accused of crimes (Bremner 1970–74; Mennel 1973b).

Research on the modern era is complicated by a new obstacle but characterized by traditional defects. Confidentiality of records poses the additional problem. Archivists and institution officials are understandably edgy about providing access to the records of living persons. Of course they must also take into account the possibility of objections from descendants of nineteenth-century delinquents. In either case, the scholar's promise to use pseudonyms or initials can sometimes allay official doubts. As noted earlier, however, the importance of the issue is deflated because few historians are interested in the case study approach, which makes the heaviest demands upon archival holdings where confidentiality is likely to be a consideration. Rather, they are content to sample published works from a variety of locations and generalize therefrom. These points can be illustrated by referring to the literature.

We begin with the exception that proves the case. Stephen Schlossman's *Love and the American Delinquent* (1977) is the most useful study because of its case study orientation. Schlossman uses court and institution records to systematically link the failures of the Wisconsin reform school to the later flounderings of the Milwaukee Juvenile Court and to put both into the context of the larger reform movements of their times. Thus the cottage school was connected to the domestic advice literature of Lydia Maria Child and Catharine Beecher, which sanctified the family as a refuge against social and economic disorder. And the juvenile court, like the playground movement, mothers' pensions, and home economics programs, reflected the greater optimism of the Progressive era. All of the latter were designed to strengthen and discipline the families of the poor with minimal reference to institutional sanctions.

Yet, as Schlossman notes, the court no less than the institution set aside "affectional discipline" in favor of a more expeditious approach. The detention center became a jail, and judges browbeat children and punished them for offenses unrelated to those that brought them into court. Reformatory and court authorities showed little interest in establishing personal relationships with the children but eagerly counted as successes those who dropped out of sight. These officials, Schlossman emphasizes, were not members of a status-conscious local elite but rather shared the disadvantaged origins of their clients (Schlossman 1977).

The only incongruous note is Schlossman's conclusion that a child-centered approach, epitomized to him by Ben Lindsey's Denver Juvenile Court, is possible. Schlossman's evidence, however, sketches fundamentally shallow and manipulative adult personalities clearly incapable of effecting such a transformation. The contradiction may not be that serious. Lindsey was a master of public relations, as much absorbed in the creation of his own image as a crusader as in spending time talking to children. Like "Daddy" George, founder of the George Junior Republic ("nothing without labor"), he gave affection to people of all ages in the course of a life filled with many interests. What set Lindsey apart was his insatiable curiosity and encompassing humanity, rare traits in any field of endeavor. But he did share some of the less attractive characteristics of Schlossman's little-known court authorities (Holl 1971; Larsen 1972; Mennel 1973b).

Like Schlossman, David Rothman is concerned with the rift between humanitarian rhetoric and neglectful practice. He utilizes conscience and convenience to describe the division in order to emphasize the pridefulness of early twentieth century reformers, particularly their faith that the new social and behavioral sciences would provide a theory of treatment based upon "individual justice." Convenience signifies the ease with which political and bureaucratic interests frustrated these ideals. Rothman shares with Schlossman (and with the reform school and juvenile court founders themselves) a belief that the downward direction of historical change is not inevitable, though neither is specific about desirable therapies or about strategies for institutionalizing them. Ryerson, reflecting the more limited view of the juvenile court implicit in the *Gault* decision (*In Re Gault*, 387 U.S. 1 [1967]), is more cautious but, like Rothman and Schlossman, believes that somewhere in the vast array of delinquency prevention programs is one that not only works but can be generally applied (Rothman 1980; Ryerson 1978; Schlossman 1977).

This faith is commendable in that it encourages at least the mention of various programs extant in given periods. It resists the determinism characteristic of other accounts such as Anthony Platt's *The Child Savers* (1977a) and Christopher's Lasch's *Haven in a Heartless World* (1977). Platt's analysis of child-saving philanthropy in late nineteenth century Illinois caricatures the role of middle-class women from Hull House who helped to create the first juvenile court, presenting them as agents of corporate capitalism primarily intent on diminishing the civil liberties and privacy of lower-class and immigrant youth. Lasch portrays social workers and psychologists as absorbed in creating therapeutic jargon in order to secure themselves as professional groups by making their audiences expert-dependent. Both of these works deny altruism as a cause of welfare activity. Lasch's, however, is more interesting, since it documents a strain of intolerance among professional groups advocating egalitarian social policies (Lasch 1973, 1977). De Tocqueville first made this connection after observing Jacksonian democracy. Lasch is intrigued by the hostility of most social scientists to the suggestion that their work, even when publicly supported, may contribute little to the diminution of crime, delinquency, and mental illness.[4]

Rothman's work deserves separate treatment here since it is the best known. *Conscience and Convenience* has a moderate appearance, being neither as harshly skeptical as Lasch and Platt nor as partial to early social workers and juvenile court proponents as a number of studies (Chambers 1963, 1971; Davis 1967; Leiby 1967; Trattner 1968). But Rothman is unpersuasive, at least insofar as his treatment of delinquency is concerned, because he does not utilize the relevant work of other scholars or respect the complexity of his subjects' thoughts and actions.[5] For example, Rothman presents the psychologist G. Stanley Hall as a key influence in the development of the juvenile court because of his supposed enthusiasm for individual case study and environmental causa-

[4]See also Henrika Kuklick's review of a related work, Burton J. Bledstein, *The Culture of Professionalism* (1976), *Journal of American History* 68 (1981):152–53. Richard Sennett, *Families against the City* (1970), a study of one middle-class Chicago neighborhood's reaction to the Haymarket Massacre (1886), illustrates yet another determinism. On the basis of extremely limited evidence, Sennett contends that demands for more police protection came mainly from nuclear families who had isolated themselves from the diversity of the city as extended families had not.

[5]The same has also been said about his discussion of mental health. See Gerald Grob's review of *Conscience and Convenience* in *Commentary* 70 (1980):75–77. See also Gerald N. Grob, "Abuse in American Mental Hospitals in Historical Perspective: Myth and Reality," *International Journal of Law and Psychiatry* 3 (1980):295–310.

tion. But a reading of Dorothy Ross's excellent though difficult study (1972) shows Hall's greatest interest to be the development of a neo-Darwinist philosophy of human development in which youthful misbehavior was a "stage" that could be little influenced by institutions. And Miriam Van Waters, the foremost figure in female corrections from 1920 to 1950, walked out of Hall's seminar after disputing his contention that a prostitute was a "type" (Mennel 1973b).

Rothman's discussion of Dr. William Healy, founder of the first mental hygiene clinic for juvenile court children, best illustrates the problem. To Rothman, the essence of Healy's representativeness was his aimless experimentalism. Supposedly, Healy dabbled with Freud but propounded no particular psychological theory in amassing *The Individual Delinquent* (1915), the book for which he is best known. This may be a proper charge to level against someone who was styling himself as a social psychologist, but Rothman has an obligation to discuss the term. Healy was clearly influenced by the studies of George Mead and Charles Cooley, who rejected the determinisms of Freud and John B. Watson and described the self as originating both in the social process and in the images that the individual constructed of other persons and objects. The premise of *The Individual Delinquent* was that human behavior was shaped largely by the self-concept the individual acquired from society. Moreover, as John Burnham has shown (1961), Healy's work marked the beginning of a more open-ended approach to the scientific study of delinquency by repudiating the monocausism of eugenicists and Lombrosian criminologists. Healy himself had first studied delinquents by taking anatomical measurements to see whether youthful offenders conformed to Lombroso's description of the born criminal. Finally, Healy's lukewarm Freudianism developed later, after the Glueck's study (1934) reported a high rate of recidivism among children treated at the Judge Baker Center (Boston) where Healy was director. This cast general doubt upon the usefulness of community mental health clinics, a movement popularized by Healy in the 1920s, and thus encouraged him to stress the familial causes of delinquency (Mennel 1973b).

Rothman's incomplete analysis of Healy's ideas is matched by his failure to probe the broader significance of the Judge Baker Center's mediocre record. No thorough study of the subject exists, but it is not difficult to speculate on the quality of the relationship that existed between the Protestant psychologists from the center and the Roman Catholic judges, politicians, and social workers in the Boston Juvenile

Court.[6] How were they supposed to react to the demand of Augusta Bronner, Healy's lifelong collaborator and second wife, for greater authority to remove delinquent children from their homes in order "to make over unworthy or stupid parents, to teach them the principles of child psychology, to alter in very fundamental ways a considerable share of mankind"? In Rothman's narrative, Catholic aid societies exist mainly to play cooperative roles (as they did in the Chicago Juvenile Court) in the emergence of the powerful secular state. His disinclination to discuss the recrudescent character of religious and cultural conflict is ironic, since his own style resembles the jeremiad of the Puritan preacher. For the mid-twentieth-century believer, therapy replaces religion to sustain the faithful in an error-prone world and nurtures the possibility that they may inherit the earth. Nothing dates Rothman's work more than the contemporary revival of interest in the religiocultural bases of life.

Rothman makes some interesting points but generally does not follow through with sustained analysis. He notes, for example, that district attorneys favored the juvenile court because it uncluttered their calendars. To what degree was this so? Rothman does not pursue this issue or related questions such as the role of local bar associations in the formation and operation of the court. On another subject, he establishes that reformatory superintendents favored military drill over psychiatric treatment as the prime agent of reform. Rothman sees this preference as a reflection of their army careers but also as a necessity, given low staff wages that attracted purportedly unskilled applicants. A complete discussion, however, would probe the connection between reform schools and military enlistment and note the high esteem that military forces then enjoyed. Doubtless some of the reform school staff were former enlisted men and therefore skilled in teaching calisthenics and drill. Morris Janowitz (1978) has noted that war and peacetime drafts were important integrators of American society in the fifty years before Vietnam. Reformatory institutions complemented this development in a minor way. The point here is not to praise reform school militarism but to explain it in the context of earlier twentieth century history instead of judging it from the inclinations of the age of therapy.

The strangest thing about Rothman's book is that it contains no analysis at all of the crime and delinquency studies of the Chicago school

[6]Morris J. Vogel, *The Invention of the Modern Hospital: Boston, 1870–1930* (Chicago: University of Chicago Press, 1980), discusses the conflict between Protestant trustees of Boston City Hospital and Irish ward politicians.

of sociology. Clifford Shaw's Chicago Area Project (1934) stressed the inevitability of delinquency in slum areas and the need to channel the energies of delinquent gangs into legitimate community and neighborhood groups that could apply pressure for better services on municipal and state welfare bureaucracies (Shaw and McKay 1942). This approach influenced a later generation of planners, especially those organizing the Community Action Programs in the War on Poverty (Marris and Rein 1973). One would think that Rothman might want to search out other anti-institutional enthusiasts even though his own interests focus upon mental patients rather than delinquent gangs.

Chicago sociologists were also great believers in the importance of the delinquent youth's own account of his life and troubles, with Shaw's *The Jack-Roller* (1930) being the model of the type. Contemporary social scientists and historians, by contrast, are interested mainly in clinical case histories, which is a pity since the major autobiographies of delinquents are among the more revealing documents of modern times. Brendan Behan's *Borstal Boy* (1959), an acid portrayal of the class hatreds embedded in British reformatory policy, can profitably be compared with the endorsement of Borstals by Healy and Benedict Alper (1941), which shows how Americans, who refused to acknowledge the existence of social classes, expressed opinions about them. The accounts of Josiah Flynt Willard (1908) and Jean Genêt (1966) are equally shattering in their effect because they put society rather than the individual youth under the microscope.

To conclude, the reader interested in gaining a comprehensive understanding of the origins of modern delinquency programs ought to supplement the accounts mentioned above with more general histories of social welfare activity. Trattner's biography (1968) of the social-work executive Homer Folks and Chambers's biography (1971) of Paul Kellogg, editor of the *Survey*, show reformers with broad interests, reflective attitudes toward their own policies, and distrust of panaceas, such as eugenics, that minimized human capacity to change. Allen Davis's study (1967) of the settlement house movement presents young men and women, often with sheltered upbringings, motivated by their compassion for the trials of recent immigrants and their confidence that the new biological and statistical sciences could improve urban life for everyone. The juvenile court was but one part of this hope, and, like related causes (child labor and consumer protection laws, etc.), it suffered from the general disillusion with social explanation that flowed from World War I and its aftermath. Roy Lubove (1965) traces this shift within social work as early practitioners defined the profession on the basis of social diagnostic skills, but later created an internal hierarchy enshrining psychoanalytic case work as "queen" in the 1920s. In all of these studies we see life through the eyes of decades other than our own and can easily imagine that some delinquents fared better than others.

V. Recent Study

Several histories touch one aspect or another of delinquency policy in the era since World War II, but there has been no interest comparable to earlier periods. The Bremner documents provide summary coverage to the early 1970s, and two political studies perceptively analyze the tangled underbrush of congressional study and Great Society policy (Bremner 1970–74; Marris and Rein 1973; Moore 1969). Some works discuss various social and psychological theories but suffer from limited knowledge of the range of therapies and of the particular reasons for the popularity of any one approach (Finestone 1976; Levine and Levine 1970; Ryerson 1978). As I noted earlier, the lack of interest may be attributed in part to disciplinary inhibitions and to the overwhelming volume and variety of programs encouraged by a welfare state that continued to expand until 1980.

There may be another, more significant reason for the lack of scholarly activity. In recent years the definition and treatment of delinquency has been most influenced by the alteration of the juvenile court following the *Gault* decision and by the growth of diversion programs predicated upon broad professional distrust of institutions. By conveying to juveniles most of the standards and safeguards of criminal law, *Gault* and related decisions undercut the court's reputation, which was both valid and hyperbolic, as a humanitarian agency. This reduction in authority was accelerated by the prevalent assumption of many community-based programs that delinquents were not guilty of crimes but were victims of social and economic deprivation (U.S. President's Commission on Law Enforcement and Administration of Justice 1967). The relevant point is that both developments accorded with the transcendental mood of historical scholarship in the late 1960s and 1970s. Current reticence, therefore, may derive from the fact that one generation's panaceas have not worked.

Why not? A standard reply is that they were never tried. The antipoverty initiatives of the Great Society were buried in Vietnam and the Middle East, and a series of conservative administrations ensured that there would be no resurrection. Such an explanation exemplifies what Charles Sanders Peirce called the method of tenacity, that is, settling doubt by adhering without reflection to original premises. A more flexible method of inquiry hints at uncomfortable truths. For example, the United States Comptroller General's Report (1975), detailing the failures and corruption of federal antidelinquency programs, would not surprise the student of early federal policy. Miriam Van Waters's report for the National Commission on Law Observance and Enforcement (1931) outlined the cruelty and neglect suffered by youthful violators of federal law. Moreover, any appraisal of recent federal programs, particularly in the area of children's rights, ought to recognize that their libertarian character left a mixed legacy. Formal rights were conveyed, but alternative policies based upon economic redistribution were frustrated.

The fundamental premise of libertarian reform was that families, group homes, and peer groups would provide suitable alternatives to the discredited courts and institutions. In fact, the family became libertarianism's most prominent victim, since the philosophy's basic expression was the quest for individual authenticity in the marketplace. In the study of social problems, this meant the atomistic proliferation of "fields" of study. The subjects were serious enough—child abuse, "parenting," and so forth—but the investigative results were often either obvious or wrong. Additionally, to the degree that study was animated by the desire to make professional status a universal social goal, it put heavy pressure on families who dissented from it. The historians' culpability here is compounded because they gave deinstitutionalization a glamorous gloss by idealizing the colonial period because of its reliance upon family government.

Disillusion, deceit, and now political opposition have flowed inexorably from the contradictions of Great Society programs. Thus Margaret Rosenheim's *Justice for the Child* (1962) became *Pursuing Justice for the Child* (1976), expressing the increasing tentativeness of veteran social investigators. Malcolm W. Klein has noted (1979) that evaluations of programs designed to keep children out of institutions have shown that the programs develop strategies ("net widening" is the operative term) to maintain their client populations, presumably at the level necessary to secure continued funding. And surely, the Reagan administration's proposed policy of block-granting many social programs is based in part upon belief that sociological study may exacerbate rather than solve life's problems. The bet is that state and local governments agree and will fund programs whose constituent demands (day care and centers for the elderly, for examples) are more pressing than those of the advice-giving industry.

There is no cause for celebration here. We currently lack only the assurance of a high government official that the administration is not "antiyouth" to know for certain that valuable programs as well as dubious research will be eliminated. Indeed, the new age arrived before the 1980 election, with many states passing laws lowering the age and increasing the number of offenses for which juveniles could be sent to criminal court. The new conservatism appears harsher than that of Potter Stewart and Warren Burger, whose dissenting opinions in the *Gault* era were based upon the belief that conveying constitutional safeguards to youthful lawbreakers was less important than providing the juvenile court more resources to fulfill its mandate.

Popular reaction to forthcoming reductions in government services is still uncertain, but there is agreement that a half-century of growth in federal and state programs has ended. Historians may or may not be apprehensive about future developments, but they generally welcome watersheds because these help to organize and explain significant blocks of time. Some scholars regard periods mainly as conveniences, but others take seriously Hegel's injunction that the importance of things becomes apparent at the moment of their disappearance—or, as he put it, the Owl of Minerva flies only at dusk. The fact of flight should encourage historians to explore the recent past. Why did psychological study enjoy such a vogue in the 1940s and 1950s? To what extent did institutions incorporate psychoanalytic techniques? Did the revival of social theory in the 1960s make a similar impact? How did the two approaches interact at various levels of government and within particular institutions? In answering these and related questions, historians should utilize case studies, biographies, and the comparative approach.

As they conduct these investigations, historians should remind themselves of the essentials of their calling. Charles Rosenberg (1979) comments, "It is no more than a truism to observe that social scientists are trained to discern and formulate patterns that can be expressed in general terms, while the historian is tied by sensibility and socialization to the particular." If so, it bears repeating, because historians embarrass themselves when they forget. History succeeds when the author addresses readers in a suggestive rather than a didactic tone in order to vivify forces and lives beyond the audience's immediate experiences. Social investigators may enhance their own studies by appreciating the difference.

REFERENCES

Abbott, Grace, ed. 1938. *The Child and the State*. 2 vols. Chicago: University of Chicago Press.

Altgeld, John P. 1886. *Our Penal Machinery and Its Victims*. Chicago: A. C. McClurg.

Ariès, Philippe. 1965. *Centuries of Childhood: A Social History of Family Life*. New York: Vintage Books.

Bailyn, Bernard. 1960. *Education in the Forming of American Society*. Chapel Hill: University of North Carolina Press.

Banner, Lois. 1973. "Religious Benevolence as Social Control: A Critique of an Interpretation," *Journal of American History* 60:23–41.

Barnard, Henry. 1854. *National Education in Europe*. Hartford: F. C. Brownell.

Beard, Charles, and Mary Beard. 1927. *The Rise of American Civilization*. New York: Macmillan.

Beard, Mary, ed. 1933. *America through Women's Eyes*. New York: Macmillan.

Beaumont, Gustave de, and Alexis de Tocqueville. 1835. *On the Penitentiary System of the United States*. Carbondale: Southern Illinois University: 1964 reprint edition.

Behan, Brendan. 1959. *Borstal Boy*. New York: Alfred A. Knopf.

Bender, Thomas. 1975. *Toward an Urban Vision: Ideas and Institutions in Nineteenth Century America*. Lexington: University Press of Kentucky.

Bledstein, Burton J. 1976. *The Culture of Professionalism: The Middle Class and the Development of Higher Education in America*. New York: Norton.

Boyer, Paul. 1978. *Urban Masses and the Moral Order in America, 1820–1920*. Cambridge: Harvard University Press.

Brace, Charles Loring. 1872. *The Dangerous Classes of New York, and Twenty Years' Work among Them*. New York: Wynkoop and Hallenbeck.

Bremner, Robert H. 1956. *From the Depths: The Discovery of Poverty in the United States*. New York: New York University Press.

————, ed. 1970–74. *Children and Youth in America: A Documentary History*. 3 vols. Cambridge: Harvard University Press.

Brenzel, Barbara M. 1975. "Lancaster Industrial School for Girls: A Social Portrait of a Nineteenth Century Reform School," *Feminist Studies* 3:40–53.

————. 1978. "The Girls at Lancaster: A Social Portrait of the First Reform School for Girls in North America, 1856–1905." Ed.D. dissertation, Harvard University.

————. 1980. "Domestication as Reform: A Study of the Socialization of Wayward Girls, 1856–1905," *Harvard Educational Review* 50:196–213.

Burleigh, Edith N., and Frances K. Harris. 1923. *The Delinquent Girl*. New York: New York School of Social Work.

Burnham, John C. 1961. "Oral History Interviews of William Healy and Augusta Bronner." Houghton Library, Harvard University.

Carlebach, Julius. 1970. *Caring for Children in Trouble*. New York: Humanities Press.

Chambers, Clarke A. 1963. *Seedtime of Reform: American Social Service and Social Action, 1918–1933*. Minneapolis: University of Minnesota Press.

———. 1971. *Paul U. Kellogg and the "Survey": Voices for Social Welfare and Social Justice*. Minneapolis: University of Minnesota Press.

Cloward, Richard, and Lloyd Ohlin. 1960. *Delinquency and Opportunity: A Theory of Delinquent Gangs*. New York: Free Press.

Cremin, Lawrence. 1961. *The Transformation of the School: Progressivism in American Education, 1876–1957*. New York: Alfred A. Knopf.

Davis, Allen F. 1967. *Spearheads for Reform: The Social Settlements and the Progressive Movement, 1890–1914*. New York: Oxford.

Deutsch, Albert. 1952. *Our Rejected Children*. Boston: Little, Brown.

Eliot, Thomas D. 1914. *The Juvenile Court and the Community*. New York: Macmillan.

Faulkner, Harold U. 1931. *The Question for Social Justice, 1898–1914*. New York: Macmillan.

Finestone, Harold. 1976. *Victims of Change: Juvenile Delinquents in American Society*. Westport, Conn.: Greenwood Press.

Flexner, Bernard, and Roger N. Baldwin. 1912. *Juvenile Courts and Probation*. New York: Century.

Flynn, Frank T. 1954. "Judge Merritt W. Pinckney and the Early Days of the Juvenile Court in Chicago," *Social Service Review* 28:20–30.

Folks, Homer. 1902. *The Care of Destitute, Neglected and Delinquent Children*. New York: Macmillan.

Foucault, Michel. 1978. *Discipline and Punish*. New York: Pantheon.

Fox, Sanford J. 1970. "Juvenile Justice Reform: An Historical Perspective," *Stanford Law Review* 22:1187–1239.

Freedman, Estelle B. 1981. *Their Sisters' Keepers: Women's Prison Reform in America, 1830–1930*. Ann Arbor: University of Michigan Press.

Genët, Jean. 1966. *Miracle of the Rose*. New York: Grove Press.

Glueck, Sheldon, and Eleanor Glueck. 1934. *One Thousand Juvenile Delinquents*. Cambridge: Harvard University Press.

Gordon, Michael. 1971. *Juvenile Delinquency in the American Novel, 1905–1965: A Study in the Sociology of Literature*. Bowling Green, Ohio: Bowling Green University Popular Press.

Griffen, Clifford S. 1960. *Their Brothers' Keepers: Moral Stewardship in the United States, 1800–1865*. New Brunswick, N.J.: Rutgers University Press.

Hagan, John. 1980. "The Legislation of Crime and Delinquency: A Review of Theory, Method and Research," *Law and Society Review* 14:603–28.

Hareven, Tamara K., ed. 1971. *Anonymous Americans: Explorations in Nineteenth-Century Social History*. Englewood Cliffs, N.J.: Prentice-Hall.

Hawes, Joseph M. 1971. *Children in Urban Society: Juvenile Delinquency in Nineteenth Century America*. New York: Oxford.

Heale, Michael J. 1976. "From City Fathers to Social Critics: Humanitarianism and Government in New York, 1790–1860," *Journal of American History* 43:21–41.

Healy, William. 1915. *The Individual Delinquent*. Boston: Little, Brown.

Healy, William, and Benedict S. Alper. 1941. *Criminal Youth and the Borstal System*. New York: Commonwealth Fund.

Holl, Jack M. 1971. *Juvenile Reform in the Progressive Era: William R. George and the Junior Republic Movement*. Ithaca: Cornell University Press.

Horlick, Allan Stanley. 1975. *Country Boys and Merchant Princes: The Social Control of Young Men in New York*. Lewisburg: Bucknell University Press.

Horwitz, Morton J. 1971. "The Emergence of an Instrumental Conception of American Law," *Perspectives in American History* 5:287–328.

Hurley, Timothy D. 1907. *The Origin of the Juvenile Court Law*. Chicago: Visitation and Aid Society.

Ignatieff, Michael. 1978. *A Just Measure of Pain: The Penitentiary in the Industrial Revolution, 1750–1850*. New York: Pantheon.

———. 1981. "State, Civil Society and Total Institution: A Critique of Recent Social Histories of Punishment." In *Crime and Justice: An Annual Review of Research*, vol. 3, ed. Michael Tonry and Norval Morris. Chicago: University of Chicago Press.

James, Howard. 1970. *Children in Trouble: A National Scandal*. New York: David McKay.

Janowitz, Morris. 1978. *The Last Half-Century: Societal Change and Politics in America*. Chicago: University of Chicago Press.

Johnson, David R. 1973. "Crime Patterns in Philadelphia, 1840–70." In *The Peoples of Philadelphia: A History of Ethnic Groups and Lower-Class Life, 1790–1940*, ed. Allen F. Davis and Mark H. Haller. Philadelphia: Temple University Press.

———. 1979. *Policing the Urban Underworld: The Impact of Crime on the Development of the American Police, 1800–1887*. Philadelphia: Temple University Press.

Jones, Mary G. 1938. *The Charity School Movement: A Study of Eighteenth Century Puritanism in Action*. Cambridge: Cambridge University Press.

Kaestle, Carl F. 1973. *The Evolution of an Urban School System: New York City, 1750–1850*. Cambridge: Harvard University Press.

Kaestle, Carl F., and Maris A. Vinovskis. 1980. *Education and Social Change in Nineteenth-Century Massachusetts*. Cambridge: Cambridge University Press.

Kammen, Michael, ed. 1980. *The Past before Us: Contemporary Historical Writing in the United States*. Ithaca: Cornell University Press.

Katz, Michael B. 1968. *The Irony of Early School Reform: Educational Innovation in Mid-Nineteenth Century Massachusetts*. Cambridge: Harvard University Press.

Kiefer, Monica. 1948. *American Children through Their Books*. Philadelphia: University of Pennsylvania Press.

Klein, Malcolm W. 1979. "Deinstitutionalization and Diversion of Juvenile Offenders: A Litany of Impediments." In *Crime and Justice: An Annual Review of Research*, vol. 1, ed. Norval Morris and Michael Tonry. Chicago: University of Chicago Press.

Lane, Roger. 1967. *Policing the City: Boston, 1822–1885*. Cambridge: Harvard University Press.

Langsam, Miriam Z. 1964. *Children West: A History of the Placing out System of the New York Children's Aid Society, 1853–1890.* Madison: State Historical Society of Wisconsin.

Larsen, Charles. 1972. *The Good Fight: The Life and Times of Ben B. Lindsey.* Chicago: Quadrangle.

Lasch, Christopher. 1973. "Origins of the Asylum." In *The World of Nations: Reflections on American History, Politics, and Culture*, ed. Christopher Lasch. New York: Alfred A. Knopf.

———. 1977. *Haven in a Heartless World: The Family Besieged.* New York: Basic Books.

Laslett, Peter. 1965. *The World We Have Lost: England before the Industrial Age.* New York: Charles Scribner's Sons.

Laurie, Bruce. 1973. "Fire Companies and Gangs in Southwark: The 1840's." In *The Peoples of Philadelphia: A History of Ethnic Groups and Lower-Class Life, 1790–1940*, ed. Allen F. Davis and Mark M. Haller. Philadelphia: Temple University Press.

Lazerson, Marvin. 1971. *The Origins of the Urban School.* Cambridge: Harvard University Press.

Leiby, James. 1967. *Charity and Correction in New Jersey: A History of State Welfare Institutions.* New Brunswick, N.J.: Rutgers University Press.

———. 1978. *A History of Social Welfare and Social Work in the United States.* New York: Columbia University Press.

Levine, Murray, and Adeline Levine. 1970. *A Social History of Helping Services.* New York: Appleton-Century-Crofts.

Lewis, W. David. 1965. *From Newgate to Dannemora: The Rise of the Penitentiary in New York, 1746–1848.* Ithaca: Cornell University Press.

Lou, Herbert H. 1927. *Juvenile Courts in the United States.* Chapel Hill: University of North Carolina Press.

Lubove, Roy. 1965. *The Professional Altruist: The Emergence of Social Work as a Career, 1880–1930.* Cambridge: Harvard University Press.

Manton, Jo. 1976. *Mary Carpenter and the Children of the Streets.* Exeter, N.H.: Heinemann.

Marris, Peter, and Martin Rein. 1973. *Dilemmas of Social Reform: Poverty and Community Action in the United States.* Rev. ed. Chicago: Aldine.

May, Margaret. 1973. "Innocence and Experience: The Evolution of the Concept of Juvenile Delinquency in the Mid-Nineteenth Century," *Victorian Studies* 18:7–29.

Mennel, Robert. 1972. "Origins of the Juvenile Court: Changing Perspectives on the Legal Rights of Juvenile Delinquents," *Crime and Delinquency* 18:68–78.

———. 1973a. "Juvenile Delinquency in Perspective," *History of Education Quarterly* 13:275–81.

———. 1973b. *Thorns and Thistles: Juvenile Delinquents in the United States, 1825–1940.* Hanover: University Press of New England.

———. 1980a. "The Family System of Common Farmers: The Early Years of Ohio's Reform Farm, 1858–1884," *Ohio History* 89:279–322.

———. 1980b. "The Family System of Common Farmers: The Origins of Ohio's Reform Farm, 1840–1858," *Ohio History* 89:125–56.

Messerli, Jonathan. 1973. *Horace Mann: A Biography*. New York: Alfred A. Knopf.

Mohl, Raymond. 1970. *Poverty in New York, 1783–1823*. New York: Oxford.

Monkkonen, Eric H. 1975. *The Dangerous Class: Crime and Poverty in Columbus, Ohio, 1860–1885*. Cambridge: Harvard University Press.

Moore, John. 1969. "Controlling Delinquency: Executive, Congressional and Juvenile, 1961–64." In *Congress and Urban Problems*, ed. Frederic N. Cleaveland. Washington, D.C.: Brookings Institution.

Muller, Norbert. 1976. "La Colonie Agricole Pénitentiaire de Mettray." Memoire, Université de Tours.

National Commission on Law Observance and Enforcement. 1931. *The Child Offender in the Federal System of Justice*. Washington, D.C.: U.S. Government Printing Office.

National Conference of Charities and Correction. 1893. *History of Child Saving in the United States*. Boston: n.p.

Owen, David. 1964. *English Philanthropy, 1660–1960*. London: Oxford.

Parker, Graham. 1976a. "The Juvenile Court Movement," *University of Toronto Law Journal* 26:140–72.

———. 1976b. "The Juvenile Court: The Illinois Experience," *University of Toronto Law Journal* 26:253–306.

Pickett, Robert S. 1969. *House of Refuge: Origins of Juvenile Reform in New York State, 1815–1857*. Syracuse: Syracuse University Press.

Pinchbeck, Ivy, and Margaret Hewitt. 1969–73. *Children in English Society*. 2 vols. London: Routledge and Kegan Paul.

Pisciotta, Alexander W. 1979. "The Theory and Practice of the New York House of Refuge, 1857–1935." Ph.D. dissertation, Florida State University.

Platt, Anthony M. 1974. "The Triumph of Benevolence: The Origins of the Juvenile Justice System in the United States." In *Criminal Justice in America*, ed. Richard Quinney. Boston: Little, Brown.

———. 1977a. *The Child Savers: The Invention of Delinquency*. 2d ed. Chicago: University of Chicago Press.

———. 1977b. Review of Schlossman, *Love and the American Delinquent*, *Crime and Social Justice* 8:80–83.

Prescott, Peter S. 1981. *The Child Savers*. New York: Alfred A. Knopf.

Reeves, Margaret. 1929. *Training Schools for Delinquent Girls*. New York: Russell Sage.

Richardson, James F. 1970. *The New York Police: Colonial Times to 1901*. New York: Oxford.

Rosenberg, Carroll Smith. 1971. *Religion and the Rise of the American City: The New York City Mission Movement, 1812–1870*. Ithaca: Cornell University Press.

Rosenberg, Charles. 1979. "Toward an Ecology of Knowledge: On Discipline, Context and History." In *The Organization of Knowledge in Modern America, 1860–1920*, ed. Alexandra Oleson and John Voss. Baltimore: Johns Hopkins University Press.

Rosenheim, Margaret K., ed. 1962. *Justice for the Child: The Juvenile Court in Transition*. New York: Free Press.

———. 1976. *Pursuing Justice for the Child*. Chicago: University of Chicago Press.

Ross, Dorothy. 1972. *G. Stanley Hall: The Psychologist as Prophet*. Chicago: University of Chicago Press.

Rothman, David J. 1971. *The Discovery of the Asylum: Social Order and Disorder in the New Republic*. Boston: Little, Brown.

———. 1974. Review of Mennel, *Thorns and Thistles*, *American Historical Review* 79:244–45.

———. 1980. *Conscience and Convenience: The Asylum and Its Alternatives in Progressive America*. Boston: Little, Brown.

Ryerson, Ellen. 1978. *The Best Laid Plans: America's Juvenile Court Experiment*. New York: Hill and Wang.

Sanders, Wiley B., ed. 1970. *Juvenile Offenders for a Thousand Years: Selected Readings from Anglo-Saxon Times to 1900*. Chapel Hill: University of North Carolina Press.

Schlossman, Steven L. 1974. "Juvenile Justice in the Age of Jackson," *Teachers College Record* 46:119–33.

———. 1977. *Love and the American Delinquent: The Theory and Practice of "Progressive" Juvenile Justice, 1825–1920*. Chicago: University of Chicago Press.

Schlossman, Steven L., and Stephanie Wallach. 1978. "The Crime of Precocious Sexuality: Female Juvenile Delinquency in the Progressive Era," *Harvard Educational Review* 48:65–94.

Schneider, John. 1980. *Detroit and the Problem of Order, 1830–1880*. Lincoln: University of Nebraska Press.

Schultz, J. Lawrence. 1973. "The Cycle of Juvenile Court History," *Crime and Delinquency* 19:457–76.

Schupf, Harriet W. 1971. "The Perishing and Dangerous Classes: Efforts to Deal with the Neglected, Vagrant and Delinquent Juvenile in England, 1840–1872." Ph.D. dissertation, Columbia University.

Sennett, Richard. 1970. *Families against the City*. Cambridge: Harvard University Press.

Shanahan, William O. 1954. *German Protestants Face the Social Question*. South Bend: University of Notre Dame Press.

Shaw, Clifford R. 1929. *Delinquency Areas*. Chicago: University of Chicago Press.

———. 1930. *The Jack-Roller: A Delinquent Boy's Own Story*. Chicago: University of Chicago Press.

Shaw, Clifford R., and Henry D. McKay. 1942. *Juvenile Delinquency in Urban Areas*. Chicago: University of Chicago Press.

Slater, Peter G. 1970. "Views of Children and of Child Rearing during the Early National Period: A Study in the New England Intellect." Ph.D. dissertation, University of California, Berkeley.

Smith, Timothy. 1957. *Revivalism and Social Reform in Mid-Nineteenth Century America*. New York: Abingdon Press.

Snedden, David. 1907. *Administrative and Educational Work of the American Reform School*. New York: Columbia University Press.

Stack, John. 1974. "Social Policy and Juvenile Delinquency in England and Wales, 1815–75." Ph.D. dissertation, University of Iowa.

Stewart, Joseph M. 1980. "A Comparative History of Juvenile Correctional Institutions in Ohio." Ph.D. dissertation, Ohio State University.

Stone, Lawrence. 1981. "Family History in the 1980's," *Journal of Interdisciplinary History* 12:51–87.

Sutherland, Neil. 1976. *Children in English-Canadian Society, 1880–1920.* Toronto: University of Toronto Press.

Teeters, Negley K. 1960. "The Early Days of the Philadelphia House of Refuge," *Pennsylvania History* 27:165–87.

Thavenet, Dennis. 1976. "'Wild Young "Uns" in Their Midst': The Beginning of Reformatory Education in Michigan," *Michigan History* 60:240–59.

Thomas, William I. 1923. *The Unadjusted Girl.* Boston: Little, Brown.

Thrasher, Frederic M. 1927. *The Gang: A Study of 1,313 Gangs in Chicago.* Chicago: University of Chicago Press.

Thurston, Henry W. 1942. *Concerning Juvenile Delinquency: Progressive Changes in Our Perspective.* New York: Columbia University Press.

Trattner, Walter I. 1968. *Homer Folks: Pioneer in Social Welfare.* New York: Columbia University Press.

Tyler, Alice Felt. 1944. *Freedom's Ferment: Phases of American Social History to 1860.* Minneapolis: University of Minnesota Press.

U.S. Comptroller General. 1975. *Report to Congress: How Federal Efforts to Coordinate Programs to Mitigate Juvenile Delinquency Proved Ineffective.* Washington, D. C.: U.S. Government Printing Office.

U.S. President's Commission on Law Enforcement and Administration of Justice. 1968. *The Challenge of Crime in a Free Society.* Washington, D.C.: U.S. Government Printing Office.

Van Waters, Miriam. 1925. *Youth in Conflict.* New York: New Republic.

Vogel, Morris J. 1980. *The Invention of the Modern Hospital: Boston 1870–1930.* Chicago: University of Chicago Press.

Willard, Josiah Flint [Josiah Flynt]. 1908. *My Life.* New York: Outing.

Wines, Enoch C., and Theodore W. Dwight. 1867. *Report on the Prisons and Reformatories of the United States and Canada.* Albany: Van Benthuysen.

———. 1880. *The State Prisons and Child Saving Institutions in the Civilized World.* Cambridge, Mass.: J. Wilson.

Wirkkala, John. 1973. "Juvenile Delinquency and Reform in Nineteenth Century Massachusetts." Ph.D. dissertation, Clark University, Worcester, Mass.

Wishy, Bernard. 1968. *The Child and the Republic.* Philadelphia: University of Pennsylvania Press.

Wohl, R. Richard. 1969. "The 'Country Boy' Myth and Its Place in American Urban Culture," *Perspectives in American History* 3:77–158.

Zuckerman, Michael. 1976. "Children's Rights: The Failure of Reform," *Policy Analysis* 2:371–85.

ADDENDUM: Two recent dissertations examine juvenile justice in the contemporary era. Gayle Clark Olson's "Law Enforcement and Juvenile Delinquency Prevention: An Historical Federal, State and Local Perspective" (Ph.D. diss., University of California, Santa Barbara, 1981) is concerned with the effects of federal intervention on local programs. John R. Sutton, "Stubborn Children: The Social Origins of Child-Regulation in the Juvenile Justice System" (Ph.D. diss., University of California, Davis, 1981) is an analysis of the "diversion-deinstitutionalization" movement.

Ronald V. Clarke

Situational Crime Prevention: Its Theoretical Basis and Practical Scope

ABSTRACT

Situational crime prevention can be characterized as comprising measures (1) directed at highly specific forms of crime (2) that involve the management, design, or manipulation of the immediate environment in as systematic and permanent a way as possible (3) so as to reduce the opportunities for crime and increase its risks as perceived by a wide range of offenders. These measures include various forms of target hardening (making the objects of crime less vulnerable), defensible space architecture (which encourages residents in housing projects to exercise territorial surveillance of the public spaces outside their dwellings), community crime prevention initatives (e.g., neighborhood watch and citizen patrol schemes), and a number of less-easily categorized measures such as improved coordination of public transport with pub closing times, or more sensitive public housing allocation policies that avoid the concentration of children in particular housing developments. Traditional criminological theories have been concerned with the etiology of crime—the fundamental social and psychological causes—and have provided little support for situational measures not aimed at "root causes." An alternative theoretical perspective that gives greater weight to situational factors in crime and to the ways these are taken into account by potential offenders provides better conceptual underpinning for situational prevention. Emphasizing offenders' decision making helps us understand why displacement of crime (e.g., to some other time or place) is by no means the inevitable result of situational measures. Various examples of successful situational measures, as well as a general pessimism regarding the effectiveness of other forms of crime control, might lead one to expect a growth in situational prevention. This is unlikely to be rapid, however, because it is difficult to persuade people and organizations to take the necessary action, particularly when, as is so often the case, risks of victimization are small.

Ronald V. Clarke is a senior member of the Home Office Research Unit, London.
Thanks are due to colleagues in the Home Office Research Unit, particularly to Mike Hough, for their comments on a draft of this paper. Figures and tables are reproduced with the permission of the Controller of Her Majesty's Stationery Office.

Finally, for some people situational prevention has unattractive connotations of "big brother" forms of state control and of a "fortress society"; it is also criticized for avoiding fundamental moral issues.

Few informed observers now believe that significant reductions in crime can be achieved through the essentially marginal adjustments that seem practically and ethically feasible in relation to policies of incapacitation (Greenwood 1979; Brody and Tarling 1980), deterrent sentencing (Beyleveld 1979; Walker 1979), or rehabilitation (Martinson 1974; Brody 1976). Recent research (see Clarke and Hough 1980 for a review) also gives little reason to think that the solution to rising crime lies in more or better policing, at least within the limits imposed by available technology and current economic conditions. The question therefore arises whether other means of preventing crime, in particular the practical measures—such as fitting safes and alarms—that people and organizations take to protect themselves might not merit greater government support. This in turn raises some important theoretical questions. Is the protection afforded to particular targets by such means purchased at the cost of displacing crime to some other time or place? If opportunities for certain kinds of crime are blocked, will offenders simply resort to more violence or displace their energies to completely different and perhaps more intractable kinds of crime? And is it the case that no real improvements in levels of crime can be achieved without tackling root psychological and social causes?

These and other questions have been addressed in the course of a program of research on "situational crime prevention" carried out by the Home Office Research Unit in England (Clarke and Mayhew 1980). This essay describes such work and attempts to place it in a broader criminological context. It will be seen that the program's approach involves greater than usual attention to situational factors in crime. This mirrors some more general trends in the social sciences, where theories that set greater store by situational determinants of behavior are supplanting predominantly "dispositional" accounts of social problems, with their emphasis on individual malfunction or maladaptation (cf. Tizard 1976; Ross 1977). This is evidenced in psychology by the development of social learning theory (Mischel 1968; Bandura 1973), behavior modification (Eysenck 1976), and environmental (Krasner 1980) and ecological (Barker 1968; Willems 1977) psychologies. In sociology a similar trend is apparent in the current popularity of interactionist accounts of behavior (cf. Downes and Rock 1979), which stress the ways people make sense of their world and adapt to its constraints and opportunities.

Situational preventive measures have demonstrated their effectiveness in some contexts and warrant further development and experimentation. Section I of this essay places situational prevention in the context of criminological theory and suggests that much offending can usefully be viewed not simply as the product of deep social, economic, and psychological causes but also as the result of deliberate choices by individuals. A substantial literature supports the commonsense observation that the attractiveness of criminal opportunities affects the likelihood that individuals will engage in crime and, to this extent, that situational prevention strategies are theoretically and practically plausible.

Section II reviews a substantial body of research that has tested various situational strategies of crime prevention. Such approaches can usefully be divided into (1) measures that increase the visibility of crimes by increasing the degree of *surveillance* to which they are potentially subject, (2) *target hardening* measures that diminish criminal opportunities by making property less vulnerable (automobile steering column locks are an example), and (3) *environmental management* measures that attempt to eliminate the targets of crime (payroll clerks, for example, are much less vulnerable to robbery if wages are paid by check rather than in cash). The lines to be drawn between these three categories are sometimes unclear: some preventive strategies exhibit characteristics of two or even three of these approaches. Nonetheless, the distinction is organizationally useful, and section II reviews the findings of major research under each of these headings.

Section III discusses "displacement," the phenomenon by which efforts to prevent crime in one context may cause an increase in crime in other contexts. Displacement can take several forms. Efforts to reduce one kind of crime (say bank robbery, by constructing bulletproof teller shields in all banks) may lead would-be robbers to increase their involvement in different crimes (e.g. robbery of retail stores). Efforts to reduce crime in a particular place (e.g. the subways) may cause shifts to crime in other places (e.g. back alleys). Efforts to reduce crime at a particular time (e.g. nighttime subway muggings) may result in crime's shifting to other times (e.g. daytime). Section III describes the range of displacement effects that have been observed and hypothesized and reviews selected research findings on whether, when, and to what extent displacement occurs.

There is reason to believe that situational prevention strategies do reduce the incidence of certain kinds of crime, even when displacement effects are taken into account. One might suppose accordingly that vigorous steps are being taken to implement situational programs. In fact, there are many fewer situational prevention programs being deployed than one might expect. Section IV reviews the practical and theoretical objections to their deployment and reflects on some of the dilemmas for public policy that they present.

I. Criminological Theory: Criminal Dispositions

Current criminological theories do not provide encouraging answers to the questions raised in the opening paragraph. Most of these theories are seeking to explain why some individuals or groups are born with, or come to acquire, a "disposition" to offend. The explanation may be sought in genetic differences of physiological functioning (e.g. slow automatic reactivity and low cortical arousal), in psychological factors of personality and upbringing (e.g. faulty conditioning of extroverted neurotics), or in sociological influences (e.g. "anomie," "subcultural," and "labeling" theories). Whatever the source of criminal dispositions, once present they are presumed to express themselves over a diverse range of conditions and circumstances. This being so, there is little to be gained by action that reduces opportunities for crime only at particular times and places. The mainstream of criminological thought would therefore prescribe measures that attempt to prevent the disposition from developing in the first place or, once developed, to eradicate it or compensate for it.

Unfortunately, most such measures suffer from a number of theoretical and practical difficulties (cf. Morris and Hawkins 1970; Wilson 1975). First, it is difficult to see what could be done about many of the social and psychological factors that have been implicated. How can parents be made, for example, to have greater love for their children or to exercise more consistent discipline? If relative deprivation is an important factor in crime, is equal prosperity for all an attainable goal? And are there any acceptable means of modifying temperament or other predisposing biological variables? Second, though correlates have frequently been demonstrated between aspects of disadvantage and crime, these have never been strong, and causal relations have never been traceable save through a number of mediating variables. This means that the results of intervention must be highly unpredictable, and, since these would be expected to manifest themselves only in the longer term, they would also be difficult to demonstrate. Third, and perhaps most important, social policies to reduce poverty and racial discrimination or to improve housing and education are desirable in their own right. They already command a broad measure of support in the community and probably do not rely to any great extent for their force on arguments about preventing crime; in any case they fall outside the direct province of criminal justice policymakers.

A criminal act does not, however, result simply and inevitably from the presence of a criminally disposed individual. The conditions for crime must be right in terms of such situational factors as the availability of a vulnerable target and an appropriate opportunity. Moreover, the motivation to offend need not be long-standing, but may result from temporary mood or pressures (Matza 1964).

A number of empirical studies over the years have, rather unsystematically, attested to the importance of such situational forces, namely:

—Burt's (1925) pioneering studies of delinquency in London, in which he showed that the higher rate of property offending in the winter months was promoted by longer hours of darkness;

—Hartshorne and May's (1928) experimental studies of deceit, in which they showed that the chances of children's behaving dishonestly on a particular occasion depended on the teacher in charge or the level of supervision afforded;

—"lost letter" and similar experiments that show, for example, that the probability of "stealing by finding" is related to the amount of money involved and to characteristics of the supposed victim (Farrington and Knight 1979);

—self-report studies showing that most individuals have committed some form of crime at one time or another (see Hood and Sparks 1970 for a review), and more recent studies (cf. Mars 1973; Ditton 1977; Henry 1978) of particular occupational groups, such as waiters and bakery roundsmen, showing that cheating and pilferage are very widespread;

—evidence (e.g. Wolfgang, Figlio, and Sellin 1972; Osborn and West 1980) that large proportions of even the more persistent delinquents desist from crime as their circumstances alter and they grow older, get married, or obtain steady jobs (cf. Trasler 1979);

—demonstrations by Wilkins (1964) and by Gould and his co-workers (Gould 1969; Mansfield, Gould, and Namenwirth 1974) that fluctuations in levels of auto crime reflect the number of opportunities as measured by the numbers of registered vehicles;

—more recent studies by Cohen and Felson (1979) showing that theft and burglary have grown as the availability and portability of valuable consumer goods have increased;

—areal studies of crime in cities (see Baldwin 1979 for a review) that have shown that the distribution of particular crimes is related to the presence of particular targets and locations such as business premises, drinking clubs, and parking lots (Engstad 1975; Poyner 1981);

—"crime specific" studies of shoplifting (Walsh 1978), vandalism (Ley and Cybrinwsky 1974; Clarke 1978), and burglary (e.g. Scarr 1973; Reppetto 1974; Brantingham and Brantingham 1975; Waller and Okihiro 1978; Walsh 1980; Maguire 1982) that have shown that characteristics of the target are related in consistent and predictable ways to the chances of victimization;

—"victim" studies of the general population showing that chances of victimization are related to features such as age and life-style (cf. Skogan 1978; Hindelang 1976);

—Newman's (1972) defensible-space findings that crime in public housing projects can be inhibited by the careful design and layout of buildings and public spaces;

—studies of residential institutions for delinquents, for example, by Clarke and Martin (1971) and Sinclair (1971), that have shown that absconding and other forms of misbehavior are powerfully related to institutional climate (Moos 1975) and regime.

Some caveats are needed at this point about the evidence reviewed above. First, most of the relationships have not been shown to be causal. Second, not all the variables (e.g. number of registered vehicles) could be manipulated in the interest of reducing crime. Third, there is little firm evidence that, even where variables could be manipulated, reductions in crime would result, since other factors might be concurrently affected. Nevertheless, these limitations do not explain why criminological theory has failed to take adequate account of situational factors (cf. Ohlin 1970; Gibbons 1971; Jeffrey 1971). The main reason seems to be that conventional criminology is concerned to explain the development of criminal dispositions—it is generally not geared to explaining why particular criminal events have occurred at particular places and particular times. In explaining the occurrence of criminal events, situational factors would have to be accorded a major role. It would also be necessary to show how they impinge on behavior, and for this purpose a useful explanatory concept seems to be that of offender decision making. In other words, an adequate theory of criminal events would have two components: first, a description of the nature and distribution of criminal opportunities (Sparks 1980) and, second, an account of how offenders' decisions are affected, not merely by facts of upbringing and personal history, but also by the circumstances and situations in which they find themselves. Such a theory would see people as choosing to take advantage of naturally arising opportunities or as deliberately creating opportunities (cf. Clarke 1982), rather than as being "passive actors" (Taylor, Walton, and Young 1973) compelled to behave criminally by deeply rooted causes. Examples of such a "choice" perspective are to be found in the more recent discussions of deterrence (cf. Cook 1980), and precursors might be seen in the work of Matza (1964) and other American naturalists.

It is not suggested that decision making will always be fully rational or properly considered. It seems more appropriate to hold to a notion of "limited rationality" in which economic explanations are tempered by psychological factors (cf. Cook 1980). For example, people's capacity and willingness to acquire and process information about the risks of crime vary widely. So do their desire for profit and their willingness to take risks. Some burglars seem to disregard completely the low probability of being intercepted by police patrols, while others take great care to avoid such an eventuality (Maguire 1982).

Few people's assessments of the risks would accurately reflect the realities, and few individuals would go through an elaborate calculation of costs and benefits for every crime. Common observation suggests that some crime is committed more or less on impulse, and that in these cases strong emotions, alcohol, or the dynamics of the peer group may play a considerable part. In addition, people adopt rules of thumb or "standing decisions" that eliminate the need to analyze every decision. As Cook (1980) explains: "Most of us have long ago adopted standing decisions to refrain from robbery and assault, no matter what the circumstances." And it could be added that others of us have decided to take advantage of certain kinds of criminal opportunities that arise. These decisions are partly affected by the individual's life circumstances—the risks of being caught for crime are much greater for college professors than for unemployed teenagers—but they are also influenced by temperament and upbringing. The notion of "standing decisions" can thus be seen to have some parallels with that of "dispositions" in more traditional criminological theory.

In order, then, to give an adequate account of a decision to commit an offense, it will be necessary to go beyond information about the offender's current circumstances and personal history to include data about the following:

1) his immediate motives and intentions;
2) his moods and feelings;
3) his moral judgments regarding the act in question and the "techniques of moral neutralization" open to him (cf. Matza 1964);
4) his perception of criminal opportunities and ability to take advantage of, or create, them; and
5) his assessment of the risks of being caught as well as of the likely consequences.

II. Preventive Implications of a Choice Model

If it is allowed that "choice" models, concerned with the explanation of criminal events as the product of conscious decisions by individuals, have some value, how do they help in answering the questions raised at the beginning of the essay? First, by emphasizing the wide range of factors that influence an offender's decisions, including his assessments of the risks, rewards, and morality of the act in question, they provide more adequate concepts with which to examine the displacement phenomenon (Reppetto 1976) and, as discussed below, in fact suggest that displacement is far from inevitable. Second, by emphasizing that crime is often as much a matter of immediate circumstances (both personal and environmental) as of background and upbringing, they help to show why preventive action directed to root social and psychological causes—where such action is practicable—may be of limited effect. Third, by encompassing in the explanatory model a substantially greater number of variables than dispositional explanations, choice theories widen the potential scope for preventive action—though it would be rash to expect, given criminology's past record, that the benefits for practice will be directly proportional to improved understanding. For instance, there is little that can be done about the vast range of misfortunes and setbacks that can befall individuals and that might raise the probability that they will behave criminally while depressed or angry.

The main preventive benefit of a "choice" model is that by emphasizing the situational context of crime it helps to focus preventive effort on specific categories of offenses rather than on crime in general; this in turn should encourage careful analysis of the chances of falling victim to particular crimes as well as of the costs and benefits of preventive action. It also provides a stronger theoretical rationale for increasing the risks to the offender and reducing his opportunities, which is the essence of "situational" prevention. Three main categories of such intervention—surveillance, design, and environmental management—are employed below for convenience, though they are not always sharply distinguished; for example, Newman achieves defensible space by designing for surveillance.

A. Surveillance

One might think that the best means of exploiting offenders' fears that they will be seen and apprehended would be enhanced police patrolling, but the evidence concerning this aspect of the police deterrent role is not encouraging. A variety of studies have suggested that increases in levels of patrolling (e.g. Bright 1969; Kelling et al. 1974) or changes in patrolling methods, such as substituting foot for vehicle patrols (e.g. Kelling and Pate 1981), have little effect on crime rates. While it is not always clear that levels of surveillance were materially altered in the experiments (see Larson's 1975 criticisms of the Kansas City study), the reasons adduced for the limited effects of police surveillance are convincing. These have to do with the fact that crime is a relatively rare event when set against the vast number of opportunities for it to occur as represented by the activities of a huge population of citizens over a considerable geographical area for the twenty-four hours of the day. Even if the police concentrate on the most dangerous locations, their chances of lighting on a crime in progress are slim. In any case, much crime occurs in private places where the police cannot be present.

It is sometimes suggested that the visibility of people going about their everyday affairs should be exploited for surveillance purposes. This might be done, for example, by encouraging people to report suspicious incidents, by offering rewards for information, or by providing more police call boxes. The available evidence suggests, however, that the public at large poses little threat to offenders. First, people frequently fail to notice a crime taking place. In one study (Gelfand et al. 1973), "shoplifting" incidents were staged in direct view of shoppers, but only 28 percent of those whose attention was attracted noticed the theft. Even if an observer becomes suspicious he might have difficulty in deciding whether an offense is being committed: a stranger may be unable to tell whether a man entering a house in slightly suspicious circumstances is an intruder or someone with a right to be there. Also, the incident may be interpreted as something other than crime. In the often-cited murder of Kitty Genovese in New York in 1964, many of the thirty-eight inactive witnesses said they thought the incident was "a lovers' quarrel" (Rosenthal 1964). A number of studies under the "bystander intervention" heading also show that witnesses to criminal incidents appear surprisingly reluctant to challenge offenders or to provide direct help to victims (cf. Latané and Darley 1970). Explanations offered for this include the fear of personal injury, the inconvenience of becoming involved, and feelings that victims may not welcome interference. The likelihood of witnesses calling the police, especially for minor offenses, may also not be great. They may feel that the police would arrive too late to take effective action, and they may in any case have difficulty reaching them. Finally, the risk may be small that witnesses will recognize offenders if they see them again by chance or, more usually, if an identification is required by the police (cf. Home Office 1976; Clifford and Bull 1978).

While there may be little real threat from the general public, offenders have much more to fear from people who are familiar with and have some commitment to defending the property, persons, or environment under threat. Leaving aside the police and other law enforcement personnel who have been discussed above, there seem to be two main categories of such people, discussed below: first, residents can protect their own homes and immediate neighborhoods; second, some employees, such as bus conductors, car park attendants, bartenders, shop assistants, and caretakers can, under certain conditions, provide effective surveillance in the places where they work.

1. *Residents*. Jacobs (1961) has argued that crime flourishes when people do not know their neighbors, when they stay behind their doors, and when they have no sense of identity with the neighborhoods in which they live. To foster the development of local communities and to increase the number of residents interacting upon the streets, she advocates accommodating people at high densities, reducing open spaces such as parks, greatly widening sidewalks, and placing shops and services in streets formerly reserved for housing.

Attractive as they may be, it is difficult to envisage her ideas being implemented on any wide scale in Great Britain or indeed elsewhere, since they tend to conflict with established planning principles of low housing densities and land-use zoning. Equally problematic is that her prescriptions may produce high levels of activity on the streets, but not a sense of community; and activity alone does not necessarily impede crime. While Luedtke (1970), Letkemann (1973), Pablant and Baxter (1975), and Duffala (1976) all found levels of pedestrian and vehicle traffic to be negatively related to the incidence of certain crimes, in most cases the effect of activity is not easily separated from other situational factors that also affect target vulnerability (such as, in the case of shops, how far their interiors are screened from the view of pedestrians by parked cars and window layout; Duffala 1976; Louv 1978). Moreover, other studies have claimed that activity may have no effect on crime (Wilcox 1974; Reppetto 1974) or, especially in more socially disorganized areas, that it may even encourage crime by providing cover for strangers to circulate (cf. Angel 1968; Suttles 1968; Brantingham and Brantingham 1975).

Jacobs's "planning" approach to enhancing surveillance can be distinguished from the "architectural" approach of Oscar Newman (1972), who has recommended that housing estates be designed to give residents a better view of vulnerable public areas and an increased sense of territorial responsibility. Newman's "defensible space" ideas have enjoyed considerable support among the public and architects alike, but it is again questionable whether they can be applied on any wide scale. Newman himself suggests that modifying existing buildings is often less realistic than installing more security hardware or employing security personnel, and even for new buildings there is little chance that defensible space would override other possibly conflicting considerations such as cost or residents' desire for privacy. Nor is it clear how far "defensible space" actually reduces crime. Newman's (1972) original work has been subject to methodological criticisms (Hillier 1973; Bottoms 1974; Mawby 1977), and he himself (Newman 1980) has modified his thesis to accord greater weight to social factors, particularly the social "mix" of the people on the estates. Furthermore, where housing projects have been modified along defensible-space lines, the benefits have not always been great, and results from a number of studies looking at defensible space features of the environment in terms of crime have usually shown design to have a rather limited effect (see Mayhew 1979 for a review).

The results of some studies undertaken by the Home Office are in line with these general conclusions regarding the modest crime prevention value of defensible space, though one of the studies concerned with residential burglary (Winchester and Jackson 1983.) produced somewhat more optimistic results. In this project, a sample of 450 houses that had been burglarized in southeast England was compared with a control sample of nonburglarized houses on the bases of: physical vulnerability in terms of design and siting, levels of occupancy, residents' security practices, and attractiveness in terms of the possible gains. Of these factors, physical site characteristics and location were found to be the most important correlates of victimization. The probability of being burglarized for the most vulnerably situated properties (as measured by a fourteen-item scale of vulnerability that included information about visibility from other houses on the road and about ease of access to the four sides of the house) was very substantially greater than for the least vulnerable.

The second Home Office study concerned vandalism in thirty-eight public housing projects in London (Wilson 1978). Measures of vandalism (based on repair records) were obtained for each of 285 separate buildings in the projects, and the buildings were also rated by the researchers on a range of "defensible space" design features. While the main correlate of vandalism for all types of buildings was the number of children accommodated, some relationships in support of Newman's ideas were found as follows:

1. The relatively small amount of damage to dwellings themselves (see fig. 1) supported the notion that impersonal and publicly accessible space is more vulnerable to damage than targets toward which residents can adopt proprietary attitudes.

2. High-rise buildings experienced more vandalism in ground floor communal areas—space to which residents' feelings of territoriality were unlikely to extend. (See table 1, where rates of vandalism are calculated for buildings of differing heights according to the number of entrances—these varied considerably in number for both high- and low-rise buildings. Damage to elevators is not included.)

3. In buildings with few resident children, vandalism was greater if entrances were impersonal and could be used as throughways to other locations. This is illustrated in table 2, which shows vandalism to elevators in buildings with two different kinds of entrances. (The differences in vandalism were much greater than differences in elevator usage.)

4. Levels of vandalism were high in large buildings (not necessarily high rises) characterized by extensive semipublic space that could not easily be supervised by residents (Wilson 1978, pp. 59–60).

The third study was concerned with vandalism to 217 freestanding telephone boxes. (These boxes, which have windows on all four sides, are large enough to take one, or at most two, standing people.) The purpose of the study was to see if the surveillance afforded to the boxes from surrounding homes protected them from deliberate damage (Mayhew et al. 1979). The factor most strongly related to the level of vandal-

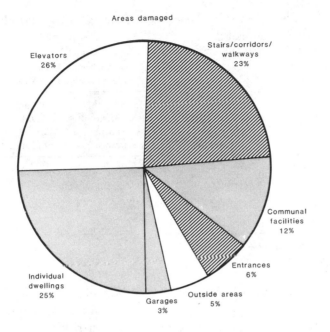

Fig. 1. Vandalism on thirty-eight housing estates in one London borough. From Wilson 1978.

ism (as measured from repair records) was a combination of patterns of renting versus homeownership and numbers of children resident in the surrounding area: boxes in areas of public housing with many children were vandalized most. Once this factor was controlled in the analysis, a small deterrent effect of overlooking windows was found (see table 3). One possible reason for the effect being no greater is that many people are away from home for much of the day. Even when home they may spend little time looking out the window, and, where the offender is careful to make no noise, defensible space designs may confer only marginal protection from crime.

More active surveillance provided by residents in the form of citizen patrols or "block watch" schemes appears little more successful. Though fear of crime may be reduced, there is not much evidence that these schemes bring about actual reductions in crime rates (cf. Washnis 1976; Cirel et al. 1977; Yin et al. 1977). Also there appear to be difficulties in recruiting enough people who are willing to give up time to exercise vigilance on behalf of others, and, more particularly, it is difficult to

TABLE 1

Building Story Height and Damage in Ground-Floor
Communal Areas

| | | Vandalism in Ground-Floor Communal Areas | |
| | | Buildings with Fewer Than One Incident per Entrance | Buildings with One or More Incidents per Entrance |
Story Height	Number of Buildings		
1–4	123	83%	17%
5	95	77	23
6–10	37	46	54
11–22	30	23	77
Total	285	70%	30%

Source: Wilson 1978.
Note: $X^2 = 46.4$; 3 df; $p < .001$.

maintain enthusiasm. This is seemingly because individuals encounter
so few incidents of crime that the effort required begins to seem disproportionate to results. The generally smaller risk of crime in Great
Britain (where the annual risk of being burglarized is three per hundred
households compared with about eight per hundred in the United States)
may be the main reason why organized community surveillance stands
little chance of flourishing there, and indeed it is telling that one isolated
vandal patrol disbanded after only a few weeks during which not a single
vandal was glimpsed at work.

TABLE 2

Buildings with Elevators: Type of Entrance
and Vandalism

| | | Vandalism to Elevators | |
Type of Entrance	Number of Buildings	Buildings with 0–4 Incidents	Buildings with 5 or More Incidents
Discrete entrance	30	70%	30%
Entrance acting as a throughway	21	24	76
Total	51	51%	49%

Source: Wilson 1978.
Note: $X^2 = 10.5$; 1 df; $p < .01$.

TABLE 3

Telephone Box Vandalism and Overlooking Windows

Number of Windows	Average Number of Vandal Incidents per Box	
	Public Housing Areas	Other Areas
Less than median	7.1	4.3
More than median	5.6	3.5
All boxes	6.4	3.9
	(N = 69)	(N = 148)

Source: Mayhew et al. 1979.

Note: The number of vandal incidents per box was measured over a twelve-month period. Boxes surrounded by predominantly public housing were more overlooked (the median number of windows was higher) than boxes elsewhere. Even so, the "window effect" for this sample was less strong ($t = 1.56; p < 0.07$; one-tailed test) than for the other ($t = 2.04; p < 0.025$; one-tailed test).

2. *Employees.* The risk of crime in shops, buses, underground stations, and parks may be such that people employed in busy public places will have far greater potential for witnessing crime then will residents, and measures to extend their surveillance capabilities might therefore be correspondingly more valuable. For example, Sturman (1978) has shown in a study undertaken in the city of Manchester that rates of vandalism to shops and schools are, respectively, 85 times and 500 times higher than to private dwellings. The potential value of the surveillance afforded by employees is illustrated by the following evidence:

1) Reppetto (1974) and Waller and Okihiro (1978) have shown that apartment blocks with doormen are much less vulnerable to burglary;

2) vandalism is a smaller problem in public housing projects in England where there is a resident caretaker or janitor (Department of the Environment 1977);

3) public telephones in places such as pubs or laundromats, which are given some supervision by staff working there, suffer almost no vandalism in comparison with those in call boxes (unpublished British Post Office records);

4) car parking lots with attendants have much lower rates of auto theft (*Sunday Times*, 9 April 1979);

5) hooliganism by soccer supporters on trains has been reduced by allowing club stewards to travel free of charge to supervise the other supporters (unpublished British Rail data);

6) shoplifting is discouraged by the presence of clerks who are there to serve the customers (Walsh 1978).

The importance of "employee" supervision can be further illustrated by the results of a Home Office study (Mayhew et al. 1976) of vandalism on different types of double-decker buses, operated either by the driver alone or with the help of a conductor. It was expected that damage to buses without conductors would be greater, since there would be much less effective supervision of the passengers. It was also thought that there would be more damage on the top deck for all buses because even when a conductor is carried, he usually rides downstairs. These predictions were generally confirmed, though damage (as recorded by research staff) on the lower deck, which was in any case uncommon, was apparently not reduced further by the presence of a conductor. The magnitude of some of the other differences was surprising: damage on the upper deck was ten times as great as on the lower deck for buses with a conductor, and twenty-five times as great for driver-only buses (see table 4). These differences were not due either to the upper deck's being used more or to its being preferred by high-risk groups such as adolescent boys.

Much of the deterrent role of conductors, caretakers, and so on, may result simply from their being around; and in many cases employing more of them, for greater parts of the day, may be all that is needed. In other cases they may need training or other kinds of assistance such as closed circuit television to help them carry out their surveillance role. Research evidence on the value of such aids is somewhat equivocal: for example, closed circuit television (CCTV) is not of proved effectiveness in shops (Home Office 1973) but has been found in a Home Office study (Mayhew et al. 1979) to be of value in the London Underground, where CCTV was provided to help staff in certain stations deal with pick-pocketing, purse-snatching, and mugging (though the latter offense was

TABLE 4

Vandalism to Double-Deck Buses

Location of Seats	Average Vandalism Score per Seat	
	One-Man-Operated Buses ($N = 48$)	Other Buses ($N = 51$)
Lower deck	0.2	0.2
Upper deck	5.1	2.4

Source: Mayhew et al. 1976.

in fact quite rare). The number of all such crimes reported before and after the installation of CCTV were compared, as well as those occurring in some nearby stations. As table 5 shows, the installation of CCTV seems to have resulted in a considerable drop in crime, without much evidence of displacement to the neighboring stations.

While more research attention has been paid to the surveillance afforded by residents, the evidence reviewed above suggests that it is through the exploitation of "employee" surveillance that the greater crime prevention gains are to be had. Not much is yet known about the conditions under which such surveillance achieves its best effects (e.g. How important is the status of the employee and the nature of his role?), but the results of the studies to date identify this as an important topic for future research.

B. *Design: Target Hardening*

The most obvious way to reduce criminal opportunities is to obstruct or "target harden"—to increase the physical security of targets of theft through the use of bolts, reinforced materials, and immobilizing devices and to protect against vandalism by installing unbreakable and paint-resistant materials and by placing vulnerable objects behind grills or meshes.

Some forms of target hardening have proved highly successful. In Great Britain, the Post Office succeeded in virtually eliminating theft from public telephone installations in the late 1960s by the wholesale replacement of vulnerable aluminum coin receptacles with stronger steel ones. In many government offices, the opportunities for employees to make personal long-distance telephone calls have been reduced by sim-

TABLE 5

Theft Offenses on the London Underground Railway before and after Installing CCTV

	Theft Offenses	
	Twelve Months before Installation	First Twelve Months after Installation
Stations with CCTV ($N = 4$)	243	66
Nearby stations ($N = 15$)	535	393

Source: Mayhew et al. 1979.
Note: $X^2 = 6.16$, 1 df; $p < 0.05$.

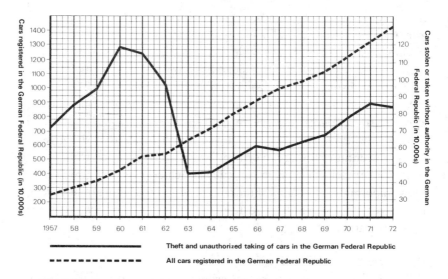

Fig. 2. Theft and unauthorized taking of cars in the German Federal Republic, and numbers of cars registered, 1957–72. From Mayhew et al. 1976.

ple devices that make it impossible to call long distance without the aid of the operator. Steering column locks were made compulsory on all cars (old and new) in West Germany in 1963, with a consequent and apparently permanent reduction of more than 60 percent in the rate of car thefts (see figure 2). There is further unexploited potential for designing out theft of and from cars, for example, by centrally activated locking systems, and through replacing keys with magnetic punch cards (Ekblom 1979). And a suggestion that offenders convicted of drunken driving should be required to equip their vehicles with a breathalyzer system connected to the ignition (only sober people would thus be able to start the car) has been given serious consideration by the legislature in Western Australia.

A final example is to be found in the "Operation Identification" schemes now popular in North America where householders are encouraged to mark valuable possessions with indelible codes that render the goods uniquely identifiable and thus of less value to the thief. Evaluations of such schemes (see Zaharchuk and Lynch 1977; Heller et al. 1975) have found a number of difficulties, including that of encouraging people to join. Participating households, however, have usually enjoyed some protection from burglary, which has been reflected in reduced overall levels of burglary in specific areas if—and this is unusual—the majority of householders have been involved.

C. *Environmental Management*

A final group of situational measures can be loosely identified under the heading of environmental management. One form of this consists in removing targets of crime from the environment. Thus the opportunities for wage snatches are reduced if employees are paid by check rather than in cash. In Sweden the problem of check frauds was dealt with in 1970 (Knutsson and Kuhlhorn 1981) principally by requiring check users to show proof of identification (see table 6). Robberies of New York City bus drivers were greatly reduced with the introduction of automated flat-fare collection (Chaiken, Lawless, and Stevenson 1974). Large-scale thefts of copper from one of Britain's major ports have been greatly reduced by the simple expedient of the port authority's refusing to accept consignments until immediately before the date of sailing. And thefts from electricity and gas meters can be eliminated where coin meters are replaced by quarterly billing.

A further variant of target removal is found in measures that disguise opportunities for crime or make temptations less blatant, even if the target is only removed from the subjective world of potential offenders. For example, the rapid repair of vandalism may prevent further attacks. Zimbardo (1973) showed that a car left in poor condition in a "rough" city district rapidly attracted further depredation. And, for whatever reasons, walls carrying murals appear not to attract graffiti to the same extent as blank walls.

TABLE 6

Check Frauds in Sweden, 1970–78

Year	Number of Offenses	Index
1970	39,337	100
1971	28,810	61
1972	7,315	19
1973	4,926	13
1974	5,800	15
1975[a]	7,069	18
1976[a]	8,279	21
1977[a]	9,228	23
1978	5,667	14

Source: Knutsson and Kuhlhorn 1981.

[a] The slight increase in check frauds in these years probably reflects a resurgence of check use in the retail trade following the initial decline in use as a result of the new measures.

Some sorts of crime have been dramatically reduced by removing not the targets but the means to commit the crimes. For example, the incidence of aircraft "skyjacking" has been reduced from an annual average of about seventy in the early 1970s to the present rate of about fifteen a year by screening passengers and baggage to detect weapons and bombs (Wilkinson 1977). Gun control, including the control of imitation firearms, is often advocated (cf. Rhodes 1977, for a recent exposition) as a method of reducing robbery and other crimes involving violence or the threat of violence. The Scottish Council on Crime (1975) has proposed that pubs in which fights are common should serve drinks in plastic containers so glasses cannot be used as offensive weapons.

Certain measures of environmental management have some but not all of the characteristics of the situational approach, and some are opportunity-reducing only in an extended sense. Insofar as a distinction can be drawn between the social and physical environments, this subgroup tends to involve manipulation of the former. Perhaps the best example, at least in a British context, is to be found in the organization of events such as soccer games. Good liaison between the police, the two soccer teams, and supporters' clubs can reduce the opportunities and temptations for vandalism and violence; arrival and departure of supporters can be better managed so as to avoid long delays; within and possibly around the grounds, routes of access to stands and occupation of stands can be controlled. Again, public transport services in many towns in Great Britain shut down before the pubs have closed, leaving some customers stranded and in high spirits—a recipe for vandalism and the theft of cars and bicycles. Coordination of late-night buses and pub closing would eliminate the precipitating conditions. Public housing allocation policies can be pursued that avoid high concentrations of children on certain sorts of estates or that place families in accommodations where parents can more easily supervise their children (cf. Wilson 1978).

Finally, some forms of environmental management whose main objectives are independent of crime control can have preventive effects. The recent law in Great Britain requiring all motorcyclists to wear crash helmets was introduced to save lives, but it had the unintended effect of reducing the theft of motorcycles—no doubt because few potential thieves have a helmet with them at the opportune time and place, and without one they run a high risk of being stopped by the police (cf. Mayhew et al. 1976).

III. Displacement

As may be clear from examples mentioned above, displacement can take a variety of forms, and it is usual to distinguish between five main types (Reppetto 1976; Gabor 1978): in response to blocked opportunities or increased risks in respect of a particular offense, an offender might attempt to commit it elsewhere (geographic displacement) or at a different time (temporal displacement), change his modus operandi (tactical displacement), choose a different target or victim (target displacement), or turn his attention to some completely different form of crime (activity-related displacement).

The dispositional bias of criminological theory has tended to reinforce popular beliefs in the inevitability of displacement ("bad will out"). People find it hard to accept that the occurrence of actions with often momentous consequences for both victim and offender can turn on apparently trivial situational contingencies of opportunities or risks. But shifts in opportunities have been shown to affect behavior such as suicide, which, not unlike many forms of crime, is usually thought to result from deep-seated motivation. Hassall and Trethowan (1972) and Brown (1979) have provided convincing evidence that the substantial reductions in suicide in Great Britain in recent years can be attributed to the reduced toxicity of the gas used in homes for cooking and heating.

Similar considerations apply to crime, though due regard must be paid to differences in motivation underlying different sorts of offenses. While situational measures are in principle applicable to any category of crime (even very determined offenders such as "skyjackers" can be stopped, albeit at substantial cost), it seems that the more "professional" the crime and the criminal, the greater the probability of displacement. Some studies (e.g. Maguire 1982) have suggested that many burglars, for example, see themselves as being in the business of stealing and would take advantage of, or seek out, any reasonable opportunity for theft of whatever kind. There is also clear evidence of displacement in crimes such as bank robbery: in Great Britain safecracking was the favored form of bank robbery until the technology of safes outreached that of the "cracksman"; over-the-counter armed robberies then became the prevalent form until preventive technology within banks displaced robberies to cash in transit. Though there was an escalation of violence at each stage in displacement (cf. Ball, Chester, and Perrott 1978), it is unlikely that all the gains made by situational measures were negated.

At the other end of the spectrum there are an enormous number of offenses committed by individuals whose engagement in crime is marginal and who would be seen by very few people as "real" criminals; a sizable proportion of the population regularly evades income tax, drives while drunk, or steals from employers or from shops. Reducing opportunities for these kinds of "everyday" offenses should result in overall gains. For instance, Decker (1972) found that the use of "slugs" in parking meters in a New York district was greatly reduced by introducing meters that incorporated a slug-rejector device and in which the last coin inserted was visible in a plastic window; few drivers would bother to park their cars in some less convenient place just because they could continue to use their slugs. Nor is it likely that reduced opportunities for these sorts of offenses would displace energies to other illegal activities. For example, if employees are stopped from using the office phone for personal use, it offends common sense to think that they will therefore turn their attention to the stationery supply. The risks to office stationery are quite independent of the difficulties of making illicit telephone calls.

But it is those offenses that are neither "professional" nor "everyday" that pose the most difficult questions about displacement. These offenses include many of the less carefully planned burglaries or auto thefts, where the offender, who may merely supplement his normal income through the proceeds of crime, has gone out with the deliberate intention of committing the offense and has sought the opportunity to do so. The difficulty posed for situational measures is one of the vast number of potential targets combined with a generally low overall level of security. Within easy reach of every house with a burglar alarm, or car with an antitheft device, are many others without such protection. For example, when steering column locks were introduced in Great Britain in 1971 they were installed only on new cars; and while the risk of these cars being stolen was reduced, the risk to older cars increased, presumably as a result of displacement (Mayhew et al. 1976). However, as West Germany's altogether happier experience with steering locks shows, it is sometimes possible to effectively protect a whole class of property in order to bring about an overall reduction in crime.

That displacement may be more likely for "professional" crime than for other kinds suggests that any general assessment of the value of situational prevention critically depends on the proportions of crime falling into these various groups. However, these proportions would be very difficult to estimate. Though available studies (see Petersilia 1980 for a review) suggest that perhaps the bulk of crime is committed by a small number of "persistent" offenders (who are not necessarily the same as "professionals"), these estimates rely exclusively upon officially recorded crime: "everyday" offenses that tend to be committed against organizations rather than individuals may be much less likely to be reported. What seems to be needed is a study (which would be very difficult to mount) involving some satisfactory combination of victim and self-report data for a sample of the whole population and for the entire spectrum of crime.

Finally, and as a footnote to this discussion that has been concerned with the reaction of specific individuals to blocked opportunities, a further reason why it would be difficult to make a precise assessment of the overall value of situational prevention is that situational measures may sometimes create opportunities for different forms of crime committed by completely different groups of offenders. For example, the movement to a "cashless" society in which financial transactions are largely computerized would greatly reduce the scope of petty pilfering but could create opportunities for crime of a very different order—large-scale computer fraud.

It is clear, then, that while displacement does not inevitably rob situational measures of their value, it poses a potential threat in every case of their application, and to defeat it may require considerable insight into the social and psychological contexts of offending.

IV. The Prospects for Situational Crime Control Strategies

To summarize the discussion to this point, it appears that situational prevention rests upon a sound basis of theoretical and empirical work that has drawn attention to the importance of immediate physical and social determinants of criminal behavior. Though some situational measures are naive or particularly prey to displacement, others have been notably successful.

A. *Practical Difficulties*

A significant expansion in situational prevention might therefore be justified, but this is unlikely to occur for one important reason: the risks of falling victim to particular crimes, either for individuals or organizations, may only rarely justify special action. For example, the loss from shoplifting for many stores is so small as to make it distinctly uneconomic for them to take preventive measures, especially where these might reduce sales. Similarly, the rather small risks of being burglarized for many householders rarely justify special measures (especially ones of doubtful effectiveness or that involve practical difficulties and substantial costs or inconvenience; cf. Gardiner and Balch 1980) beyond the purchase of homeowner's insurance.

Given these practical realities, it is not surprising that crime-prevention publicity campaigns that simply exhort people to take preventive measures by reminding them of risks of which they may already be aware seem largely ineffective, at least when measured in terms of behavioral change. Two "lock-up-your car" campaigns, one mounted by a local police force (Burrows and Heal 1979) and the other a much larger press and television campaign covering a large part of northern England (Riley and Mayhew 1980), have recently been the subject of Home Office evaluations. In both cases, before and after measures were taken for experimental and control areas, and in addition to the collection of auto theft statistics, security checks were made on parked vehicles. One result for the larger of the two studies, involving some 25,000 vehicles checked by the police, is shown in table 7. As will be seen, there was no evidence that people were more careful about locking their cars after the campaign, and a similar result was obtained in the smaller study. A third evaluation of an antivandalism campaign, making use of a parallel research design and using repair records for schools, housing estates, and public telephone installations to measure vandalism, also found no campaign effects (cf. Riley and Mayhew 1980).

It therefore seems that for those offenses where the risks to particular individuals are small, but where society would benefit from an overall reduction, some other means are needed for encouraging people to take the necessary preventive measures. Some of the possible ways, such as persuading insurance companies to offer discounted premiums to people who protect their houses, or passing laws like those existing in some European countries that make it an offense to leave parked cars unlocked, have recently been discussed by Pease (1979) and by Gardiner and Balch (1980). Whereas Pease is willing to entertain still more radical ideas, such as making the help of the police in dealing with shoplifters conditional on demonstrated efforts by the shopkeeper to prevent the offense, Gardiner and Balch conclude that even the more moderate proposals are frequently seen to be impractical or distasteful. Greater research understanding of these barriers to implementation is urgently needed—indeed, it might even be held that there is now a much clearer idea about the kind of preventive measures that should be taken in respect to particular forms of crime than about how to get them implemented. This

TABLE 7

Percentage of Cars Found to Be Completely
Secure in Checks Made by the Police, before and
after a Publicity Campaign

Area	Before Campaign	After Campaign
Campaign area	85.2	84.5
	(7,006)	(6,732)
Control area	83.1	82.4
	(6,232)	(5,239)

Source: Riley and Mayhew 1980.
Note: The number of cars involved in each check is given in parentheses.

is just as true of those cases where action depends not on individual members of the public but on organizations, private or otherwise. The organizations in question may not benefit greatly from the measures and may indeed be given considerable inconvenience and expense. There may also be problems of achieving the necessary cooperation between agencies.

These difficulties are illustrated by a Home Office "demonstration project" intended to help a local authority education department in tackling vandalism in some of its schools (Gladstone 1980). One proposal involved replacing windows in the schools' specially vulnerable areas with toughened glass. This scheme failed because ordering and storing the new glass would have required a considerable reorganization of the local authority's maintenance department. Another unsuccessful idea was a "good neighbor" scheme in which people living in the vicinity of schools would be encouraged to report suspicious incidents to the police. To implement this scheme required the cooperation of the education department, the schools' head teachers, and two different branches of the local police—those for crime prevention and community relations— and, in the event, despite backing from the education department, this cooperation could not be achieved.

B. *Other Difficulties*

Purely practical problems of implementation are only one set of reasons why the progress of situational prevention may not be rapid. Among criminologists, situational prevention will have to contend with the new orthodoxy of "nothing works," and in some quarters it will also raise the ghosts of positivism by its essentially quantitative stance. Its insistence on the specificity of preventive measures will also attract the hostility of those who see crime not as a self-contained problem but as an indicator of more general social malaise; they may feel that situational prevention deprives them of a useful lever for promoting broader social, economic, and educational reforms. These critics might also see the approach as little more than an attempt to shore up a socially divisive and inequitable system of law enforcement that should be attacked at its very roots. It can only be replied that there is a case for seeing incremental change as a safer strategy for reform, and that situational prevention does not exclude other action. In addition, most criminologists would probably agree that it would be better for the burden of crime reduction to be gradually shifted away from the criminal justice system, which may be not only ineffective but selective and punitive in its operation, to preventive measures whose social costs may be more equitably distributed among all members of society. One danger to be guarded against— perhaps through codes of security that would be legally binding on car manufacturers, builders, local transport operators, and so forth—is that the attention of offenders might be displaced away from those who can afford to purchase protection to those who cannot (cf. Wilson and Schneider 1978). Another is that those who have paid for their own protection may be less willing to see increased public expenditure on law enforcement services—which is a problem for political solution.

There are other more general worries. Situational measures can be too readily identified with their more unattractive aspects (barbed wire, heavy padlocks, guard dogs, and private security forces). And in some of their more sophisticated forms (closed circuit television surveillance and electronic intruder alarms) they provoke fears, on the one hand, of "big brother" forms of state control and, on the other, of a "fortress society" in which citizens scuttle from one protected environment to another in perpetual fear and suspicion of their fellows. Against these criticisms, it should be said that situational measures need not always be obtrusive and need not infringe individual liberties or lower the quality of life. Steel cash compartments in telephone booths are indistinguishable from aluminum ones, and steering column locks are automatically brought into operation by removing the ignition keys of cars. Defensible-space housing designs have the advantage of promoting feelings of neighborliness and safety, and better transport arrangements for soccer supporters could substantially improve enjoyment of the game.

A more fundamental difficulty than any of the above is that people often seem more disturbed by what offending represents—a threat to the moral order—than by its material consequences. Simply preventing crime is therefore not enough, because what is really wanted is the moral improvement of offenders: people should not *want* to disobey the law. In large measure, however, crime may be the price paid for some important freedoms: freedom of self-expression, freedom from oppressive forms of state control, and freedom from claustrophobic family ties or social obligations. Infringements of these freedoms—even in the cause of reducing crime—are likely to be strongly resisted, and it is unlikely that our own society could come to emulate the greater orderliness of some other, perhaps more constrained and regulated countries, such as Japan (Clifford 1976). For us the best hope for reducing crime—despite the various objections discussed above—may still lie in a more thorough-going application of the situational approach, piecemeal and laborious as this may be.

REFERENCES

Angel, Schlomo. 1968. *Discouraging Crime through City Planning*. Working Paper no. 75. Berkeley: University of California.

Baldwin, John. 1979. "Ecological and Areal Studies in Great Britain and the United States." In *Crime and Justice: An Annual Review of Research*, vol. 1, ed. Norval Morris and Michael Tonry, pp. 29–66. Chicago and London: University of Chicago Press.

Ball, John, L. Chester, and R. Perrott. 1978. *Cops and Robbers: An Investigation into Armed Robbery*. London: Andre Deutsch.

Bandura, Albert. 1973. *Aggression: A Social Learning Analysis*. Englewood Cliffs, N.J., and London: Prentice-Hall.

Barker, Roger G. 1968. *Ecological Psychology*. Stanford, Calif.: Stanford University Press.

Beyleveld, Derek. 1979. "Deterrence Research as a Basis for Deterrence Policies," *Howard Journal of Penology and Crime Prevention* 18:135–49.

Bottoms, Anthony E. 1974. Review of O. Newman, *Defensible Space, British Journal of Criminology* 14:204–6.

Brantingham, Paul J., and Patricia L. Brantingham. 1975. "The Spatial Patterning of Burglary," *Howard Journal of Penology and Crime Prevention* 14:11–24.

Bright, John A. 1969. "The Beat Patrol Experiment." Home Office Police Research and Development Branch. Unpublished.

Brody, Stephen R. 1976. *The Effectiveness of Sentencing*. Home Office Research Study no. 35. London: H.M. Stationery Office.

Brody, Stephen R., and Robert Tarling. 1980. *Taking Offenders out of Circulation*. Home Office Research Study no. 64. London: H.M. Stationery Office.

Brown, James H. 1979. "Suicide in Britain: More Attempts, Fewer Deaths, Lessons for Public Policy," *Archives of General Psychiatry* 36:1119–24.

Burrows, John, and Kevin Heal. 1979. "Police Car Security Campaigns." In *Crime Prevention and the Police*, ed. John Burrows, Paul Ekblom, and Kevin Heal. Home Office Research Study no. 55. London: H.M. Stationery Office.

Burt, Cyril. 1925. *The Young Delinquent*. London: University of London Press.

Chaiken, Jan M., Michael W. Lawless, and Keith A. Stevenson. 1974. *Impact of Police Activity on Crime: Robberies on the New York City Subway System*. Report no. R-1424-N.Y.C. Santa Monica, Calif.: Rand Corporation.

Cirel, Paul, Patricia Evans, Daniel McGillis, and Debra Whitcomb. 1977. *Community Crime Prevention—Seattle, Washington—An Exemplary Project*. National Institute of Justice, Law Enforcement Assistance Administration, U.S. Department of Justice. Washington, D.C.: U.S. Government Printing Office.

Clarke, Ronald V., ed. 1978. *Tackling Vandalism*. Home Office Research Study no. 47. London: H.M. Stationery Office.

————. 1982. "Crime Prevention through Environmental Management and Design." In *Abnormal Offenders, Delinquency and the Criminal Justice System*, ed. John C. Gunn and David P. Farrington. New York and London: Wiley.

Clarke, Ronald V., and J. Mike Hough, eds. 1980. *The Effectiveness of Policing*. Farnborough, Hants: Gower.

Clarke, Ronald V., and Patricia M. Mayhew, eds. 1980. *Designing out Crime*. London: H.M. Stationery Office.

Clarke, Ronald V., and David N. Martin. 1971. *Absconding from Approved Schools*. Home Office Research Study no. 12. London: H.M. Stationery Office.

Clifford, Brian R., and Ray Bull. 1978. *The Psychology of Person Identification*. London: Routledge and Kegan Paul.

Clifford, William. 1976. *Crime Control in Japan*. Lexington, Mass., Toronto, and London: Lexington Books.

Cohen, Lawrence E., and Marcus Felson. 1979. "Social Change and Crime Rate Trends: A Routine Activity Approach," *American Sociological Review* 44:588–608.

Cook, Philip J. 1980. "Research in Criminal Deterrence: Laying the Groundwork for the Second Decade." In *Crime and Justice: An Annual Review of Research*, vol. 2, ed. Norval Morris and Michael Tonry, pp. 211–68. Chicago and London: University of Chicago Press.

Decker, John F. 1972. "Curbside Deterrence: An Analysis of the Effect of a Slug Rejector Device, Coin View Window and Warning Labels on Slug Usage in New York City Parking Meters," *Criminology*, August, pp. 127–42.

Department of the Environment. 1977. *Housing Management and Design*. Lambeth Inner Area Study. IAS/IA/18. London: Department of the Environment.

Ditton, Jason. 1977. *Part-time Crime: An Ethnography of Fiddling and Pilferage*. London: Macmillan.

Downes, David, and Paul Rock, eds. 1979. *Deviant Interpretations*. Oxford: Martin Robertson.

Duffala, Dennis C. 1976. "Convenience Stores, Armed Robbery, and Physical Environmental Features," *American Behavioral Scientist* 20:227–46.

Ekblom, Paul. 1979. "A Crime-Free Car?" *Research Bulletin*, no. 7, pp. 28–30 (London, Home Office Research Unit).

Engstad, Peter A. 1975. "Environmental Opportunities and the Ecology of

Crime." In *Crime in Canadian Society*, ed. Robert A. Silverman and James J. Teevan, Jr. Scarborough, Ont.: Butterworths.

Eysenck, Hans J., ed. 1976. *Case Studies in Behavior Therapy*. Boston and London: Routledge and Kegan Paul.

Farrington, David P., and Barry J. Knight. 1979. "Two Non-reactive Field Experiments on Stealing from a 'Lost' Letter," *British Journal of Social and Clinical Psychology* 18:277–84.

Gabor, Thomas. 1978. "Crime Displacement: 'The Literature and Strategies for Its Investigation,'" *Crime and Justice* 6:100–106.

Gardiner, John A., and George I. Balch. 1980. "Getting People to Protect Themselves." In *Policy Implementation: Penalties or Incentives*, ed. John Brigham and Don W. Brown. Beverly Hills, Calif.: Sage Publications.

Gelfand, Donna M., Donald P. Hartmann, Patrick Walder, and Brent Page. 1973. "Who Reports Shoplifting? A Field Experimental Study," *Journal of Personality and Social Psychology* 23:276–85.

Gibbons, Don C. 1971. "Observations on the Study of Crime Causation," *American Journal of Sociology* 77:262–78.

Gladstone, Francis J. 1980. *Co-ordinating Crime Prevention Efforts*. Home Office Research Study no. 62. London: H.M. Stationery Office.

Gould, Leroy C. 1969. "The Changing Structure of Property Crime in an Affluent Society," *Social Forces* 48:50–59.

Greenwood, Peter. 1979. "Rand Research on Criminal Careers." In *Progress to Date*. Santa Monica, Calif.: Rand Corporation.

Hartshorne, Hugh, and Mark A. May. 1928. *Studies in the Nature of Character*. Vol. 1. *Studies in Deceit*. New York: Macmillan.

Hassall, Christine, and W. H. Trethowan. 1972. "Suicide in Birmingham," *British Medical Journal* 1:717–18.

Heller, Nelson B., William W. Stenzel, Allen D. Gill, Richard A. Kolde, and Stanley R. Schimerman. 1975. *Operation Identification—An Assessment of Effectiveness. National Evaluation Program—Phase I Summary Report*. National Institute of Criminal Justice, Law Enforcement Assistance Administration, U.S. Department of Justice. Washington, D.C.: U.S. Government Printing Office.

Henry, Stuart. 1978. *The Hidden Economy*. Oxford: Martin Robertson.

Hillier, B. 1973. "In Defense of Space," *RIBA Journal*, November, pp. 539–44.

Hindelang, Michael J. 1976. *Criminal Victimization in Eight American Cities*. Cambridge, Mass.: Ballinger.

Home Office. 1973. *Shoplifting and Thefts by Shop Staff*. Report of a Home Office Working Party on Internal Shop Security. London: H.M. Stationery Office.

———. 1976. *Report of the Departmental Committee on Evidence of Identification in Criminal Cases (Devlin Report)*. H.C. 338. London: H.M. Stationery Office.

Hood, Roger G., and Richard F. Sparks. 1970. *Key Issues in Criminology*. London: Weidenfeld and Nicolson.

Jacobs, Jane. 1961. *The Death and Life of Great American Cities*. New York: Random House.

Jeffrey, C. Ray. 1971. *Crime Prevention through Environmental Design*. Beverly Hills, Calif.: Sage Publications.

Kelling, George L., and Tony Pate. 1981. "A Study of Foot Patrol: The Newark Experiment," *Research Bulletin no. 11*, pp. 30–32 (London, Home Office Research Unit).

Kelling, George L., Tony Pate, Duane Dieckman, and Charles E. Brown. 1974. *The Kansas City Preventive Patrol Experiment*. Washington, D.C.: Police Foundation.

Knutsson, Johannes, and Eckhart Kuhlhorn. 1981. *Macro-Measures against Crime*. Information Bulletin no. 1. Stockholm: National Swedish Council for Crime Prevention.

Krasner, Leonard. 1980. *Environmental Design and Human Behavior*. Oxford: Pergamon.

Larson, Richard C. 1975. "What Happened to Patrol Operations in Kansas City? A Review of the Kansas City Preventive Patrol Experiment," *Journal of Criminal Justice* 3:267–97.

Latané, Bibb, and John M. Darley. 1970. *The Unresponsive Bystander: Why Doesn't He Help?* New York: Appleton-Century-Crofts.

Letkemann, Peter. 1973. *Crime as Work*. Englewood Cliffs, N.J.: Prentice-Hall.

Ley, David, and R. Cybrinwsky. 1974. "The Spatial Ecology of Stripped Cars," *Environment and Behavior* 6:53–67.

Louv, R. 1978. "Cutting Convenience Crime: A Little Social Science Ties-up a Lot of Robbers," *Human Behavior* 7:37–38.

Luedtke, Gerald, and Associates. 1970. *Crime and the Physical City: Neighborhood Design and Techniques for Crime Reduction*. Springfield, Va.: National Technical Information Service.

Maguire, Mike (in collaboration with Trevor Bennett). 1982. *Burglary in a Dwelling*. London: Heinemann.

Mansfield, Roger, Leroy C. Gould, and J. Zvi Namenwirth. 1974. "A Socio-economic Model for the Prediction of Societal Rates of Property Theft," *Social Forces* 52:462–72.

Mars, Gerald. 1973. "Hotel Pilferage: A Case Study of Occupational Theft." In *The Sociology of the Workplace*, ed. Mary Warner. London: Allen and Unwin.

Martinson, Robert. 1974. "What Works? Questions and Answers about Prison Reform," *Public Interest* 35:22–54.

Matza, David. 1964. *Delinquency and Drift*. New York: Wiley.

Mawby, Rob I. 1977. "Defensible Space: A Theoretical and Empirical Appraisal," *Urban Studies* 14:169–79.

Mayhew, Patricia M. 1979. "Defensible Space: The Current Status of a Crime Prevention Theory," *Howard Journal of Penology and Crime Prevention* 18: 150–59.

Mayhew, Patricia M., Ronald V. Clarke, John N. Burrows, J. Mike Hough, and Stuart W. Winchester. 1979. *Crime in Public View*. Home Office Research Study no. 49. London: H.M. Stationery Office.

Mayhew, Patricia M., Ronald V. Clarke, Andrew Sturman, and J. Mike Hough. 1976. *Crime as Opportunity*. Home Office Research Study no. 34. London: H.M. Stationery Office.

Mischel, Walter. 1968. *Personality and Assessment*. New York: Wiley.

Moos, Rudolph H. 1975. *Evaluating Correctional and Community Settings*. London and New York: Wiley.

Morris, Norval, and Gordon Hawkins. 1970. *The Honest Politician's Guide to Crime Control*. Chicago: University of Chicago Press.

Newman, Oscar. 1972. *Defensible Space: Crime Prevention through Urban Design*. New York: Macmillan.

———. 1980. *Community of Interest*. New York: Anchor Press/Doubleday.

Ohlin, Lloyd E. 1970. *A Situational Approach to Delinquency Prevention*. Washington, D.C.: Youth Development and Delinquency Prevention Administration, U.S. Department of Health, Education, and Welfare.

Osborn, Stephen S., and Donald J. West. 1980. "Do Young Delinquents Really Reform?" *Journal of Adolescence* 3:99–114.

Pablant, P., and J. C. Baxter. 1975. "Environmental Correlates of School Vandalism," *Journal of the American Institute of Planners* 41:270–79.

Pease, Ken. 1979. "Some Futures in Crime Prevention," *Research Bulletin*, no. 7, pp. 31–35 (London, Home Office Research Unit).

Petersilia, Joan. 1980. "Criminal Career Research: A Review of Recent Evidence." In *Crime and Justice: An Annual Review of Research*, vol. 2, ed. Norval Morris and Michael Tonry, pp. 321–79. Chicago: University of Chicago Press.

Poyner, Barry. 1981. *"Crime Prevention and the Environment: Street Attacks in City Centres*. Police Research Bulletin 37. London: Home Office.

Reppetto, Thomas A. 1974. *Residential Crime*. Cambridge, Mass.: Ballinger.

———. 1976. "Crime Prevention and the Displacement Phenomenon," *Crime and Delinquency* 22:166–77.

Rhodes, Robert P. 1977. *The Insoluble Problems of Crime*. New York: Wiley.

Riley, David, and Patricia M. Mayhew. 1980. *Crime Prevention Publicity: An Assessment*. Home Office Research Study no. 63. London: H.M. Stationery Office.

Rosenthal, Abraham M. 1964. *Thirty-eight Witnesses*. New York: McGraw-Hill.

Ross, Laurence. 1977. "The Intuitive Psychologist and His Shortcomings: Distortions in the Attribution Process." In *Advances in Experimental Social Psychology*, vol. 10, ed. Leonard Berkowitz. New York: Academic Press.

Scarr, Harry A. 1973. *Patterns of Burglary*. U.S. Department of Justice. Washington, D.C.: U.S. Government Printing Office.

Scottish Council on Crime. 1975. *Crime and the Prevention of Crime*. Scottish Home and Health Department. Edinburgh: H.M. Stationery Office.

Sinclair, Ian A. 1971. *Hostels for Probationers*. Home Office Research Study no. 6. London: H.M. Stationery Office.

Skogan, Wesley G. 1978. *Victimization Surveys and Criminal Justice Planning*. Visiting Fellowship Program Report. Washington, D.C.: National Institute of Law Enforcement and Criminal Justice.

Sparks, Richard F. 1980. "Criminal Opportunities and Crime Rates." In *Indicators of Crime and Criminal Justice: Quantitative Studies*, ed. Stephen E. Feinberg and Albert J. Reiss, Jr. Bureau of Justice Statistics, Department of Justice. Washington, D.C.: U.S. Government Printing Office.

Sturman, Andrew. 1978. "Measuring Vandalism in a City Suburb." In *Tackling Vandalism*, ed. Ronald V. Clarke. Home Office Research Study no. 47. London: H.M. Stationery Office.

Suttles, Gerald D. 1968. *The Social Order of the Slum: Ethnicity and Territory in the Inner City*. Chicago: University of Chicago Press.

Taylor, Ian, Paul Walton, and Jock Young. 1973. *The New Criminology*. London: Routledge and Kegan Paul.

Tizard, Jack. 1976. "Psychology and Social Policy," *Bulletin of the British Psychological Society* 29:225–33.

Trasler, Gordon B. 1979. "Delinquency Recidivism and Desistance," *British Journal of Criminology* 19:314–22.

Walker, Nigel D. 1979. "The Efficacy and Morality of Deterrents," *Criminal Law Review*, March, pp. 129–44.

Waller, Irvin, and Norman Okihiro. 1978. *Burglary: The Victim and the Public*. Toronto: University of Toronto Press.

Walsh, Dermot P. 1978. *Shoplifting: Controlling a Major Crime*. London: Macmillan.

———. 1980. *Break-ins: Burglary from Private Houses*. London: Constable.

Washnis, George J. 1976. *Citizen Involvement in Crime Prevention*. Lexington, Mass.: D. C. Heath.

Wilcox, S. 1974. "The Geography of Robbery." In *The Pattern and Control of Robbery*, vol. 3, ed. F. Feeney and A. Weir. Davis: University of California.

Wilkins, Leslie T. 1964. *Social Deviance*. London: Tavistock.

Wilkinson, Paul. 1977. *Terrorism and the Liberal State*. London: Macmillan.

Willems, Edwin P. 1977. "Reactions of Models to Methods in Behavioral Ecology." In *Ecological Factors in Human Development*, ed. Harry McGurk. Amsterdam: North-Holland.

Wilson, James Q. 1975. *Thinking about Crime*. New York: Basic Books.

Wilson, L. A., and A. L. Schneider. 1978. *Investigating the Efficacy and Equity of the Public Initiatives in the Provision of Private Safety*. Eugene, Oreg.: Institute of Policy Analysis.

Wilson, Sheena. 1978. "Vandalism and 'Defensible Space' on London Housing Estates." In *Tackling Vandalism*, ed. Ronald V. Clarke. Home Office Research Study no. 47. London: H.M. Stationery Office.

Winchester, Stuart W., and Hilary M. Jackson. 1983. "Residential Burglary: The Limits of Prevention." Home Office Research Unit. In preparation.

Wolfgang, Marvin, Robert E. Figlio, and Thorsten Sellin. 1972. *Delinquency in a Birth Cohort*. Chicago: University of Chicago Press.

Yin, Robert K., Mary E. Vogel, Jan M. Chaiken, and Deborah R. Both. 1977. *Citizen Patrol Projects*. National Evaluation Program Phase I Summary Report. National Institute of Law Enforcement and Criminal Justice. Law Enforcement Assistance Administration, U.S. Department of Justice. Washington, D.C.: U.S. Government Printing Office.

Zaharchuk, Ted, and Jennifer Lynch. 1977. *Operation Identification: A Police Prescriptive Package*. Ottawa: Ministry of Solicitor General.

Zimbardo, Philip G. 1973. "A Field Experiment in Autoshaping." In *Vandalism*, ed. Colin Ward. London: Architectural Press.

David P. Farrington

Randomized Experiments on Crime and Justice

ABSTRACT

An experiment investigates the effect of changes in one factor (the independent variable) on another (the dependent variable). The independent variable is under the control of the researcher. A randomized experiment is one in which people (or other units) are assigned to conditions according to a table of random numbers, with every person having the same probability of being assigned to each condition. These experiments are especially useful for testing causal hypotheses. Their unique advantage over other methods is their high internal validity, or high ability to demonstrate the effect of one factor on another. The randomization ensures that people assigned to one condition are equivalent in every possible way to those assigned to another condition, within the limits of statistical fluctuation.

Despite their methodological advantages, very few randomized experiments have been carried out on crime and justice topics. Most have investigated the effects of providing special help for offenders, and in most cases this help proved no more effective in reducing reoffending than did existing alternative treatment methods. It is difficult to arrange randomized experiments because program administrators are unwilling to relinquish control of assignment to experimenters, and because of ethical problems of denial of treatment. Randomized experiments are most feasible when the effects of a treatment are unknown and when it is impossible to treat everyone. Because of their high internal validity, hypotheses should be tested, and technologies should be evaluated, using randomized experiments whenever possible.

This essay outlines some of the uses, advantages, and problems of randomized experiments on crime and justice. Section I defines terms and contrasts experimentation with other possible research methods.

David P. Farrington is University Lecturer in Criminology, Cambridge University.
I am very grateful to Alfred Blumstein, Sheldon Messinger, Michael Tonry, and Nigel Walker for helpful comments on an earlier draft of this essay.

Section II describes major criminological experiments in three areas: (*a*) programs to help offenders and potential offenders in their natural environment, (*b*) police, courts, and penal institutions, and (*c*) committing and reporting crimes. Section III reviews major methodological, practical, and ethical problems arising in randomized experiments, and section IV, the conclusion, discusses when these experiments are feasible and desirable.

The emphasis throughout is on methodological issues rather than on substantive results, although some important findings are described. Comprehensive coverage of all the results and methodological issues of randomized experiments in crime and justice is, of course, not possible in an essay of this length. Only experiments published in English are included. In most cases these have been carried out in North America, Great Britain, Australia, New Zealand, the Netherlands, and the Scandinavian countries.

I. Introduction

A. *The Meaning of Randomized Experiments*

The word "experiment" is often used loosely to refer to any social action (especially if innovative) whose ultimate effects are uncertain. Following this definition, most methods of dealing with crime are experimental in nature (cf. Mannheim 1965). The word "experiment" has a different, and somewhat more precise, meaning in this essay. It refers to a systematic attempt to investigate the effect of variations in one factor (the independent variable) on a second (the dependent variable).

It is easiest to explain the nature of experimentation by discussing a specific example. Berg (Berg et al. 1978; Berg, Hullin, and McGuire 1979) wanted to investigate the relative effectiveness of two court dispositions, adjournment (continuance) and social work supervision, in the treatment of truancy. Both dispositions were being used by the juvenile court in Leeds, England. A retrospective study (Berg et al. 1977) suggested that adjournment was more effective than supervision in reducing subsequent truancy. However, the juveniles chosen for adjournment may have been different in some way from those chosen for supervision, and these preexisting differences may have caused the difference in outcome.

The best way to ensure that people receiving one treatment are equivalent to those receiving another is to assign them at random to the treatments. Providing that a reasonably large number of people are randomly assigned, those receiving one treatment will be equivalent, within the limits of statistical fluctuation, to those receiving another. It is then possible to disentangle the effects of the treatments from the effects of extraneous variables (uncontrolled differences between the groups). With the cooperation of the Leeds juvenile court, Berg carried out an experiment in which truants were randomly assigned either to adjournment or to supervision. During a six-month follow-up period, the supervised juveniles were more often truants and committed more criminal offenses, suggesting that adjournment was the more effective disposition in preventing truancy and delinquency.

In this example, the independent variable was the form of the disposition. The major dependent variable was truancy, and there was also a second dependent variable, delinquency. The random assignment meant that the adjourned and supervised groups were equivalent in extraneous factors that might have been related to truancy and delinquency (e.g. age, sex, social class, and school performance) and that might have been used as a basis for the dispositions in the uncontrolled situation. Therefore, in some way the subsequent differences in truancy and delinquency must have been produced by the different dispositions.

The defining feature of an "experiment" is the control of the independent variable. Berg assigned each juvenile to adjournment or supervision. In his retrospective study, the dispositions had, as usual, been under the control of the juvenile court magistrate. This essay is concerned with randomized experiments. In Berg's study, juveniles were assigned to adjournment or supervision by reference to a table of random numbers. In randomized experiments, there is control of both independent and extraneous variables.

The control of extraneous variables by randomization is similar to, but not exactly the same as, control of extraneous variables in the physical sciences by holding physical conditions (e.g. temperature, pressure) constant. Randomization ensures that the average unit in one treatment group is approximately equivalent to the average unit in another before the treatment is applied. Holding physical conditions constant ensures a more exact equivalence of experimental units, but the theory of experimental control is the same in both cases.

B. *Advantages of Randomized Experiments*

An experiment is designed to test a causal hypothesis about the effect of changes in one variable on changes in another. A hypothesis cannot be tested experimentally unless it can be expressed in these terms. In the classic model of scientific progress, a series of testable causal hypotheses is derived from each theory. If each hypothesis is tested in an experiment, the pattern of results can be compared with the pattern of theoretical predictions. On the basis of this comparison, and taking into account other considerations such as the complexity of a theory, it is possible to conclude that one theory is preferable to another. Ideally, each experiment should be one link in a chain of cumulative knowledge, guided by theory. In practice, well-developed, explicitly specified, falsifiable theories are rare in criminology, and the hypotheses tested by experiments are usually isolated rather than systematic tests of a larger theory.

Following Campbell and Stanley (1966) and Cook and Campbell (1979), the methodological adequacy of any test of a causal hypothesis can be assessed on four major criteria. *Statistical conclusion validity* refers to whether the two variables of interest really are related. *Internal validity* refers to whether a change in one variable really did produce a change in another. *Construct validity* refers to what the theoretical constructs are that underlie the measured variables; and *external validity* refers to how far the results can be generalized to different persons, settings, and times.

The unique advantage of randomized experiments over other methods is high internal validity. There are many threats to internal validity that are eliminated in randomized experiments but are serious in nonexperimental research. In particular, selection effects, owing to differences between the kinds of people in one condition and those in another, are eliminated. Because of the equivalence produced by randomization, observed effects cannot be attributed to history (events other than the treatment), maturation (people getting older), testing (increasing familiarity with measures), instrumentation (changes in methods of measurement), or statistical regression to the mean.[1] Another advantage of randomized experiments is that there is no ambiguity about the direction of causal influence.

---

[1]Statistical regression to the mean is based on the assumption that any measured score is a combination of two components, a true score and a randomly distributed error component. If a sample is chosen on the basis of high pretest scores, in many cases the error component will have increased the measured score above the true score. On the posttest, the error components will again be randomly distributed about the true score, so that the measured score of these people will decrease back toward the true score. Similarly, if a sample is chosen on the basis of low pretest scores, their measured scores will tend to increase on the posttest, purely because of this statistical fluctuation.

C. *Selection of Randomized Experiments*

This essay is concerned with randomized experiments on crime and justice. It includes projects such as Berg's, in which some measure of offending was a dependent variable, and projects on the operation of some aspect of the criminal justice system: police, courts, and penal institutions. It also includes studies of why people commit offenses and of reactions to offenses and offenders.

The emphasis is on experiments carried out in real-life settings. In the quest for increased control over independent and extraneous variables, many researchers conduct experiments in laboratories with students as subjects. The price that usually has to be paid for increased control is loss of construct and external validity, at least when these are defined in relation to real-life problems and settings. Randomized experiments are included in this essay only if they are concerned with real-life problems and settings, and those conducted on campuses are not included. It is unfortunate that researchers rarely attempt to investigate construct and external validity by replicating their experiments with different operational definitions of independent and dependent variables, different people, and different settings. The studies included in this essay should be highest, on all kinds of validity, of all kinds of criminological research, and this is the major reason for reviewing them.

The discussion so far is deliberately oversimplified. There can be several independent variables, several dependent variables, and complex experimental designs. For example, a *factorial* design might include two independent variables, each investigated at three levels (high, medium, and low). If each level of one variable was studied in combination with ("crossed" with) each level of the other, people would be assigned to one of nine conditions. Because experimentation on crime and justice is at an early stage of development, most experiments have relatively simple designs. Berg's study had only one independent variable with two levels, and this is typical.

Matching and randomization can be combined in a design. For example, in the classic Cambridge-Somerville study (Powers and Witmer 1951), 325 pairs of boys were matched on rated delinquency potential, and one member of each pair was chosen at random to receive the special treatment. This design reduces the number of sources of variation and so makes it more possible to detect any effect of the treatment. However, it can create problems in statistical analysis. Many statistical tests (e.g. chi-squared) are based on an underlying assumption of independent random samples, and matched groups are clearly not independent.

It might be thought that another method of ensuring equivalent groups would be to give all treatments to the same people in a random order, and this is the method favored in behavior modification research (see e.g. Farrington 1979a). However, in these "within-subjects" designs people who receive one treatment second are not necessarily the same as those who receive the other treatment second, because of the different effects of the treatments received first. It is possible to estimate the effects of prior treatments by comparing treated and untreated groups, but this requires a "between-subjects" design. Pure within-subjects designs are not discussed in this essay because they are likely to have lower internal validity than between-subjects designs.

The dependent variable can be measured after the manipulation of the independent variable or both before and after, as in a pretest-posttest design. An advantage of pretest measurement is that it can help to verify that the random assignment was successful in producing equivalent groups. A disadvantage is that the pretest may affect the posttest in some way, although it is possible to control for this in more complex designs.

In randomized experiments, each person has the same probability as each other person of being assigned to each condition, but these probabilities are not necessarily the same for all conditions. For example, Dobson and Cook (1979) carried out an experiment in which the probabilities of assignment to the four conditions were .286, .286, .300, and .129. Unequal assignment probabilities are necessary when programs can deal only with a limited number of clients at any given time.

Random assignment can be achieved most securely by reference to a table of random numbers. Assigning cases by tossing a coin, as was done in some of the earlier experiments (e.g. Powers and Witmer 1951), and even in some of the later ones (e.g. Lichtman and Smock 1981), is less satisfactory, because of the possibility that human errors and biases may spoil the randomization. Assigning alternate cases to experimental and control groups (e.g. Rosenberg 1964) may also be unsatisfactory if the scheduling of the cases is not random but can be manipulated in some way.

Although most randomized experiments involve persons, other experimental units, such as areas or institutions, could be randomly assigned. In practice, units other than persons are seldom sufficiently numerous for the randomization to ensure that those in each condition are equivalent. For example, Tornudd (1968) carried out an experiment in which three towns out of six were chosen at random to have lower probabilities of prosecuting persons arrested for drunkenness. With such

small numbers of experimental units, the randomization could not ensure equivalence, and some other method such as matching might as well
be used.[2] This essay concentrates on experiments with a minimum
number per condition of about fifty, which in practice means randomization of persons.

D. *Other Methods*

Extraneous variables can be controlled in advance of research by
randomization or by prospective matching. They can be controlled after
research has been carried out by retrospective matching or by some kind
of statistical analysis that estimates the relation between two variables
while holding others constant. Persons in different conditions of an
experiment can be matched on a small number of variables that are likely
to be related to the dependent measure (e.g. age, sex, race, type of
current offense, number of previous convictions) or on a large number of
variables by equating prediction scores.[3] Whatever method is used, the
major problem with matching is that it cannot ensure equivalence on all
extraneous variables, but only on a subset. It can always be argued that
differences in outcomes reflect differences in unmatched extraneous
variables rather than differences in treatments.

There are other problems. Generally, matching is inefficient; only
subsamples of those studied can be matched. If an experiment involves
matched pairs and one member of a pair is lost from the study, the other
member should also be excluded. This can lead to considerable attrition
and small final samples. Another problem is that matched groups are not
necessarily representative of populations, limiting the generalizability of
results. For example, if a group of people who were fined was matched
retrospectively with an imprisoned group, the matched fined group
might be unrepresentative of all fined offenders and the matched im-

[2] To understand why randomization ensures closer equivalence with larger samples,
imagine drawing samples of 10, 100, or 1,000 unbiased coins. With 10 coins, just over 10
percent of the samples would include 2 or less, or 8 or more, heads. With 100 coins, just
over 10 percent of the samples would include 41 or less, or 59 or more, heads. With 1,000
coins, just over 10 percent of the samples would include 474 or less, or 526 or more, heads.
It can be seen that, as the sample size increases, the proportion of heads in it fluctuates in a
narrower and narrower band around the mean figure of 50 percent.

[3] A prediction score is an estimate that a person will be rearrested or reconvicted within a
specified period. For example, in the parole research of Nuttall et al. (1977), the prediction
score was based on sixteen variables. On the employment variable, 1 was added to each
person's score if he was unemployed, 1 was deducted if he was self-employed, and 2 was
deducted if he was employed full time. These numbers were determined by the relation
between employment and reconviction. There was a straight-line relation between the
total prediction score and the probability of reconviction, so two people with the same
prediction score were effectively matched on their likelihood of being reconvicted.

prisoned group unrepresentative of all imprisoned offenders. Artifactual differences between the groups could be produced by their scores regressing to different means.[4]

Naturally occurring (uncontrolled) situations can be analyzed as though they involve relations between independent and dependent variables, by applying methods of statistical control such as partial correlations.[5] These analyses always have lower internal validity than randomized experiments. It is desirable, in nonexperimental or "quasi-experimental" research, to consider threats to internal validity systematically and to attempt to deal with them (see e.g. Campbell and Ross 1968; Farrington 1977; Ross, Campbell, and Glass 1970; Schnelle and Lee 1974).

As already mentioned, an experiment is especially suitable for testing a hypothesis about the influence of one factor on another. Remember that Berg was interested in testing the hypothesis that adjournment was more effective than supervision as a treatment for truancy. The experimental method is unsuitable in the absence of such causal hypotheses. Hypothesis-testing research should always be preceded by hypothesis-generating research, which need not be experimental. Indeed, unstructured interviews or participant observation may be more effective than experiments in generating hypotheses, although experiments are usually more effective in testing hypotheses. Berg, for instance, preceded his experiment with a retrospective, nonexperimental study of records.

Experiments are usually more suitable to establish whether changes in an independent variable produce changes in a dependent variable than to determine the relative importance of or interactions between many independent variables. Berg demonstrated that the case disposition influenced truancy and delinquency, but he did not establish the relative influence of the disposition and other variables such as age, sex, and social class. Many factors such as age and sex could not be manipulated as independent variables, except in simulation experiments. Correlational research, using methods such as path analysis, multiple regression,

---

[4]Regression to the mean is explained in note 1 above. If matched samples are drawn from two populations with different true mean scores, the mean scores of the samples will tend to move toward their respective population means between a pretest and a posttest.

[5]A correlation coefficient measures the strength of the relation between two variables. A partial correlation measures the strength of the relation between two variables independently of their associations with a third variable (see e.g. Blalock 1972).

and log-linear modeling,[6] may be more suitable for establishing relative importance and interactions. Similarly, experimentation, with its static independent variable/dependent variable design, is not very suitable for investigating reciprocal influences between variables.[7]

While a given experiment can demonstrate whether a change in A produces a change in B, it will not usually establish the variables or processes that intervene between A and B. For example, Berg did not demonstrate *why* adjournment was more effective than supervision. One possibility is that the educational welfare officers who usually dealt with adjourned cases put great emphasis on getting the children back to school, while the social workers who dealt with supervised cases put more emphasis on understanding the child's problems. Any experiment is likely to leave loose ends of this kind, often generating further testable hypotheses. The interpretation of any experiment may be easier if it includes interviews and observations.

E. *Difficulties of Reviewing Randomized Experiments*

Published randomized experiments on crime and justice topics are rare. In a review of community programs for the prevention and treatment of juvenile delinquency, Wright and Dixon (1977) could identify only ninety-six that provided empirical data, and only forty-seven of these were described in published sources. Only twenty-seven had randomized or matched samples, and only nine projects combined randomization with an outcome measure of delinquent behavior and a follow-up period of at least six months.

Similar conclusions about the rarity of randomized experiments and frequency of unpublished reports are reached in other reviews. Logan (1972) found that only twenty-three out of one hundred projects evaluating crime and delinquency programs, and having at least a quasi-

[6]Path analysis is a method of investigating causal relationships between variables (see e.g. Land 1969). It makes use of a path diagram, which shows the effect of each variable on each other one. The strength of each effect is estimated by means of a path coefficient, which is analogous to a partial correlation coefficient (see note 5 above). Multiple regression analysis is a method of investigating how a number of independent variables combine to predict a dependent variable (see e.g. Blalock 1972). While path analysis and multiple regression analysis are generally based on variables measured on interval scales (such as height and weight), log-linear modeling is a method for use with variables classified in categories (see e.g. Fienberg 1980). The log-linear method can be used to show the strength of the relation between two categorical variables independently of a third.

[7]A reciprocal influence between two variables, A and B, occurs if a change in A produces a change in B, and a change in B produces a change in A.

experimental design, used random assignment. Sechrest, White, and Brown (1979, p. 76) referred to the problem of "fugitive literature," namely technical reports, unpublished papers, or articles published in out-of-the-way places. In addition to their low accessibility, such reports often were of poor quality, because they never had to undergo the rigorous reviewing process typical of reputable academic journals.

The most extensive bibliography of realistic randomized experiments was compiled by Boruch, McSweeny, and Soderstrom (1978). They noted among the major problems the ambiguity or absence of information about whether an experiment involved randomization and the promiscuous use of the word "experimentation." Under the heading "criminal and civil justice" they were able to list reports on seventy-four projects, of which thirty-six were unpublished. Criminal and civil justice was one of the categories about which they were most confident that they had identified a notable majority, if not the entire population, of projects. However, their list includes hardly any of the British randomized experiments.

The present review has been similarly impeded by absence and ambiguity of information. For example, a statement such as "two control groups were randomly chosen to match the treatment group closely on major variables" (Glaser 1964, p. 209) is not unusual. Again, Sarason and Ganzer (1973, p. 443) stated that their "assignment of subjects to conditions was essentially random but was occasionally influenced by weekly admission rates." Only projects that were clearly randomized experiments are reviewed here, not including the above two examples.

Despite their methodological advantages, randomized experiments constitute a tiny fraction of all research on crime and justice. This is because they are very difficult to carry through successfully. One aim of this essay is to describe these difficulties, partly because no researcher should embark on a randomized experiment without being aware of them, but also in the hope that they can be overcome.

F. *Summary*

This essay is concerned with *experiments on crime and justice*, investigating the effects of changes in independent variables on dependent variables. It is further concerned with *randomized* experiments in which each person is assigned to each condition at random, and with randomized experiments in *real-life settings*. Such experiments are especially useful for testing causal hypotheses. Their unique advantage over other methods is their high internal validity, or high ability to demonstrate the effect of one factor on another.

II. The Uses of Randomized Experiments

A. *Helping People in the Natural Environment*
Table 1 summarizes the major published randomized experiments that have been concerned with helping offenders and potential offenders in the natural environment (the community or the school) to stop offending. Detailed criteria for inclusion in this table are given in Appendix 1. It should be noted that the descriptions of investigators, subjects, design, and results are extremely abbreviated. For example, in the Empey and Lubeck (1971) experiment, the subjects were repeat offenders aged 15–17, excluding sex offenders, drug addicts, the mentally retarded, and psychiatric cases. The original reports must be consulted for full details of the experiments.

The help given, often labeled "counseling" in table 1, was nonspecific and heterogeneous in most cases. For example, in the Cambridge-Somerville study evaluated by McCord (1978), the 325 treated boys received regular friendly attention from counselors and whatever medical and educational services were needed. The counselors talked to the boys, took them on trips and to recreational activities, tutored them in reading and arithmetic, encouraged them to participate in the YMCA and summer camps, played games with them at the project's center, encouraged them to attend church, alerted ministers and priests to their problems, kept in close touch with the police, and visited families to give advice and general support (see McCord and McCord 1959).

The methodological problems of these kinds of experiments are discussed in detail in section III. Attempting to summarize the results shown in table 1, it seems that the special help that was provided was usually ineffectual in reducing offending, at least in comparison with the more usual treatments received by the control groups. In sixteen of the twenty-two experiments, there was no significant difference in recidivism between the helped and control groups.

In two of the other six cases, the group receiving special help had a higher recidivism rate. The experiment by Berg and his colleagues (1978) has already been discussed in some detail. In the second Community Treatment Project (Palmer 1974; CTP2), the delinquents were classified as needing or not needing institutional treatment. Those who needed

TABLE 1

Experiments on Helping People in the Natural Environment

Investigators	Subjects	Design	Results
Berg et al. (1978)—UK	96 M & F truants	(1) adjourned (2) supervised	(1) lower reoffending in 6 months
Binder & Newkirk (1977)	Youths referred by police	(1) behavioral program (2) no treatment	(1) fewer rearrests in 1 year
Byles and Maurice (1979)—Canada	305 M & F juveniles caught by police	(1) family therapy (2) traditional youth bureau	N.S.D. recidivism in 2 years
Ditman et al. (1967)	301 M & F drunks	(1) alcohol clinic (2) Alcoholics Anonymous (3) no treatment	N.S.D. rearrests in at least 1 year
Empey & Erickson (1972)	150 M recidivists	(1) community program including guided group interaction (2) probation	N.S.D. rearrests in 4 years
Empey & Lubeck (1971)	261 M recidivists	(1) community program including guided group interaction (2) institution	N.S.D. recidivism in 1 year
Folkard, Smith & Smith (1976)—UK	900 M & F probationers	(1) intensive probation (2) regular probation	N.S.D. reconvictions in 2 years
Hackler & Hagan (1975)	353 M youths in 4 public housing projects	(1) supervised work (2) teaching machine testing (3) control	N.S.D. delinquency in 4 years
Lamb & Goertzel (1974)	110 M sentenced to jail	(1) community program (2) jail	N.S.D. parole revocation in 6 months
Lichtman & Smock (1981)	503 M probationers	(1) intensive probation (2) regular probation	N.S.D. reconvictions in 2–3 years

Study	Sample	Treatment groups	Outcome
McCord (1978)	650 schoolboys	(1) counseled (2) no treatment	N.S.D. convictions in 30 years
Meyer, Borgatta & Jones (1965)	381 schoolgirls	(1) counseled (2) control	N.S.D. court appearances in 3 years
O'Donnell, Lydgate & Fo (1979)	553 M & F referred youths	(1) had buddies (2) control	N.S.D. rearrests in 3 years
Palmer (1974)—CTP1	802 M delinquents	(1) community treatment (2) institution	(1) lower revocations in 2 years
Palmer (1974)—CTP2	106 M delinquents needing/not needing institutionalization	(1) community treatment (2) institution	If need institution, (1) higher reoffending in 18 months. Otherwise, N.S.D.
Quay & Love (1977)	568 M & F referred juveniles	(1) counseled (2) control	(1) lower rearrests in about 1 year
Reckless & Dinitz (1972)	1,094 schoolboys	(1) classes to improve self-concept (2) control classes	N.S.D. police contacts and self-reported delinquency in 3 years
Reimer & Warren (1957)	3,793 M parolees	(1) low caseload (2) regular case oad	N.S.D. major arrests in 23 months
Rose & Hamilton (1970)—UK	394 M arrested juveniles	(1) cautioned and supervised (2) cautioned	N.S.D. recidivism in 2 years
Rossi, Berk & Lenihan (1980)—LIFE	432 M former prisoners	(1) job counseling (2) unemployment benefit (3) both (4) control	(2) and (3) lower rearrests in 1 year
Rossi, Berk & Lenihan (1980)—TARP	3,982 M & F former prisoners	(1)(2)(3) unemployment benefit (4) job counseling (5)(6) control	N.S.D. rearrests in 1 year
Venezia (1972)	123 M & F delinquents	(1) unofficial probation (2) counsel and release	N.S.D. referral to probation in 6 months

Notes: N.S.D. = not significantly different; United States research unless otherwise stated.

institutional treatment had a higher reoffending rate if they were treated in the community rather than in an institution. Those who did not need institutional treatment offended at the same rate in the two conditions.

None of the four experiments showing a lower recidivism rate for the helped group is entirely persuasive. Binder and Newkirk's (1977) positive results are complicated by a later unpublished report that indicated their program had the desired effects in one town but not in another. Palmer's (1971, 1974) positive results in the first Community Treatment Project (CTP1) may reflect parole revocation criteria rather than reoffending patterns. According to Lerman (1975), the community treatment and institutional groups had equal rearrest rates but different probabilities of having their parole revoked after an arrest. Lerman concluded that the Community Treatment Project had succeeded in changing the discretionary decision-making behavior of adult correctional officials but had had no appreciable effect on the behavior of the youths.

Quay and Love's (1977) positive findings were challenged by Mrad (1979). Mrad showed that, when days in the program were added to the follow-up period afterward, the counseled group had an average rearrest rate of 40 percent in an average 400 days, while the control group had an average rearrest rate of 45 percent in an average 450 days. In reply, Quay and Love (1979) argued that there was a significant difference if the cutoff point for both groups was set at 300 days. Whether the program led to a lasting decrease in the rearrest rate seems uncertain.

Rossi, Berk, and Lenihan (1980) reported that special financial help for former prisoners decreased rearrests for property crimes in the "LIFE" project, although the difference was barely significant, at the .05 level in a one-tailed test.[8] This result was not replicated in their "TARP" experiment, although they argued in this case that the effects of financial help in decreasing reoffending had been canceled out by its effects in increasing unemployment.

The sixteen experiments reporting no significant effects will not be discussed in detail here. In some instances a real effect of treatment may have been masked by some other factor. However, the results summarized in table 1 are in agreement with the hypothesis that existing

---

[8] A one-tailed statistical test investigates whether an effect is present in one direction only. A two-tailed test investigates whether there is a significant deviation in either direction from chance expectation. A result that is barely significant at the .05 level in a one-tailed test (i.e., with a probability of .05 of being obtained by chance) would not be significant at the .05 level in a two-tailed test. With the sample sizes commonly used in social science research, such a result generally indicates a weak relationship.

methods of helping people in the natural environment are no more effective in reducing reoffending than existing alternative treatment methods. The theoretical implications of this conclusion will not be discussed in detail here, in view of the concentration on method. One possible conclusion is that being friendly to offenders, discussing their problems with them, and attempting to build up relationships with them are ineffective methods of changing delinquent and criminal behavior.

B. *Experiments on Police, Courts, and Institutions*

Table 2 summarizes the major published randomized experiments on police, courts, and institutions. As before, detailed criteria for inclusion are given in Appendix 1. The experiments in table 2 are more heterogeneous than those in table 1. The majority (twelve) were attempts to help institutionalized delinquents or prisoners to stop offending. Of these twelve, eight reported no significant difference in recidivism between helped and control groups.

Of the four experiments that succeeded in reducing the recidivism of institutionalized groups, two (Berntsen and Christiansen 1965; Shaw 1974) were attempts to help prisoners deal with the problems they faced after release (e.g. accommodation and employment). Why they were successful is uncertain. According to Shaw (1974, p. 94), "the most likely way in which the experimental situation may have influenced the results was by raising the interest of the welfare officers." It is unfortunate that Fowles's (1978) experiment, which was almost a replication of Shaw's, found that the special counseling in prison was ineffectual. The reason the casework institution was more effective than traditional or group counseling institutions in Williams's (1970) research is also unclear.

The fourth experiment showing positive results, Adams's "PICO" project (1970), demonstrates an interaction between types of people and types of treatment. Institutionalized delinquents were divided into those thought amenable and those thought nonamenable to the individual counseling treatment, and both groups were then randomly assigned to treated and control groups. The "treated amenable" group had the lowest rate of return to custody, while the "treated nonamenable" group had the highest rate. A problem in this experiment is that, while sixteen hundred youths were randomly assigned, the analysis was based on the first one hundred released in each condition (amenable or nonamenable, treatment or control). The randomization ensured comparability of all treated and all control youths, but whether treated youths released first were comparable to control youths released first is less certain.

TABLE 2
Experiments on Police, Courts, and Institutions

Investigators	Subjects	Design	Results
Adams (1970)	400 institutionalized delinquents rated amenable or nonamenable	(1) counseled (2) control	(1) amenable lowest return to custody in 33 months (1) nonamenable highest
Annis (1979)—Canada	150 M prisoners	(1) group therapy (2) control	N.S.D. reconvictions in 1 year
Ares, Rankin & Sturz (1963)	726 defendants	(1) pretrial release recommended (2) control	(1) more released, more dismissed/acquitted
Baker & Sadd (1981)	666 M defendants in felony cases	(1) helped in court, given job counseling (2) processed normally by court	(1) more dismissed. N.S.D. rearrests in 1 year
Berntsen & Christiansen (1965)—Denmark	252 prisoners	(1) counseled (2) control	(1) lower reconvictions in at least 6 years
Bond & Lemon (1981)—UK	120 M & F magistrates	(1) regular training (2) deferred training	(1) less concerned with deterrence and protection of society in 1 year
Cornish & Clarke (1975)—UK	173 M institutionalized delinquents	(1) therapeutic community (2) traditional training	N.S.D. reconvictions in 2 years
Earle (1973)	174 M police	(1) stressful training (2) nonstressful training	(2) fewer disciplinary actions in 2 years
Fowles (1978)—UK	290 M prisoners	(1) counseled (2) control	N.S.D. reconvictions in 1 year

Study	Sample	Conditions	Results
Goldman (1979)	302 civil cases	(1) conference & deadline (2) control	(1) dealt with more quickly
Jesness (1971a)	281 M institutionalized delinquents	(1) 20-bed unit (2) 50-bed unit	N.S.D. revocations in 5 years
Jesness (1971b)	1,173 M institutionalized delinquents	(1) treated according to I-level (2) regular living units	N.S.D. revocations in 2 years
Jesness (1975)	913 M institutionalized delinquents	(1) psychodynamic institution (2) behavioral institution	N.S.D. violations in 2 years
Kassebaum, Ward & Wilner (1971)	512 M prisoners	(1) small-group counseling (2) large-group counseling (3) control	N.S.D. rearrests in 3 years
Lenihan (1977)	120 defendants	(1) telephone available (2) telephone not available	(1) more released
Rosenberg (1964)	2,954 defendants in personal injury cases	(1) mandatory pre-trial conference (2) not mandatory	(1) cases take longer but recover more money
Shaw (1974)—UK	176 M prisoners	(1) counseled (2) control	(1) lower reconvictions in 2 years
Stapleton & Teitelbaum (1972)	1,131 M juveniles in court	(1) legally represented (2) not represented	(1) dismissed more in one of two cities
Waldo & Chiricos (1977)	281 prisoners	(1) work release (2) control	N.S.D. in self-reported and official arrests in 46 months
Williams (1970)—UK	610 institutionalized youths	(1) casework institution (2) group-counseling institution (3) traditional institution	(1) lower reconvictions in 2 years

Notes: N.S.D. = not significantly different; United States research unless otherwise stated.

Of the other eight experiments summarized in table 2, seven were on court processes and one (Earle 1973) was on police training. Earle contrasted the usual stressful training method with a nonstressful method and found that 6.3 percent of the nonstressful group were subject to disciplinary actions in a two-year follow-up period, compared with 18.3 percent of the stressful group. These percentages would be significantly different at the .05 level on a one-tailed chi-squared test, although such a test would be invalid in the light of the combination of matching and randomization in the design. The stress and non-stress groups were not significantly different in commendations and complaints.

The seven court experiments all had significant results. In the Manhattan bail project (Ares, Rankin, and Sturz 1963; Botein 1965) defendants recommended for pretrial release by the project staff were more likely to be released than those not recommended. Similarly, in the Vera court employment project (Baker and Sadd 1981), defendants included in the project were more likely to have their cases dismissed than the control group, although the two groups were equally likely to be rearrested during a one-year follow-up period.

Rosenberg (1964) studied the effect of having a mandatory pretrial conference in personal injury cases and found that cases in the mandatory group tended to take longer but to recover more money. Goldman (1979) studied the effect of two preappeal procedures, namely a conference between adversaries and an order setting time deadlines for critical events. He found that cases subject to these procedures were dealt with more quickly and were just as well briefed and argued before the appellate judges as other cases.

In Bond and Lemon's (1981) experiment, comparing magistrates who received the regular training during their first year with those who deferred their training until after the end of this year, the training seemed to make the magistrates less concerned with deterrence and the protection of society. The training consisted of instruction on the nature of the magistrates' court and its role in the judicial system and included a number of visits to penal institutions.

Lenihan (1977) investigated the effect of making a telephone available to defendants awaiting trial in a detention house and reported that those who had the telephone were more likely to be released before their trials. This difference was significant at the .05 level only in a one-tailed test.[9]

[9]See note 8 above.

Interestingly, the district attorney's office and the courts opposed and effectively blocked acceptance of the telephone after the experiment. The courts liked to have defendants in custody because this ensured their appearance on the appointed day, and the district attorney found it easier to conduct plea bargaining with defendants in custody. The telephone was eventually installed in the detention house after a riot by the inmates that was attributed to overcrowding. As Lenihan (1977, p. 582) wryly commented, "so speaks the power of violence over the power of social research."

The final experiment, by Stapleton and Teitelbaum (1972), studied the effect of providing legal representation for juveniles in two courts. One juvenile court was legalistic in orientation, for example, allowing tests of the admissibility of evidence and clearly separating adjudication and disposition, while the other had a traditional welfare orientation. The legal representation was effective in securing more dismissals in the legalistic court, but not in the welfare court. The welfare court would proceed without witnesses and a plea, it did not respect the privilege against self-incrimination, and the judge would enter a finding on different grounds from the original petition.

Readers may be surprised by the exclusion from table 2 of the Kansas City Preventive Patrol Experiment (Kelling et al. 1976), which is perhaps the most famous experiment on policing. It was reported that fifteen beats were randomly divided into three groups, five reactive (responding only to calls for service), five control (with one car per beat), and five proactive (with two or three cars per beat). The three groups of beats did not differ in crimes reported either to the police or in a victimization survey.

The Kansas City experiment controlled the independent variable of police patrolling strategy, although some commentators (e.g. Larson 1975; but see Risman 1980) have argued that the three policing strategies were not functionally distinct. However, the randomization procedure did not control extraneous variables. If fifteen beats were randomly assigned, this would be too small a number to ensure equivalence on extraneous variables.[10] As Fienberg, Larntz, and Reiss (1976) pointed out, it seems unlikely that the beats were randomly assigned, since the reactive beats were at the corners and in the middle of the experimental area. This is confirmed by Pate, Kelling, and Brown's (1975) statement that the police selected the configuration of beats that best suited the

[10]See note 2 above.

department's operational concerns. The Kansas City project was therefore not a randomized experiment.

C. *Experiments on Committing and Reporting Crimes*

A summary table is not provided for these experiments because they are less important than those summarized in tables 1 and 2. Experiments on committing crimes are typically concerned with marginal or trivial criminal behavior, and experiments on reporting crimes are some distance away from the criminal justice system. Both have been reviewed elsewhere (Farrington 1979b), and so a comprehensive coverage is not attempted here.

In experiments on committing crimes, members of the public are usually given an opportunity to be dishonest. These experiments can be reactive, involving direct contact between experimenters and subjects, or nonreactive. One of the first reactive studies was carried out by Feldman (1968). He pretended to pick up money in the street and offered it to members of the public, asking if they had dropped it. The subjects had an opportunity to claim the money dishonestly. The same method has been used by Farrington and Kidd (1977).

Feldman also gave cashiers and store clerks too much money when buying items, providing an opportunity for them to keep the money dishonestly; Korte and Kerr (1975) also used this method. Bickman (1971) left coins in telephone booths and asked users of the booths whether they had picked up the coins. Again, the users had an opportunity to keep the money dishonestly. This method has also been used by others (Franklin 1973; Kleinke 1977; Sroufe et al. 1977). These experiments have shown that stealing is greater with victims who are lower class and unattractive.

The nonreactive experiments have mostly used the "lost letter" technique. Hornstein, Fisch, and Holmes (1968), Hornstein (1970), and Tucker et al. (1977) left wallets containing cash in an envelope on the street for members of the public to pick up. Farrington and Knight (1979, 1980) and Knox and McTiernan (1973) also left cash in an apparently lost letter on the street, which members of the public could choose to post honestly or keep dishonestly. These experiments have shown that stealing is greater when the amount of money is larger, when the apparent victim is dissimilar to the subject, and when the apparent victim is male rather than female.

One of the most realistic experiments on committing crimes was carried out by Schwartz and Orleans (1967). Taxpayers were randomly assigned to three groups, and each person was interviewed during the month before income tax returns were filed. One interview stressed moral reasons for paying income tax, one stressed the threat of sanctions for nonpayment, and the third mentioned neither. There was also a randomly chosen noninterviewed group. Schwartz and Orleans found that the amount of income tax paid (in comparison with the previous year) was significantly greater in the moral appeal group than in the other three, suggesting that this moral appeal was the most effective of these methods in decreasing tax evasion.

Experiments on reporting crimes have usually studied shoplifting. Typically, the experimenter has arranged for an apparent shoplifting incident to take place in a store and has then investigated the willingness of members of the public to report it to the staff of the store. Steffensmeier and Terry (1973) and Steffensmeier and Steffensmeier (1977) found that shoplifters dressed as hippies were more likely to be reported than those dressed conventionally, but this result was not obtained by Gelfand et al. (1973).

The series of experiments carried out by Bickman is the most extensive. He found that reporting was greater when the shopper had had an unpleasant interaction with the shoplifter (Bickman and Green 1975) and when the shopper was encouraged to report by another person (Bickman and Rosenbaum 1977; Bickman 1979), but less when the shopper had had an unpleasant interaction with the salesclerk (Bickman 1976). Promises of anonymity or rewards by the store did not affect reporting (Bickman and Helwig 1979).

One of the most realistic series of experiments concerned with reactions to offending has focused on the reactions of employers. Typically, applications for jobs have been sent to employers, either mentioning or not mentioning previous convictions, to investigate if a criminal record affects whether an applicant is called for an interview. Schwartz and Skolnick (1962) found that a conviction for assault considerably reduced the likelihood of a positive response from an employer, and an acquittal on an assault charge was almost as bad.[11] These results were replicated in Canada by Palys (1976).

The effects of convictions for other kinds of offenses have also been studied. Buikhuisen and Dijksterhuis (1971) in Holland reported that

[11]This may not have been a randomized experiment. Schwartz and Skolnick (1962, p. 135) note that "employers were not approached in preselected random order, due to a misunderstanding of instructions on the part of the law student who carried out the experiment."

convictions for theft and for drunken driving both reduced employers' positive responses, but Boshier and Johnson (1974) replicated the experiment in New Zealand and discovered that only the theft conviction had this effect. In Canada, Erickson and Goodstadt (1979) found that a conviction for possessing marijuana significantly decreased positive responses.

Experiments on why people commit crimes and on how people react to offenses and offenders can increase our knowledge of these topics, especially if direct observational measures are used. Most of our knowledge about offending is derived by indirect methods, from official statistics or self-reports. The challenge to researchers is to study offending in controlled situations with high construct and external validity in relation to what most people would call "real crimes."

III. Problems of Randomized Experiments

A. *The Independent Variable*

The methodological problems discussed in this section are especially pertinent to randomized experiments of the sort listed in tables 1 and 2. Some of the problems also apply to nonexperimental studies, which in general present greater difficulties of interpretation than experiments. Many of the points raised here are set out as a checklist, in Appendix 2, that may be consulted by persons writing or reading reports of experiments.

Randomized experiments can be used purely for evaluation of existing technologies or practices (such as the pretrial conference; see Rosenberg 1964). In order to advance knowledge, they are best used to test causal hypotheses derived from an underlying theory. It is often unclear whether a criminological experiment is intended to evaluate a technology or to test a causal hypothesis (or both). Many experiments seem to have been inspired by the vague hope that various kinds of help would tend to rehabilitate offenders. It is often difficult to decide what theoretical constructs were being measured by what operational definitions.

The exact nature of the treatments given in experiments is often unclear. When they are described in detail, there is often disagreement about the theoretical labels that should be given to them. Kassebaum, Ward, and Wilner (1971) gave extensive details about their "group counseling." The detailed description permitted Quay (1977) to argue that the service was delivered by minimally trained and inexpert personnel, and consequently that adequate group counseling was not pro-

vided. Similarly, Vosburgh and Alexander (1980) argued that the treatment given in the Cambridge-Somerville study was "friendly visiting" rather than "individual psychotherapy." Lerman (1975) pointed out that the "community treatment" group in Palmer's (1971) project actually spent far more time in an institution than receiving community treatment. All these arguments revolve round the issue of construct validity.

The information given in experiments about the nature of the treatment is usually insufficient to permit replication. The most basic information about time spent in the program or attendance of clients at sessions is often missing. Sechrest and Redner (1979) have drawn attention to the problem of "integrity" of treatment, by which they mean the extent to which the treatment plan was carried out as intended. Again, documentation on this is often missing.

Treatments specified at the beginning of an experiment may change over time. Especially with innovative treatments, administrators may wish to correct perceived defects and make improvements. If researchers wish to assure themselves that the treatments have not changed, continuous monitoring is necessary. A related problem is that the existence of the experiment may cause official policies to change. Clarke and Cornish (1972) reported that the number of juveniles sent to the institution they were studying declined after the experiment began, because the classifying center was concerned that juveniles might not receive the most suitable treatment. Whether classifying staff can predict which youths will respond best to which regimes is doubtful. For example, in another English experiment Williams (1970) found that psychologists' predictions of reconviction were less accurate if they took into account the institution to which a boy was sent than if they did not. The psychologists expected the least disturbed boys to do best in the traditional institution, and the most disturbed boys to do worst, but the reverse proved to be the case.

Treatments may also vary with place and with treatment staff. Attempts are often made to select staff who are sympathetic to the particular treatment they are giving (e.g. Cornish and Clarke 1975). However, this makes it difficult to disentangle the effects of the treatment from the effects of the staff. This disentangling is possible if staff are randomly assigned to treatments, but against this is might be argued that the effects of a treatment depend on the staff giving it. In view of the history of negative results in criminological evaluation, the best solution may be to carry out an initial experiment in which staff are carefully assigned to give treatments the highest possible chance of success.

If a treatment is successful in the initial experiment, a subsequent study could be carried out in which staff were randomly assigned to treatments.

Few researchers have attempted to investigate the possibility of a "Hawthorne" effect, namely that any kind of special concern or attention given to clients might lead to an improvement in their behavior. This effect is more likely in a treatment group than in a control group. To allow for it, more than one treatment group could be included in an experiment.

The external validity of an experiment may be low if, as is common, treatment staff are unusually enthusiastic and expert. It may be that manipulations that have the desired effect in a small-scale experiment would not have the same effect if implemented as routine social policy. One possible reason why LIFE was more successful than TARP (Rossi, Berk, and Lenihan 1980) is that the former was administered by a research team and the latter by state unemployment benefit officers. Other problems of implementation have been discussed by Pillemer and Light (1979). For example, the beneficial effect of a program may depend on how many other people receive it.

A problem that arises in institutional research on treatment regimes is to disentangle the effects of the regimes from those of existing inmates. For example, in a comparison between two institutions by Jesness (1975), 15–17-year-old boys were randomly assigned to the institutions. In addition, all 14-year-olds went to one and all 18-year-olds to the other. These boys were not included in the experiment, but they might have influenced the 15–17-year olds who were. In carrying out research in existing institutions, it might be desirable to run the experiment for a while without collecting data, until nonrandomly assigned inmates have been cleared from the institutions, as Williams (1970) did. It is sometimes possible to avoid this problem by conducting research in a new institution (e.g. Kassebaum, Ward, and Wilner 1971).

It is often difficult to ensure that all members of the treatment group receive the treatment while all members of the control group do not. Some subjects in the treatment group may refuse the treatment. For example, Stapleton and Teitelbaum (1972) were concerned with the effect of legal representation on the outcomes of juvenile court cases, but they could not randomly determine which juveniles would be legally represented and which would not. Those in the experimental group were offered legal representation, but only 70.7 percent accepted this offer; 11.8 percent were represented by other lawyers, and 17.5 percent

chose not to be represented. Of the control-group juveniles who were not offered legal representation, 26.4 percent nevertheless had legal representatives. Similar problems occurred in Rosenberg's (1964) research on the effects of pretrial conferences.

The problem of refusal of treatment can sometimes be dealt with by asking for cooperation before randomizing, but the results of an experiment carried out with only cooperative clients may be difficult to generalize to the whole population of clients. This may not matter. If a treatment could be implemented only with cooperative clients, external validity may be important only in relation to such people.

There are other obstacles to complete separation of treatments. Agency personnel who are responsible for one treatment may be attracted by the other and may incorporate elements of it into their own program (e.g. Jesness et al. 1975). There may be contamination of one treatment by another if both are being given within the same institution, with the inmates sharing some facilities (e.g. Cornish and Clarke 1975). The blurring of the distinction between treated and control groups increases the likelihood of concluding that the treatment had no effect.

Another issue connected with the control of the independent variable centers on differential attrition of people from treated and control groups. It might be argued that people who do not successfully complete the treatment should be eliminated from the treatment group, in order to carry out a fair test of the effects of the treatment. However, the elimination of treatment failures sacrifices the benefits of randomization, since the groups will no longer be comparable. It could be done if the subjects had been placed in matched pairs before being randomly assigned, because if one member of a pair was a treatment failure both could be eliminated from the analysis. However, this would reduce the generalizability of the results.

Very few experiments can arrange for a truly "untreated" control group and therefore obtain a measure of the absolute effect of any treatment. It is more feasible to compare two varieties or strengths of the same treatment. For example, in Fowles's (1978) experiment on welfare help for prisoners, those in the experimental group had an average of ten contacts with the welfare officer, compared with an average of two for the control group.

If two treatments are compared and the first proves better than the second, it is impossible to know whether either is better or worse than no treatment. Similarly, if two treatments appear to be equally effective, it is impossible to know whether they are both better than, both worse than, or both just as good as no treatment. Instead of concluding that "nothing works," one could instead conclude that "everything works (equally well)."

If two varieties of the same treatment are compared, there may be insufficient variation in the independent variable to produce a detectable effect. For example, Folkard, Smith, and Smith (1976) found that "intensive" probation had no significant effect on reconviction rates of probationers. However, the "intensive" group had an average number of contacts with their probation officer per month of about 3, compared with the control group's average of about 1.5. This experiment shows that variations within the range of 1.5–3 contacts per month with a probation officer had no effect on reconviction, but it leaves open the possibility that variations over a wider range (e.g. up to 30 contacts per month) might have an effect.

It might be argued that an experiment involving really intensive probation would be pointless, because such a degree of probation would never be introduced as a penal policy. Even if this is true, it is still important for theoretical reasons to know whether variations in the intensity of probation within any range have an effect on reconviction rates. This might give some clue about whether the theory underlying probation practice is true or false. As Sechrest and Redner (1979) pointed out, it is important to investigate the relation between strength of treatment and effectiveness and to attempt to determine if there is an optimal strength.

It is also desirable to know under what boundary conditions (ranges of values) of other variables a treatment has an effect on reoffending, but little progress has been made toward answering this question. For example, with reference to the research of Kassebaum, Ward, and Wilner (1971), 1–2 hours of group counseling per week may not have a detectable effect if the other 166–67 hours are spent in a prison, but it may have an effect if the other 166–67 hours are spent in some other environment.

It is often difficult to manipulate only one independent variable. Changing one factor often leads to changes in others. For example, Jesness (1965, 1971a) was interested in comparing twenty-boy and fifty-boy living units in an institution, but the inmate/staff ratio was much greater in the larger unit. Perhaps because of this, the regime in the fifty-boy unit was much more controlling and punitive, whereas the regime in the twenty-boy unit was more informal, allowing greater willingness of the staff to involve themselves in the boys' problems. It is common for treatments to vary along many different dimensions, making it difficult to know which aspect of a treatment was responsible for any observed effect. There may also be a long causal chain of intervening factors linking the independent and dependent variables, again making it difficult to know which factor really produced the effect.

Many experimenters have been criticized for failing to allow for an interaction between individuals and treatments—for individuals responding in different ways to different treatments. To investigate this in an experiment, it is necessary to have prior hypothesis-generating research to stratify people, and then to assign treatments at random within classes of individuals. The most extensive attempt to match individuals to treatments was the Preston typology experiment of Jesness (1971b), based on I-level.[12] This did not succeed in demonstrating interaction effects. The simple amenable/nonamenable classification of Adams (1970) appeared to be more successful in this respect.

B. *The Dependent Variable*

As with the independent variable, the choice of the dependent variable should be guided by theory. Most experimental treatments seem to have been primarily intended to rehabilitate offenders, hence the usual dependent variable has been some measure of the recidivism of the treated offenders. However, merely measuring recidivism makes it impossible to discriminate between rehabilitation and individual deterrence as a reason for reduced offending. Any attempt to distinguish between these would require interviewing offenders.

As in nonexperimental research, dependent measures should be reliable and valid. The most common measures have been based on official records of offending, which have many known problems. For example, official records are the tip of the iceberg of offenses committed, use legal rather than behavioral categories, and are subject to unreliable recording procedures (for a discussion of some problems of official records, see e.g. Farrington 1979c). There are many reasons it may be desirable to interview the subjects of the research, and these interviews could include a self-reported delinquency measure. Reckless and Dinitz (1972) had self-reported delinquency as a dependent variable in their experiment, and Waldo and Chiricos (1977) had self-reports of arrests.

The independent variable manipulation should not be able to bias the

---

[12]The Preston study, like the Community Treatment Project, used a typology derived from I-level (Interpersonal Maturity level) theory to classify delinquents. According to this theory, each person can become fixed at one of seven levels of maturity, each requiring a different method of rehabilitative treatment (see Austin 1977; Beker and Heyman 1972).

measurement of the dependent variable. As already noted, Lerman (1975) argued that the positive results in the Community Treatment Project were caused by the experimental condition's affecting the probability of parole revocation after an offense. Perhaps the most objective dependent variable would be an observational measure of offending. However, with the exception of some of the experiments described in section IIC above, few researchers have attempted this, because of the difficulty of arranging controlled situations in which people can commit offenses. Observational methods in criminal justice have been discussed by McCall (1975).

There are other common problems. For example, how long should the follow-up period be and when should it start? Tables 1 and 2 show that most follow-up periods were three years or less. It can be argued that the follow-up period should be relatively short if the focus of interest is on the effects of treatment. Any effects might be strongest immediately after the treatment and then become attenuated with time. On the other hand, it may be informative to compare short-term effects with long-term outcomes. Conclusions derived from a short-term follow-up may be the same as (e.g. Kantrowitz 1977) or different from (e.g. Waldo and Griswold 1979) those obtained after a longer period.

There is a major problem with a short follow-up period when the dependent measure is reconviction and if there is a delay of several months between the offense and the reconviction. In this case it would be desirable to extend the follow-up period so that the offense-conviction interval is a relatively small part of it, or to define reoffending according to the date of the offense rather than the date of the reconviction. Experiments measuring reconvictions during a one-year follow-up period (e.g. Fowles 1978) seem unsatisfactory because they exclude people who have reoffended but have not yet been reconvicted.

Problems arise when institutional and community treatments are to be compared, in regard to the start of the follow-up period. If the follow-up period begins on release for the institutional group and on sentence for the community group, the groups will be at risk during different age ranges and time periods, so that the benefits of randomization in ensuring comparability are lost. This problem can be avoided if the treatment period is the same in each case and if the follow-up period begins at the end of treatment. However, there is then the difficulty of what to do about persons in the community group who offend during the treatment period. The exchange between Quay and Love (1977, 1979) and Mrad

(1979) partly revolved around this issue. The problem of when to start the follow-up period can sometimes be avoided by modifying the underlying theory. If the treatment is intended to prevent or reduce crime by the treated person for any reason (including incapacitation), the follow-up period can include time spent in an institution.

In many cases it might be desirable to have pretest and posttest measures of the dependent variable, in an attempt to detect changes in behavior over time. Empey and Lubeck (1971) and Empey and Erickson (1972) had such before and after measures. However, in order to draw conclusions about changes over time, it is necessary to control for threats to internal validity such as maturation, history, and regression (see above).

As an example, apprehension and court processing may be caused by and follow an unusually high rate of offending. If offending rates fluctuate about some average level, they would be lower after apprehension than before it, even if they were unaffected by the official processing. This problem of regression to the mean is the basis of the criticism by Maltz et al (1980) of the "suppression effect" of Murray and Cox (1979). Murray and Cox found that youths' arrest rates were significantly lower after intervention than before it, and Maltz and his colleagues pointed out that these results could be produced by regression rather than by the intervention.

This phenomenon occurs in experimental evaluations of treatment effects, but it does not spoil the evaluation. For example, in the Silverlake experiment (Empey and Lubeck 1971), the community group declined from an average of 2.71 known offenses per person in the year before intervention to 0.73 in the year after. The corresponding decline for the institutional group was from 2.66 to 0.74. This experiment was designed to show the relative effect on offending of the community and institutional programs, and it demonstrates that the two treatments were equally effective. It was not designed to show whether either treatment led to an increase or a decrease in the offending rate, and threats to valid inference, such as regression to the mean, do not permit conclusions about this.

The simplest dependent variable is the dichotomy "rearrested or not" during a certain period. More complex measures are possible, for example, including rates of offending, types of crimes committed, and changes in other aspects of life such as employment or earnings (which are not considered here). It is sometimes difficult to obtain an accurate measure of types of crimes committed from official records (e.g. because of the legal categories used, plea bargaining, and the "principal offense" rule[13] in England, which may hide subsidiary offenses).

The major problem of measures other than the simple dichotomy arises from differential time at risk. A person may be incarcerated after his first rearrest and then not be at risk of committing further offenses during the follow-up period. Even if time at risk can be equated (or if rates of offending per month are calculated), age during time at risk may still vary, and again the benefits of randomization in ensuring comparability will be lost. Except for experiments in which almost everyone is rearrested (e.g. Jesness 1971a), the most satisfactory dependent variable obtainable from official records may be the customary arrested/nonarrested dichotomy.

The difference between percentages rearrested in treated and control groups may be statistically but not practically significant. Providing samples are large enough, small differences will be statistically significant. It is desirable for an experimenter to assess the size of effect (e.g. percentage difference) that would have practical significance and then calculate the sample size that would be needed to obtain statistical significance with this size of effect. Something similar to this was done by Baker and Sadd (1981), who reported that the size of their sample provided a .90 probability of detecting a decrease in recidivism from 30 percent to 20 percent.

A conventional significance test estimates the probability of rejecting the null hypothesis (that a treatment has no effect) when it is true, but the probability of failing to reject the null hypothesis when it is false (called type 2 error, reflecting the "power" of a statistical test) is also important. This is rarely considered by experimenters, although it and other statistical issues have been discussed by Riecken and Boruch (1974) and Rezmovic (1979).

Strictly speaking, many statistical tests can be used only when subjects are randomly sampled. However, even in randomized experiments, statistical problems can arise, and it is common for the data collected to violate the underlying assumptions of the statistical tests used. Some violations are not serious. For example, Lunney (1970) has shown that, with an experimental design and equal numbers of people in each

---

[13]If a person is convicted of several offenses on the same occasion, one of these is chosen as the "principal offense," and this determines the offense classification of the conviction. The principal offense is the one that receives the most severe disposition or, if two offenses receive the same disposition, the one with the highest maximum penalty.

condition, analysis of variance can be used even with a dichotomous dependent variable. The most serious problems are likely to arise in designs combining matching and randomization, since many statistical tests are based on the assumption that all observations are independent. With a design such as that used in the Cambridge-Somerville study, where boys were chosen at random for treatment from within matched pairs, it seems essential to use a technique such as the Wilcoxon T or the one-sample Student's t.[14]

C. *Practical Problems of Randomized Experiments*

A major practical problem is to convince program administrators of the desirability of randomization. Many people responsible for criminal justice programs do not see the need for randomization, as the following reply by Gottheil (1979, p. 71) to criticisms from Roesch (1978) shows: "Community-based programs require community-based funding, if not from the start then at least after some demonstration period. This is another factor in the reluctance to add a costly evaluation to a budget that must be approved periodically by a succession of local officials or agencies, including some of those most likely to resist an innovative program. Experienced program administrators might also point out that, regrettably, local officials tend not to be impressed with statistically sophisticated—albeit sound—evaluation reports. It is unrealistic to expect that provision of an experimental design to enable evaluation research on diversion will receive the highest priority, no matter what the inclinations and skills of the program administrator."

Objections by program administrators may be based on ethical considerations, and these are discussed in section IIID. There is certainly a widespread belief that randomized experiments are expensive and time-consuming (e.g. Boruch 1976). This is partly because such experiments have to be done prospectively and cannot be done retrospectively. Allowing time for pilot work, randomly assigning a sufficient number of cases, an adequate follow-up period, data analysis, and writing up a report, it is doubtful if a worthwhile criminological experiment could be completed within five years. Publication delays may even reach ten years (see e.g. Lenihan 1977).

Program administrators may be unwilling to relinquish control of the assignment to the experimenter, even when randomization has been

---

[14]The Wilcoxon T test is a nonparametric test of whether two groups of matched subjects are significantly different (see e.g. Siegel 1956). The one-sample Student's t test is a parametric test of the same thing (see e.g. Edwards 1969).

accepted. There are many examples in the literature of randomization designs that broke down for one reason or another, and some of these have been reviewed by Conner (1977). He concluded that randomization was likely to break down when exceptions were allowed and when the procedure was not controlled by the research staff. For example, in Ross and Blumenthal's (1974) research on sanctions for drinking drivers, the judges were allowed to give different sanctions in "exceptional" cases, but the exceptional cases amounted to 50 percent in one condition. If people are to be screened out of an experiment, the screening should occur before the randomization. This may limit the generalizability of the results, but it saves the experiment. It is often desirable in an experiment to check that the randomization has been successful in producing equivalent groups.

Another practical problem is the extent to which the researchers and program administrators should be integrated and part of the same agency. Being part of an agency may make it easier for researchers to get permission for a randomized experiment, but it may make it more difficult for them to carry out an objective evaluation. The action team needs to believe that what they are doing is worthwhile (cf. Empey 1980), and they may feel threatened by the researchers and so not give full cooperation. This kind of rivalry apparently occurred in the Clarke and Cornish (1972) experiment.

Ideally, the program administrators and the subjects should be ignorant of the experimental conditions and hypotheses, to avoid problems such as experimenter expectancy and demand characteristics.[15] This is usually difficult to arrange. In the Berg et al. (1978) study, the experiment was kept secret from the juveniles and from the treatment staff (educational welfare officers and social workers). However, in the Fricot Ranch study (Jesness 1965, 1971a), the experiment was suggested by the treatment staff, who thought they could do a better job with smaller living units. Too little research has been done on the effects on participants and treatment staff of knowing about different aspects of a realistic experiment.

Many practical problems faced in randomized experiments also arise in nonexperimental research. For example, unpredictable events can

[15]The experimenter's expectations can bias the results, for example, if he or she unwittingly behaves differently to different groups or communicates expectations to the subjects in some subtle way. Also, unintentional cues in the experiment may function as demand characteristics indicating to subjects how they are expected to behave. These and other "nonspecific treatment effects" have especially been identified in laboratory experiments (see e.g. Miller 1972).

spoil any research, as floods spoiled Ross and Blumenthal's (1975) traffic violation experiment. Dishonesty of interviewers can also arise in any research, as discussed by Rezmovic, Cook, and Dobson (1981). These researchers and Conner (1977) comment on the lack of information in published reports about these kinds of practical problems and call for more communication of research experience as well as research methodology.

The best answer to practical problems is to demonstrate that they can be overcome. This review shows that the belief that it is impossible to carry out randomized experiments is incorrect. It may be that program administrators will see the desirability of randomized experimentation if the advantages and disadvantages of this method, compared with other possible methods, are discussed with them in detail.

D. Ethical Problems

Many of the ethical issues arising in randomized experiments are similar to those arising in other kinds of research. This applies, for example, to privacy, confidentiality, and informed consent. It has been pointed out that, from a methodological viewpoint, it is desirable for the subjects to be ignorant of the experimental conditions. This clashes with the belief that subjects should give their informed consent. The effect of informed consent on the results of an experiment is not known with any certainty. More research is needed of the kind carried out by Singer (1978), who demonstrated that the requirement of informed consent significantly decreased the willingness of people to be interviewed about sensitive topics.

One problem arising especially in experiments centers on the denial of treatment to certain people. This would be difficult to justify if there were sufficient resources to treat everyone and if the treatment was known to be beneficial. However, if the effects of the treatment were known, it would be unnecessary to carry out an experiment to investigate them. If the effects of the treatment are unknown, it is possible to justify withholding the treatment from a small number of people in order to establish what the effects are.

Resources are often insufficient to treat everyone, and in these cases randomization may be seen as one of the fairest methods of selecting clients for treatment. Wortman and Rabinowitz (1979) carried out an interesting experiment to investigate attitudes toward assignment methods, and although it was done with students it is sufficiently important to cite. Students were told that they had been selected for an "innovative educational program" either on merit, according to need, at random, or on the basis of first come, first served. They were asked to rate the fairness of these selection methods, and they rated the randomization method as fairest. It would be desirable to replicate this research with the general public and with other kinds of programs. Ethical discussions should be illuminated by empirical research of this kind.

Binder, Monahan, and Newkirk (1976) justified not treating all referrals to their diversion program on the grounds that their small staff was inadequate. They argued (p. 137) that: "When one does not have substantial reason to believe that a service is actually beneficial, society is rightly more tolerant of controlled experimentation. Indeed, it is becoming increasingly accepted and even legislated that those who would offer the public a supposed boon are obliged to verify empirically the beneficial nature of their service." When resources are sufficient to treat everyone, it may be better to delay rather than deny treatment (cf. Lenihan 1977).

A basic rule that might be followed is that subjects should not be harmed by participating in research. Many experimenters randomly assign subjects either to the usual treatment or to something believed to be better (or preferred by the subjects). For example, people who would normally be committed to an institution might be randomly assigned either to an institution or to some kind of community treatment (cf. Empey and Lubeck 1971). One problem with this is that what is best for the individual is not necessarily best for the community. Ethical issues arise if people who would normally be in institutions commit offenses while in the community as part of an experiment. The experimental community treatment could be justified if it could be shown that, during a period of several years beginning with the date of the sentence, the community group did not commit more offenses than the institutionalized group. Again, the best way to establish this is by means of a randomized experiment.

Experimenters usually err on the side of caution, and this sometimes may spoil the design of the research. For example, in the Kansas City Preventive Patrol Experiment, it seems likely that policing strategies were not randomly assigned to beats because of concern for the protection of the public. Kelling et al. (1976, p. 614) stated that "the geographical distribution of beats avoided clustering reactive beats together or at an unacceptable distance from proactive beats. Such clustering could have resulted in decreased response time in the reactive beats."

Diener and Crandall (1978) pointed out that one approach frequently used in evaluating whether a project is ethical is to consider whether its likely benefits (usually consisting of, or consequent upon, advancement of knowledge) outweigh its likely costs (e.g. in terms of deception, invasion of privacy, or harm caused to subjects). The problem is how to assess likely benefits and costs. It would be desirable to carry out a careful review of costs and benefits in past experiments, compared with those in other kinds of research (or in the absence of research). This would require more information about research than is usually published, and it would also need to be done with hindsight. It cannot be attempted within the scope of this essay.

Legal and constitutional problems also arise in randomized experiments but cannot be discussed here. Some have been reviewed by Winick (1981).

IV. Conclusion

Randomized experiments are especially useful for testing causal hypotheses and evaluating well-defined technologies. Their unique advantage over other methods is their high internal validity, or high ability to demonstrate the effect of one factor on another. Such experiments have been carried out to investigate the effect of helping offenders in the natural environment; on the operation of police, courts, and penal institutions; and on why people commit offenses and how they react to offenses and offenders.

In the real world there are many factors influencing many other factors. No single experiment could unravel and explicate all the causal influences. Randomized experiments in crime and justice would be more useful if they were links in a chain of cumulative knowledge, guided by well-developed, explicitly specified, falsifiable theories. The ultimate aim might be to derive equations specifying how one factor is functionally dependent on a number of others, within specified time intervals. This stage of development is a long way off, but it might appear more attainable if researchers would bear in mind this model of scientific progress when designing their experiments.

Despite their advantages, relatively few randomized experiments on crime and justice have been carried out, because of their formidable methodological, practical, and ethical problems. No researcher should embark on such an experiment without being aware of these problems. The challenge to researchers is to identify where randomized experiments are feasible and to demonstrate that their theoretical and practical benefits outweigh their costs.

There are some causal hypotheses, such as the role of broken homes in producing delinquency, that could never be tested in randomized experiments, at least in Western society at present. Some variables, such as age and sex, cannot be manipulated realistically. Events that have already happened, such as changes in the law, could not be investigated experimentally, since experiments must be prospective. Randomized experiments are most feasible when the effects of a treatment are unknown and when it is impossible to treat everyone. It would be economical to evaluate social and penal policies in small-scale experiments before a great deal of money is spent implementing them on a large scale, but this has rarely happened.

It is clear that there are differing views about the desirability of randomized experiments. After carrying out one such experiment, Clarke and Cornish (1972, p. 21) concluded that "it is particularly unlikely that its widespread use [i.e., the widespread use of randomized experimentation] at present would significantly advance our knowledge about institutional treatment in ways that could not be otherwise achieved." They essentially argued in favor of correlational research, using methods such as retrospective matching and statistical control of variables, on the grounds that the reduction in internal validity is outweighed by the reduction in ethical and practical problems.

On the other hand, the National Academy of Sciences Panel on Research on Rehabilitative Techniques strongly advocated randomized experiments: "We believe that randomized experiments can be carried out with minimal risk to individual rights. We further believe that this minimal risk is justifiable in light of the need for valid information and the potential benefits to society that would result from successful rehabilitation" (Sechrest, White, and Brown 1979, p. 17).

At present, efforts to weigh the methodological attractiveness of randomized experiments against their ethical and practical problems must be essentially subjective. My own view is that, because of their high internal validity, attempts should be made to test hypotheses and evaluate technologies using randomized experiments wherever possible.

Appendix 1
Selection of Major Experiments in Tables 1 and 2

The aim in tables 1 and 2 is to summarize the major published realistic randomized experiments on crime and justice. The only reference in these tables that is not to a published report is Williams (1970), and a less detailed description of this experiment has been published (Williams 1975). When an experiment has been described in more than one publication, the later one has usually been cited, except when the earlier one contains more extensive information.

As indicated in section IE, this review has been greatly hindered by a lack of key information in published reports and by an often confusing presentation of results. Martinson (1976) was not entirely unfair when he observed that reviewing one of Palmer's research reports was like translating the Moscow telephone directory into Swahili, and a similar comment could be made about other researchers. In the interests of clarity, Appendix 2 provides a checklist of key questions that need to be answered in a report on an experiment.

The distinction between tables 1 and 2 was sometimes arbitrary. For example, the court employment project of Baker and Sadd (1981) could have been included in either table. It was placed in table 2 because defendants were seen and helped in court, but the attempts to help defendants get jobs in the community could equally have justified its placement in table 1.

The requirement that experiments should be realistic led to the exclusion of all simulation experiments. For example, several English researchers have studied decision making by magistrates by asking them, within an experimental design, how they would sentence certain cases (e.g. Hine, McWilliams, and Pease 1978; Shea 1974). Other researchers have compared decision making by magistrates and judges in simulation experiments with their real nonexperimental decisions (e.g. Ebbesen and Konecni 1975; Kapardis and Farrington 1981). Other simulations—for example, the famous Stanford prison experiment[16] (e.g. Haney, Banks, and Zimbardo 1973; see also Banuazizi and Movahedi 1975)—have also been eliminated. Any experiment carried out on a campus or involving college students as subjects has been excluded.

Experiments that were primarily on methodological issues, as opposed to substantive questions about criminal behavior or the criminal justice system, have also been excluded. The investigation of the effect of different methods of administration of a self-reported delinquency questionnaire on admission rates by Hindelang, Hirschi, and Weis (1981) is an example of such a study. Also, experiments with institutionalized

---

[16]In the Stanford prison experiment, people were randomly assigned to be "guards" and "prisoners" in a simulated prison environment.

delinquents or prisoners as subjects that did not attempt to change their offending behavior (e.g. Stumphauzer 1972) were eliminated.

Experiments were included only if the number of persons in each condition was at least fifty or so. This size is necessary for the random assignment to achieve reasonably equivalent groups and also to stand any chance of obtaining statistically significant results with percentage differences between groups of the order of 10 percent or 15 percent. The smallest experiment included is that by Berg et al. (1978), which had fifty-one in one group and forty-five in the other. The largest experiment excluded is the Seattle Atlantic Street Center project (Berleman and Steinburn 1967; Berleman, Seaberg, and Steinburn 1972), which had fifty-two in one group and thirty-nine in another.[17] Other experiments excluded because of sample size were Alexander and Parsons (1973), Barkwell (1980), Berman (1975, 1978), Bowman (1959), Lee and Haynes (1978, 1980), Seidman, Rappaport, and Davidson (1980), Shore and Massimo (1979), Stuart, Jayaratne, and Tripodi (1976), and Zacker and Bard (1973).

As far as possible, the size of the sample specified in tables 1 and 2 is that originally randomly assigned between the conditions, but it is often difficult to establish this. The sample size is often different for different purposes. For example, Ditman et al. (1967) randomly assigned 301 chronic drunkenness offenders, but they presented the results for 241 with complete records. The figure of 301 is shown in table 1. The sample size may increase as the research progresses. In their research on the "buddy system," Fo and O'Donnell's (1975) sample of 442 increased to O'Donnell, Lydgate, and Fo's (1979) sample of 553. The larger size of 553 is shown in table 1.

All the experiments based on units other than people had to be excluded on the grounds of sample size (e.g. Buikhuisen 1974; Tornudd 1968; with towns). Similarly, all the studies of policing based on areas were eliminated (e.g. Feld 1978; Schnelle et al. 1975, 1977, 1978, 1979). Most of these involved essentially within-subjects designs, which are not included here.

Only experiments that, as far as could be ascertained, clearly involved randomization were included. Some of the exclusions were very close to

---

[17]This project was not excluded solely on the grounds of sample size but also because of its serious attrition rate of about 25 percent and its replacement procedure. Whenever a youth dropped out of the treatment group, he was replaced by a youth from the control group (see Berleman 1980). Since the youths who dropped out were probably different from those who stayed in the program, this replacement procedure probably led to nonequivalent groups.

random assignment. The diversion experiment of Baron, Feeney, and Thornton (1973) was excluded because juveniles were dealt with by the project (using family therapy) on four days a week and by the regular intake unit on the other three days. This design does not ensure equivalence on extraneous variables unless the days are varied at random, and they were merely changed monthly (see Baron and Feeney 1976). Similarly, the experiments of Ross and Blumenthal (1974, 1975) were excluded because the experimental conditions were confounded with months and with weeks. In both experiments, the random assignment broke down.

The "design" column in tables 1 and 2 gives basic information about differences between groups. As in the rest of the columns, it is necessary to consult the reports to obtain full information about the design. For example, in the Ditman et al. (1967) experiment, all drunkenness offenders were fined $25, given a thirty-day suspended sentence, and required to abstain from alcohol for a year before being randomly assigned to the three conditions. The tables concentrate on the randomly assigned groups. As another example, in addition to the three randomly assigned groups of Kassebaum, Ward, and Wilner (1971), there were two non-randomized samples (voluntary small group counseling and voluntary controls). Similarly, in addition to the two randomly assigned groups of Empey and Erickson (1972), there were two nonrandomized samples (an institutionalized one and another community one).

The "results" column concentrates on the results obtained with the randomized groups, usually in relation to reoffending. Apart from police and court research, experiments were excluded if they did not provide some measure of reoffending (e.g. Persons 1966; Reid and Shyne 1969; Rezmovic, Cook, and Dobson 1981; Wood 1979). The results are usually as reported by the researchers, with no summary measure of strength of association. The nonsignificant results sometimes included considerable percentage differences (e.g. Ditman et al. 1967, varying from 56 percent to 69 percent rearrest rates). As mentioned in the text, the converse is also true, with significant results sometimes reflecting small percentage differences and having unimpressive significance levels (such as .05 in a one-tailed test). When varying follow-up periods are given, the longest one is included in the tables. For example, in the Fricot ranch experiment of Jesness (1971a), the boys from the twenty-bed living unit had a lower parole revocation rate after one year, but there was no difference between the groups after five years.

Where there seems to be some doubt about the researchers' statement of results, the tables show my conclusion. For example, O'Donnell, Lydgate, and Fo (1979) reported that their "buddy" group had a lower rearrest rate if they had previous major arrests and a higher rearrest rate if they had no previous major arrests. Both of these relations were significant at .05 on one-tailed tests. The use of one-tailed tests seems illegitimate in the absence of prior directional hypotheses. To test these hypotheses, the researchers should have stratified the sample on previous arrest records before randomization, and there is no evidence that they did this. There is no mention of it in their first published paper (Fo and O'Donnell 1974). Furthermore, there is some doubt that the randomization had made the groups equivalent in previous arrest records. Whereas 40.6 percent of those with no previous major arrests were in the control group, this was true of only 31.5 percent of those with a previous major arrest. Therefore the groups with no previous major arrests and with a previous major arrest were combined in presenting the results in table 1, with the nonsignificant results shown.

Finally, it might be noted that the experiments discussed in section IIC above do not in general fulfill the exacting requirements for inclusion in tables 1 and 2. In particular, they usually do not have fifty people randomly assigned to each condition. Excluded from section IIC are experiments on the effects of television violence on aggressive behavior (e.g. Feshbach and Singer 1971; Parke et al. 1977), on the grounds that this behavior is even further removed from real crime than is dishonesty. Also excluded are behavioral attempts to reduce stealing (e.g. McNees et al. 1976; Switzer, Deal, and Bailey 1977), since they involved within-subjects designs.

Appendix 2
A Checklist for Realistic Randomized Experiments

I dedicate this checklist to all reviewers of the literature who have been frustrated by inadequate information in research reports.

1. What was the hypothesis to be tested? What theory was it derived from?
2. Was the research project an experiment? Did the researchers have control over the independent variables?
3. Were subjects (or other units) randomly assigned to the experimental conditions?
4. What was the design? Did it include any matching? Did it allow for any interaction between individuals and treatments?

5. What were the operational definitions of the independent variables? What did the program consist of in practice? Was it constant over time and place?

6. Who administered the program? Special research staff or regular agency personnel?

7. What did the control condition consist of in practice? Along how many dimensions did the program and control conditions differ?

8. What were the number and characteristics of the people who were randomly assigned? From what population were they chosen?

9. Was there differential attrition from experimental conditions?

10. Who controlled the randomization? Was it monitored? Was its success checked?

11. What did the subjects, treatment staff, and others know or think about the experiment?

12. What were the operational definitions of the dependent variables? How adequate was any measure of offending?

13. Could the results have been affected by the choice of dependent measures (e.g. because of their sensitivity)? Could any dependent measure have been contaminated by an independent variable condition?

14. Were there comparable before and after measures of offending?

15. What was the follow-up period? Was it the same for all conditions?

16. Were the statistical tests appropriate to the data?

17. What was the strength of each effect, as opposed to statistical significance? What strength of effect could have been detected by the experiment?

18. Was the project cost-effective in relation to theoretical and practical benefits?

19. How far can the results be generalized to other places, samples, and operational definitions of variables?

Since this essay began with a discussion of a recent English experiment (Berg et al. 1978), it is appropriate to end by drawing attention to a recent American one (the TARP experiment of Rossi, Berk, and Lenihan 1980), which is notably good in providing answers to the questions above. The TARP experiment was a follow-up to the LIFE experiment (described in the same book); the latter appeared to show that financial aid given to a high-risk group of former prisoners by special research staff reduced the former prisoners' property offending. TARP was designed to see if this result could be replicated on a larger scale, with more representative samples of former prisoners, and when the program was administered by regular agency personnel.

One of the major ambiguities in the book concerns attrition from experimental conditions. On page 61, it is stated that there were a small number of refusals (1–2 percent) to participate in the project, but on page 67 the proportion given a prerelease interview is shown as 100 percent in all groups. It must be presumed, therefore, that the refusers were eliminated before randomization. Another uncertainty centers on the amount of information the former prisoners and agency staff had about the experiment. As an example of anxious moments that often arise in research, the book reports that one of the major newspapers ran a story headlined "Cash for Crooks," emphasizing that murderers and rapists were being given cash handouts.

A particularly good feature of the research was the careful checking of the dependent variable of offending, which revealed the inadequacy of state records and forced the researchers to collect local records. The cost-benefit question is one of the most difficult to answer. The TARP experiment cost $3,400,000 but was competently designed and executed. It showed conclusively that payments to former prisoners as administered by TARP did not decrease arrests for property crimes.

REFERENCES

Adams, Stuart. 1970. "The PICO Project." In *The Sociology of Punishment and Correction*, ed. Norman Johnston, Leonard Savitz, and Marvin E. Wolfgang. New York: Wiley.

Alexander, James F., and Bruce V. Parsons. 1973. "Short-Term Behavioral Intervention with Delinquent Families: Impact on Family Process and Recidivism," *Journal of Abnormal Psychology* 81:219–25.

Annis, Helen M. 1979. "Group Treatment of Incarcerated Offenders with Alcohol and Drug Problems: A Controlled Evaluation," *Canadian Journal of Criminology* 21:3–15.

Ares, Charles E., Ann Rankin, and Herbert Sturz. 1963. "The Manhattan Bail Project," *New York University Law Review* 38:67–92.

Austin, Roy L. 1977. "Differential Treatment in an Institution: The Preston Study," *Journal of Research in Crime and Delinquency* 14:177–94.

Baker, Sally H., and Susan Sadd. 1981. *Diversion of Felony Arrests*. Washington, D.C.: National Institute of Justice.

Banuazizi, Ali, and Siamak Movahedi. 1975. "Interpersonal Dynamics in a Simulated Prison: A Methodological Analysis," *American Psychologist* 30: 152–60.

Barkwell, Lawrence. 1980. "Differential Probation Treatment of Delinquency."
   In *Effective Correctional Treatment*, ed. Robert R. Ross and Paul Gendreau.
   Toronto: Butterworth.
Baron, Roger, and Floyd Feeney. 1976. *Juvenile Diversion through Family Counsel-
   ing*. Washington, D.C.: National Institute of Law Enforcement and Criminal
   Justice.
Baron, Roger, Floyd Feeney, and Warren Thornton. 1973. "Preventing De-
   linquency through Diversion," *Federal Probation* 37(1):13–18.
Beker, Jerome, and Doris S. Heyman. 1972. "A Critical Appraisal of the
   California Differential Treatment Typology of Adolescent Offenders,"
   Criminology 10:3–59.
Berg, Ian, Margaret Consterdine, Roy Hullin, Ralph McGuire, and Stephen
   Tyrer. 1978. "The Effect of Two Randomly Allocated Court Procedures on
   Truancy," *British Journal of Criminology* 18:232–44.
Berg, Ian, Roy Hullin, and Ralph McGuire. 1979. "A Randomly Controlled
   Trial of Two Court Procedures in Truancy." In *Psychology, Law and Legal
   Processes*, ed. David P. Farrington, Keith Hawkins, and Sally M. Lloyd-
   Bostock. London: Macmillan.
Berg, Ian, Roy Hullin, Ralph McGuire, and Stephen Tyrer. 1977. "Truancy
   and the Courts: Research Note," *Journal of Child Psychology and Psychiatry*
   18:359–65.
Berleman, William C. 1980. *Juvenile Delinquency Prevention Experiments*. Wash-
   ington, D.C.: Office of Juvenile Justice and Delinquency Prevention.
Berleman, William C., James R. Seaberg, and Thomas W. Steinburn. 1972.
   "The Delinquency Prevention Experiment of the Seattle Atlantic Street
   Center: A Final Evaluation," *Social Service Review* 46:323–46.
Berleman, William C., and Thomas W. Steinburn. 1967. "The Execution and
   Evaluation of a Delinquency Prevention Program," *Social Problems* 14:413–23.
Berman, John. 1975. "The Volunteer in Parole Program: An Evaluation,"
   Criminology 13:11–13.
———. 1978. "An Experiment in Parole Supervision," *Evaluation Quarterly*
   2:71–90.
Berntsen, Karen, and Karl O. Christiansen. 1965. "A Resocialization Experi-
   ment with Short-Term Offenders." In *Scandinavian Studies in Criminology*, vol.
   1, ed. Karl O. Christiansen. London: Tavistock.
Bickman, Leonard. 1971. "The Effect of Social Status on the Honesty of
   Others," *Journal of Social Psychology* 85:87–92.
———. 1976. "Attitude toward an Authority and the Reporting of a Crime,"
   Sociometry 39:76–82.
———. 1979. "Interpersonal Influence and the Reporting of a Crime," *Personality and Social Psychology Bulletin* 5:32–35.
Bickman, Leonard, and Susan K. Green. 1975. "Is Revenge Sweet? The Effect
   of Attitude towards a Thief on Crime Reporting," *Criminal Justice and Behavior*
   2:101–12.
Bickman, Leonard, and Helen Helwig. 1979. "Bystander Reporting of a Crime:
   The Impact of Incentives," *Criminology* 17:283–300.
Bickman, Leonard, and Dennis P. Rosenbaum. 1977. "Crime Reporting as a

Function of Bystander Encouragement, Surveillance, and Credibility," *Journal of Personality and Social Psychology* 35:577–86.

Binder, Arnold, John Monahan, and Martha Newkirk. 1976. "Diversion from the Juvenile Justice System and the Prevention of Delinquency." In *Community Mental Health and the Criminal Justice System*, ed. John Monahan. New York: Pergamon.

Binder, Arnold, and Martha Newkirk. 1977. "A Program to Extend Police Service Capability," *Crime Prevention Review* 4:26–32.

Blalock, Hubert M. 1972. *Social Statistics*. 2d ed. New York: McGraw-Hill.

Bond, Rod A., and Nigel F. Lemon. 1981. "Training, Experience, and Magistrates' Sentencing Philosophies: A Longitudinal Study," *Law and Human Behavior* 5:123–39.

Boruch, Robert F. 1976. "On Common Contentions about Randomized Field Experiments." In *Evaluation Studies Review Annual*, vol. 1, ed. Gene V. Glass. Beverly Hills, Calif.: Sage.

Boruch, Robert F., A. John McSweeny, and E. Jon Soderstrom. 1978. "Randomized Field Experiments for Program Planning, Development, and Evaluation: An Illustrative Bibliography," *Evaluation Quarterly* 2:655–95.

Boshier, Roger, and Derek Johnson. 1974. "Does Conviction Affect Employment Opportunities?" *British Journal of Criminology* 14:264–68.

Botein, Bernard. 1965. "The Manhattan Bail Project: Its Impact on Criminology and the Criminal Law Processes," *Texas Law Review* 43:319–31.

Bowman, Paul H. 1959. "Effects of a Revised School Program on Potential Delinquents," *Annals of the American Academy of Political and Social Science* 322:53–61.

Buikhuisen, Wouter. 1974. "General Deterrence: Research and Theory," *Abstracts on Criminology and Penology* 14:285–98.

Buikhuisen, Wouter, and Fokke P. H. Dijksterhuis. 1971. "Delinquency and Stigmatization," *British Journal of Criminology* 11:185–87.

Byles, John A., and A. Maurice. 1979. "The Juvenile Services Project: An Experiment in Delinquency Control," *Canadian Journal of Criminology* 21:155–65.

Campbell, Donald T., and H. Laurence Ross. 1968. "The Connecticut Crackdown on Speeding," *Law and Society Review* 3:33–53.

Campbell, Donald T., and Julian C. Stanley. 1966. *Experimental and Quasi-Experimental Designs for Research*. Chicago: Rand McNally.

Clarke, Ronald V. G., and Derek B. Cornish. 1972. *The Controlled Trial in Institutional Research*. London: H.M. Stationery Office.

Conner, Ross F. 1977. "Selecting a Control Group: An Analysis of the Randomization Process in Twelve Social Reform Programs," *Evaluation Quarterly* 1:195–244.

Cook, Thomas D., and Donald T. Campbell. 1979. *Quasi-Experimentation*. Chicago: Rand McNally.

Cornish, Derek B., and Ronald V. G. Clarke. 1975. *Residential Treatment and Its Effects on Delinquency*. London: H.M. Stationery Office.

Diener, Edward, and Rick Crandall. 1978. *Ethics in Social and Behavioral Research*. Chicago: University of Chicago Press.

Ditman, Keith S., George G. Crawford, Edward W. Forgy, Herbert Mosko-
witz, and Craig Macandrew. 1967. "A Controlled Experiment on the Use
of Court Probation for Drunk Arrests," *American Journal of Psychiatry* 124:
160–63.

Dobson, Douglas, and Thomas J. Cook. 1979. "Implementing Random Assignment: A Computer-Based Approach in a Field Experimental Setting," *Evaluation Quarterly* 3:472–89.

Earle, Howard H. 1973. *Police Recruit Training*. Springfield, Ill.: C. C. Thomas.

Ebbesen, Ebbe B., and Vladimir J. Konecni. 1975. "Decision Making and
Information Integration in the Courts: The Setting of Bail," *Journal of Personality and Social Psychology* 32:805–21.

Edwards, Allen L. 1969. *Statistical Analysis*. 3d ed. New York: Holt, Rinehart
and Winston.

Empey, LaMar T. 1980. "Field Experimentation in Criminal Justice: Rationale
and Design." In *Handbook of Criminal Justice Evaluation*, ed. Malcolm Klein and
Katherine Teilman. Beverly Hills, Calif.: Sage.

Empey, LaMar T., and Maynard L. Erickson. 1972. *The Provo Experiment*.
Lexington, Mass.: D. C. Heath.

Empey, LaMar T., and Steven G. Lubeck. 1971. *The Silverlake Experiment*.
Chicago: Aldine.

Erickson, Pat G., and Michael S. Goodstadt. 1979. "Legal Stigma for Marijuana
Possession," *Criminology* 17:208–16.

Farrington, David P. 1977. "The Effects of Public Labelling," *British Journal of
Criminology* 17:112–25.

———. 1979a. "Delinquent Behaviour Modification in the Natural Environment," *British Journal of Criminology* 19:353–72.

———. 1979b. "Experiments on Deviance with Special Reference to Dishonesty." In *Advances in Experimental Social Psychology*, vol. 12, ed. Leonard
Berkowitz. New York: Academic Press.

———. 1979c. "Longitudinal Research on Crime and Delinquency." In *Crime
and Justice*, vol. 1, ed. Norval Morris and Michael Tonry. Chicago: University
of Chicago Press.

Farrington, David P., and Robert F. Kidd. 1977. "Is Financial Dishonesty a
Rational Decision?" *British Journal of Social and Clinical Psychology* 16:139–46.

Farrington, David P., and Barry J. Knight. 1979. "Two Nonreactive Field
Experiments on Stealing from a 'Lost' Letter," *British Journal of Social and
Clinical Psychology* 18:277–84.

———. 1980. "Stealing from a 'Lost' Letter: Effects of Victim Characteristics,"
Criminal Justice and Behavior 7:423–36.

Feld, Scott L. 1978. "Deterrence: For the Prevention and Cure of Litter,"
Evaluation Quarterly 2:547–60.

Feldman, Roy E. 1968. "Response to Compatriot and Foreigner Who Seek
Assistance," *Journal of Personality and Social Psychology* 10:202–14.

Feshbach, Seymour, and Robert D. Singer. 1971. *Television and Aggression*. San
Francisco: Jossey-Bass.

Fienberg, Stephen E. 1980. *The Analysis of Cross-Classified Categorical Data*. 2d ed.
Cambridge:MIT Press.

Fienberg, Stephen E., Kinley Larntz, and Albert J. Reiss. 1976. "Redesigning the Kansas City Preventive Patrol Experiment," *Evaluation* 3:124–31.

Fo, Walter S. O., and Clifford R. O'Donnell. 1974. "The Buddy System: Relationship and Contingency Conditions in a Community Intervention Program for Youth with Nonprofessionals as Behavior Change Agents, "*Journal of Consulting and Clinical Psychology* 42:163–69.

———. 1975. "The Buddy System: Effect of Community Intervention on Delinquent Offenses," *Behavior Therapy* 6:522–24.

Folkard, M. Steven, David E. Smith, and David D. Smith. 1976. *IMPACT.* Vol. 2. London: H.M. Stationery Office.

Fowles, A. J. 1978. *Prison Welfare.* London: H.M. Stationery Office.

Franklin, Bill J. 1973. "The Effects of Status on the Honesty and Verbal Responses of Others," *Journal of Social Psychology* 91:347–48.

Gelfand, Donna M., Donald P. Hartmann, Patrice Walder, and Brent Page. 1973. "Who Reports Shoplifters? A Field-Experimental Study," *Journal of Personality and Social Psychology* 25:276–85.

Glaser, Daniel. 1964. *The Effectiveness of a Prison and Parole System.* Indianapolis: Bobbs-Merrill.

Goldman, Jerry. 1979. "Resolution of Appellate Litigation: A Controlled Experiment," *Evaluation Quarterly* 3:557–82.

Gottheil, Diane L. 1979. "Pretrial Diversion: A Response to the Critics," *Crime and Delinquency* 25:65–75.

Hackler, James C., and John L. Hagan. 1975. "Work and Teaching Machines as Delinquency Prevention Tools: A Four-Year Follow-up," *Social Service Review* 49:92–106.

Haney, Craig, Curtis Banks, and Philip Zimbardo. 1973. "Interpersonal Dynamics in a Simulated Prison," *International Journal of Criminology and Penology* 1:69–97.

Hindelang, Michael J., Travis Hirschi, and Joseph G. Weis. 1981. *Measuring Delinquency.* Beverly Hills, Calif.: Sage.

Hine, Jean, William McWilliams, and Ken Pease. 1978. "Recommendations, Social Information, and Sentencing," *Howard Journal of Penology and Crime Prevention* 17:91–100.

Hornstein, Harvey A. 1970. "The Influence of Social Models on Helping." In *Altruism and Helping Behavior,* ed. Jacqueline Macaulay and Leonard Berkowitz. New York: Academic Press.

Hornstein, Harvey A., Elisha Fisch, and Michael Holmes. 1968. "Influence of a Model's Feeling about His Behavior and His Relevance as a Comparison Other on Observer's Helping Behavior," *Journal of Personality and Social Psychology* 10:222–26.

Jesness, Carl F. 1965. *The Fricot Ranch Study.* Sacramento: California Youth Authority.

———. 1971a. "Comparative Effectiveness of Two Institutional Treatment Programs for Delinquents," *Child Care Quarterly* 1:119–30.

———. 1971b. "The Preston Typology Study," *Journal of Research in Crime and Delinquency* 8:38–52.

————. 1975. "Comparative Effectiveness of Behavior Modification and Trans-actional Analysis Programs for Delinquents," *Journal of Consulting and Clinical Psychology* 43:758–79.

Jesness, Carl F., Tom S. Allison, Paul M. McCormick, Robert F. Wedge, and Mary L. Young. 1975. *An Evaluation of the Effectiveness of Contingency Contracting with Delinquents*. Sacramento: California Youth Authority.

Kantrowitz, Nathan. 1977. "How to Shorten the Follow-up Period in Parole Studies," *Journal of Research in Crime and Delinquency* 14:222–26.

Kapardis, Andreas, and David P. Farrington. 1981. "An Experimental Study of Sentencing by Magistrates," *Law and Human Behavior* 5:107–21.

Kassebaum, Gene, David Ward, and Daniel Wilner. 1971. *Prison Treatment and Parole Survival*. New York: Wiley.

Kelling, George L., Tony Pate, Duane Dieckman, and Charles E. Brown. 1976. "The Kansas City Preventive Patrol Experiment: A Summary Report." In *Evaluation Studies Review Annual*, vol. 1, ed. Gene V. Glass. Beverly Hills, Calif.: Sage.

Kleinke, Chris L. 1977. "Compliance to Requests Made by Gazing and Touching Experimenters in Field Settings," *Journal of Experimental Social Psychology* 13:218–23.

Knox, Robert E., and Timothy J. McTiernan. 1973. "Lost Letters and Social Responsibility in Dublin," *Social Studies* 2:511–18.

Korte, Charles, and Nancy Kerr. 1975. "Response to Altruistic Opportunities in Urban and Nonurban Settings," *Journal of Social Psychology* 95:183–84.

Lamb, H. Richard, and Victor Goertzel. 1974. "Ellsworth House: A Community Alternative to Jail," *American Journal of Psychiatry* 131:64–68.

Land, Kenneth C. 1969. "Principles of Path Analysis." In *Sociological Methodology 1969*, ed. Edgar F. Borgatta. San Francisco: Jossey-Bass.

Larson, Richard C. 1975. "What Happened to Patrol Operations in Kansas City?" *Journal of Criminal Justice* 3:267–97.

Lee, Robert, and Nancy M. Haynes. 1978. "Counseling Juvenile Offenders: An Experimental Evaluation of Project CREST," *Community Mental Health Journal* 14:267–71.

————. 1980. "Project CREST and the Dual-Treatment Approach to Delinquency: Methods and Research Summarized." In *Effective Correlational Treatment*, ed. Robert R. Ross and Paul Gendreau. Toronto: Butterworth.

Lenihan, Kenneth J. 1977. "Telephones and Raising Bail: Some Lessons in Evaluation Research," *Evaluation Quarterly* 1:569–86.

Lerman, Paul. 1975. *Community Treatment and Social Control*. Chicago: University of Chicago Press.

Lichtman, Cary M., and Sue M. Smock. 1981. "The Effects of Social Services on Probationer Recidivism: A Field Experiment," *Journal of Research in Crime and Delinquency* 18:81–100.

Logan, Charles H. 1972. "Evaluation Research in Crime and Delinquency: A Reappraisal," *Journal of Criminal Law, Criminology, and Police Science* 63:378–87.

Lunney, Gerald H. 1970. "Using Analysis of Variance with a Dichotomous

Dependent Variable: An Empirical Study," *Journal of Educational Measurement* 7:263–69.

McCall, George J. 1975. *Observing the Law*. Washington, D.C.: U.S. Government Printing Office.

McCord, Joan. 1978. "A Thirty-Year Follow-up of Treatment Effects," *American Psychologist* 33:284–89.

McCord, Joan, and William McCord. 1959. "A Follow-up Report on the Cambridge-Somerville Youth Study," *Annals of the American Academy of Political and Social Sciences* 322:89–96.

McNees, M. Patrick, Daniel S. Egli, Rebecca S. Marshall, John F. Schnelle, and Todd R. Risley. 1976. "Shoplifting Prevention: Providing Information through Signs," *Journal of Applied Behavior Analysis* 9:399–405.

Maltz, Michael D., Andrew C. Gordon, David McDowall, and Richard McCleary. 1980. "An Artifact in Pretest-Posttest Designs: How It Can Mistakenly Make Delinquency Programs Look Effective," *Evaluation Review* 4:225–40.

Mannheim, Hermann. 1965. *Comparative Criminology*. London: Routledge and Kegan Paul.

Martinson, Robert M. 1974. "What Works? Questions and Answers about Prison Reform," *Public Interest* 35:22–54.

———. 1976. "California Research at the Crossroads," *Crime and Delinquency* 22:180–91.

Meyer, Henry J., Edgar F. Borgatta, and Wyatt C. Jones. 1965. *Girls at Vocational High*. New York: Russell Sage.

Miller, Arthur G., ed. 1972. *The Social Psychology of Psychological Research*. New York: Free Press.

Mrad, David F. 1979. "The Effect of Differential Follow-up on Rearrests: A Critique of Quay and Love," *Criminal Justice and Behavior* 6:23–29.

Murray, Charles A., and Louis A. Cox. 1979. *Beyond Probation*. Beverly Hills, Calif.: Sage.

Nuttall, Christopher P., Elizabeth E. Barnard, A. J. Fowles, A. Frost, William H. Hammond, Pat Mayhew, Ken Pease, Roger Tarling, and Mollie J. Weatheritt. 1977. *Parole in England and Wales*. London: H.M. Stationery Office.

O'Donnell, Clifford R., Tony Lydgate, and Walter S. O. Fo. 1979. "The Buddy System: Review and Follow-up," *Child Behavior Therapy* 1:161–69.

Palmer, Ted B. 1971. "California's Community Treatment Program for Delinquent Adolescents," *Journal of Research in Crime and Delinquency* 8:74–92.

———. 1974. "The Youth Authority's Community Treatment Project," *Federal Probation* 38(1):3–14.

Palys, Theodore S. 1976. "An Assessment of Legal and Cultural Stigma Regarding Unskilled Workers," *Canadian Journal of Criminology and Corrections* 18:247–57.

Parke, Ross D., Leonard Berkowitz, Jacques P. Leyens, Stephen G. West, and Richard J. Sebastian. 1977. "Some Effects of Violent and Nonviolent Movies on the Behavior of Juvenile Delinquents." In *Advances in Experimental Social Psychology*, vol. 10, ed. Leonard Berkowitz. New York: Academic Press.

Pate, Tony, George L. Kelling, and Charles Brown. 1975. "A Response to

'What Happened to Patrol Operations in Kansas City?'" *Journal of Criminal Justice* 3:299–330.

Persons, Roy W. 1966. "Psychological and Behavioral Change in Delinquents Following Psychotherapy," *Journal of Clinical Psychology* 22:337–40.

Pillemer, David B., and Richard J. Light. 1979. "Using the Results of Randomized Experiments to Construct Social Programs: Three Caveats." In *Evaluation Studies Review Annual*, vol. 4, ed. Lee Sechrest, Stephen G. West, Melinda A. Phillips, Robin Redner, and William Yeaton. Beverly Hills, Calif.: Sage.

Powers, Edwin, and Helen Witmer. 1951. *An Experiment in the Prevention of Delinquency*. New York: Columbia University Press.

Quay, Herbert C. 1977. "The Three Faces of Evaluation: What Can Be Expected to Work," *Criminal Justice and Behavior* 4:341–54.

Quay, Herbert C., and Craig T. Love. 1977. "The Effect of a Juvenile Diversion Program on Rearrests," *Criminal Justice and Behavior* 4:377–96.

———. 1979. "Effects of a Juvenile Diversion Program on Rearrests: A Reply to Mrad," *Criminal Justice and Behavior* 6:31–33.

Reckless, Walter C., and Simon Dinitz. 1972. *The Prevention of Juvenile Delinquency*. Columbus: Ohio State University Press.

Reid, William J., and Ann W. Shyne. 1969. *Brief and Extended Casework*. New York: Columbia University Press.

Reimer, Ernest, and Martin Warren. 1957. "Special Intensive Parole Unit," *NPPA Journal* 3:222–29.

Rezmovic, Eva L. 1979. "Methodological Considerations in Evaluating Correctional Effectiveness: Issues and Chronic Problems." In *The Rehabilitation of Criminal Offenders: Problems and Prospects*, ed. Lee Sechrest, Susan O. White, and Elizabeth D. Brown. Washington, D.C.: National Academy of Sciences.

Rezmovic, Eva L., Thomas J. Cook, and L. Douglas Dobson. 1981. "Beyond Random Assignment: Factors Affecting Evaluation Integrity," *Evaluation Review* 5:51–67.

Riecken, Henry W., and Robert F. Boruch. 1974. *Social Experimentation*. New York: Academic Press.

Risman, Barbara J. 1980. "The Kansas City Preventive Patrol Experiment: A Continuing Debate," *Evaluation Review* 4:802–8.

Roesch, Ronald. 1978. "Does Adult Diversion Work? The Failure of Research in Criminal Justice," *Crime and Delinquency* 24:72–80.

Rose, Gordon, and R. A. Hamilton, 1970. "Effects of a Juvenile Liaison Scheme," *British Journal of Criminology* 10:2–20.

Rosenberg, Maurice. 1964. *The Pretrial Conference and Effective Justice*. New York: Columbia University Press.

Ross, H. Laurence, and Murray Blumenthal. 1974. "Sanctions for the Drinking Driver: An Experimental Study," *Journal of Legal Studies* 3:53–61.

———. 1975. "Some Problems in Experimentation in a Legal Setting," *American Sociologist* 10:150–55.

Ross, H. Laurence, Donald T. Campbell, and Gene V. Glass. 1970. "Determining the Social Effects of a Legal Reform: The British 'Breathalyser' Crackdown of 1967," *American Behavioral Scientist* 13:493–509.

Rossi, Peter H., Richard A. Berk, and Kenneth J. Lenihan. 1980. *Money, Work, and Crime*. New York: Academic Press.

Sarason, Irwin G., and Victor J. Ganzer. 1973. "Modeling and Group Discussion in the Rehabilitation of Juvenile Delinquents," *Journal of Counseling Psychology* 20:442–49.

Schnelle, John F., Robert E. Kirchner, Joe D. Casey, Paul H. Uselton, and M. Patrick McNees. 1977. "Patrol Evaluation Research: A Multiple-Baseline Analysis of Saturation Police Patrolling during Day and Night Hours," *Journal of Applied Behavior Analysis* 10:33–40.

Schnelle, John F., Robert D. Kirchner, Frank Galbaugh, Michelle Domash, Adam Carr, and Lynn Larson. 1979. "Program Evaluation Research: An Experimental Cost-Effectiveness Analysis of an Armed Robery Intervention Program," *Journal of Behavior Analysis* 12:615–23.

Schnelle, John F., Robert E. Kirchner, M. Patrick McNees, and Jerry M. Lawler. 1975. "Social Evaluation Research: The Evaluation of Two Police Patrolling Strategies," *Journal of Applied Behavior Analysis* 8:353–65.

Schnelle, John F., Robert E. Kirchner, John W. Macrae, M. Patrick McNees, Richard H. Eck, Stana Snodgrass, Joe D. Casey, and Paul H. Uselton. 1978. "Police Evaluation Research: An Experimental and Cost-Benefit Analysis of a Helicopter Patrol in a High Crime Area," *Journal of Applied Behavior Analysis* 11:11–21.

Schnelle, John F., and J. Frank Lee. 1974. "A Quasi-Experimental Retrospective Evaluation of a Prison Policy Change," *Journal of Applied Behavior Analysis* 7:483–96.

Schwartz, Richard D., and Sonya Orleans. 1967. "On Legal Sanctions," *University of Chicago Law Review* 34:274–300.

Schwartz, Richard D., and Jerome H. Skolnick. 1962. "Two Studies of Legal Stigma," *Social Problems* 10:133–42.

Sechrest, Lee, and Robin Redner. 1979. "Strength and Integrity of Treatments in Evaluation Studies." In *How Well Does It Work?* Washington, D.C.: National Institute of Law Enforcement and Criminal Justice.

Sechrest, Lee, Susan O. White, and Elizabeth D. Brown, eds. 1979. *The Rehabilitation of Criminal Offenders: Problems and Prospects*. Washington, D.C.: National Academy of Sciences.

Seidman, Edward, Julian Rappaport, and William S. Davidson. 1980. "Adolescents in Legal Jeopardy: Initial Success and Replication of an Alternative to the Criminal Justice System." In *Effective Correctional Treatment*, ed. Robert R. Ross and Paul Gendreau. Toronto: Butterworth.

Shaw, Margaret. 1974. *Social Work in Prison*. London: H. M. Stationery Office.

Shea, Michael A. 1974. "A Study of the Effect of the Prosecutor's Choice of Charge on Magistrates' Sentencing Behavior," *British Journal of Criminology* 14:269–72.

Shore, Milton F., and Joseph L. Massimo. 1979. "Fifteen Years after Treatment: A Follow-up Study of Comprehensive Vocationally-Oriented Psychotherapy," *American Journal of Orthopsychiatry* 49:240–45.

Siegel, Sidney. 1956. *Nonparametric Statistics for the Behavioral Sciences*. New York: McGraw-Hill.

Singer, Eleanor. 1978. "Informed Consent: Consequences for Response Rate and Response Quality in Social Surveys," *American Sociological Review* 43: 144–62.

Sroufe, Ralph, Alan Chaikin, Rita Cook, and Valerie Freeman. 1977. "The Effects of Physical Attractiveness on Honesty: A Socially Desirable Response," *Personality and Social Psychology Bulletin* 3:59–62.

Stapleton, W. Vaughan, and Lee E. Teitelbaum. 1972. *In Defense of Youth.* New York: Russell Sage.

Steffensmeier, Darrell J., and Renee H. Steffensmeier. 1977. "Who Reports Shoplifters? Research Continuities and Further Developments," *International Journal of Criminology and Penology* 5:79–95.

Steffensmeier, Darrell J., and Robert M. Terry. 1973. "Deviance and Respectability: An Observational Study of Reactions to Shoplifting," *Social Forces* 5:417–26.

Stuart, Richard B., Sirinika Jayaratne, and Tony Tripodi. 1976. "Changing Adolescent Deviant Behavior through Reprogramming the Behavior of Parents and Teachers: An Experimental Evaluation," *Canadian Journal of Behavioral Science* 8:132–43.

Stumphauzer, Jerome S. 1972. "Increased Delay of Gratification in Young Prison Inmates through Imitation of High-Delay Peer Models," *Journal of Personality and Social Psychology* 21:10–17.

Switzer, E. Beth, Terrence E. Deal, and Jon S. Bailey. 1977. "The Reduction of Stealing in Second Graders Using a Group Contingency," *Journal of Applied Behavior Analysis* 10:267–72.

Tornudd, Patrik. 1968. "The Preventive Effects of Fines for Drunkenness." In *Scandinavian Studies in Criminology*, vol. 2, ed. Nils Christie. London: Tavistock.

Tucker, Lyle, Harvey A. Hornstein, Stephen Holloway, and Kenneth Sole. 1977. "The Effects of Temptation and Information about a Stranger on Helping," *Personality and Social Psychology Bulletin* 3:416–20.

Venezia, Peter S. 1972. "Unofficial Probation: An Evaluation of Its Effectiveness," *Journal of Research in Crime and Delinquency* 9:149–70.

Vosburgh, William W., and Leslie B. Alexander. 1980. "Long-Term Follow-up as Program Evaluation: Lessons from McCord's Thirty-Year Follow-up of the Cambridge-Somerville Youth Study," *American Journal of Orthopsychiatry* 50:109–24.

Waldo, Gordon P., and Theodore A. Chiricos. 1977. "Work Release and Recidivism: An Empirical Evaluation of a Social Policy," *Evaluation Quarterly* 1:87–108.

Waldo, Gordon P., and David Griswold. 1979. "Issues in the Measurement of Recidivism." In *The Rehabilitation of Criminal Offenders: Problems and Prospects*, ed. Lee Sechrest, Susan O. White, and Elizabeth D. Brown. Washington, D.C.: National Academy of Sciences.

Williams, Mark. 1970. *A Study of Some Aspects of Borstal Allocation.* London: Home Office Prison Department, Office of the Chief Psychologist.

———. 1975. "Aspects of the Psychology of Imprisonment." In *The Use of Imprisonment*, ed. Sean McConville. London: Routledge and Kegan Paul.

Winick, Bruce J. 1981. "A Preliminary Analysis of Legal Limitations on Reha-
bilitative Alternatives to Corrections and on Correctional Research." In *New
Directions in the Rehabilitation of Criminal Offenders*, ed. Susan E. Martin, Lee B.
Sechrest, and Robin Redner. Washington, D.C.: National Academy Press.

Wood, Michael T. 1979. "Random Assignment to Treatment Groups: A Strategy for Judicial Research," *Criminology* 17:230–41.

Wortman, Camille B., and Vita C. Rabinowitz. 1979. "Random Assignment:
The Fairest of Them All." In *Evaluation Studies Review Annual*, vol. 4, ed. Lee
Sechrest, Stephen G. West, Melinda A. Phillips, Robin Redner, and William
Yeaton. Beverly Hills, Calif.: Sage.

Wright, William E., and Michael C. Dixon. 1977. "Community Prevention and
Treatment of Juvenile Delinquency," *Journal of Research in Crime and Delinquency* 14:35–67.

Zacker, Joseph, and Morton Bard. 1973. "Effects of Conflict Management
Training on Police Performance," *Journal of Applied Psychology* 58:202–8.